Trans and Genderqueer S
in Medieval Hagiogra

Hagiography beyond Tradition

The study of sanctity in medieval Europe is starting to elicit cutting-edge, innovative and genuinely interdisciplinary scholarship that destabilizes what people have conventionally considered to be hagiography. This is demonstrated in the topic range of panels sponsored by the Hagiography Society at recent landmark medievalist conferences. While hagiography has traditionally been understood only in religious terms, recent scholarship moves beyond such frameworks to consider alternate ways of identifying and representing exemplary people. So doing, such research emphasises modern cultural analogies and resonances with medieval figures.

It is not enough, however, to approach saints' lives with a "sexy" modern framework. The best scholarship is rooted in analytical rigour, close attention to context(s), and a keen awareness of the potential pitfalls of anachronism, all the while accepting that anachronism can often be productive. This series provides a home for the kind of work that negotiates that border between the traditional and the contemporary and encourages scholarship enhanced by interventions drawn from celebrity studies, trans studies, crip theory, animal and monster studies, the history of senses and the emotions, media studies, and beyond. Rather than considering hagiography as a single genre, the series is open to expanding the ways in which we imagine how people come to be offered for veneration, as well as the media and genres in which they are fashioned, represented, and celebrated.

Series Editor
Alicia Spencer-Hall, Queen Mary University of London

Editorial Board
Martha Newman, University of Texas
Sarah Salih, King's College London
Bill Burgwinkle, University of Cambridge
Virginia Burrus, Syracuse University

Trans and Genderqueer Subjects in Medieval Hagiography

Edited by
Alicia Spencer-Hall
and Blake Gutt

Amsterdam University Press

Cover illustration: "We have always been here", by Jonah Coman

Cover design: Coördesign, Leiden
Lay-out: Crius Group, Hulshout

ISBN	978 94 6298 824 8
e-ISBN	978 90 4854 026 6 (pdf)
DOI	10.5117/9789462988248
NUR	684

© Alicia Spencer-Hall & Blake Gutt / Amsterdam University Press B.V., Amsterdam 2021

All rights reserved. Without limiting the rights under copyright reserved above, no part of this book may be reproduced, stored in or introduced into a retrieval system, or transmitted, in any form or by any means (electronic, mechanical, photocopying, recording or otherwise) without the written permission of both the copyright owner and the author of the book.

Every effort has been made to obtain permission to use all copyrighted illustrations reproduced in this book. Nonetheless, whosoever believes to have rights to this material is advised to contact the publisher.
Printed and bound by CPI Group (UK) Ltd, Croydon CR0 4YY

Table of Contents

Acknowledgements   9

Introduction   11
    Alicia Spencer-Hall and Blake Gutt

Following the Traces
Reassessing the Status Quo, Reinscribing Trans and Genderqueer Realities

1. Assigned Female at Death   43
   Joseph of Schönau and the Disruption of Medieval Gender Binaries
   Martha G. Newman

2. Inherited Futures and Queer Privilege   65
   Capgrave's *Life of St Katherine*
   Caitlyn McLoughlin

3. Juana de la Cruz   87
   Gender-Transcendent Prophetess
   Kevin C.A. Elphick

4. Non-Standard Masculinity and Sainthood in Niketas David's *Life* of Patriarch Ignatios   109
   Felix Szabo

Peripheral Vision(s)
Objects, Images, and Identities

5. Gender-Querying Christ's Wounds   133
   A Non-Binary Interpretation of Christ's Body in Late Medieval Imagery
   Sophie Sexon

6. Illuminating Queer Gender Identity in the Manuscripts of the *Vie de sainte Eufrosine*   155
   Vanessa Wright

7   The Queerly Departed   177
    Narratives of Veneration in the Burials of Late Iron Age Scandinavia
        Lee Colwill

Genre, Gender, and Trans Textualities

8   *St Eufrosine*'s Invitation to Gender Transgression   201
        Amy V. Ogden

9   Holy Queer and Holy Cure   223
    Sanctity, Disability, and Transgender Embodiment in *Tristan de Nanteuil*
        Blake Gutt

10 The Authentic Lives of Transgender Saints   245
    Imago Dei and *imitatio Christi* in the *Life* of St Marinos the Monk
        M.W. Bychowski

Epilogue   267
    Beyond Binaries: A Reflection on the (Trans) Gender(s) of Saints
        Mathilde van Dijk

Appendix   281
    Trans and Genderqueer Studies Terminology, Language, and Usage Guide

Index   331

List of Figures

Figure 4.1   Mosaic portrait of Ignatios in N. tympanum of the Hagia
             Sophia   119
             The Byzantine Institute, The Byzantine Institute
             and Dumbarton Oaks Fieldwork Records and Papers,
             photograph c. late 1920s-2000s, Dumbarton Oaks,
             Trustees for Harvard University, Washington, D.C.

Figure 5.1	Psalter and Prayer Book of Bonne of Luxembourg New York, Metropolitan Museum of Art, The Cloisters MS. 69.86, fol. 328r. CC0 1.0 Universal	144
Figure 5.2	Psalter and Prayer Book of Bonne of Luxembourg New York, Metropolitan Museum of Art, The Cloisters MS. 69.86, fol. 331r. CC0 1.0 Universal	145
Figure 6.1	Paris, Bibliothèque de l'Arsenal, MS 5204, fol. 87v.	163
Figure 6.2	Brussels, Bibliothèque royale de Belgique, MS 9229-30, fol. 61v.	166
Figure 6.3	The Hague, Koninklijke Bibliotheek, MS 71A 24, fol. 61v.	167
Figure 6.4	Munich, Bayerische Staatsbibliothek München, MS Clm 10177, fol. 373v.	170
Figure E.1	The Lamentation of Christ Courtesy of the Hôpital Notre Dame à La Rose, Lessen, Belgium	273

Acknowledgements

The scholarly networking and initial research that resulted in this collection was sponsored by the Hagiography Society. This volume shares the spirit of many insightful and collaborative research conversations that came about with the Society's support, and the commitment of these scholars to uncovering what was always already there: trans identities and experiences in medieval hagiography.

The editors would like to thank Shannon Cunningham and Amsterdam University Press for their ongoing support for this project, and particularly for their pledge to keep the Terminology, Language and Usage Guide a freely available resource. Gratitude is owed to all those who commented on and contributed to the Guide: friends, colleagues, and anonymous online interlocutors. Any remaining errors or omissions are, of course, our own.

We are profoundly grateful to the volume's contributors for their rigorous scholarship, alongside the trust they have placed in our editorial vision. We are deeply appreciative to Jonah Coman, creator of the volume's cover image, for lending us a share of his artistic vision. Thanks are due, too, to all those who have paved the way for this volume, including but not limited to: Aren Z. Aizura, Moya Bailey, S. Bear Bergman, Talia Mae Bettcher, Marquis Bey, b. binaohan, Kate Bornstein, John Boswell, Judith Butler, Gabrielle M.W. Bychowski, Bill Burgwinkle, Joan Cadden, B. Camminga, V. Varun Chaudhry, Simone Chess, Carsten Balzer/Carla LaGata, Andrea Long Chu, Jonah Coman, Trystan Cotten, Leah DeVun, Carolyn Dinshaw, Emmett Harsin Drager, Aniruddha Dutta, Lee Edelman, Ruth Evans, Leslie Feinberg, Elizabeth Freeman, Jack Halberstam, Cáel M. Keegan, Anna Kłosowska, Grace Lavery, Karma Lochrie, Clovis Maillet, Robert Mills, Adam Miyashiro, Marcia Ochoa, Mary Rambaran-Olm, Raina Roy, Julia Serano, C. Riley Snorton, Sandy Stone, Susan Stryker, Trudy (@thetrudz), Salvador Vidal-Ortiz, and Karl Whittington.

Blake would like to thank the Michigan Society of Fellows, Don Lopez, and Linda Turner for the postdoctoral scholarship that allowed the completion of this project. Enormous gratitude is due to all the interlocutors who shared their time and energy with me and the various elements of this project: Catherine Brown, Bill Burgwinkle, Gabrielle M.W. Bychowski, David Caron, Simone Chess, Shane DuBay, Joey Gamble, Scott Larson, Peggy McCracken, Brendan McMahon, Misha Mihailova, Anthony Revelle, Megan Steffen. I will forever be thankful for Alicia, without whom this project would not exist, and I would be sadder and less wise. 'Engage.'

Alicia would like to thank the kind, generous souls who have supported this project, and this co-editor, from this collection's earliest imaginings. Shannon, the best editor a medievalist could want, who, amongst other things, has shown me that Midwest surely is best – if she's there, Sean and Theo and Stella too. Blake, the best partner an editor could dream of, the best friend anyone could ever ask for. A toast to our handsome sea-faring sons: 'tea, earl grey, hot.' Sara, Kamala, Iwona, the people who lift me up when my feet and my feelings seem stuck to the floor, who without sugar-coating or silver-lining remind me of all that blue sky out there and in here too. And Jon, as ever, the eagle to my shark: would you like an egg?

Introduction

Alicia Spencer-Hall and Blake Gutt

Abstract
The Introduction sets out the rationale for the collection, and the significance and scope of trans studies, in the Middle Ages and beyond. It includes concise coverage of key scholarship in the field, contextualizing the volume and its chapters accordingly. It concludes with a chapter-by-chapter snapshot of the collection as a whole, explaining the thematic structures underpinning the volume's analytical work.

Keywords: medieval studies, gender studies, gender theory, trans studies

In hir pioneering study, *Transgender Warriors*, Leslie Feinberg writes: 'I couldn't find *myself* in history. No-one like me seemed to have ever existed'.[1] Working for transgender rights entails striving towards the visibility and acceptance of transgender lives. Yet something more than tolerance of trans people's physical existence in the present is required. That something is full ideological existence – the ability to imagine a transgender past, and a transgender future. In this volume, 'transgender' is employed as a broad umbrella, including genderqueer, genderfluid, and non-binary identities, and is also used as a rubric for discussing ways of being that disrupt normative notions of binary gender/sex.[2] We reference both transgender and genderqueer subjects in the title of the volume precisely to indicate

---

1 Feinberg, *Transgender Liberation*, p. 11. See also Bychowski in this volume: pp. 245-65; 'Ze/Hir' in the Appendix (p. 325).
2 The syntax of phrases such as 'trans and non-binary identities' may suggest that 'non-binary' and 'trans' are parallel but mutually exclusive terms. Our usage, however, is intended to convey that non-binary identities *are* trans (that is, to avoid the assumption that trans identities must be binary), which may be the unintended impression when trans identities are discussed without the explicit mention of non-binary identities. See 'Trans(gender)' (pp. 316-17) and 'Non-Binary' (p. 306) in the Appendix.

Spencer-Hall, Alicia, and Blake Gutt (eds), *Trans and Genderqueer Subjects in Medieval Hagiography*. Amsterdam, Amsterdam University Press 2021
DOI: 10.5117/9789462988248_INTRO

that both formations operate against – and through – the same normative socio-cultural structures. 'Transgender', as a category, is a subset of 'queer', understood as defiant and often explicitly political non-normativity. Queerness encompasses sexualities and gender identities deemed 'atypical' in their cultural setting, as well as a mode of being in the world that questions dominant norms. Trans theories and readings emerge from the framework of queer theory, and owe much to its innovations. Yet 'trans' cannot be fully contained within the borders of 'queer'. If queer was the call, trans is one of many responses. Trans scholarship brings its insights to bear through specific ways of feeling, knowing, and attending to sources that explore resonances between trans, genderqueer, and gender non-conforming lives across history. The term 'subjects' does double duty in the collection's title, referring to individuals *and* to topics, traces, and resonances which destabilize modern impositions of fixed binary gender on premodern culture(s).

Feinberg begins hir history with St Joan of Arc (d. 1431), whose claims of holy visions, and successful military leadership, resulted in a heresy trial that culminated in execution, based in considerable part on the charge of cross-dressing. Joan has served as a rallying point for trans identity, and exemplifies the ways that religion intersects with medieval trans and genderqueer lives.[3] Joan wore masculine clothing, and fulfilled a role socially understood as masculine, in response to (perceived) divine contact. The chapters in this volume demonstrate that non-normative gender expressions, identities, and embodiments were, in the medieval period, very often imbricated with religion. This could sometimes, as in the case of Joan, leave individuals in a double bind, caught between sanctity and heresy. Since medieval theorizations of gender often drew on religion to explain non-normativity, religion – broadly defined – is a logical starting point and a highly productive source. This material impels the response of modern researchers, both trans and cis, from the sexologist Magnus Hirschfeld (d. 1935), to Feinberg, to the contributors to this volume. Medieval artefacts call out to us for recognition just as we call out to them for representation.

M.W. Bychowski's work demonstrates that, whether or not Joan was transmasculine, Joan's life was constrained by socio-cultural norms that were not only gendered, but virulently transphobic.[4] Joan's death was the direct result of medieval transphobia. Joan is thus a productive figure for exploring the link between trans lives and sanctity. Yet in France, white supremacists,

---

3   Feinberg, *Transgender Liberation*, pp. 12-14; Bychowski, 'Patron Saint'.
4   'Patron Saint'.

whose racist ideology is intertwined with trans- and queerphobia, now claim the saint as their own.[5] Essentialized as the 'Maid of Orléans' and scrubbed of queerness, Joan has become a potent white nationalist symbol. Trans history is an ongoing project of reclamation; the hegemony will not easily loosen its grip. The continuing discussion around Joan's life and death indicates the complex intersections of identity-based oppressions. The far-right's Joan, emblematic of whiteness, cannot be queer; the queer Joan can never be a white supremacist icon. Dismantling cis-heteronormativity entails the dismantling of co-relative and compounding discriminatory structures, including white supremacy.[6]

'Transgender' is not just an identity, or a form of embodiment, but a way of disrupting normative and essentializing frameworks. Transphobia is the stigmatization of ways of being that do not conform (or are *perceived as not conforming*) to socio-culturally normate, binarized delineations of 'gender-appropriate' roles, appearances, affects, embodiments, and identities. Transphobia may target individuals who do not consider themselves to be transgender because it is a practice that functions to enforce normativity, and lacks nuanced understanding of the structures it seeks to eradicate, or the lives made possible by and within them. Examinations of culture that draw on transgender viewpoints, affects, and theorizations are not only valuable for trans individuals, who may encounter new ways of recognizing and understanding their own experiences, but also for cisgender individuals, for whom trans readings may catalyse the interrogation of previously unquestioned socio-cultural norms.

This volume employs a transgender lens to undertake a cross-temporal investigation of medieval literature, philosophy and religion: each chapter employs the insights of twentieth- and twenty-first-century trans theory to read medieval texts. With two exceptions – Felix Szabo discusses a Byzantine eunuch saint, and Lee Colwill analyses burials in Late Iron Age Scandinavia linked to the magico-religious practice of *seiðr* – the chapters focus on Catholicism, the dominant religion in medieval Western Europe. As the contributions to this volume amply demonstrate, the co-incidence of medieval representations of non-normative gender with representations of holiness is no coincidence. There is a deep structural connection between these categories of exceptional life, not only in medieval Catholicism. Further comparative study is warranted to tease out the imbrications of religiosity and gender variance. Hagiography as addressed by this volume

5   Lichfield, 'Struggle'; News Wires, 'French Far-Right'.
6   young shaq realness, Twitter thread.

is interdisciplinary: not only textual, but visual, material, cultural. Not only saints are holy. Beyond its role in institutional canonization, hagiography is the broader practice of memorializing, and reanimating, spiritually significant lives. Audiences turn to these lost lives, seeking the emotional and haptic traces of existences that illuminate their own experiences.[7] Hagiographies are narratives of becoming, possibility, and immanence.[8] They are not how-to manuals for becoming a saint, examples for the reader to rigidly emulate, but guides to recognizing and honouring the sanctity within oneself, offering moments of communion. The isolated trans and/or genderqueer reader finds that they are no longer alone; communities of readers assemble around saints, though separated by space and time. Modern trans memoirs function as autohagiography: these records of exceptional lives affirm the presence of trans individuals, serving as beacons whose light reveals the possibilities suppressed by normative culture.[9] From members of the trans community lost to violence or suicide, to iconic leaders and activists such as Sylvia Rivera and Marsha P. Johnson, modern-day trans saints abound.[10] Once again, their hagiographies are not instruction manuals, but texts that offer companionship as readers unravel what it means to live authentically, as themselves.[11] Transness is not merely compatible with holiness; transness itself is holy. Trans sanctity, as a mode of radical authenticity, creates a spiritual kinship that is not necessarily religious. For example, Feinberg, with whose words we began this Introduction, was a secular Jewish thinker. Similarly, the study of medieval hagiography, with its intrinsically Catholic worldview, owes much to the contributions of non-Christians.

We do not argue that 'transgender' is somehow an ahistorical or historically transcendent framework, but rather that the patterns of thought enabled by trans theory resonate with the content of the texts under consideration, animating the development of productive new readings. Medieval and modern conceptions of gender – what it is, how it is produced, why it matters – differ. Yet in both periods, there are gender norms, and transgressions thereof. By challenging assumptions that persist among modern scholars of the medieval period, this collection sheds revealing light on medieval understandings and experiences of gender. Simultaneously,

7   On emotional and haptic engagement, see Spencer-Hall, *Medieval Saints*, pp. 107-45.
8   On becoming, see Light, 'Trans/Mystical', pp. 9-14. Also see the 'FTM' (pp. 294-95) and 'MTF' (pp. 303-04) in the Appendix.
9   On autohagiography, see: Spencer-Hall, *Medieval Saints*, pp. 147-92; 193-242.
10 Bychowski, 'Rest in Power'; Ellison and Hoffman, 'Afterward'.
11 See: Bornstein, *Danger*; Mock, *Redefining Realness*; Sullivan, *Laughed in Pleasure*.

these analyses challenge us to think more critically about 'common-sense' understandings of how gender works today.

The trans past is not a playground. It is unethical to cleave historical trans subjects from the lived realities of their modern descendants, mobilizing trans life as an abstract concept. It is inherently transphobic for cis scholars to instrumentalize trans history for the purposes of building an academic career without explicitly making the connection to, and advocating for, trans lives today.[12] Nor can contemporary trans studies fully comprehend the current situation without understanding and acknowledging the complex history/ies of trans existence. Trans lives have never been monolithic. Traces of non-normative gender in the past reveal productive, affirmative possibilities; medieval imbrications of transness and sanctity are a case in point.

Transgender identity is too often defined in the negative, becoming legible for the cis majority primarily through the pain and dysphoria often associated with the incongruence of an individual's identified gender with their assigned gender, and with the governing gender 'regime'. We therefore hold space in this volume for gender euphoria: for all the moments, short and long, subtle and transcendent, in which the realization and enactment of one's identified gender produces a powerful and specific joy.[13] Being trans is not only about what feels wrong; it is about what feels right. Transgender euphoria resonates with mystical ravishment – both entail, as Ellis Light writes, 'fully embodied comfort and joy in oneself and one's orientation towards creation'.[14] In this way, 'trans modes of reading allow us to connect with medieval mysticism on its own terms'.[15] As a critical tool, transgender readings are about feeling otherwise; to 'sense transgender', following Cáel M. Keegan, is to experience 'a desiring feeling for what might otherwise go unrealized'.[16] In this Introduction, we set the stage for the transgender readings that follow by briefly summarizing the current state of trans rights, and the current state of the fields in which this volume intervenes. We work back from the present to the medieval period, demonstrating the ways in which trans pasts are emerging through the current theoretical and activist landscape, and why these pasts are so significant in the present.

---

12   See: Bychowski and Kim, 'Introduction', pp. 33-34.
13   See Light, 'Trans/Mystical'.
14   Ibid., p. 32.
15   Ibid., p. 21.
16   Keegan, *Lana and Lilly Wachowski*, p. 6.

Trans lives and trans rights in 2020: A (very) brief overview

In May 2019, the World Health Organization officially de-pathologized trans identities, one of the most significant advances in recent decades in acknowledging the validity of trans and genderqueer existence.[17] Other legal landmarks include the availability of neutral (X) gender markers for non-binary people on identification documents in more than fifteen US states, as well as in countries including Australia, Canada, and Iceland. Similar recognition of non-binary or 'third gender' identities occurs in countries such as Argentina, India, Nepal, and Pakistan.[18] In 2017, Danica Roem became the first openly transgender candidate to be elected to the state legislature in Virginia (USA). In 2020, Pakistan's Aisha Mughal attended the UN Convention on the Elimination of all Forms of Discrimination against Women, becoming the first openly trans person to participate in the Convention's forty-year tenure.

Transgender people are increasingly visible in Western anglophone (primarily American) culture. Notable figures include actress Laverne Cox, writer and activist Janet Mock, and former Olympic athlete Caitlyn Jenner. In 2014, Cox was the first openly trans person to appear on the cover of *Time* magazine, in the June 'Transgender Tipping Point' issue.[19] The same year, she became the first openly trans person to be nominated for a Primetime Emmy Award in an acting category, for her role as trans woman Sophia Burset in the Netflix show *Orange is the New Black*. Cox once more made Emmy history in 2015, winning a Daytime Creative Arts Emmy Award in the Outstanding Special Class as executive producer for the documentary *Laverne Cox Presents: The T Word*.

This increase in visibility, however, does not generally extend to trans men or non-binary people. Trans women bear the brunt of the public gaze: they are rendered emblematic of what it is to be trans, and are thus disproportionately vulnerable to transphobic abuse, up to and including murderous violence, with trans women of colour doubly marginalized.[20] Trans men are often rendered invisible – deliberately so, in the case of certain anti-trans campaigners, who depict trans women as conniving, perverted, and potentially violent men, while infantilizing trans men as vulnerable

---

17 World Health Organization, 'Gender Incongruence'; Transgender Europe, 'World Health Organisation'.
18 Movement Advancement Project, 'Identity Document'; Wikipedia, 'Legal Recognition'.
19 Steinmetz, 'Tipping Point'.
20 GLAAD, 'Transgender Day of Remembrance'.

young lesbians suffering the effects of internalized misogyny, who have been confused or tricked into 'abandoning' their womanhood. In this way, transphobic rhetoric seeks to present transmasculine and transfeminine identities as fundamentally different phenomena. Non-binary identities are typically least understood, often derided as fabricated or attention-seeking.

In June 2019 – Pride month – the Vatican's Congregation for Catholic Education published a pamphlet denying the validity of LGBTQ+ identities. According to this text, queer identities are 'founded on nothing more than a confused concept of freedom in the realm of feelings and wants, [...] as opposed to anything based on the truths of existence'.[21] Gender theories which affirm LBGTQ+ identities are declared to 'annihilate the concept of "nature"', and threaten the 'anthropological fact' of the nuclear family.[22] Whilst exposure to religion is typically protective against suicide for cis-heterosexual individuals, a recent study concluded that it was 'positively associated with suicidal thoughts and behaviours' for LGB individuals.[23] On the evidence of this study, as well as the Vatican's overtly transphobic pamphlet, the same is likely to be true of trans and genderqueer individuals. However, religion can also be a powerfully affirming facet of a trans person's life.[24] In the medieval period, trans and gender non-conforming identities were often understood as indicating proximity to, rather than distance from, the divine. This volume is part of the ongoing work to affirm holiness as entirely compatible with trans identities, and to offer historically grounded refutation of theological transphobia. Jonah Coman offered a fulsome rebuttal of the Vatican's pamphlet on Twitter, demonstrating that the text's assertions contradict the Catholic tradition and history it claims to protect.[25]

In 2018, the British government opened a public consultation on proposed reforms to the Gender Recognition Act (GRA) (2004), aimed at simplifying the process of obtaining legal recognition of one's identified gender. The initial report noted that the GRA 'perpetuate[d] the outdated and false assumption that being trans is a mental illness', whilst being 'overly intrusive, humiliating and administratively burdensome'.[26] However, the consultation unleashed a so-called 'debate' on the validity of trans existence. Trans Exclusionary Radical Feminists (TERFs) have gained prominence in

21 Congregation for Catholic Education, 'Towards a Path', p. 11.
22 Ibid., p. 14; pp. 20-21 (p. 20).
23 Lytle et al, 'Association of Religiosity'.
24 See, for example, Pulitano, 'Ceremonies'.
25 Coman, Twitter. Coman revisits themes of transness and sanctity in the cover image he created for the present volume.
26 Minister for Women and Equalities, *Reform*, p. 21.

the UK, spreading transmisogynistic rhetoric popularized by academics including Janice Raymond in the 1970s and 1980s, and gathering momentum through support from well-known figures such as J.K. Rowling.[27] Reportedly, submitted responses to the consultation were overwhelmingly in favour of reform.[28] And yet, in June 2020, newspapers announced that the Conservative Government does not intend to implement any changes.[29] Alarmingly, there were indications instead that long-established trans rights may be rolled back. At the time of writing (July 2020), the trans community is redoubling their fight, whilst preparing for the worst.

In the USA, the Trump administration has enacted legislative changes ranging from removing requirements for agencies receiving government funding to treat trans people equally, to banning transgender individuals from serving in the military.[30] In 2018, a memo revealed that the administration was considering implementing a legal definition of 'sex' as 'either male or female, unchangeable, and determined by the genitals that a person is born with'.[31] This attempt to define trans people out of existence would also, of course, be devastating for intersex people. Trans people responded on social media with the hashtag #WontBeErased. In spite of all the hostility, in spite of its very material, very deadly effect on trans lives, trans life continues to flourish. The internet allows trans people to talk, rather than merely being talked about. The open structures of the web challenge hierarchical distributions of power. Therefore, we cite Twitter and Wikipedia proudly: these are communal tools that allow disenfranchised populations to document their experiences. More than ever, trans voices are being heard. In June 2020, the Supreme Court of the United States ruled that Title VII of the Civil Rights Act (1964) offers protection from workplace discrimination to LGBT+ employees.[32] This is a landmark victory – but the struggle continues. In May 2020, for instance, the Hungarian parliament ended recognition for trans and intersex people, 'replac[ing] the category of "sex" on the civil registry with [...] "sex assigned at birth"'.[33]

---

27 Raymond, *Empire*; Lewis, 'British Feminism'. Although the term 'TERF' was coined as a descriptor, it is now claimed to be a slur by many anti-trans feminists. Trans-exclusionary voices now describe themselves as 'gender-critical'. See 'TERF' and 'Gender-Critical' in the Appendix: p. 314 and p. 297 respectively. On Rowling, see: Montgomerie, 'Addressing'.
28 Stonewall, 'Statement'.
29 Cowburn, 'Groups'.
30 National Center for Transgender Equality, 'Administration'.
31 Green, Benner, and Pear, 'Defined Out of Existence'.
32 Supreme Court of the United States, Bostock v. Clayton County.
33 ILGA-Europe, 'Hungary Rolls Back Legal Protections'.

Visibility and history

The greater visibility of trans identities in contemporary culture has led some to turn to a faulty version of history in order to justify transphobia. Were there transgender people in the Middle Ages? The question itself is, as M.W. Bychowski points out, 'a bit absurd'.[34] For one, it is rooted in the conceptualization of trans identity as an aberrant product of twenty-first century culture. How quaint, that 2000-something predilection for transgender lives! That is how future historians – how we – will remember trans identities, so the transphobic logic goes. And yet, history does not remember faithfully, nor are historians necessarily the most efficient messengers of past insights. Marginalized identities are often written out of the historical record by those with the privilege of formulating 'historical truth'. The Middle Ages is frequently viewed as a time 'where men were men, women were women, everyone was the same race and practiced the same faith, and no one was corrupted by technology, sexuality or democracy'.[35] This is not how any medievalist worth their salt would put it.

Disingenuous interrogation of the presence of trans people in history is rarely about the factual specifics of the past alone. If talking about medieval trans lives is 'anachronistic', then 'trans-ness [is] not an inextricable part of humanity or gender diversity'.[36] The transphobes' dream is an imaginary medieval past in which everyone knows their (gendered) place. Similar themes emerge in the usage of the Middle Ages by the alt-right and beyond: those who fantasize a past in which everyone who mattered was straight, cisgender, white, and Christian.[37] White supremacists and fascists weaponize the Middle Ages to justify their hatred; as a discipline, medieval studies itself is the product and progenitor of structural racism and intersectional oppressions.[38]

'If the medieval past (globally) is being weaponized for the aims of extreme, violent supremacist groups, what are you doing, medievalists, in your classrooms?', asked Dorothy Kim in 2017.[39] The question remains as urgent as ever. We must uplift the voices of medievalists of colour, of queer medievalists, of trans medievalists, of disabled medievalists, of women

---

34 Bychowski, 'Transgender People?'.
35 Amy Kaufman, interviewed in Porterfield, 'Medieval Mindset'.
36 Bychowski, 'Transgender People?'.
37 Kim, 'Charlottesville', 'Teaching'; Rambaran-Olm, 'Misnaming'.
38 Medievalists of Color, 'On Race'; Medievalists of Color, 'Race in the Profession'; Miyashiro, 'Decolonizing'; Rambaran-Olm, 'Misnaming'; 'White Supremacy'.
39 Kim, 'Teaching'.

medievalists, of non-Christian medievalists: of the modern representatives of all the groups that some seek to erase by weaponizing the Middle Ages. We must affirm the value of avowedly situated and embodied scholarship, because all scholarship is situated and embodied. Hegemonic, unmarked situations and bodies have for too long been allowed to masquerade as 'normality' and 'neutrality'. Hundreds of years separate us from medieval subjects, but time can be queered.[40] The past can be felt, and is often closer than we think.

State of the field (1): Academic trans studies

Trans studies is too broad, too deep, and too well-established to be summarized efficiently in the space available here – this in itself is a wonderful thing.[41] The field's major theoretical propositions can be traced from its inception to the present along the following trajectory. Sandy Stone's 'The Empire Strikes Back' and Susan Stryker's 'My Words to Victor Frankenstein' are foundational 1990s texts that position trans studies as a vibrant – and very necessary – opposition to gender essentialism, giving trans people a voice within academic discourse. Stryker and Paisley Currah revisited the fundamentals of trans theory in 'Postposttranssexual', the inaugural keywords edition of *TSQ: Transgender Studies Quarterly* (2014).[42] Trans theory has been situated as the ungrateful evil twin of queer theory; a contention that can be variously dismissive and productive, as demonstrated by Stryker and V. Varun Chaudhry.[43] Writing in 2019, Andrea Long Chu is more fatalistic: 'Trans studies is the twin that queer studies ate in the womb.' 'Trans studies is over', she proclaims, and '[i]f it isn't, it should be.'[44] We disagree, though the provocation is welcome. There is much work left to do.

Academic trans studies is disproportionately white, for which it is undoubtedly the poorer. White-centric frameworks from the global North are not the only ways to think and understand trans identities and bodies. The insistent focus on trans-ness and/as whiteness erases trans people of

---

40   On queer temporalities see: Edelman, *No Future*; Love, *Feeling Backward*; Dinshaw, *Getting Medieval*; *How Soon?*. On trans time(s), see: DeVun and Tortorici, 'Trans*historicities'; Mills, *Seeing Sodomy*, pp. 81-132.
41   Stryker and Aizura, *Reader 2*; Stryker and Whittle, *Reader*.
42   Whittington's entry for 'Medieval' demonstrates the significance of medieval contexts for trans identities.
43   Stryker, 'Evil Twin'; Chaudhry, 'Centering'.
44   Chu and Drager, 'After Trans Studies', p. 103.

colour and their experiences, reproducing racialized normativity within the trans community itself.[45] To avoid reinscribing the violence of colonial and white-supremacist regimes of gender, it is essential to foreground intersectionality, especially the role of racialization, bringing the lived histories of multiply marginalized individuals centre stage. The term 'transgender' itself can erase or overwrite indigenous frameworks of gender.[46] In the past few years, long-standing efforts to decolonize trans studies have begun to gain (more) traction within academic publications. In 2014, a special issue of *TSQ*, edited by Aren Z. Aizura et al., was devoted to 'decolonizing the transgender imaginary'. C. Riley Snorton's book, *Black on Both Sides* (2017), was a landmark in Black trans studies, analysing the parallel structures subtending the production of gender and race, and the ways that chattel slavery (re)shaped paradigms of gender.[47] Snorton's book is, to date, the most visible example of the ascendency of Black trans studies.[48] Much of the most cutting-edge work in trans studies is online only, often written in non-academic jargon and from outside the academic community. Gatekeeping of what counts as theorization, who gets to speak about trans identities, and which forms of discourse are valid, is an obstacle both to the production and dissemination of work by marginalized scholars, and to the progress of the entire field.

Trans studies features on more curricula than ever. The rise of trans studies – and recognition of trans identities – in the Academy has, however, provoked considerable backlash. In 2018, *The Guardian* published an open letter from a network of academics employed in the UK, first signed by Kathleen Stock, a prominent anti-trans philosopher.[49] The network contends that trans-inclusive policies stifle 'academic freedom'. Yet debating the validity of trans lives is no mere academic exercise; it has real-world impact within and beyond the classroom. Numerous junior scholars have testified to the ways in which transphobic – and 'gender-critical' – discourse excludes and harms.[50] The *Confronting Trans Antagonism* digital toolkit, first made available online in 2018, is an invaluable resource for trans-affirming

---

45 Aizura et al., 'Transgender Imaginary'; Bey, 'Trans*-ness of Blackness'; binaohan, *decolonizing*; Camminga, 'Umbrella?'; Dutta and Roy, 'Decolonizing'; Ellison et al, 'Issue of Blackness'; Paramo, 'Transphobia'; Snorton, *Black on Both Sides*.
46 binaohan, *decolonizing*, pp. 25-36.
47 Snorton, *Black on Both Sides*.
48 See also: Bey, 'Trans*-ness of Blackness'; Ellison et al., 'Issue of Blackness'.
49 Stock (and signatories), 'Academics'.
50 See: Spicer, 'Stuck in Between'; t philosopher, 'Leaving'.

pedagogy.[51] That such a toolkit is even necessary testifies to the routine nature of transphobia in the classroom. Transphobia must be addressed not only in pedagogy, but also in the profession of academia.

State of the field (2): medieval trans studies

Trans medievalism, as a field, has flourished in recent years. Arguably the most prominent and innovative scholar is M.W. Bychowski, whose website, *Transliterature: Things Transform* is a crucial resource for researchers. Bychowski is a pioneer in medieval trans studies, establishing the discipline through her extensive publications and her commitment to increasing the visibility of medieval trans scholars and scholarship at international conferences.[52] In 2019, Bychowski co-edited and co-wrote the Introduction for a special edition of *Medieval Feminist Forum*, 'Visions of Medieval Trans Feminism', with Dorothy Kim.[53] This Introduction charts the scholarly work accomplished and the changing political landscape since 2016. The piece is an outstanding primer on the stakes and trajectory of premodern trans studies. Bychowski and Kim map the intersections of medieval feminist studies and medieval trans studies, and discuss the experience of being a trans woman scholar in the Academy. As we write, there is only one out trans scholar of medieval studies in a permanent academic position, worldwide. Cis scholars working in trans studies must centre the voices of their trans colleagues.

Whilst trans scholars remain, by and large, in precarious academic positions, work in medieval trans studies is increasingly visible, and increasingly embraced by the institutional 'mainstream'. Robert Mills' monograph, *Seeing Sodomy in the Middle Ages*, which offers numerous transgender readings of medieval French and English literature and art, was awarded the Society for French Studies' R. Gapper Book Prize in 2015.[54] Jessica A. Boon won the Society for Medievalist Feminist Scholarship's 2019 'Best Article' award, for her essay on trans saint Juana de la Cruz.[55] If the floodgates are not exactly opening, there is a noticeable efflorescence of premodern trans scholarship receiving the imprimatur of 'respectable' academic presses – including

---

51 Buchanan et al., *Toolkit*. See also Coman, 'Ally'.
52 Bychowski, *Transliterature: Things Transform*; 'Isle'; 'Reconstructing'; 'Trans Textuality'.
53 Bychowski and Kim, 'Visions'; 'Introduction'.
54 See also Mills, 'Visibly Trans?'
55 On Juana, see also Elphick in this volume: pp. 87-107.

the present volume. The 2019 special issue of the *Journal for Early Modern Cultural Studies* on Early Modern trans studies, edited by Simone Chess, Colby Gordon, and Will Fisher is another landmark, soon to be joined by the collection *Trans Historical: Gender Plurality Before the Modern*, edited by Masha Raskolnikov, Greta LaFleur, and Anna Kłosowska (forthcoming, Cornell University Press). Such scholarship has been largely anglocentric thus far, at least in terms of works reaching wider academic audiences. Nevertheless, things are changing on this front too, with medieval trans studies gaining currency beyond anglophone contexts. Here, we think particularly of Clovis Maillet's 2020 French-language study, *Les genres fluides : de Jeanne d'Arc aux saintes trans* (*Fluid Genders: From Joan of Arc to Trans Saints*).

The vibrancy of premodern trans studies is further evidenced by the urgent, revelatory work being done by doctoral candidates. Blake Gutt's 2018 article 'Transgender Genealogy in *Tristan de Nanteuil*', written during his PhD, included a manifesto for future work in the field, insisting upon the validity and value of trans theory in and for medieval studies. In 2020, Ellis Light was awarded Fordham University's Department of English Graduate Essay Prize for their chapter 'Trans/Mystical: The Euphoria of Blood, Milk, and Sweat in Julian of Norwich's *Revelation*'. This work was explicitly inspired by Bychowski and Kim's special issue of *Medieval Feminist Forum*; clearly medieval trans scholarship is responding to a keenly felt need.[56]

Some of the most important work in medieval trans studies is being done by the most precariously situated scholars: graduate students, early career researchers, those without permanent positions.[57] Securely employed scholars – who are almost always cis – must use their status to support marginalized trans colleagues, practically and intellectually. Cis privilege also means that trans studies is more readily accepted as valuable when it is undertaken by non-trans researchers. Medieval trans studies undoubtedly benefits from the sensitive and thoughtful engagement of cis scholars. Indeed, the field owes a significant debt to the queer and feminist work that paved the way for the emergence of the discipline, as outlined below. However, cis scholars should be mindful not to let their presence crowd out trans voices, and should actively create space for their trans colleagues to flourish. The current volume uplifts the work of early career trans and genderqueer scholars, and offers a model of ethical and engaged cis-authored scholarship.

56   Light, 'Trans/Mystical', p. 1.
57   Medievalists of Color, 'Youngest'.

Terms of engagement (1)

Queer and feminist scholars have been instrumental in highlighting the ways in which hagiography routinely confounds essentialist, binaristic expectations of sex and gender. We must acknowledge, however, that these fields have largely excluded academics of colour, and continue to do so to this day. Feminism in medieval studies has almost always meant white feminism, with very little engagement with global or transnational feminism, womanism, or, more recently, critical race studies. Similarly, queer medieval studies has centred whiteness, ignoring theoretical strands such as queer of colour critique. Since the 1980s, (white) feminist medievalists have worked to redress the stark gender imbalance in the canon. Women, let alone female saints, were largely absent. Through the publication of paradigm-exploding criticism, scholars including Caroline Walker Bynum and Barbara Newman have made the lives of female saints both accessible and relevant.[58] Central to the feminist recovery of neglected sources is close attention to the particularities of female saints' lives, as a distinct corpus and in terms of individual women. Whilst traditional(ist) scholarship held that holy women were passive and submissive, feminist criticism foregrounds the gender dynamics at play. Saints negotiate with patriarchal-ecclesiastical authorities to claim power for themselves. They collaborate with male confessors and hagiographers to co-create their textual identities and to formulate new kinds of theology, directly inspired by their gendered subject position. Feminist criticism thus interrogates how sanctity alters the rules of the gender 'game'.

Bynum's hugely influential *Jesus as Mother*, for instance, demonstrates that Jesus was routinely portrayed as a maternal figure in the Middle Ages. Born of the Virgin Mary alone, his body is fundamentally female. As such, women are not simply sinners, but fully capable of divinity. Bynum re-conceptualizes 'extreme' female asceticism as an affirmative act for holy women.[59] Saints mortify their flesh not to destroy or to negate their bodies to reach God, but instead to find transcendence by inhabiting their bodies as fully, as intensely, as possible. To embrace the (female) body is to embrace divinity. Jesus' gender fluidity is an archetype of a broader pattern in medieval spiritual texts. Whereas monks might position themselves as brides of Christ, following the example of the erotically charged Song of

---

58   Bynum, *Jesus as Mother*; *Holy Feast*; *Fragmentation*; B. Newman, *Virile Woman*; *Sister of Wisdom*. On feminist hagiographical studies see, for a start, Hollywood, *Soul*; Lochrie, *Translations*.
59   *Holy Feast*; *Fragmentation*.

Songs, pious women were often considered to become more virile.[60] Whilst underscoring that transgression of gender boundaries was commonplace in medieval religion, 'pre-trans studies' feminist analyses tended to emphasise a limited fluidity, a movement between fixed male and female polarities, subverting but not surpassing the binary itself. A more recent strand of critique conceptualizes saints as transcending the gender binary entirely, inhabiting a 'third' gender.[61]

Queer and feminist scholarship highlights the sexualization of saints: the ways that holy women and men become subject to the consuming gaze of desiring worshippers, alongside their own highly eroticized mystical encounters with Christ. Worship can be an intimate act between queer subjects. Gender is not necessarily the operative factor, what matters is the transcendent trajectory of pious desire: worshipper to saint, saint to God. Depictions of saintly nudity and vulnerability during torture closely resemble modern pornography, as noted by scholars including Robert Mills, Bill Burgwinkle, and Cary Howie.[62] Critics' juxtaposition of queerness and sanctity articulates the evident, yet heretofore unspeakable, truth: not only did queer medieval people exist, but medieval religion was fundamentally queer.[63] The religious gaze was never (merely) heterosexual. The uncritical assumption that 'heterosexuality' was the norm – or even existed as such – in the Middle Ages radically limits comprehension of sources from the period.[64]

Trans studies is additive, not derivative. The objective is not to replace feminist and queer readings, but rather to expand upon the possibilities that these readings offer. At the same time, trans studies indicates where such readings have overwritten or erased trans potentialities, while continuing to insist on the paramount importance of the availability and co-existence of multiple interpretations. While productively nuancing other readings, medieval trans studies must also be receptive to critique, and must collaborate with related fields. For example, there exists a large corpus of work on medieval 'hermaphrodites', much of it flawed by the simplistic equation of mythical hermaphrodites with historical intersex bodies and

---

60 For an example, see Elphick in this volume, pp. 90-94.
61 McDaniel, *Third Gender*; Murray, 'One Flesh'; Spencer-Hall, *Medieval Saints*, pp. 55-59.
62 Mills, *Suspended Animation*, pp. 106-44 (p. 109); Burgwinkle and Howie, *Sanctity and Pornography*.
63 See also: Burrus, *Sex Lives*; Boswell, *Same-Sex Unions*, pp. 108-61; *Christianity*; Campbell, *Gift*; 'Translating'; Gaunt, 'Straight Minds'; Mills, 'Delight'; Hollywood, 'Queering'; *Sensible Ecstasy*; Lees and Watt, 'Age and Desire'; Lochrie, 'Mystical Acts'.
64 Schultz, 'Heterosexuality'.

lives. Recent scholarship in medieval intersex studies has reassessed and revised these harmful assumptions.[65] Karl Whittington, for instance, asks whether individuals identified as trans in medievalist work would better be understood as intersex at times.[66]

Terms of engagement (2)

A commitment to rigorous attention to historical sources is a hallmark of trans medievalist work. In order to counter transphobic, misogynist, and/or queerphobic arguments that rely on interpretations of the Bible, biblical paratexts, and Christian traditions, we return to these sources to see what the texts actually say.[67] This allows us to challenge marginalizing biblical interpretation by contextualizing it within a fluid tradition of Christian inquiry into the nature of being human.[68] Another essential tool is commitment to a non-teleological, non-linear historicism, capable of exploring how the past offers new ways of being in the present and future. The past is present in the now; seeing trans lives in medieval sources is affirming in meaningful ways, including politically.[69] Anti-theoretical approaches contend that objectivity about the past is not only possible, but the benchmark for the work of professional historians. This is an untenable position, which reinscribes the hegemonic status of the very subject positions that currently pass for objective. Ways of seeing, thinking and being that are produced by marginalization are not simply of 'special interest' to those directly impacted by oppressions; they are essential, challenging the notion of any 'singular', 'objective' history, and revealing the seeds of resistance that were always already there.

Before trans studies, medieval studies was already home to a considerable body of work on 'transvestite' saints.[70] Disguise is a recurrent motif, casting gender expressions that might also be read as trans identities as forms of deception. This pernicious trope – often a product of the critic rather than the

---

65   Notable work on medieval intersex identities includes the 2018 special edition of *postmedieval* edited by Ruth Evans, comprising an Introduction (Evans, 'Gender') that summarizes the latest scholarship.
66   'Medieval Intersex', p. 240.
67   Bychowski, 'On Genesis'; DeVun, 'Heavenly Hermaphrodites'.
68   Strassfeld and Henderson-Espinoza, 'Trans*/Religion'.
69   Gutt, 'Anamorphosis'; Evans, 'Gender', pp. 120-22.
70   For bibliography, see: Whittington, 'Medieval Intersex', p. 240 n.11.

text itself – forecloses the affirmative interpretation of trans identities.[71] This is not to say that characters in medieval texts do not cross-dress. Rather, the reflexive assumption that non-normative gender expressions can *only* ever indicate cross-dressing is reductive. Trans studies offers multiple, nuanced ways of reading and interpreting texts. Historical sources come with their own problems. They are imperfect or unavailable; we don't have access to medieval trans lives described by medieval trans individuals. However, we do have evidence that medieval individuals thought about gender in complex ways. Hagiography is not biography, but these texts showcase what medieval people were told to believe, the ways that gender was being considered and discussed, and the questions that were being asked that these texts tried to answer: trans lives could be envisioned and, therefore, trans lives could be lived.

Research is not just about flipping binaries but also about reading, discovering, different *kinds* of gender. Christ, for example, may be read as genderqueer, trans, or beyond gender.[72] Kathryn M. Ringrose proposes that medieval eunuchs inhabited a third gender, a proposition equally forwarded by several scholars of hagiography, in response to the ways that saints' lives negotiate, and at times explode, simplistic gender binaries.[73] Leah DeVun draws from medical, alchemical, and theological texts to reveal 'Christ him/herself as a hermaphrodite, the perfect combination of contraries – masculine and feminine, human and divine – in one body'.[74] Gutt's study of St Fanuel foregrounds the ways in which, in some hagiographic contexts at least, gender transgressions do not foreclose secure gendered identities.[75]

The fact that senior scholars see value in revisiting their own past interpretations clearly indicates the significance of transgender as an optic.[76] In the present volume, Martha G. Newman transports us into her own scholarly history, revisiting arguments from her 2003 article about a monk named Joseph, and re-visioning the monastic not as 'a woman in disguise', but as a trans man.[77] Newman offers a blueprint for ethical scholarship: the

---

71   Davis, 'Crossed Texts'; Anson, 'Female Transvestite'; Grayson, 'Disruptive Disguises'. In this volume, see also Wright (pp. 155-76) and Bychowski (pp. 245-65); 'Transvestite' in the Appendix: p. 322.
72   DeVun, 'Heavenly Hermaphrodites', pp. 137-39.
73   Ringrose, 'Shadows'. On eunuchs, see also: Ringrose, *Perfect Servant*; Tougher, *Eunuch*; 'Holy Eunuchs!'; Szabo in this volume: pp. 109-29.
74   'The Jesus Hermaphrodite', p. 195.
75   'Anamorphosis'.
76   See, e.g.: Karras and Linkinen, 'Revisited', revising arguments in Karras and Boyd, 'Interrogation' and '"Ut cum muliere"'.
77   M.G. Newman, 'Real Men'.

ways that scholars, particularly cis-heterosexual scholars, can and should return to earlier work rooted in trans-exclusionary (or trans-minimizing) paradigms. Such reassessment is also necessary on the macro-level, as disciplinary norms, standard methodologies, and default assumptions are revisited, and thereby improved. The necessity – and fruitfulness – of this work is demonstrated in Colwill's chapter in this volume, which shows what is to gain when the gendered biases that permeate archaeology as a field are challenged.[78] The assumption of gender binarism skews findings, in archaeology as elsewhere.

The scope of the present volume is relatively narrow; we focus on a subset of cultural artefacts, using a particular theoretical approach. We therefore recognize that there are significant intersections of identity that are not substantively addressed in this collection. These include queer sexualities; racial and geographic diversity (almost all of the sources addressed are western European, and all assume whiteness as default); disability; and class. Colwill and Szabo's chapters examine Late Iron Age Scandinavia and the Byzantine Empire respectively, while Gutt's chapter considers the intersection of trans and crip embodiments. Regarding the question of class, the subjects discussed in this collection are all extraordinary in some way, belonging to an elite class of holiness.

The decolonization of trans studies is imperative.[79] From the Indian subcontinent to North America, European colonization is responsible for the stigmatization and eradication of indigenous gender identities that colonizers viewed as 'unnatural'.[80] The link between transphobia and white supremacy is well attested.[81] The racial(ized) histories of trans identities is a critical area of research, and far-reaching analyses of the connection between racialization and trans embodiment(s) have been published in the last few years.[82] Such projects are especially urgent since trans women of colour are the focus of the most deadly form of transphobia: transmisogynoir.[83] In terms of this collection, productive future work might examine Western Christian notions of trans identity, exceptionality and sanctity alongside non-Western models of 'exceptional' and/or holy trans identities, for example

---

78   Pp. 177-97, especially 179-82, 186-87, 191-93.
79   Aizura et al, 'Transgender Imaginary'; binaohan, *decolonizing*.
80   Picq, 'Decolonizing'.
81   Paramo, 'Transphobia'; also 'White Supremacy' in the Appendix, pp. 324-25.
82   Bey, 'Trans*-ness of Blackness'; Camminga, 'Umbrella?'; Dutta and Roy, 'Decolonizing'; Ellison et al, 'Issue of Blackness'; Snorton, *Black on Both Sides*.
83   See 'Transmisogynoir' in the Appendix: p. 320.

the hijras of the Indian subcontinent, and indigenous North American Two-Spirit individuals.[84]

Overview of the collection

The first section of the volume focuses on the traces of queer medieval lives, and reinscribing trans and genderqueer realities by critiquing assumptions that reproduce the status quo. Martha G. Newman's chapter examines an equivocal narrative told about a twelfth-century German monk named Joseph, offering its readers by turns an essentialist portrayal of gendered disguise and a portrait of a self-actualized trans man. Caitlyn McLoughlin analyses John Capgrave's fifteenth-century *Life of St Katherine* within a queer genealogical framework, whilst addressing the saint's relative privilege through the lens of homonormativity. Kevin C.A. Elphick's examination of gender fluidity and liminality in the *Life* and sermons of Juana de la Cruz demonstrates that her use of imagery that transcends gender is contiguous, and compatible, with earlier hagiographic sources and with her Franciscan heritage. Through the case study of Patriarch Ignatios, Felix Szabo explores the sacred masculinity available to eunuch saints: were eunuchs really capable of saintly behaviour?

The second section of the collection addresses objects, images and identities – and trans and genderqueer ways of looking at them. Sophie Sexon examines imagery of Christ's wounds in Books of Hours and prayer rolls, reading this sacred body as non-binary. Vanessa Wright explores corporeal, sartorial, and gestural signifiers of gender and identity in illuminations of the *Vie de sainte Eufrosine* in three fourteenth-century Parisian manuscripts. Lee Colwill's chapter investigates four remarkable burials in Late Iron Age Scandinavia, exploring the evidence for connecting the magico-religious practice of *seiðr* with transgressive gender performances.

The final section considers imbrications of gender and genre. Reflecting on the Old French *Vie de sainte Eufrosine*, Amy V. Ogden considers the role of gender transgression in the poet's pedagogical techniques. Blake Gutt combines trans and crip theory to read the character of Blanchandin·e in a fourteenth-century French text, *Tristan de Nanteuil*, in which impairment, cure, and gender transformation function as tools of a hagiographic narrative. Analysing an extract from Magnus Hirschfeld's *Transvestites* on St Marinos,

---

84 See 'Hijra' (p. 301) and 'Two-Spirit' (p. 324) in the Appendix.

M.W. Bychowski repurposes Hirschfeld's theories to read medieval trans saints through the frame of authenticity.

In her Epilogue, Mathilde van Dijk situates the essays in this collection as descendants of a feminist tradition which insists upon the complexity of gender identity. Van Dijk maintains that medieval texts are particularly useful in the fight for trans and genderqueer rights today: they testify to the inherent instability of the gender binary, whilst proffering different models of conceptualizing gender.

The chapters are presented in thematic units; however, many other fruitful combinations are possible. For example, St Eufrosine unites Ogden and Wright's chapters, and each can be productively juxtaposed with Bychowski's chapter on St Marinos, and Newman's chapter on brother Joseph, two other AFAB monks. The authenticity of the trans soul, foregrounded by Bychowski, resonates with Sexon's assessment of a genderqueer Christ who offers potent representation of genders beyond the binary, and Elphick's study of Mother Juana's divine prenatal regendering. Sexon's analyses demonstrate that the perfect divinity of Christ's body depends upon its 'imperfection' – his wounds. Gutt's chapter centres a disabled body, and examines the structures that bind sacred, physically impaired, and transgender embodiment(s) together. This exploration complements Colwill's discussion of skeletal remains, which lays bare the complex physical means by which trans embodiments are constituted, interpreted, or denied. Queer lineages and non-normative genealogies link Ogden, McLoughlin and Gutt's contributions. Szabo's treatment of the Byzantine eunuch saint Patriarch Ignatios adds context to St Eufrosine's self-presentation as a eunuch, explored by Ogden and Wright.

The chapters in this collection represent the cutting-edge of medieval(ist) trans studies and theoretically inflected hagiographical scholarship. This volume is a call to arms. On the one hand, this is a corpus of contextually rigorous, politically engaged scholarship which offers a model for similar progressive research. On the other hand, the collection levies a challenge to scholars across disciplines: how might we reflect upon the past, rethink the past and our role, as academics, in producing it? How can we do justice to our sources, and ourselves? How might we support those with skin in the nominally historical game, professionally and personally? In this spirit, we offer the Appendix to the volume, the 'Trans and Genderqueer Studies Terminology, Language, and Usage Guide'. Historical representation matters, linguistic representation too. Chapters in this volume demonstrate the productivity – the necessity – of trans and genderqueer historical scholarship.

As a complement, the Guide offers practical support for doing such work without perpetuating historical anti-trans and anti-queer injustices.

'History hurts, but not only,' observes Lauren Berlant.[85] No matter how traumatic, history has the potential to inspire 'optimism in response to the oppressive presence of what dominates or is taken for granted. Political emotions are responses to prospects for change: fidelity to those responses is optimistic, even if the affects are dark.'[86] This collection sits at that very crossroad, of joyful optimism constituted by the realization that things must change, that history must do more, must do better, than the status quo of trans-exclusionary work.

Acknowledgements

Many thanks to M.W. Bychowski for her helpful comments on an earlier draft of this piece.

Bibliography

Aizura, Aren Z., Trystan Cotten, Carsten Balzer/Carla LaGata, Marcia Ochoa, and Salvador Vidal-Ortiz, eds., 'Decolonizing the Transgender Imaginary', *TSQ: Transgender Studies Quarterly*, 1.3 (2014).

Anson, John, 'The Female Transvestite in Early Monasticism: The Origin and Development of a Motif', *Viator*, 5 (1974), 1-32.

Berlant, Lauren, *Cruel Optimism* (London: Duke University, 2011).

Bey, Marquis, 'The Trans*-ness of Blackness, the Blackness of Trans*-ness', *TSQ: Transgender Studies Quarterly*, 4.2 (2017), 275-95.

binaohan, b., *decolonizing trans/gender 101* (Toronto: biyuti, 2014).

Boon, Jessica A., 'At the Limits of (Trans)Gender: Jesus, Mary, and the Angels in the Visionary Sermons of Juana de la Cruz (1481-1534)', *Journal of Medieval and Early Modern Studies*, 48.2 (2018), 261-300.

Bornstein, Kate, *A Queer and Pleasant Danger: A Memoir* (Boston: Beacon, 2012).

Boswell, John, *Christianity, Social Tolerance, and Homosexuality: Gay People in Western Europe from the Beginning of the Christian Era to the Fourteenth Century* (Chicago: University of Chicago, 1980).

—, *Same-Sex Unions in Pre-Modern Europe* (New York: Villard, 1994).

---

85 Berlant, *Cruel Optimism*, p. 121.
86 Ibid.

Buchanan, Blu, Ellen Samuels, Aren Aizura, Alana M. Berry, Lisa Hoffman-Kuroda, and Hannah Kagan-Moore, *Confronting Trans Antagonism in the Academy: A Digital Toolkit*, 14 December 2018 <https://docs.google.com/document/d/e/2PACX-1vSd3UlkNkvEMURQc6mKU3nwicfhhQeBvsXQl9kbw_zK2Ac3QQ8YBm8q_HUSSTETOabtB3Kfsd4SJDQZ/pub#h.tptu4ru5suh4> [accessed 5 January 2019].

Burgwinkle, Bill, and Cary Howie, *Sanctity and Pornography in Medieval Culture: On the Verge* (Manchester: Manchester University, 2010).

Burrus, Virginia, *The Sex Lives of Saints: An Erotics of Ancient Hagiography* (Philadelphia: University of Pennsylvania, 2004).

Bychowski, M.W., 'On Genesis: Transgender and Subcreation', *TSQ: Transgender Studies Quarterly*, 6.3 (2019), 442-47 <https://doi.org/10.1215/23289252-7549598> [accessed 18 August 2019].

——, 'The Isle of Hermaphrodites: Disorienting the Place of Intersex in the Middle Ages', *postmedieval*, 9.2 (2018), 161-78 <https://doi.org/10.1057/s41280-018-0079-1> [accessed 18 August 2019].

——, 'The Patron Saint of Dysphoria: Joan of Arc as Transgender', *Transliterature: Things Transform*, 28 May 2019 <http://www.thingstransform.com/2019/05/the-patron-saint-of-dysphoria-joan-of.html> [accessed 22 August 2019].

——, 'Reconstructing the Pardoner: Transgender Skin Operations in Fragment VI', in *Writing on Skin in the Age of Chaucer*, ed. by Nicole Nyffenegger and Katrin Rupp (Berlin: De Gruyter, 2018), pp. 221-50.

——, 'Rest in Power: The Digital Iconography of Transgender Saints', *Transliterature: Things Transform*, 6 September 2016. <http://www.thingstransform.com/2016/09/rest-in-power-digital-iconography-of.html> [accessed 11 June 2020].

——, *Transliterature: Things Transform* <http://www.thingstransform.com> [accessed 29 August 2019].

——, 'Trans Textuality: Dysphoria in the Depths of Medieval Skin', *postmedieval*, 9.3 (2018), 318-33 <https://doi.org/10.1057/s41280-018-0090-6> [accessed 22 January 2019].

——, 'Were there Transgender People in the Middle Ages?', *The Public Medievalist*, 1 November 2018 <https://www.publicmedievalist.com/transgender-middle-ages/> [accessed 27 August 2019].

Bychowski, M.W., and Dorothy Kim, eds., 'Visions of Medieval Trans Feminism', *Medieval Feminist Forum*, 55.1 (2019) <https://ir.uiowa.edu/mff/vol55/iss1/> [accessed 20 February 2020].

——, 'Visions of Medieval Trans Feminism: An Introduction', *Medieval Feminist Forum*, 55.1 (2019), 6-41 <https://ir.uiowa.edu/mff/vol55/iss1/2/> [accessed 18 February 2020].

Bynum, Caroline Walker, *Fragmentation and Redemption: Essays on Gender and the Human Body in Medieval Religion* (New York: Zone, 1991).

—, *Holy Feast and Holy Fast: The Religious Significance of Food to Medieval Women* (Berkeley: University of California, 1987).

—, *Jesus As Mother: Studies in The Spirituality of The High Middle* Ages (Berkeley: University of California, 1982).

Campbell, Emma, *Medieval Saints' Lives: The Gift, Kinship and Community in Old French Hagiography* (Cambridge: Brewer, 2008).

—, 'Translating Gender in Thirteenth-Century French Cross-dressing Narratives: *Le Roman de Silence* and *La Vie de Sainte Euphrosine*', *Journal of Medieval and Early Modern Studies*, 49.2 (2019), 233-64.

Camminga, B. 'Where's Your Umbrella?: Decolonisation and Transgender Studies in South Africa', *Postamble*, 10.1 (2017) <https://www.academia.edu/31979917/Wheres_Your_Umbrella_Decolonisation_and_Transgender_Studies_in_South_Africa> [accessed 16 June 2019].

Chaudhry, V. Varun, 'Centering the "Evil Twin": Rethinking Transgender in Queer Theory', *GLQ*, 25.1 (2019), 45-50 <https://doi.org/10.1215/10642684-7275278> [accessed 29 August 2019].

Chess, Simone, Colby Gordon, and Will Fisher, eds., 'Early Modern Trans Studies', *Journal for Early Modern Cultural Studies*, 19.4 (2019).

Chu, Andrea Long, and Emmett Harsin Drager, 'After Trans Studies [A Dialogue]', *TSQ: Transgender Studies Quarterly*, 6.1 (2019), 103-11 <https://doi.org/10.1215/23289252-7253524> [accessed 22 August 2019].

Coman, Jonah (@MxComan), [Twitter thread responding to Vatican's Congregation for Catholic Education 2019 pamphlet on gender], 10 June 2019 <https://threadreaderapp.com/thread/1138201535169597441.html> [accessed 30 August 2019].

—, 'Be My Ally: A Guide to Being a Trans Ally for Academics', 2019 <www.bit.do/BeMyAlly> [accessed 4 June 2020].

Congregation for Catholic Education, '"Male and Female He Created Them": Towards a Path of Dialogue on the Question of Gender Theory in Education', 2 February 2019 [circulated June 2019] <http://www.educatio.va/content/dam/cec/Documenti/19_0997_INGLESE.pdf> [accessed 27 August 2019].

Cowburn, Ashley, 'Cross-party LGBT+ Groups Unite to Condemn Boris Johnson's "Plans to Scrap Trans Self-Identification"', *The Independent* [online], 19 June 2020 <https://www.independent.co.uk/news/uk/politics/trans-rights-lgbt-gender-recognition-act-boris-johnson-liz-truss-a9575256.html> [accessed 1 July 2020].

Davis, Stephen J., 'Crossed Texts, Crossed Sex: Intertextuality and Gender in Early Christian Legends of Holy Women Disguised as Men', *Journal of Early Christian Studies*, 10.1 (2002), 1-36.

DeVun, Leah, 'Heavenly Hermaphrodites: Sexual Difference at the Beginning and End of Time', *postmedieval*, 9.2 (2018), 132-46 <https://doi.org/10.1057/s41280-018-0080-8> [accessed 18 November 2018].

—, 'The Jesus Hermaphrodite: Science and Sex Difference in Premodern Europe', *Journal of the History of Ideas*, 69.2 (April 2008), 193-218.

DeVun, Leah, and Zeb Tortorici, eds., 'Trans*historicities', *TSQ: Transgender Studies Quarterly*, 5.4 (2018).

Dinshaw, Carolyn, *Getting Medieval: Sexualities and Communities, Pre- and Postmodern* (Durham: Duke University, 1999).

—, *How Soon is Now? Medieval Texts, Amateur Readers, and the Queerness of Time* (Durham: Duke University, 2012).

Dutta, Aniruddha, and Raina Roy. 'Decolonizing Transgender in India: Some Reflections', *TSQ: Transgender Studies Quarterly*, 1.3 (2014), 320-36.

Edelman, Lee, *No Future. Queer Theory and the Death Drive* (Durham: Duke University, 2004).

Ellison, Joy, and Nicholas Hoffman, 'The Afterward: Sylvia Rivera and Marsha P. Johnson in the Medieval Imaginary', *Medieval Feminist Forum*, 55.1 (2019), 267-94.

Ellison, Treva, Kai. M. Green, Matt Richardson, and C. Riley Snorton, eds., 'The Issue of Blackness,' *TSQ: Transgender Studies Quarterly*, 4.2 (2017).

Evans, Ruth, 'Gender Does Not Equal Genitals', *postmedieval*, 9.2 (2018), 120-31 <https://doi.org/10.1057/s41280-018-0088-0> [accessed 18 November 2018.]

—, ed., 'Medieval Intersex: Language and Hermaphroditism', *postmedieval*, 9.2 (2018).

Feinberg, Leslie, *Transgender Liberation: A Movement Whose Time Has Come* (New York: World View Forum, 1992) <https://www.workers.org/book/transgender-liberation-a-movement-whose-time-has-come/> [accessed 19 February 2020].

—, *Transgender Warriors* (Boston: Beacon, 1996).

Gaunt, Simon, 'Straight Minds / 'Queer' Wishes in Old French Hagiography: *La Vie de Sainte Euphrosine*', *GLQ*, 1 (1995), 439-57.

GLAAD, 'Transgender Day of Remembrance: Nov 20', *glaad.org* <https://www/glaad.org/tdor> [accessed 2 July 2020].

Grayson, Saisha, 'Disruptive Disguises: The Problem of Transvestite Saints for Medieval Art, Identity, and Identification', *Medieval Feminist Forum*, 45 (2009), 138-74.

Green, Erica L., Katie Benner, and Robert Pear, '"Transgender" Could Be Defined Out of Existence Under Trump Administration', *New York Times* [online], 21 October 2018 <https://www.nytimes.com/2018/10/21/us/politics/transgender-trump-administration-sex-definition.html> [accessed 19 February 2020].

Gutt, Blake, 'Medieval Trans Lives in Anamorphosis: Looking Back and Seeing Differently (Pregnant Men and Backward Birth)', *Medieval Feminist Forum*, 55.1 (2019), 174-206.

—, 'Transgender Genealogy in *Tristan de Nanteuil*', *Exemplaria*, 30.2 (2018), 129-46.

Hollywood, Amy, 'Queering the Beguines: Mechthild of Magdeburg, Hadewijch of Anvers, Marguerite Porete' in *Queer Theology: Rethinking the Western Body*, ed. by Gerard Loughlin (Oxford: Blackwell, 2007), pp. 163-75.

—, *Sensible Ecstasy: Mysticism, Sexual Difference, and the Demands of History* (Chicago: University of Chicago, 2002).

—, *The Soul as Virgin Wife: Mechthild of Magdeburg, Marguerite Porete, and Meister Eckhart* (Notre Dame: University of Notre Dame, 1995).

ILGA-Europe, 'Hungary Rolls Back Legal Protections, Puts Trans and Intersex People at Risk', *ilga-europe.org*, 19 May 2020 <https://ilga-europe.org/resources/news/latest-news/hungary-rolls-back-legal-protections-puts-trans-and-intersex-people-risk> [accessed 10 June 2020].

Karras, Ruth Mazo, and David Lorenzo Boyd, 'The Interrogation of a Male Transvestite Prostitute in Fourteenth-Century London', *GLQ*, 1 (1995), 459-65.

—, '"Ut cum muliere": A Male Transvestite Prostitute in Fourteenth-Century London', in *Premodern Sexualities*, ed. by Louise Fradenburg and Carla Frecerro (London: Routledge, 1996), pp. 99-116.

Karras, Ruth Mazo and Tom Linkinen, 'John/Eleanor Rykener Revisited', in *Founding Feminisms in Medieval Studies: Essays in Honor of E. Jane Burns*, ed. by Laine E. Doggett and Daniel E. O'Sullivan (Woodbridge: Boydell & Brewer, 2016), pp. 111-24.

Keegan, Cáel M., *Lana and Lilly Wachowski* (Urbana: University of Illinois, 2018).

Kim, Dorothy, 'Medieval Studies Since Charlottesville', *Inside Higher Ed*, 30 August 2018 <https://www.insidehighered.com/views/2018/08/30/scholar-describes-being-conditionally-accepted-medieval-studies-opinion> [accessed 19 February 2020].

—, 'Teaching Medieval Studies in a Time of White Supremacy', *In the Middle*, 28 August 2017 <http://www.inthemedievalmiddle.com/2017/08/teaching-medieval-studies-in-time-of.html> [accessed 20 February 2020].

Lees, Clare, and Diane Watt, 'Age and Desire in the Old English *Life of St Mary of Egypt*: A Queerer Time and Place?', in *Middle-Aged Women in the Middle Ages*, ed. by Sue Niebryzdowski (Woodbridge: Brewer, 2011), pp. 53-67.

Lewis, Sophie, 'How British Feminism Became Anti-Trans', *The New York Times* [online], 7 February 2019 <https://www.nytimes.com/2019/02/07/opinion/terf-trans-women-britain.html> [accessed 18 August 2019].

Lichfield, John, 'The 600-year Struggle for the Soul of Joan of Arc', *The Independent* [online], 5 January 2012 <https://www.independent.co.uk/news/world/europe/the-600-year-struggle-for-the-soul-of-joan-of-arc-6284992.html> [accessed 1 July 2020].

Light, Ellis, 'Trans/Mystical: The Euphoria of Blood, Milk, and Sweat in Julian of Norwich's *Revelation*', in *Bodily Fluids and Forms of Community in Medieval Devotional Literature* (Ph.D. dissertation in preparation, Fordham University, 2020).

Lochrie, Karma, *Margery Kempe and Translations of the Flesh* (Philadelphia: University of Pennsylvania, 1991).

—, 'Mystical Acts, Queer Tendencies', in *Constructing Medieval Sexuality*, ed. by Karma Lochrie, Peggy McCracken, and James S. Schultz (Minneapolis: University of Minnesota, 1997), pp. 180-200.

Love, Heather, *Feeling Backward: Loss and the Politics of Queer History* (Cambridge: Harvard University, 2009).

Lytle, Megan C., John R. Blosnich, Susan M. De Luca, and Chris Brownson, 'Association of Religiosity with Sexual Minority Suicide Ideation and Attempt', *American Journal of Preventive Medicine,* 54.5 (2018), 644-51.

Maillet, Clovis, *Les genres fluides : de Jeanne d'Arc aux saintes trans* (Paris: Arkhê, 2020).

McDaniel, Rhonda L., *The Third Gender and Aelfric's "Lives of Saints"* (Kalamazoo: Medieval Institute, 2018).

Medievalists of Color, 'Race in the Profession', *medievalistsofcolor.com* <https://medievalistsofcolor.com/category/race-in-the-profession/> [accessed 17 January 2020].

—, 'On Race and Medieval Studies', *medievalistsofcolor.com*, 1 August 2017 <https://medievalistsofcolor.com/statements/on-race-and-medieval-studies/> [accessed 20 February 2020].

—, 'The Youngest of Old Fields', *medievalistsofcolor.com*, <http://medievalistsofcolor.com/statements/the-youngest-of-old-fields/> [accessed 2 July 2020].

Mills, Robert, *Seeing Sodomy in the Middle Ages* (Chicago: Chicago University, 2014).

—, *Suspended Animation: Pain, Pleasure and Punishment in Medieval Culture* (London: Reaktion, 2005).

—, 'Visibly Trans? Picturing Saint Eugenia in Medieval Art', *TSQ: Transgender Studies Quarterly*, 5.4 (2018), 540-64 <https://doi.org/10.1215/23289252-7090017> [accessed 27 August 2019].

—, '"Whatever You Do is a Delight to Me!": Masculinity, Masochism and Queer Play in Representations of Male Martyrdom', *Exemplaria*, 13.1 (2001), 1-37.

Minister for Women and Equalities (Rt Hon Penny Mordaunt, MP), *Reform of the Gender Recognition Act – Government Consultation*, July 2018 <https://www.gov.uk/government/consultations/reform-of-the-gender-recognition-act-2004> [accessed 19 February 2020].

Miyashiro, Adam, 'Decolonizing Anglo-Saxon Studies: A Response to ISAS in Honolulu', *In the Middle*, 29 July 2017 <http://www.inthemedievalmiddle.com/2017/08/teaching-medieval-studies-in-time-of.html> [accessed 20 February 2020].

Mock, Janet, *Redefining Realness: My Path to Womanhood, Identity, Love and So Much More* (New York: Atria, 2014).

Montgomerie, Katy, 'Addressing the Claims in JK Rowling's Justification for Transphobia', *Medium*, 16 June 2020 <https://medium.com/@completelykaty/addressing-the-claims-in-jk-rowlings-justification-for-transphobia-7b6f761e8f8f> [accessed 1 July 2020].

Movement Advancement Project, 'Identity Document Laws and Policies', *lgbtmap.org*, last updated 18 February 2020, <https://www.lgbtmap.org/equality-maps/identity_document_laws> [accessed 19 February 2020].

Murray, Jacqueline, 'One Flesh, Two Sexes, Three Genders?', in *Gender and Christianity in Medieval Europe: New Perspectives*, ed. by Lisa Bitel and Felice Lifschitz (Philadelphia: University of Pennsylvania, 2008), pp. 34-51.

Natanson, Hannah, '"It's All White People": Allegations of White Supremacy are Tearing Apart a Prestigious Medieval Studies Group', *The Washington Post* [online], 19 September 2019 <https://www.washingtonpost.com/education/2019/09/19/its-all-white-people-allegations-white-supremacy-are-tearing-apart-prestigious-medieval-studies-group/> [accessed 19 February 2020].

National Center for Transgender Equality, 'The Discrimination Administration', *transequality.org* <https://transequality.org/the-discrimination-administration> [accessed 19 February 2020].

Newman, Barbara, *From Virile Woman to WomanChrist: Studies in Medieval Religion and Literature* (Philadelphia: University of Pennsylvania, 1995).

—, *Sister of Wisdom: St. Hildegard's Theology of the Feminine* (Oakland: University of California, 1987).

Newman, Martha G., 'Real Men and Imaginary Women: Engelhard of Langheim Considers a Woman in Disguise', *Speculum*, 78 (2003), 1184-1213.

News Wires, 'French Far-Right Decries Choice of Mixed-Race Joan of Arc in Orléans', *France 24*, 23 February 2018 <https://www.france24.com/en/20180223-france-joan-arc-french-far-right-decries-orleans-choice-mixed-race-festival> [accessed 19 February 2020].

Paramo, Michael, 'Transphobia is a White Supremacist Legacy of Colonialism', *Medium*, 17 July 2018 <https://medium.com/@Michael_Paramo/transphobia-is-a-white-supremacist-legacy-of-colonialism-e50f57240650> [accessed 16 June 2019].

Picq, Manuela P., 'Decolonizing Indigenous Sexualities: Between Erasure and Resurgence', in *The Oxford Handbook of Global LGBT and Sexual Diversity Politics* [online], ed. by Michael Bosia, Sandra M. McEvoy, and Momin Rahman (June 2019) <https://doi.org/10.1093/oxfordhb/9780190673741.013.23> [accessed 14 August 2020].

Porterfield, Katie, 'A Medieval Mindset', *MTSU Magazine* [online], 29 January 2016 <https://mtsunews.com/a-medieval-mindset/> [accessed 10 June 2020].

Pulitano, Jay, 'Transgender Religious Naming Ceremonies', *glaad.org*, 17 June 2014 <https://www.glaad.org/blog/transgender-religious-naming-ceremonies> [accessed 19 February 2019].

Rambaran-Olm, Mary, 'Anglo-Saxon Studies [Early English Studies], Academia and White Supremacy', *Medium*, 27 June 2018 <https://medium.com/@mrambaranolm/anglo-saxon-studies-academia-and-white-supremacy-17c87b360bf3> [accessed 20 February 2020].

—, 'Misnaming the Medieval: Rejecting "Anglo-Saxon" Studies', *History Workshop*, 4 November 2019 <www.historyworkshop.org.uk/misnaming-the-medieval-rejecting-anglo-saxon-studies/> [accessed 19 February 2020].

Raskolnikov, Masha, Greta LaFleur, and Anna Kłosowska, eds., *Trans Historical: Gender Plurality Before the Modern* (Ithaca: Cornell University, forthcoming 2021).

Raymond, Janice, *The Transsexual Empire: The Making of the She-Male* (London: Women's Press, 1980).

Ringrose, Kathryn M., 'Living in the Shadows: Eunuchs and Gender in Byzantium', in *Third Sex, Third Gender: Beyond Sexual Dimorphism in Culture and History*, ed. by Gilbert Herdt (New York: Zone, 1996), pp. 85-109.

—, *The Perfect Servant: Eunuchs and the Social Construction of Gender in Byzantium* (Chicago: University of Chicago, 2003).

Schultz, James A., 'Heterosexuality as a Threat to Medieval Studies', *Journal of the History of Sexuality*, 15.1 (2006), 14-29.

Snorton, C. Riley, *Black on Both Sides: A Racial History of Trans Identity* (Minneapolis: University of Minnesota, 2017).

Spencer-Hall, Alicia, *Medieval Saints and Modern Screens: Divine Visions as Cinematic Experience* (Amsterdam: Amsterdam University, 2018).

Spicer, Puck, 'Stuck in Between: My Experience in Philosophy as a Trans and Non-Binary Student', *MAP UK*, 3 October 2018 <https://www.mapforthegap.org.uk/post/stuck-in-between-my-experience-in-philosophy-as-a-trans-and-non-binary-student> [accessed 28 August 2019].

Steinmetz, Katy, 'The Transgender Tipping Point', *Time* [online], 29 May 2014 <https://time.com/135480/transgender-tipping-point/> [accessed 19 February 2020].

Stock, Kathleen, (and signatories), 'Academics are Being Harassed over their Research into Transgender Issues', *The Guardian* [online], 18 October 2018 <https://www.theguardian.com/society/2018/oct/16/academics-are-being-harassed-over-their-research-into-transgender-issues> [accessed 29 August 2019].

Stone, Sandy, 'The Empire Strikes Back: A Posttranssexual Manifesto', *Camera Obscura*, 10.2 (29) (1992), 150-76.

Stonewall, 'Statement on Reports that Key Gender Recognition Act Reforms are Set to be Dropped', *stonewall.org.uk*, 14 June 2020 <https://www.stonewall.org.uk/about-us/news/statement-reports-key-gender-recognition-act-reforms-are-set-be-dropped> [accessed 1 July 2020].

Strassfeld, Max, and Robyn Henderson-Espinoza, eds., 'Trans*/Religion', *TSQ: Transgender Studies Quarterly*, 6.3 (2019).

Stryker, Susan, 'My Words to Victor Frankenstein Above the Village of Chamounix: Performing Transgender Rage', *GLQ*, 1.3 (1994), 237-54.

—, 'Transgender Studies: Queer Theory's Evil Twin', *GLQ*, 10.2 (2004), 212-15.

Stryker, Susan, and Aren Z. Aizura, eds., *The Transgender Studies Reader 2* (New York: Routledge, 2013).

Stryker, Susan, and Paisley Currah, eds., 'Postposttranssexual: Key Concepts for a Twenty-First-Century Transgender Studies', *TSQ: Transgender Studies Quarterly*, 1.1-2 (2014).

Stryker, Susan, and Stephen Whittle, eds., *The Transgender Studies Reader* (New York: Routledge, 2006).

Sullivan, Lou, *We Both Laughed In Pleasure: The Selected Diaries of Lou Sullivan 1961-1991*, ed. by Ellis Martin and Zach Ozma (New York: Nightboat, 2019).

Supreme Court of the United States, Bostock v. Clayton County, 17-1618, 590 U. S. ___ (2020) <https://www.supremecourt.gov/opinions/19pdf/17-1618_hfci.pdf> [accessed 1 July 2020].

Tougher, Shaun, *The Eunuch in Byzantine History and Society* (New York: Routledge, 2008).

—, 'Holy Eunuchs! Masculinity and Eunuch Saints in Byzantium', in *Holiness and Masculinity in the Middle Ages*, ed. by P.H. Cullum and Katherine J. Lewis (Cardiff: University of Wales, 2004), pp. 93-108.

t philosopher, 'I Am Leaving Academic Philosophy Because of its Transphobia Problem', *Medium*, 30 May 2019 <https://medium.com/@transphilosopher33/i-am-leaving-academic-philosophy-because-of-its-transphobia-problem-bc618aa55712> [accessed 19 July 2019].

Transgender Europe, 'World Health Organisation Moves to End Classifying Trans Identities as Mental Illness', *tgeu.org*, 18 June 2018 <https://tgeu.org/world-health-organisation-moves-to-end-classifying-trans-identities-as-mental-illness/> [accessed 19 February 2020].

Whittington, Karl, 'Medieval', *TSQ: Transgender Studies Quarterly*, 1.1-2 (2014), 125-29.

—, 'Medieval Intersex: In Theory, Practice, and Representation', *postmedieval*, 9.2 (2018), 231-47 <https://doi.org/10.1057/s41280-018-0085-3> [accessed 18 November 2018].

Wikipedia, 'Legal Recognition of Non-Binary Gender', last updated 9 June 2020, <https://en.wikipedia.org/wiki/Legal_recognition_of_non-binary_gender> [accessed 12 June 2020].

World Health Organization, 'Gender Incongruence', *ICD-11: International Classification of Diseases 11th Revision* [website], last updated May 2019, <http://id.who.int/icd/entity/411470068> [accessed 20 February 2020].

young shaq realness (@BasicBitching), [Twitter thread unpacking interconnection of racism and transphobia], 1 July 2020 <https://threadreaderapp.com/thread/1278377502969380872.html> [accessed 2 July 2020].

About the authors

ALICIA SPENCER-HALL is an Honorary Senior Research Fellow at Queen Mary University of London (UK). Her research interests include: medieval hagiography, disability, gender, digital culture, and film and media studies. Her first monograph, *Medieval Saints and Modern Screens: Divine Visions as Cinematic Experience* was published by Amsterdam University Press in 2018, and is now available Open Access. Her second book, *Medieval Twitter*, is forthcoming with ARC Humanities. Catch her on Twitter (@aspencerhall), or at her blog, Medieval, She Wrote (medievalshewrote.com).

BLAKE GUTT is a postdoctoral scholar with the Michigan Society of Fellows (University of Michigan, USA). He specializes in thirteenth- and fourteenth-century French, Occitan and Catalan literature, and modern queer and trans theory. Blake's current research project examines representations of gender transition and transformation in medieval European literary texts. He has published on the trans Middle Ages in *Exemplaria* (2018), *Medieval Feminist Forum* (2019), and most recently in *postmedieval*'s 10th Anniversary Special Issue on Race, Revulsion and Revolution (2020). He is working on a monograph on medieval and modern epistemological systems, developed from his doctoral thesis (University of Cambridge, 2018).

Following the Traces

Reassessing the Status Quo

Reinscribing Trans and Genderqueer Realities

1   Assigned Female at Death

Joseph of Schönau and the Disruption of Medieval Gender Binaries

Martha G. Newman

Abstract
Sometime after 1188, Engelhard of Langheim composed a story about a Cistercian monk named Joseph. Engelhard insisted Joseph was a woman, but he also undercut normative assumptions to display gender fluidities for which he lacked a conceptual vocabulary. He preserved a binary gender system that controlled the dangers of a woman in a male monastery. Yet his willingness to ventriloquize Joseph's male voice presents a Joseph who, with God's help, successfully performed his male trans identity, while his depiction of Joseph's death suggests Joseph's soul miraculously became female after he died. Engelhard did not explicitly acknowledge either possibility, but in a world in which the miraculous could break naturalized categories, both transitions remain beneath the surface of his tale.

Keywords: Cistercian, Engelhard of Langheim, Hildegund of Schönau, nuns, exempla, gender fluidity

Sometime in the last decade of the twelfth century, the Cistercian author Engelhard of Langheim dedicated a collection of stories to the nuns of the Franconian abbey of Wechterswinkel. Engelhard's tales portray things that are not what they seem. The Eucharist looks like bread but is really the body of Christ, sweat is perfume, woollen cloth is purple silk, and monks are not always as holy as they appear. Engelhard's last story, which depicts the life of a young monk named Joseph and his death at the Cistercian abbey of Schönau, continues this theme.[1] 'This man was a woman although no one knew it', Engelhard proclaims as he begins his tale, this time asserting distinctions between male and female as the reality that could not be discerned from visible signs.[2] But his story about the invisibility of gender differences diverges from his tales of the Eucharist and other holy objects. Whereas most of Engelhard's stories teach how to imagine connections between the signs provided by everyday objects and an invisible and transcendent reality, the story of Joseph breaks connections between visible signs and the binary categories of gender that behaviours and physical characteristics conventionally signify. Engelhard could not find in Joseph's outward appearance and behaviour markers that referenced normative gender distinctions. Ultimately he resorted to the physical characteristics of Joseph's body to assert that Joseph was and would always be a woman. Nonetheless, Engelhard's choices in constructing and narrating his tale undercut his normative assumptions and display transgender possibilities that he did not have the conceptual vocabulary to acknowledge.

I first wrote about brother Joseph in the early years of the twenty-first century. In an article entitled 'Real men and imaginary women: Engelhard of Langheim considers a woman in disguise', I analysed the tale in the context of cross-dressing. There, I referred to Joseph as 'Hildegund' – the name the monks eventually assign Joseph after his death – and I argued that the story illuminates its author's confused efforts to appropriate characteristics of female religiosity in order to celebrate his monastery's male holiness.[3] I remain interested in the author's confusions, but these last fifteen years have changed my perspective. I wrote – and still write – as a cisgender,

---

1   Engelhard's story collection has been partially edited by Griesser ('Exempelbuch', pp. 55-73). Schwarzer edited the last tale ('Vitae', pp. 515-29), usually known as the story of Hildegund of Schönau (*Bibliotheca hagiographica latina* no. 3936). I cite Schwarzer's edition except in cases where the manuscripts diverge. All translations from Latin, whether from this text or others, are my own.
2   'Femina fuit hic homo; nemo cognovit'. Schwarzer, 'Vitae', p. 516.
3   Newman, 'Real Men', pp. 1184-1213. I relied on Marjorie Garber's insights in *Vested Interests*, where she discusses the ways cross-dressing creates space for a 'third gender'. Although the concept of a 'third gender' remains useful, I now recognize the essentialist assumptions in the concept of transvestism and the way an emphasis on disguise can erase transgender possibilities. I am grateful to C. Libby for our conversation about disguise and for sharing forthcoming work. We need to reexamine other medieval saints who once were considered transvestites. For the older literature, see Anson, 'Female Transvestite'; and Patlagean, 'L'histoire'. For the latest work, see, for example, Bychowski (pp. 245-65), Wright (pp. 155-76) and Ogden (pp. 201-21) in this volume. On 'Hildegund', see Hotchkiss, *Clothes*; and Liebers, *Geschichte*.

heterosexual feminist, interested in the cultural construction of gendered categories. My earlier essay accepted Engelhard's gender essentialism, emphasizing the figure of Hildegund and the possibilities she offers for medieval women.[4] I offer this essay to rethink what I once took for granted.[5] A focus on Joseph rather than on Hildegund offers glimpses of multiple and mutable medieval genders while also demonstrating the operations of power that inscribe normative categories.[6] Engelhard wrote at a time when religious women had started to follow the customs of Cistercian men, and the structure of his story preserves a normative, binary gender system that reinforces the physical separation of monks and nuns. At the same time, his story encourages a process of religious formation that nuns and monks could share, and it offers a protagonist whose identity undercuts fixed categories in multiple ways. In offering multiple readings of Joseph's stories, I question direct lines and identifications between the past and the present but suggest the possibility that, to use Carolyn Dinshaw's term, a medieval past and an imagined future can still find ways to 'touch'.[7]

The story of brother Joseph

We know of brother Joseph from five accounts that Cistercian monks composed in Latin over a span of fifty years, from about 1188 to 1240. Other shortened versions appear in later collections of exempla.[8] There is no evidence for Joseph's life outside of these tales. The five descriptions of Joseph's life contain common elements but they are not identical, suggesting that their authors heard different versions of the tale. In two, the authors identify their informants as someone who knew Joseph at Schönau; in a third, the author himself claims to have been Joseph's friend, teacher, and fellow novice. Such variations are common among the oral and written stories that late twelfth- and early thirteenth-century Cistercians circulated between their communities. In many cases, written accounts of miraculous events and holy figures provide the visible tips of an extensive substratum of oral

---

4 As 'Hildegund' is Joseph's dead name, I will only use it when quoting Engelhard. See 'Dead Name; Dead-Naming; Dead Name' in the Appendix: p. 292.
5 See also Karras and Linkinen, 'Revisited'.
6 See Mills, 'Visibly Trans?', p. 541.
7 Dinshaw, *Getting Medieval*, p. 47; Devun and Tortorici, 'Trans, Time, and History', pp. 530-31.
8 For analysis of the five versions of this story, see McGuire, 'Written Sources', pp. 247-54, and Newman, 'Real Men'. Joseph also appears in the *vita* of Eberard of Commeda [*Bibliotheca hagiographica latina* no. 2361]; see de Visch, *Vita*.

tales.⁹ These stories often claim witnesses and informants to confirm their veracity, but their variations undermine this testimony, suggesting that the witnesses authenticate the stories rhetorically rather than legally. Whether or not Joseph lived and died at Schönau, the Cistercian authors present his story as if it were plausible, exemplary, and one to be admired.

Engelhard of Langheim appears to be the first to record Joseph's story. Born and educated in Bamberg before he joined the Franconian abbey of Langheim, Engelhard was a collector of Cistercian exempla and an author who wrote to and about religious women.¹⁰ His tales for the nuns of Wechterswinkel offer one of the first extant texts written by Cistercian monks for religious women interested in following Cistercian customs.¹¹ It appears that Engelhard sent an earlier version of the collection to his friend Erbo, abbot of Prüfening, and that his composition contains stories that circulated orally among male communities. Sometime after 1188, he added more stories to his collection, including the tale of brother Joseph, and he sent it to the nuns at Wechterswinkel in recompense for an unspecified favour the nuns had done for him. Thus, he did not compose his stories for women alone. Nor do his stories articulate a distinctive form of female spirituality that differs from that of men. Instead, they assume that the nuns would be interested in tales about Cistercian monks. In fact, Engelhard's stories address monks and nuns as a single social group that bypassed male sacerdotal authority on one hand, and a specifically female religiosity on the other. In describing everyday objects and behaviours that were not what they seemed, they suggest that both male and female monastics could find sacramental potential in the labour and prayer associated with their religious life.¹² The story of Joseph further reflects Engelhard's interest in addressing

9   See Newman, 'Making Cistercian Exempla', pp. 45-66.
10 His extant texts include correspondence with Erbo, abbot of Prüfening; a *vita* of the nun and canoness Mechthild of Diessen; a meditation on the life of the Virgin Mary; and a collection of Cistercian exempla dedicated to the Cistercian nuns of Wechterswinkel. For his letters, see Griesser, 'Engelhard von Langheim und Abt Erbo von Prüfening'; for the *vita*, see *Vita de B. Mathilde Virgine* [*Bibliotheca hagiographica latina*, 5686], *AASS* 7 May, pp. 436-49, now translated by Lyon in *Noble Society*, pp. 163-219. The meditation on the life of the Virgin is unedited, but can be found in Poznań, Biblioteka Raczyńskich Rkp.156, fols. 3r-26v.
11 Scholars long considered Wechterswinkel as one of the first houses of Cistercian women in German-speaking lands, but Wagner (*Urkunden*) has shown that much of the evidence for this affiliation dates to the thirteenth century. Nonetheless, the twelfth-century nuns at Wechterswinkel founded two communities that followed Cistercian customs, established granges, and rededicated their community in honor of the Virgin Mary. By the early thirteenth century, they were clearly affiliated with the Cistercian order; it may be that Engelhard wrote these nuns as they were considering adopting Cistercian customs.
12 Newman, *Cistercian Stories*, pp. 138-48.

an audience of both monks and nuns, but it also demonstrates the limits of the Cistercians' gendered language of sanctity. Influenced especially by Bernard of Clairvaux's sermons on the Song of Songs, twelfth-century Cistercian monks employed feminine imagery to describe their spiritual development, and they considered their souls as the Bride of the *Song* who longed for the divine embrace of her Bridegroom Christ.[13] Engelhard's story suggests that this Cistercian language of gender fluidity resonated differently when addressed to an audience of both monks and nuns. By implying the possibility of actual, rather than metaphorical, movement between genders, the tale nearly slipped from Engelhard's control. Only by asserting from the beginning that Joseph was a woman did Engelhard constrain such slippage within the realm of metaphor and reinscribe a normative gender essentialism.

Engelhard's presentation of Joseph's story is unusual. He wrote most of his tale in Joseph's voice, allowing Joseph to recount his adventures and trials, and he framed Joseph's tale with his own introduction, conclusion, and interpretation. Engelhard often composed in the present tense, frequently used direct dialogue to make the action immediate for his audience, and occasionally appended personal comments, but Joseph's is the only tale that he constructed in the first person. Scholars have long pondered the significance of the 'I' in medieval texts, especially when writings about the self rely on established models and patterns and do not distinguish between history and fiction.[14] The late eleventh and twelfth centuries saw a growth in first-person narratives, many of which were monastic accounts depicting a path of conversion to religious life loosely modelled on Augustine's *Confessions*.[15] Rarer are authors who wrote in the voice of another person. The technique does appear in stories of dream visions in which a first-person account of solitary experience is at a remove from the text in which the vision is recorded. This use of the first person asserts a story's veracity, allowing the audience to hear the narrator recount their experiences orally.[16] Engelhard's use of the first person has the same ef-

---

13 See, most recently, Engh, *Gendered Identities*. See also Newman, 'Crucified by the Virtues', pp. 192-209.

14 See Schmitt's discussion of medieval autobiography (*Conversion*, pp. 44-50), and McNamer's discussion of the relation between the author's and the recipient's 'I' (*Affective Meditation*, pp. 67-73).

15 Schmitt, *Conversion*, pp. 57-62. These include the writings of John of Fécamp, Otloh of Saint-Emmeran, Guibert of Nogent, and Aelred of Rievaulx.

16 See the account of the conversion of Herman the Jew (Schmitt, *Conversion*), which relies on a first-person narration of Herman's dream. See also Thomas of Cantimpré's *vita* of Christina

fect, and he may have chosen this technique as a means of enhancing the immediacy of his tale. Yet Engelhard nowhere claims to have heard Joseph speak. Rather, he remarks that he relied on information provided by a monk at Langheim who had been present at Joseph's death and funeral. Even with this information, the chain of transmission breaks down, for it is unlikely that this informant heard Joseph tell his story. Engelhard constructs Joseph's account as an extension of Joseph's deathbed confession at which only the prior was present. The informant, if he even existed, must have heard the story from the prior before transmitting it to Engelhard. Joseph's language is thus Engelhard's construction. The tension between Engelhard's presentation of Joseph's voice and the narrative framing that constrains the story creates possibilities within the tale that Engelhard did not explicitly acknowledge.

Although Joseph's deathbed tale is an extension of his confession, it is a description of his life rather than an enumeration of his sins. The story is filled with the sorts of wondrous events that Cistercian storytellers such as Engelhard loved to collect. Joseph informs the prior he was born near Cologne and, as a child, accompanied his father on a pilgrimage to Jerusalem after his mother's death. The father died in Tyre, leaving Joseph in the care of an untrustworthy servant who stole his possessions and left him destitute. Eventually, pilgrims helped him return to Europe. In Rome, he received an education, 'begging letters in the schools just as I had begged scraps at the door'.[17] Once back in Cologne, he served in the household of the archbishop. This prelate, who was in the midst of a dispute with the emperor Frederick Barbarossa over an episcopal election at Trier, asked Joseph to transport a letter to the pope in Verona in hope that Joseph's youth might avoid the suspicion of Frederick Barbarossa's men. As Joseph neared Augsburg his traveling companion abandoned him, leaving him with a sack filled with stolen goods. Caught with the sack, Joseph was tried and sentenced to be hung. While imprisoned, he convinced a priest of his innocence by showing him the hidden message for the pope, and he proved his innocence to the rest of the community by undergoing an ordeal of hot iron. The people released him and caught the real thief, whom they hung.

But Joseph's problems were not over. The thief's relatives resented Joseph's acquittal, and they captured him, cut the thief from the gibbet, and suspended Joseph in his place. 'And yet', Joseph continues, 'as all human aid had ceased, divine aid arrived, and a good angel of God was sent to me as

---

the Astonishing in *Collected Saints' Lives*; and Gardiner, *Visions*, especially pp. xxiii-xxv.

17   'Adjeci studium et didici litteras, mendicans illas in scholis sicut in ostiis bucellas'. Schwarzer, 'Vitae', p. 517.

solace'.[18] The angel supported his feet, comforted him with a sweet taste and smell, and explained that the beautiful music he heard was the sound of angels transporting the soul of his sister to heaven. In three years, Joseph learned, he would receive a similar reception. He remained on the gibbet for three days until local shepherds noticed him, cut him down, and fled in fear when his body, still supported by the angel, floated gently to the ground. Much to his surprise, Joseph discovered he was already in Verona. He completed his errand, returned to Cologne and, at the recommendation of a female recluse, entered the Cistercian monastery of Schönau in gratitude for the divine aid he received. 'I came here', he informs the prior, 'as an act of thanks in response to God because he kept me clean and unblemished in this world'.[19] Now, he explains, the day foretold for his death has arrived. He soon dies, on the day he had predicted.

A transgender monk

Throughout his account of his life and adventures, Joseph uses male pronouns and masculine endings for his nouns and adjectives. By giving Joseph a male voice, Engelhard reveals non-normative possibilities that he did not have the language to acknowledge. One possibility is that Joseph is a transgender man. Engelhard did not have the conceptual vocabulary to articulate Joseph's trans identity but, as Blake Gutt argues, our modern ability to notice medieval gender fluidities provides a corrective to the idea that non-normative genders are a recent phenomenon.[20] Engelhard leaves traces in his account that can touch the present and help imagine the future.[21] Engelhard depicts Joseph as a person who lives his life as a man, who proves his truthfulness before God through an ordeal, and who chooses to become a Cistercian monk. To see Joseph as a trans man rather than as a woman in disguise is to assume that his performance of masculinity is neither a disguise nor a choice but rather the realization of his identity.

Joseph enacts patterns of masculinity that were familiar to members of the Cistercian order. Cistercian monks frequently told tales of young men whose adventures and experiences convinced them to join a monastery to

18 'Attamen humano cessante auxilio, affuit divinum, et angelus Dei bonus mihi missus in solatium'. Ibid., p. 519.
19 'Sic veni huc in gratiarum actione responsurus Deo, quia mundum et immaculatum custodivit ab hoc seculo'. Ibid. This is a quotation from the Epistle of James, 1:27.
20 Gutt, 'Transgender Genealogy', p. 130. See also Gutt, 'Medieval Trans Lives'.
21 Devun and Tortorici, 'Trans, Time, and History', pp. 530-31, Dinshaw, p. 47, *Getting Medieval*.

avoid the dangers of the world. Such accounts appear in a variety of forms, including exempla, sermons, letters, and first-person accounts of conversion. Aelred of Rievaulx, for instance, described his temptations at the Scottish court of King David and his eventual decision to enter a Cistercian abbey, while Bernard of Clairvaux sought to convince scholars in Paris as well as numerous young knights to abandon the dangers of the world for the monastery.[22] Bernard's parables provide allegorical accounts of young knights, often described as 'delicate' or 'inexperienced', who endure trials that teach them to combat vice, embrace virtue, and learn to trust in God.[23] For the most part, Joseph's description of his adventures follows this pattern. He too is an innocent and inexperienced youth, buffeted by the dangers of the world and supported by divine aid when abandoned by human assistance. Cistercian monks, accustomed to stories of such conversions, would have heard little unusual in his tale. One of the few comments that could have signalled Joseph's difference is his assertion that he entered Schönau to thank God for keeping him 'pure and unblemished in this world'. Many Cistercian stories tell of youths who succumb to temptations before they convert, while the idea of preserving purity is often associated with female sanctity. Nonetheless, Engelhard recounts other stories of monks who are also concerned about maintaining their virginity and the purity of their bodies, so even here, Joseph fits into a pattern attributed to Cistercian men. His comment might have served as a clue for those in Engelhard's audience who had already heard Engelhard declare that Joseph was a woman, but it would not have seemed out of the ordinary for those who assumed he was a man.

Engelhard's multiple voices, and his interest in the contrast between appearance and invisible reality opens up the possibility that Joseph is a trans man. Engelhard frames Joseph's story, told in Joseph's voice, with an introduction that declares that 'this man was a woman'. This statement implies that Joseph was assigned female at birth, but it also assumes that this natal categorization was both true and fixed. Engelhard's assertion at Joseph's death, that the monks think it was a woman who died, furthers his presentation of gender as unalterable. The authors of the later accounts of Joseph's life explicitly present Joseph's masculinity as a disguise, suggesting that he adopts male clothing for reasons of safety when he and his father embark on their pilgrimage, that he lives in ever-present fear of discovery,

---

22 See Aelred of Rievaulx, *On Spiritual Friendship*; Bernard of Clairvaux, *Letters* 108-114, pp. 156-172; and Bernard of Clairvaux, "Sermon on Conversion", in *Sermons*, pp. 31-79.

23 On Bernard of Clairvaux's parables, see Bruun, *Parables*.

and that he enacts stereotypically female characteristics such as vanity and sexual attractiveness.[24] Engelhard's Joseph, however, does none of these things. In fact, when Engelhard speaks in Joseph's voice, he undermines this position, since Joseph does not present himself as a disguised woman, but as a man. Furthermore, Engelhard remarks that the female recluse who recommends Joseph to Schönau 'knew the secrets of his conscience', but nonetheless advised him to enter a male monastery.[25] He twice mentions the recommendation of this holy woman, suggesting that it is one of the reasons the monks at Schönau did not further investigate Joseph's background. In retrospect, her advice suggests that she both knows of Joseph's assigned sex and recognizes his male identity as genuine. Although Engelhard explicitly employs the idea that Joseph is not what he seems, hiding a female reality under his male dress, he also implies a contrast between the appearance of Joseph's body and the invisible reality of his male identity. Engelhard may have consciously chosen to tell Joseph's story in Joseph's male voice in order to confirm the veracity of the story, but this choice also implies that, despite his physical characteristics, Joseph is really a man.

Engelhard's narration of the arc of Joseph's life reveals patterns that resonate with trans experience. Scholars have argued that queer and trans lives construct identities outside of the normative social structures and temporal progressions from which they have often been excluded, especially outside of progressions based on biological procreation. Queerness can create alternative ways of 'being in the world', including new understandings of birth and development.[26] In medieval Europe conversion to a religious life offered such an alternative by providing a way to escape structures and temporalities based on procreation.[27] In Engelhard's ventriloquizing of Joseph's voice, Joseph never suggests that he was assigned female at birth. Instead, he articulates three alternative births, each of which is also marked by a death. Joseph experiences the first as a child, at the death of his mother, when his father vows to take him

---

24 'Vita Hildegundis', in *AASS* 2 April: pp. 778-88; Caesarius of Heisterbach, *Dialogus Miraculorum*, I, c. 40, pp. 47-53.
25 '[S]pecialiter ei commendatus ab inclusa sancta que secreti hujus sola creditor conscia'. Schwarzer, 'Vitae', p. 517.
26 See, for instance, Edelman, *No Future*, pp. 5-8; Halberstam, *Queer Art*, pp. 2-3, 98. Gutt, in 'Transgender Genealogy', employs Deleuze and Guattari to retheorize this antisocial turn and show how a story can create queer socialities.
27 Insistence on celibacy often breaks familial expectations of marriage and procreation. See, for instance, the life of Christina of Markyate, especially the analysis by Head, 'Marriages', pp. 75-102.

to Jerusalem if God permits Joseph to live. In explaining this to the prior, Joseph attributes his life to God rather than to his parents. His father's death in Tyre initiates a second birth: Joseph became an orphan and enters a life characterized by difficulty and struggle. Joseph's near-death experience on the gibbet marks the beginning of his third birth, one that culminates in his entrance into the monastery of Schönau. Conversion to monastic life traditionally seemed a rebirth in which a convert 'put off the old man and took on the new'.[28] In Joseph's case, this rebirth is further accentuated by the angel's intervention and the vision of his sister's soul ascending to heaven. Both imply that he had embarked on a new path that led to heaven. Joseph's three births reflect a spiritual formation modelled on a Christian progression of grace, struggle, and salvation, a progression that also appears in Bernard of Clairvaux's parables.[29] Joseph's self-narration performs a male identity familiar to the monks, but it also articulates the development of a particular Christian identity in which Joseph could disassociate himself from biological progressions and familial structures.

Finally, Joseph recognizes his difference by attributing it to divine beneficence, not to his own choice. He begins his story by telling the prior that after his death, 'you will marvel at what you will find in me, although it is not customary. For God did great things for me; let my response to these gifts be fitting. If it will not bore you to hear this, I will tell you what miraculous things God did in me'.[30] It is possible to read this statement as Joseph's – or Engelhard's – recognition that the brothers at Schönau would marvel when they discovered that Joseph's bodily morphology seemingly revealed him to be a woman. But this statement is actually more ambiguous. Joseph thinks the prior will marvel at what the monks found 'in him' (*'in me'*), and he repeats the phrase a sentence later when he speaks of the miraculous things done in him (*'in me'*). His use of this preposition shifts the focus from the appearance of his body, suggesting that the monks would discover a gift from God that Joseph had incorporated into himself. It implies that Joseph's identity as a man is neither a choice nor a disguise but rather a divine gift.

28 See Ephesians 4.22, and the Cistercians' description of conversion in their *Exordium parvum* c. 15, in Waddell, *Narrative and Legislative Texts*, p. 434.

29 On resurrection and resuscitation in saints' lives, see Spencer-Hall, *Medieval Saints*, pp. 83-87.

30 'Invenietis in me, quod miremini, sed non oportet. Magna mihi fecit Deus; dignum esset, quod responderem beneficiis ejus. Si non tedet vobis audire, referam vobis, quid miraclorum fecit Deus in me'. Schwarzer, 'Vitae'. p. 517.

Female at death

A reading enabled by modern trans theory, which reveals Joseph as a trans man, is not the only way of approaching non-normative gender in Engelhard's tale. The idea of Joseph as trans separates his male gender from the appearance of his body but it also assumes that his male identity is a fixed, transcendent reality. A second reading of Engelhard's story, however, suggests a gender fluidity in which Joseph miraculously changes from male to female at death. This possibility is what the monks at Schönau experience. They know Joseph as a man, and, even after he dies, they initially celebrate his holiness as a man who had a vision of his sister's salvation and a foreknowledge of his own death. Only after Engelhard articulates his confidence that Joseph 'was accepted by Christ in an odour of sanctity and led in peace by an angel of peace' does he offer another miracle in which a man suddenly becomes a woman.[31] Strikingly, the signs of this miracle are verbal more than physical. Unlike the authors of later versions of the story who linger on the appearance of Joseph's body, noting breasts constricted by a bandage 'lest they flopped or hung down and showed her to be a woman while she lived', Engelhard downplays this uncovering.[32] He remarks only that 'this little body was stripped to be washed, but only by a few and likewise only for the briefest time. Immediately it was re-covered with astonishment and wonder'.[33] Instead, the uncovering is verbal. In comparison to the few who saw Joseph's body, 'for everyone else, the news was uncovered (*detegitur*) that this was a woman who had died, and the abbot, who was giving his commendation, changed (*transivit*) the gender (*genus*) from masculine to feminine'.[34] This act creates a moment of linguistic recognition in which 'all those who are literate are astounded, hearing a woman commended', and it produces a cathartic moment in which the monastic community praises and blesses God for his gifts.[35] By this point, Engelhard is working to control

---

31 '[A]cceptus ipse Christo in odorem suavitatis et deductus in pace ab angelis pacis'. Ibid., p. 520.
32 '[Q]ua constricta fuerant ubera, ne fluerent aut dependerent'. *Vita S. Hildegundis Virginis* AASS 5.32, p. 787.
33 'Tollitur ex more corpusculum, nudatur ad lavandum, a paucis tamen idemque brevissimum; nam protinus est cum stupore et admiratione retectum'. Schwarzer, 'Vitae', p. 520.
34 'Ceterum fama detegitur cunctis, feminam esse, que obiit et in commendatione, quam abbas interim fecit, genus masculinum in femininum transivit'. Ibid. Every version of the story emphasizes that the abbot changed the Latin gender markers of his prayers, suggesting that the Cistercians found this an essential element of the narrative.
35 'Stupent litterati omnes, audientes feminam commendari, et inter longa suspiria mirabantur virtutem Christi'. Schwarzer, 'Vitae', p. 520.

the story, and the miracle he wants to emphasize is the ability of a woman to live as a monk without detection. Unacknowledged but suggested by the structure of his account, however, is that the monks experience a different miracle, in which Joseph only becomes a woman after death.

The miraculous, like the queer, breaks an order of things that has become naturalized. The idea that a man could become a woman or a woman become a man upends a Biblical anthropology that assumes God created two sexes distinguished by bodily characteristics. Nonetheless, the miraculous possibility that a monk could experience the transformation of his gendered or sexed identity remained within the cultural parameters of Cistercian monasticism. One of the stories that Cistercian monks circulated describes a monk who asks an angel to help him control his sexual desires; the angel, in a dream, removes his penis and the monk's temptations disappear.[36] Similarly, the community at the Cistercian abbey of Villiers celebrated their abbot William whose body at death had 'no vestige of [male] genitals except for a clear smooth area, bright and pure'.[37] Even more central to Cistercian culture were Bernard of Clairvaux's sermons on the Song of Songs, which encouraged monks to identify with the female figures in the Canticles. In providing a model for the soul's progression as it learns to participate in divine love, Bernard suggests that his monks can overcome the foolishness of young women, develop the productivity of a mother, and identify with the Bride's love and longing as she seeks and encounters her Bridegroom. As Line Cecilie Engh argues, Bernard encourages monks to perform the Bride so that they may ultimately become better men.[38] Engelhard's story of Joseph, however, holds out the possibility that a performance of the Bride might actually transform monks into women. Did Joseph's body after death reflect the female quality of his perfected soul as it became a Bride of Christ, united with the divine in heaven?

Normative confusions

Engelhard's introductory and concluding commentary, and his description of Joseph's death, constrain these non-normative readings of Joseph's gender. By

---

36   Herbert of Clairvaux, *Liber*, 1.3, pp. 10-11.
37   'Nec apparuit in loco dicto aliquod vestigium genitalium nisi sola planities plana, clara et munda, reverberans oculos intuentium claritate nimia'. *Cronica Villariensis monasterii*, ed. G. Waitz, MGH SS 25:202.
38   Engh, *Gendered Identities*, pp. 405-8. See also Bynum, 'Jesus as Mother', pp. 110-65.

insisting that Joseph was always a woman, Engelhard denies the possibility that performing the Bride might make monks female. He also denies that Joseph's performance of maleness was a divine gift that showed he was a man. Instead, by proclaiming at the outset that '[t]his man was a woman, although no one knew it', Engelhard prepares his audience to interpret Joseph's narrative within a fixed, binary system of sexual categories in which physical morphology signals gender. Furthermore, although Joseph uses masculine endings in his own narrative, the scribe wrote feminine endings into the rubrics, and Engelhard employs female pronouns and endings in his introduction and conclusion.[39] This gives the story an organizational structure that tries to assert that Joseph was always female. Engelhard describes the abbot shifting to feminine pronouns in his commemoration, and notes that the monks of Schönau refused to use the name 'Joseph' in their obituary, since 'Joseph signified the masculine and not the feminine'.[40] The monks eventually settle on the label 'maid of God'. Only in later accounts do the authors determine that Hildegund is the name that Joseph was assigned at birth.

Engelhard's insistence that Joseph is a woman limits the fluid possibilities within his story, but this tactic creates other problems for Engelhard. The Cistercians had long criticized other religious groups for an unwillingness to segregate men and women. Engelhard's tale, as well as any circulation of an oral version of Joseph's story, could have opened the Cistercians to the same charges they had levelled at others. Engelhard's account dulls such criticism, however. He emphasizes that Joseph arrived at Schönau with the recommendation of the holy recluse, and he insists that Joseph entered the monastery '*regulariter*', that is, according to the rules.[41] He articulates Joseph's recognition that the monks will not find him 'customary', but insists that Joseph's behaviour is a fitting response to God's gifts. He describes Joseph's purity, giving no hints of sexual impropriety, and he depicts the monks' modesty in their very brief observation of Joseph's body.[42] In fact, Engelhard asserts that Joseph converts to Cistercian life because it replicates the sense of heavenly contact that he experienced while supported by the

---

39 A single exception: Engelhard once uses *gloriosus* (glorious) rather than *gloriosa* in his commentary. Schwarzer, 'Vitae', p. 517.
40 '[Q]uia Joseph masculum, et non feminam significaret'. Ibid., p. 521.
41 'Intravit regulariter intromissus'. Ibid., p. 516.
42 In this, Engelhard's story differs from Byzantine stories of transformation, in which monks who lived as male but were assigned female at death were accused of fathering children. On this, see Bychowski (pp. 245-65) and Szabo (pp. 109-29) in this volume.

angel.[43] Despite the seeming irregularity of Joseph's presence, Engelhard uses the story to praise the special holiness of his order.

Engelhard also controls against criticism by suggesting that it is difficult for the monks at Schönau to discern normative female characteristics from Joseph's appearance and behaviour. However, such a difficulty undermines the gender essentialism that Engelhard works to establish and solidify. Again, Engelhard's approach to the story differs from that of later authors who depict feminine characteristics that remain unchanged despite Joseph's appearance. Caesarius of Heisterbach, for example, describes Joseph as vain, interested in inspecting his appearance in a mirror, and he recounts that another monk claims that he could not look at Joseph without temptation.[44] Caesarius enjoys the irony of recognizing what the characters in his story do not see. For Engelhard, however, the problem is not that the monks at Schönau cannot recognize signs of femininity that are in plain sight. Rather, the signs themselves are unclear. Despite his efforts, Engelhard can neither find nor describe characteristics that clearly distinguish men from women. As a result, he comes close to articulating a third, non-normative conception of gender, in which male-female differences evaporate and, following Paul in Galatians 3:28, 'all are one in Jesus Christ.'[45]

Engelhard tries to use the dichotomy of strength and weakness to separate male and female but he cannot maintain weakness as a clear sign that Joseph is a woman. Initially, his categories seem distinct. Not only was '[t]his man a woman', but the monks at Schönau should have noticed that Joseph was female since 'her weakness frequently proclaimed it. What could she do? She did not know how to act like a man since the nature of her sex prevented it, especially among us where all of our sex are strong'.[46] Yet at the same time, Joseph's weakness is no different from that of the monks around him. Engelhard describes Joseph's weariness and exhaustion, but then asks: 'What in this seems female, what is to be suspected as foreign and new?'[47]

43 'Reor et hoc ordinis nostris qualecunque preconium, quod virgo Christi tot agonibus fatigata, nec victa, dum ab angelo transitus sui tempus et felicitatem agnovit, nusquam sibi tutius Deoque laudabilius quam in religione nostra finiri se credidit'. Schwarzer, 'Vitae', p. 520.
44 Caesarius of Heisterbach, *Dialogus Miraculorum*, I, c. 40, pp. 46-53.
45 Engelhard employs Pauline ideas of strength and weakness in his *Vita de B. Mathilde Virgine*, primarily to note Mechthild's strength. He does not make her male, but compares her to a list of strong women. On Galatians 3.28, see Meeks, 'Image', pp. 165-208; and Kahl, 'No Longer Male', pp. 37-49. On a third gender in early medieval saints' lives, see McDaniel, *Third Gender*.
46 'Femina fuit hic homo; nemo cognovit, quamquam hoc infirmitas crebra clamaverit. Quid faceret? viriliter agere noluit, obstitit sexus natura, maxime apud nos, ubi cuncta sunt fortia.' Schwarzer, 'Vitae', p. 516.
47 'Sed quid in illa videre femineum, quid alienum aut novum suspicari?' Ibid., pp. 516-17.

There was nothing uniquely female in Joseph's behaviour. Engelhard tells of other male novices who became weary and despaired of their ability to endure Cistercian life; in fact, this was something he experienced himself when a novice. Even as an adult, he thought it possible for a monk to show a 'female' weakness, for in a letter to his friend Erbo of Prüfening, he develops an elaborate humility trope through which he confesses that he himself 'is a woman' because he does not have the strength to do manly things.[48] The weakness with which Engelhard tries to characterize women could also describe the condition of men.

In fact, Joseph does not remain weak. Like other monks who model their development on Cistercian stories and sermons, Joseph gradually moves beyond feminine weakness to became strong. As a result, Engelhard's language becomes contradictory. At times, he suggests that God works through female weakness, for Joseph is a 'delicate girl in whom the virtue of God and the wisdom of Christ could mock the devil'.[49] Yet this young woman also overcomes her sex, acting as 'a weak woman who had forgotten her sex, who entered and finished the battle, and who triumphed over the enemy'.[50] Like the young knights in Bernard of Clairvaux's parables who fight against temptations and learn to become strong, Joseph too 'valiantly (*fortiter*) but briefly undertook to perform strong (*fortes*) battles in war, so that as victory was achieved by this weak (*infirmiori*) knight over the strong (*forti*) enemy, so glory increased for the king'.[51] At this point, Engelhard's interpretation dovetails with Joseph's own narration, for whether as a young man or as a young woman, Joseph resembles other virtuous monks in fighting valiantly to overcome weakness and become strong.

Having tried, and failed, to maintain a dichotomy between female weakness and male strength, Engelhard returns to an essentialist separation of male and female by suggesting gendered reactions to Joseph's story. He tells his audience, 'I wish this to be a wonder for women but an example for men, so that while women boast about her, men are ashamed that today we are not lacking women who dare strong things for Christ, while the majority

---

48 'Fateor, mulier sum ego, uiris me non comparo, patrem me fore non deopto, uirtute dico, non dignitate.' Griesser, 'Engelhard von Langheim und Abt Erbo von Prüfening', p. 25.
49 '[Q]uod in puella tam tenera diabolo illusisset Dei virtus et dei sapientia Christi.' Schwarzer, 'Vitae', p. 520.
50 '[F]ragilis hec oblita sit sexum, inierit atque finierit prelium, triumpharit inimicum'. Ibid.
51 'Fortiter siquidem et non diu in bello factura fortes pugnas aggressa est, ut regi suo tanto cresceret gloria, quanto [in]firmiori militi fieret a forti hoste victoria'. Ibid.

of men follow the weakness of women'.[52] In some of the manuscripts of the story, Engelhard goes still further, telling his readers: 'I do not encourage this in women, for while many are equal in strength, they are unequal in fate, and often the stronger falls at the same turning point in battle at which the weaker triumphs'.[53] At this point, Engelhard dissolves the dichotomy between male strength and female weakness with which he began his tale. Now men have become weak and women dare to be strong, so much so that the sexes have become equal in strength and can only be distinguished by fortune. In fact, Engelhard ends his exemplum by asking monks to identify with Joseph's 'female' weakness, and to take to heart the message that God would reward the weak. Weakness is no longer a natural condition of women, but has become a characteristic of men that they should fight to overcome.

A story for Cistercian nuns

Engelhard assumed that both men and women would read his story, but he hoped that monks and nuns would read it differently. This gendered response reflects the circumstances around the composition and transmission of his text. In dedicating his collection to the nuns of Wechterswinkel, he demonstrates his supposition that nuns would be interested in stories of Cistercian monks. This gift further supports the likelihood that these nuns already followed Cistercian customs or were interested in doing so. Exactly what Cistercian customs they might have adopted, however, is not clear. Twelfth-century Cistercian women 'followed the institutes of the Cistercian brothers', but we do not know the extent to which such communities adapted male customs for the use of women.[54] One twelfth-century observer, Herman of Tournay, describes women in the diocese of Laon as living 'according to the *ordo* of Cîteaux, which many men and hardened youth fear to undertake';

---

52 'Velim hanc miraculo feminis, viris exemplo, ut glorientur ille, illi erubescant, quod hodieque non desint in feminis, que pro Christo audeant fortia, quod in viris pars maxima mulierum sectantur infirma.' Ibid.

53 'Nulli tamen feminarum similia suaserim, quia multis par fortitudo, sed dispar est fortuna, et eodem belli discrimine sepe cadit fortior, quo vincit infirmior.' Ibid. This second sentence appears in the two copies of Engelhard's story collection now in the Biblioteka Raczyńskich in Poznań, Poland, but not in a manuscript produced at the male monastery of Prüfening. It is possible that the Poznań manuscripts, filled with Engelhard's texts for and about women, may have been intended for female communities.

54 As Berman and others have argued, women who 'followed the institutes of the Cistercian brothers' should be considered Cistercian nuns (Berman, 'Cistercian Nuns', pp. 853-55). See also Lester, *Cistercian Nuns*, pp. 83-84.

he portrays women who not only worked at weaving and sewing, which he understands to be women's work, but who also harvested, cut down trees, and cleared the fields, imitating 'in all things the monks of Clairvaux'.[55] Engelhard's depiction of female strength as equal to that of men suggests that he thought women were capable of living as did men, and that their struggles with the difficulties of Cistercian life would be no different from those of men. But he also assumed that his audiences lived in communities that were segregated by sex. In suggesting that the women of Wechterswinkel should admire Joseph but not imitate him, Engelhard makes clear that he did not want women to become monks. His story of Joseph offers to both men and women a progression from weakness to strength, but it also insists they remain in gender-specific spaces.

Engelhard understood male and female as divinely established categories, naturalized by God's creation of humanity and displayed through bodily characteristics. Furthermore, he considered sexual difference as intertwined with grammatical distinctions, so that the gender of names and pronouns signifies sexual categories. Still, he inhabited a monastic culture in which monks could identify with the female Bride in the Song of Songs, and religious women could enact the virile strength needed to adopt the customs and institutes of their male counterparts. His story of Joseph displays this fluidity. The language of his story corresponds with his understanding of his audience's social position, as he thought that monks and nuns could follow the same customs and enact the same processes of spiritual formation in which they, like Joseph, could learn to overcome weakness and become strong. Nonetheless, he sought to keep such gender fluidities within the realm of metaphor, and to maintain a real and physical separation between female and male. By placing Joseph in the category of people and things that look one way but are another, he insisted that Joseph was always a woman, whom divine grace had made capable of acting as if she were a man, and he ignored the possibility that Joseph instead may always have been a man.

Nonetheless, Engelhard's story also contains elements that unsettle medieval Christian gender binaries and touch the medieval to the present. In trying to control against the dangers of a woman in a male monastery, Engelhard blurred the signs of gender difference. His willingness to ventriloquize Joseph's voice shows that language could create a Joseph who,

---

55 'Ordinem Cistellensem, quem multi virorum et robustorum juvenum aggredi metuunt'; 'vitamque Clarevallensium monachorum per omnia imitantes'. Herman of Tournay, *De miraculis*, PL 156: 1001-02.

with God's help, successfully performs his trans identity. Yet Engelhard's language also suggests a Joseph who miraculously became a woman after death. Engelhard did not elaborate on either possibility, but in a world in which the miraculous could break naturalized categories and disrupt the normal order of things, they both remain just beneath the surface of his tale. Engelhard may have employed Joseph's tale to limit female behaviours and assert normative genders, but his tale also undermines fixed binaries, and it suggests that medieval religious communities could provide a space for transgender possibilities and expressions of gender fluidity.

Bibliography

Manuscripts

Engelhard of Langheim's Exempla Book, Poznań, Poland, Biblioteka Raczyńskich Rkp.156, fols. 49^v-97^v.

Engelhard of Langheim's Exempla Book, Poznań, Poland. Biblioteka Raczyńskich Rkp.173, fols. 42^r-101^r.

Primary sources

Aelred of Rievaulx, *Spiritual Friendship*, trans. by Lawrence C. Braceland, ed. by Marsha Dutton (Collegeville: Cistercian Publications, 2010).

Bernard of Clairvaux, *The Letters of Bernard of Clairvaux*, trans. by Bruno Scott James (Kalamazoo: Cistercian Publications, 1998).

—, *Sermons on Conversion*, trans. by Marie-Bernard Saïd (Kalamazoo: Cistercian Publications, 1981).

Bibliotheca hagiographica latina antiquae et mediae aetatis, 2 vols. (Brussels: Société des Bollandistes, 1898-1901).

Caesarius of Heisterbach, *Dialogus Miraculorum*, ed. by Joseph Strange, 2 vols. (Cologne: Heberle, 1951).

Cronica Villariensis monasterii, ed. by G. Waitz, in *Monumenta Germania Historica, Scriptores* 25 (Hannover: Hansche, 1880), pp. 195-209.

Engelhard of Langheim, *Vita de B. Mathilde Virginis*, ed. by Gottfrird Henschen, *Acta Sanctorum* 7 May, 436-449 (Paris: Victor Palmé, 1866).

Gardiner, Eileen, ed., *Visions of Heaven & Hell before Dante* (New York: Italica, 1989).

Griesser, Bruno, 'Engelhard von Langheim und Abt Erbo von Prüfening: Neue Belege zu Engelhards Exempelbuch', *Chistercienser-Chronik*, 67/68 (1964), 22-37; 76 (1969), 20-24.

—, 'Engelhard von Langheim und sein Exempelbuch für die Nonnen von Wechterswinkel', *Cistercienser-Chronik*, 65/66 (1963), 55-73.

Herbert of Clairvaux, *Liber visionum et miraculorum Clarevallensium*, ed. by Giancarlo Zichi, Graziano Fois, and Stefano Mula (Turnhout: Brepols, 2017).

Herman of Tournay, *De miraculis sanctae Mariae Laudunensis*, in *Patrologia Latina, cursus completus*, ed. by J.-P. Migne, 221 vols. (Paris: Migne, 1841-1865), 156: 961-1016.

Lyon, Jonathan R., trans., *Noble Society: Five Lives from Twelfth-Century Germany* (Manchester: Manchester University, 2017).

Schwarzer, Joseph, 'Vitae und Miracula aus Kloster Ebrach', *Neues Archiv der Gesellschaft für ältere deutsche Geschichtskunde*, 6 (1881), 515-29.

Thomas of Cantimpré, *The Collected Saints' Lives*, ed. and trans. by Barbara Newman and Margot King (Turnhout: Brepols, 2008).

Visch, C. de, ed., *Vita reverendi in Christo patris ac domini D. Adriani ... vitae aliorum duorum veterum monachorum ord. Cisterc. sanctitatis opinione illustrium, Eberardi cognominati vulgo de Commeda...* ([Dunes] 1655).

'Vita Hildegundis', in *Acta Sanctorum*, 2 April, 778-88 (Paris: Victor Palmé, 1866).

Waddell, Chrysogonus, ed., *Narrative and Legislative Texts from Early Cîteaux* (Cîteaux: Commentarii cistercienses, 1999).

Wagner, Heinrich, *Urkunden und Regesten des Frauenklosters Wechterswinkel*, Quellen und Forschungen zur Geschichtes des Bistums und Hochstifts Würzburg 70 (Würzburg: Kommissionsverlag Ferdinand Schöningh, 2015).

Secondary sources

Anson, John, 'The Female Transvestite in Early Monasticism: The Origin and Development of a Motif', *Viator*, 5 (1974), 1-32.

Berman, Constance, 'Were There Twelfth-Century Cistercian Nuns?' *Church History*, 68 (1999), 824-64.

Bruun, Mette B., *Parables: Bernard of Clairvaux's Mapping of Spiritual Topography* (Leiden: Brill, 2007).

Bynum, Caroline Walker, 'Jesus as Mother and Abbot as Mother: Some Themes in Twelfth-Century Cistercian Writing', in *Jesus as Mother: Studies in the Spirituality of the High Middle Ages* (Berkeley: University of California, 1982), pp. 110-65.

DeVun, Leah, and Zeb Tortorici, 'Trans, Time, and History', *Transgender Studies Quarterly*, 5.4 (2018), 518-39.

Dinshaw, Carolyn, *Getting Medieval: Sexualities and Communities, Pre- and Postmodern* (Durham: Duke University, 1999).

Edelman, Lee, *No Future: Queer Theory and the Death Drive* (Durham: Duke University, 2004).

Engh, Line Cecilie, *Gendered Identities in Bernard of Clairvaux's Sermons on the Song of Songs: Performing the Bride* (Turnhout: Brepols, 2014).

Garber, Marjorie, *Vested Interests: Cross-Dressing and Cultural Anxiety* (New York: Routledge, 1992).

Gutt, Blake, 'Medieval Trans Lives in Anamorphosis: Looking Back and Seeing Differently (Pregnant Men and Backward Birth)', *Medieval Feminist Forum*, 55.1 (2019), 174-206.

—, 'Transgender Genealogy in *Tristan de Nanteuil*', *Exemplaria*, 30.2 (2018), 129-46.

Halberstam, J., *The Queer Art of Failure* (Durham: Duke University, 2011).

Head, Thomas, 'The Marriages of Christina of Markyate', *Viator*, 21 (1990), 75-102.

Hotchkiss, Valerie R, *Clothes Make the Man: Female Cross Dressing in Medieval Europe* (New York: Garland, 1996).

Kahl, Brigitte, 'No Longer Male: Masculinity Struggles behind Galatians 3:28', *Journal for the Study of the New Testament*, 79 (2001), 37-49.

Karras, Ruth Mazo and Tom Linkinen, 'John/Eleanor Rykener Revisited', in *Founding Feminisms in Medieval Studies: Essays in Honor of E. Jane Burns*, ed. by Laine E. Doggett and Daniel E. O'Sullivan (Woodbridge: Boydell & Brewer, 2016), pp. 111-24.

Lester, Anne, *Creating Cistercian Nuns: The Women's Religious Movement and Its Reform in Thirteenth-Century Champagne* (Ithaca: Cornell University, 2011).

Libby, C., 'The Historian and the Sexologist: Revisiting the Transvestite Saint', *Transgender Studies Quarterly*, Special Issue: Europa (forthcoming Summer 2021).

Liebers, Andrea, *"Eine Frau War Dieser Mann", Die Geschichte der Hildegund von Schönau* (Zürich: eFeF-Verlag, 1989).

McDaniel, Rhonda L., *The Third Gender and Aelfric's "Lives of Saints"* (Kalamazoo: Medieval Institute, 2018).

McGuire, Brian Patrick, 'Written Sources and Cistercian Inspiration in Caesarius of Heisterbach', *Analecta Cisterciensia*, 35 (1979), 227-82.

McNamer, Sarah, *Affective Meditation and the Invention of Medieval Compassion* (Philadelphia: University of Pennsylvania, 2009).

Meeks, Wayne, 'Image of the Androgyne: Some Uses of a Symbol in Earliest Christianity', *History of Religions*, 13 (1974), 165-208.

Mills, Robert, 'Visibly Trans? Picturing Saint Eugenia in Medieval Art,' *Transgender Studies Quarterly*, 5.4 (2018), 540-64.

Newman, Martha G., 'Making Cistercian Exempla or, the Problem of the Monk Who Wouldn't Talk', *Cistercian Studies Quarterly*, 46.1 (2011), 45-66.

—, 'Real Men and Imaginary Women: Engelhard of Langheim Considers a Woman in Disguise', *Speculum*, 78 (2003), 1184-1213.

—, Newman, Martha G. 'Crucified by the Virtues: Monks, Lay Brothers, and Women in Thirteenth-Century Cistercian Saints' Lives', in *Gender and Difference in the*

Middle Ages, ed. by Sharon Farmer and Carol Braun Pasternack (Minneapolis: University of Minnesota, 2003), pp. 192-209.

—, *Cistercian Stories for Nuns and Monks: The Sacramental Imagination of Engelhard of Langheim* (Philadelphia: University of Pennsylvania, 2020).

Patlagean, Evelyne, 'L'histoire de la femme déguisée en moine et l'évolution de la sainteté féminine à Byzance', *Studi medievali*, 3rd. ser., 17.2 (1976), 597-623.

Schmitt, Jean-Claude, *The Conversion of Herman the Jew: Autobiography, History, and Fiction in the Twelfth-Century*, trans. Alex J. Novikoff (Philadelphia: University of Pennsylvania, 2003).

Spencer-Hall, Alicia, *Medieval Saints and Modern Screens: Divine Visions as Cinematic Experience* (Amsterdam: Amsterdam University, 2018).

About the author

MARTHA G. NEWMAN is Associate Professor of Medieval History and Religious Studies at the University of Texas (USA). Her new book, *Cistercian Stories for Nuns and Monks: The Sacramental Imagination of Engelhard of Langheim* (University of Pennsylvania Press, 2020), analyses late twelfth-century tales about Cistercian monks that illuminate the religiosity of Cistercian nuns. She is author of *The Boundaries of Charity: Cistercian Culture and Ecclesiastical Reform* (Stanford University Press, 1996) and essays on monastic culture, medieval gender, and labour. Between 2007 and 2016, she also served as the founding Chair of the Department of Religious Studies at U.T.-Austin.

2 Inherited Futures and Queer Privilege

Capgrave's *Life of St Katherine*

Caitlyn McLoughlin

> **Abstract**
> This chapter considers John Capgrave's *Life of St Katherine* within a queer genealogical framework in order to contribute to a queer historical archive. Procreative and generative language and detail early in the narrative explicitly open the *vita* to a reading that considers the text itself as offspring in a genealogical line of reproduced texts. Thus the chapter also understands this textual procreation as representative of a particularly genderqueer temporality. Finally, this chapter offers an intersectional consideration of Katherine's characterization in order to assess how different social privileges and subjugations effect and enable her veneration, complicating essentialist notions of gendered social position and female sanctity.
>
> **Keywords:** queer, genderqueer, temporalities, futurity, hagiography, privilege, St Katherine, John Capgrave

Queer historicism transgresses temporal boundaries through affective connections based on identification and recognition between individuals and communities.[1] A twenty-first century reading of John Capgrave's verse *Life of Saint Katherine of Alexandria* (c. 1445) shows how certain authorial modes of textual production foreground a future for queer readers by developing alternative pathways to inheritance, although these rely on Katherine's privileged subjectivity. Homonormativity, first theorized by Lisa Duggan in 2002, refers to 'a politics that does not contest dominant

---

1   Halberstam theorizes the notion of 'perverse presentism', whereby methodological and interpretive insights from the present are applied to the past (*Female Masculinity*, pp. 52-53).

heteronormative assumptions and institutions but upholds and sustains them while promising the possibility of a demobilized gay constituency and a privatized, depoliticized gay culture anchored in domesticity and consumption'.[2] Capgrave's endorsement of marriage and biological reproduction likewise prefigures modern homonormative uses of established familial institutions as pathways to legitimacy. This method of political validation is recognizable in various modern campaigns for the legalization of same sex marriage, which often emphasize(d) monogamous commitment and conservative values as characteristics of 'good' and loving couples, regardless of partners' genders. Challenging the normative function of familial inheritance, this chapter re-evaluates ideals that shaped the social circumstances of gendered subjects in fifteenth-century England. In the *Life of Saint Katherine*, Capgrave (d. 1464) – an Augustinian friar and scholastic theologian – presents a paradoxical Katherine, whose resistance to normative social institutions is complicated by the reinforcement of 'proper' adherence to expected social positions and gendered proclivities. For modern readers seeking a queer medieval genealogy, Katherine's holy celibacy and formulation of gendered social positions can be claimed as queer subjectivity. Katherine functions as a religious and political model for both men and women, and Capgrave's text itself is produced through a series of textual comminglings that powerfully evoke genderqueer reproduction. However, this purposeful reading must reconcile the text's rejection of binary subjectivity with Katherine's extraordinary status and privilege as a basis for her heavenly inheritance and ultimate endurance as a spiritual ideal.

In league with legends

In the Prologue to the *Life of Saint Katherine*, Capgrave explains how his source was derived from a long-lost biography originally composed in the fourth century in Greek by Katherine's disciple Athanasius. This version was then translated into Latin and subsequently buried by a fifth-century scholar named Arrek. It was later found by a parson of Saint Pancras in London, who began to translate it into English, but died before completing the work. Capgrave describes himself coming upon the half-finished translation, which was composed in an obscure dialect that he deems

---

2   Duggan, 'New Homonormativity', p. 179.

'dark language' ('derk langage').³ He therefore decides to translate it into proper English, and to supplement missing details with an authoritative Latin source. The details of the obscure unfinished English version and the supplemental Latin source remain unknown, and Capgrave's account of discovering the text in such fashion is unsubstantiated. Yet Capgrave's history generally traces the evidence we do have: early Greek versions of Saint Katherine's life date to the seventh and eighth centuries, but the first full account of her passion is found in an eleventh-century Latin version known as the *Vulgate*. The *Vulgate* most likely served as the source material for Jacobus de Voragine's version in the *Legenda Aurea* (c. 1260), which was the source material for many more extant legends of the *Life* including those in the *South England Legendary*, the *Scottish Legendary*, and Caxton's *Golden Legend*, as well as an anonymous prose version in Middle English (c. 1420).⁴ Capgrave could have drawn on a number of existing sources to compose his version, supplying his textual genealogy simply as a stylistic narrative technique.⁵ These accounts of Katherine's life focus almost exclusively on the bureaucratic, hagiographically prosaic elements of her story: the saint's brief time as a learned regent, her passion, and her martyrdom. Capgrave's verse version, however, attends insistently to intimate aspects of Katherine's life – particularly her heritage and youth, her eventual conversion to Christianity, and her mystical marriage to Christ – which frame her rejection of normative cultural values as the marker of her higher calling.⁶

Capgrave's *Life*, which survives in four fifteenth-century manuscripts, contains about 8,000 lines of rhyme royal verse divided into a prologue and five books.⁷ After detailing his discovery of the text, Capgrave fills the first book with details of Katherine's birth, education, ancestry, and coronation. Katherine's parents, King Costus and Queen Meliades, are described as being old when Katherine is born, and Capgrave compares them to other 'geriatric' holy parents including Abraham and Sarah (Genesis 17:1-18).⁸ As

3   Capgrave, *Life*, Prologue, ll. 208-09. All modern English translations are my own. References to the Middle English text, supplied parenthetically and/or in corresponding endnotes by book and line number(s), are to Winstead's edition (Capgrave, *Life*).
4   See Lewis, *Cult*, pp. 9-11; 'A King'.
5   See Winstead's 'Introduction' in Capgrave, *Life*, p. 6.
6   The only other versions that include these details are the Middle English prose version (c. 1420), as well as texts in the Middle Dutch tradition. On the latter texts, see: van Dijk, 'Martyrs'; Williams-Krapp, *Legendare*, pp. 425-46.
7   See Bibliography for a list of extant manuscripts.
8   I, ll. 176-89. Joachim and Anne, also discussed here, are not named in the Bible, but feature in the apocryphal Gospel of James (1-5).

Katherine grows into adolescence, King Costus has a walled castle built for her, wherein she spends most of her time studying. Katherine eventually becomes so learned that she outwits 310 philosophers and scholars gathered by her father to challenge her.[9] When the kingdom is left without a ruler after King Costus's death, Meliades immediately calls a parliament to confirm Katherine's claim to the throne. While the lords assent to Katherine's rule, her subjects quickly become dissatisfied with her devotion to study and lack of a husband:

> 'We have a queen: she keeps to herself;
> She loves nothing but books and school.
> She lets all our enemies ride and run throughout the land,
> She is always studying and alone.
> This will bring us all to wreck and to sorrow!
> If she had a lord, all might be well[.]'[10]

As queen, Katherine's ambivalence towards marriage generates substantial conflict in the kingdom.

The entirety of Capgrave's second book is devoted to debate over the need for Katherine to marry. However, Katherine maintains that she will only consider marrying a man who is peerless, all-knowing, mighty, rich but generous, fair, and most importantly, immortal.[11] Book III describes a visit from the Virgin Mary to an old hermit named Adrian, going on to detail Katherine's conversion and mystical marriage to Christ. On the Virgin's instruction, Adrian breaks into Katherine's castle, informs her that Christ has chosen her for a wife, and takes her to the desert, where they are met by the Virgin Mary.[12] Adrian baptizes Katherine before she marries Christ, who gives her a wedding ring made of chalcedony, then instructs Adrian to teach Katherine about his Incarnation and promptly returns from whence he came.[13] After eight days, the Virgin Mary tells Katherine that her mother has died in her absence, and that Katherine will be tortured and killed by a pagan emperor.[14] Capgrave then introduces Maxentius, a

---

9   I, ll. 400-27.
10 "'We have a qween: sche comyth among no men; | Sche loveth not ellys but bookys and scole. | Let all oure enmyes in lond ryde or ren, | Sche is evyr in stody and evermore sole. | This wille turne us all to wrake and to dole! | But had sche a lord, yet all myth be wele'" (I, ll. 862-67).
11 II, ll. 1401-56.
12 III, ll. 376-1002.
13 III, ll. 1107-344.
14 III, ll. 1430-57.

Persian emperor who came to power but was quickly deposed in Rome, now seeking Christians to persecute. The rest of Book IV details Katherine's confrontations with Maxentius after he invades Alexandria. Capgrave recounts various exchanges between Katherine, the emperor, and the fifty philosophers he gathers to debate her.[15] She eventually convinces the philosophers of Christ's divinity and they convert, establishing Katherine's seminal Christian authority.

Book V records the numerous resultant martyrdoms: the converted philosophers are burned; Maxentius's converted wife is tortured before she is beheaded and thrown to the dogs; the empress's knight Porphirius converts, retrieves her body, and is likewise beheaded and given to the dogs.[16] Capgrave also reveals the miracles that surround these violent deaths. The philosophers die in the fire, but their bodies are left untouched by the flames.[17] After Maxentius has Katherine beaten and imprisoned, she is tended by angels; and after Katherine prays that God will destroy a torture wheel meant for her, a lightning bolt strikes the contraption, sending wheels and spokes flying through the air.[18] When Katherine is finally beheaded, milk flows from her neck instead of blood and angels carry her body to Mount Sinai, where an oil font with curative powers appears.[19] At this point, Capgrave's text ends suddenly, without the invocation to the saint asking for her favourable intercession to God that is characteristic of medieval hagiographies. This abrupt and atypical ending leaves the text, and the reader's relationship with Katherine, open-ended and mutable.

Problem child

Katherine's refusal to biologically reproduce extends beyond the characteristic idealization of virginity in medieval saints' lives to become part of Capgrave's textual preoccupation with procreation.[20] Capgrave presents a genderqueer theory of authorship that subverts maternal imagery to imagine

15 IV, ll. 819-2059.
16 V, ll. 1415-1596.
17 V, ll. 288-308.
18 V, ll. 883-945; ll. 1303-65.
19 V, ll. 1912-52.
20 While she emphasizes the function of virginity in medieval hagiography, Winstead importantly points out that saints' lives often 'worked not to propagate enduring values of medieval Christianity, but to invest partisan views of topical issues with the authority of tradition' (p. 5). See also: Salih, *Versions of Virginity*; Bernau, Evans and Salih, *Medieval Virginities*.

textual production. For modern readers, 'queer' means that which falls outside the norm, alongside moments or actions that contravene normative behaviours or expectations – in this case, those specifically regarding gender – which allow for or produce transgressive results.[21] Lee Edelman's theorization of 'the Child' identifies the production of biological offspring as 'central to the compulsory [heteronormative] narrative of reproductive futurism'.[22] This 'reproductive futurism' ensures human survival and affords unending opportunities for cultural, social, and political redemption through the heterosexual reproduction of children. Each successive generation brings the opportunity for a new and more fully articulated identity, one that is ideally heteronormative. In contrast, Edelman argues that queerness is antithetical to any form of production.

Opposing the heteronormative conception of reproductive futurity, Edelman embraces antisociality, sterility, and the disruption of majoritarian social and political order. Just such a queer rejection of reproductive futurism emerges in the *Life of Saint Katherine*. Katherine spends her adolescence and young adulthood alone, studying within her garden walls. Her antisociality becomes a problem when her subjects deem her rule incompetent, and demand that she marry to demonstrate proper sociability. Katherine's refusal to take a husband, and her ultimate martyrdom, glorify her sterile existence and the end of her royal line. Her self-isolation and sterility lead to the disruption of social and political order: an unchallenged foreign power invades Alexandria and slaughters Katherine's people. However, Katherine's rejection of heteronormative modes of production and subsequent cultivation of cultural chaos results in her textual memorialization; she ultimately fits within a hagiographical lineage that articulates subversive and non-normative futures. Working within a literary genre that welcomes and celebrates immediate and distant futures independent of biological reproduction, Capgrave produces a text that is well suited to a queer historical archive unbound by normative conceptions of reproduction. Following Heather Love, throughout the twentieth century, these normative conceptions have been constructed via an understanding of queerness as 'perverse, immature, sterile, [and] melancholic [...] provok[ing] fears about the future [while] also recall[ing] the past'.[23] Essential to the construction

---

21   I follow Sedgwick's formulation of queerness as 'the open mesh of possibilities, gaps, overlaps, dissonances and resonances, lapses and excesses of meaning, when the constituent elements of anyone's gender, of anyone's sexuality aren't made (or *can't* be made) to signify monolithically' (*Tendencies*, p. 8). See also: 'Queer' in this volume's Appendix: p. 311.
22   Edelman, *No Future*, p. 21, square brackets indicate my addition for clarity.
23   Love, *Feeling Backward*, p. 6.

of a queer archive, 'reading for backwardness' finds value in 'regressive' or nonproductive identities deemed to be lagging behind by modernization efforts that sought to move humanity forward by abandoning those marked inferior or 'backwards'.[24] Katherine's antisociality and sterility are of value to Capgrave, who works them into signs of heavenly preordination.

Before Capgrave imagines alternative futures, the *Life*'s extended prologue focuses on origins, beginning with the queer geneses of the text. Although Capgrave engenders Katherine's textual existence and recapitulates her history, she most likely never actually lived. Capgrave is forthright about the fact that his account is not original, but instead, a translation of several other translations: the product of a lineage of male authorship. The first Latin translation of Katherine's life was supposedly written by Arrek, who was so desirous to learn as much as he could of Katherine that he lived in Alexandria for twelve years: '[t]o know of this [Katherine's textual life] both the spring and the well'.[25] Arrek's hopeful characterization of Alexandria as a 'spring' ('spryng') or source lends a metaphoric layer to Capgrave's fixation on origins. Capgrave recounts that one hundred years after Athanasius completed his Greek transcription of Katherine's life, Arrek 'did sow it anew, | For out of Greek he translated, | This holy life, into Latin'.[26] The characterization of Arrek's translation as being 'sown' ('i-sowe') draws on shared imagery of sexual intercourse and writing as acts of begetting, reinforcing an understanding of texts as offspring.[27] Following this metaphor, Arrek's translation retains some of the features of Athanasius's Greek parent text, but also emerges as a unique Latin progeny.

Earlier in the Prologue, Capgrave explains the translation efforts of an anonymous priest who was very pale due to the 'great labour he had in his life | To seek [Katherine's] life for eighteen years'.[28] Capgrave emphasizes the arduous physicality of finding and writing Katherine's life, characterizing the task as a 'labour'.[29] The embodied nature of this textual production

24   Ibid.
25   'This [what he had previously heard of Katherine] made him sekere into that londe to wende, | To know of this bothe the spryng and the welle, | If any man coude it any pleynere telle' (Prologue, ll. 180-82).
26   'did it new i-sowe, | For owt of Grew he hath it fyrst runge, | This holy lyff, into Latyne tunge' (Prologue, ll. 173-75).
27   '"souen": 4a. to beget; be begotten of seed', *Middle English Dictionary*. 'Sown' is used with a sexual connotation later in Book III (ll. 637-44).
28   'For grete labour he had in his lyve | To seke [Katherine's] liffe yerys thyrtene and fyve' (Prologue, ll. 48-49).
29   '"labour": 4b. pain, sickness, disease; also, the active phase of an intermittent disease; ~ of birth', *Middle English Dictionary*.

intensifies when the priest finds Katherine's *Life* after receiving a vision in a dream: a well-dressed figure, holding a disintegrating book, tells the priest that he must eat it, and warns that he will not succeed in his translation if he does not comply.[30] The priest is hesitant, countering: "'I may in no way get them [the boards and leaves of the book] into my mouth: | My mouth is small and they are so great, | They will break my jaws and my throat'".[31] While this image incorporates the medieval conception of reading or learning as a sort of mastication, the priest's anxiety and the graphic account of the way the book will affect his body inverts the process of birth: the priest's throat becomes a birth canal, at risk of breaking or tearing.[32] But the visionary figure is persistent, instructing the priest to "'[r]eceive it boldly'" and "'hide it in [his] womb'", where "'[i]t shall not grieve [him] neither in his back nor side'".[33] Finally the vision tells the priest that "'in [his] womb it [the book] will be sweet'" ("'in thi wombe it wyll be swete'"), which presents textual consumption as a type of incubation, threatening pain and complication, but also promising pleasure and fulfilment.[34] In the fifteenth century, 'womb' ('wombe') was used to refer to the stomach or any bodily cavity, including the uterus.[35] By instructing the priest to hide the book that holds the story of St Katherine in his 'womb', the man in the vision foregrounds a genderqueer textual birth. Additionally, the priest describes the book as 'food' ('mete') and as having 'rotten' ('roten') covers. These characterizations rely on an understanding of the book as organic, living, and susceptible to decay. Capgrave queerly humanizes the text by presenting a queer production process: a male, textual pregnancy.[36] Over nearly 250 lines, Capgrave's explication of the text's complicated creation functions as a labour that results in the 'birth' of a new *textual* life of Saint Katherine, one that is dependent on 'sowing' and 'begetting' between men. This version of saintly femininity, which is conceived of by men and serves

---

30 Prologue, l. 90.

31 "'I may in noo wyse into my mouth hem gete: | My mouth is small and eke thei be so grete, | Thei wyll brek my chaules and my throte'" (Prologue, ll. 95-97).

32 Considering gendered uses of the body in Carolingian monastic orders, Coon links the relationship between teeth or the capability for 'masticat[ion] of the divine word' and virility as indicated by the Benedictine Rule (*Dark Age Bodies*, pp. 88-95 [p. 88]).

33 "Receyve it boldly [...] in thi wombe it hyde | It schal not greve thee neyther in bak ne syde" (Prologue, ll. 101-03).

34 Prologue, l. 104.

35 "'wombe'": 1a. (a) The human stomach; also *fig.* and in *fig.* context; ~ skin, the lining of the stomach; 5a. (a) The human uterus, womb; also *fig.*; specif. the womb of the Virgin Mary; also, the vaginal canal, vagina', *Middle English Dictionary*.

36 Prologue, ll. 94-98.

as a model for both men and women, results in a textual object that modern readers can understand as both androgynous and genderqueer, further establishing a queer historical lineage.

In order to make Katherine's life more 'openly known to women and men', Capgrave must endure one more stage of textual labour and deliver Katherine's life from the nearly incomprehensible 'dark language' of the anonymous priest.[37] But before ending the Prologue, Capgrave presents his own beginnings: 'If you wish to know who I am | My country is Norfolk, of the town of Lynne | [...] God gave me grace never to cease | To follow the steps of my fathers before | Which to the rule of Augustine were sworn'.[38] Capgrave provides an abundance of originary information, his own included, establishing the text as one concerned with genealogies on multiple levels. Capgrave interjects frequently throughout the remainder of his text. Reference to the self signals a shift in late-medieval narration and challenges previous modes of writing and hagiographic authorship, in which authors would often remain anonymous to keep focus on the holy subjects of their texts.[39] Capgrave's uninhibited voice brings life to the vernacular composition of the *Life*, imbuing it with a distinct personality. Additionally, Capgrave's inclusion of himself in his text serves as a sort of genetic marking that reinforces and strengthens his hereditary ties to both text and narrative.

While Capgrave presents Katherine as an exceptional figure worthy of veneration, he also highlights her scholarly endeavours and touts her continuous rejection of various social expectations, often doing so in personal terms. For instance, in his prologue to Book III, Capgrave calls for Katherine's support and comfort: 'I apply myself directly to this work; | Thou blessed maiden, comfort me in this. | Because thou were so learned and also a clerk, | Clerks must love thee – it stands to reason'.[40] Capgrave here seems to personally identify with Katherine on a scholarly level. This reinforcement of his respect for her scholastic achievement transgresses the ideal gendering typical of medieval literature and social thought, that would

---

37 'Therfor wyl I thee serve so as I can | And make thi lyffe, that more openly it schalle | Be know abowte of woman and of man' ['Therefore I will serve you as well as I can | And make your life more plainly understood | among women and men'] (Prologue, ll. 44-46).
38 'If ye wyll wete what that I am | My cuntré is Northfolke, of the town of Lynne; | [...] Godd geve me grace nevyr for to blynne | To follow the steppes of my faderes before | Whech to the rewle of Austen were swore' (Prologue, ll. 239-45).
39 See: Coakley, *Women*; Kieckhefer, *Unquiet Souls*.
40 'I dresse me now streyt onto this werk; | Thow blyssyd may, comfort thou me in this. | Because thou were so lerned and swech a clerk, | Clerkes must love thee – resoun forsoth it is' (III, ll. 36-39).

associate reason with men and emotion with women. Capgrave's account of Katherine's complicated origins (both as a 'historical' character and as a physical book) establishes a genderqueer beginning for a narrative and legacy that offers non-normative possibilities for conceiving of production.

Institutional privilege

Throughout the body of the text, Capgrave upholds conservative social institutions such as marriage and childbearing, but simultaneously glorifies Katherine's rejection of them. Karen Winstead points out that Capgrave addressed these kinds of 'complex social and philosophical issues' for a broad audience of readers, as evidenced in Book II during a long debate about 'a woman's fitness to rule' which 'sets forth contradictory yet equally compelling arguments about government, tradition, and gender, and [...] concludes with no clear-cut winner'.[41] Capgrave's effective presentation of these issues critically relies on Katherine's occupation of intersecting social positions.[42] While she is marginalized because of her gender and her religion, her inherited nobility and her social class afford political belonging that facilitates her extraordinary refusals of gender norms. Katherine's classed and gendered position in the ruling elite demonstrates her value within and for dominant cultural systems. Her refusal of prescribed modes of marriage and reproduction in favour of alternative enactments are shown to be heavenly ordained, and thus, indisputable. Taken with Emma Campbell's understanding of spiritual marriage as 'an attempt to think beyond the human limits of kinship and desire to glimpse other – potentially queer – alternatives', Capgrave's *Life* provides an opportunity to consider the role that social privilege plays in the enactments of gender/queer alternatives.[43] Capgrave presents Katherine as a complex figure who assimilates various attributes of sanctity broadly and the extant legendary Katherine texts specifically, ventriloquizing Katherine's privileged – if non-conformist – voice in order to disperse various theological ruminations. This layered presentation of character is complicated by Katherine's refusal of the expectations placed

---

41 Winstead, 'Introduction' in Capgrave, *Life*, pp. 7-8.

42 In 1989, Kimberlé Crenshaw theorized intersectionality as a means to examine the relationships between socio-economic and socio-cultural categories and identities, and thereby analyse how multiple identities, including gender, class, and race, interact in experiences of exclusion and marginalization: 'Demarginalizing'.

43 Campbell, *Gift*, p. 96. See also Salih's discussion (pp. 66-97) of the 'plurality of identity positions' (p. 67) offered by the topos of *sponsa Christi* in *Versions of Virginity*.

upon her, and the immediate physical persecution but eventual (eternal) glory this occasions. Ultimately, Katherine leverages her privileged positions of ruler and scholar to achieve even greater honour as a bride of Christ and virgin saint, securing her future – made possible by inherited social positions – as one of the most popular and venerated figures of the late medieval period.

Katherine's 'duty' to her people and country is marriage to a suitable consort and the subsequent production of an heir to ensure continuity of rulership, a textual detail that foregrounds her tenuous access to power. Capgrave depicts her uncle, the Duke of Tyre, as an antagonistic force who fails to understand Katherine's fate and future sanctity, instead equating her political and general worth with her ability and willingness to reproduce. He chides: "'What benefit was it to us that you were born | If you will not do right as they did – | I mean your father and mother before you?'"[44] While Capgrave's reader knows Katherine's ultimate destiny as bride of Christ, the Duke can only understand Katherine's purpose within the terms of biological reproduction, or rather, reproductive futurism. By reminding her that she would not be in a privileged position on the throne had her parents not taken such care in raising her, and more importantly, in producing her, the Duke presents reproduction as the critical function of Katherine's inheritance. The saint's refusal of the requirements of her rank and gender communicates her political inadequacy – reinforcing the notion that women do not belong in politics – but she adapts and eventually relies on those very institutions to build and foster her exceptional status as virgin martyr.

Katherine's advisors continue to wield power over her, emphasizing the political impact of matrimony and insisting that Katherine's retention of power is entirely dependent on marriage. Meliades avers that her daughter's desire to marry only a man who is immortal, rich, generous, and so forth is perilous since no such man exists, while implying that failure to marry and reproduce spells certain deposition.[45] Up to this point, Meliades is the only other woman in the text, and Capgrave's portrayal of her 'proper' enactment of female nobility starkly contrasts with Katherine's rejection of it.[46] When Katherine reasserts her intention to remain unmarried, Meliades declares that she 'bewails' ('wayle') the day Katherine was born,

---

44 "'What boote was it to us that ye were born | If that ye wyll not do ryght as thei dede – | I mene youre fadyr and modyr yow beforn?'" (II, ll. 1065-67).
45 II, ll. 1014-29.
46 Meliades, daughter of the king of Armenia, is characterized as acceptably regal and exceptionally beautiful (I, ll. 218-23). She is initially anxious about her ability to conceive, and subsequently about Katherine's opposition to marriage (I, ll. 176-79).

foreseeing that Katherine's stubbornness will bring about her own early death.[47] Katherine's refusal to marry thus effectively kills off both her existing and potential biological familial lines. Reflecting Campbell's argument that queerness emerges from 'the orthodox ideological aims of hagiographic texts which use marriage as a metaphor for divine union', Katherine trades a normative conception of feminine power, dependent on marriage and reproduction, for a genderqueer power made possible through virginity and martyrdom.[48]

Katherine deflects all arguments for the necessity of her marriage in favour of her solitary academic life. Capgrave's portrayal of Katherine as a distracted ruler provides a nuanced presentation of saintliness. She is faced with an ethical dilemma requiring a choice between serving her people and serving her own desires. At this point in the text, Katherine knows nothing of Christianity. Combined with her rejection of marriage and political obligation, her decision to remain enclosed in her study appears particularly selfish, further complicating her later exemplary, saintly status. After hearing the first argument urging her to wed at a special parliament organized for just that purpose, Katherine admits silently to herself:

> 'If I conceal my decision [to remain a virgin scholar], then shall I fall
> Angering all my people here [...]
> Yet I greatly wonder why my heart is set
> On a point that I cannot abandon,
> And yet it is against my own law,
> Which I am sworn to keep and to defend.'[49]

Katherine explicitly acknowledges that she is breaking the law by refusing to marry and acting in a way that does not best serve her people. This self-interest translates to a lack of governing proficiency and signals that Katherine is out of place in the political realm. Capgrave's detailed account of Katherine's refusal to marry for the good of her people, despite the knowledge that it would be just and lawful, suggests individual agency. But as a future virgin saint, marrying a man is a step that Katherine *cannot*

---

47   II, l. 1040-50 (1040).
48   Campbell, *Gift*, p. 96
49   "'If I concelle my counsell | than schall I falle | In indignacyon of all my puple here; | If I denye her askyng in this halle | And tell no cause, I put hem more in dwere [...] | Yet wondyr I sore that my hert is sett | On swech a poynte that I cannot let, | And yet it is agens myne owyn lawe, | Whech I am swore to kepe and to defende'" (II, ll. 169-77).

take.⁵⁰ Katherine's dilemma is resolved with an alternative marriage to the unlikely man she had long ago anticipated. Her mystical union with Christ affords her power in the eternal realm and absolves her of her selfish conceit: Christ chose Katherine for his wife before she was even born, so *of course* she desired to remain unwed. Katherine's unwillingness to compromise, as well as its effects – her poor diplomacy – are reconfigured as divine will.

Katherine's earthly privilege – determined by her socio-political status, virtue, and beauty – marks her for marriage to a high-calibre human husband, while her spiritual exceptionality leads to her mystical marriage to Christ. When the Virgin Mary instructs the hermit Adrian to travel to Alexandria to convert Katherine, she tells him that although Katherine's council laboriously used "'many methods and strategies'" ("'many a wyle, | And many a mene'") to convince her to marry, they failed.⁵¹ The Virgin reveals that she herself, however, had "ordained [Katherine] a lord | To whom she shall in purity agree to be married'".⁵² The Virgin continues, telling Adrian about Katherine's impressive lineage, honour, and virtue as well as her goodness, skill, and pedigree: "'[Y]ou [shall] know she is a queen – | Rich, royal, wise, and also fair, | For in this world there have been none like her'".⁵³ The Virgin Mary praises Katherine's inherited wealth and status, wisdom, and beauty, thereby identifying Katherine as an idealized and privileged model of femininity. Earlier in her conversation with Adrian, the Virgin refers to Katherine as a 'sweet flower' ('swete floure'), also noting Katherine's physical appeal.⁵⁴ An emphasis on feminine beauty mirrors the reasons given by Katherine's advisors for her earthly marriage: her beauty is reworked within the context of mystical betrothal, further solidifying the substitution of marriage to an earthly prince for marriage to a heavenly one. When the Virgin notes that Katherine is childless, instead of lamenting like Katherine's advisors, she substitutes religious devotion and piety for biological children, telling Adrian, "'[Katherine] has no children, neither has she any heir, | For if she believes, she shall love better the hair shirt |

---

50 While numerous married women were canonized and venerated, the overtly 'saintly' parts of their lives only began after the deaths – or sometimes, conversions – of their husbands. Some married couples maintained chaste marriages as an act of devotion, but often after having children. See Winstead, *Virgin Martyrs*; Elliot, *Spiritual Marriage*; Karras, *Sexuality*, pp. 36-78.
51 III, ll. 192-94.
52 "'For I myselve have ordeynd hir a lorde | To whom sche schall in clennesse well acorde'" (III, ll. 195-96).
53 "'Fyrst of alle, thu whyte sche is a qween – | A rych, a reall, a wys, and eke a fayre, | For in this worlde swech no moo there been'" (III, ll. 204-206).
54 III, l. 201.

Than any fine linens after that she [will] be drawn | Unto my service and to my Son's law'".[55] Winstead points out the double meaning of the word 'reynes' ('fine linen'): in addition to referencing the fine cloth of Rennes, Brittany, the term 'can also mean "the male generative organ" (MED, 'reine' 2b)'.[56] This innuendo draws out Katherine's modification of earthly marriage into something chastely spiritual. Christ's 'law' ('lawe') is shown to be more alluring than any temporal cultural or social expectation and so Capgrave renders blasphemous any possibility *other* than Katherine's spiritual marriage to Christ. Although Katherine's conversion marks her as a minority figure within pagan territory, it also signals the assumption of an extremely powerful position with the dominant, Christian majority of her late-medieval readership.

Katherine's rejection of earthly marriage may subvert expectations of her position, but she subsequently attains spiritual power through martyrdom. Katherine's enduring popularity surpasses that of many other saints. During Capgrave's lifetime, Katherine's cult was one of the most popular in England and parts of Europe; in contemporaneous texts including the *Book of Margery Kempe*, Katherine is often named as one of Christ's primary saintly spouses.[57] Katherine's social position required her engagement with the world around her – she had property to manage and family to quarrel with – bolstering her relatability amongst a medieval readership. In her textual afterlives, Katherine's power and character is shown to be multivalent and familiar. After all, by presenting virginal and holy women, Capgrave and other hagiographers sought not to inspire readers to direct imitation, but instead to motivate them to be better Christians. By providing Katherine with a suitable bridegroom immediately after her rejection of the pleas of her advisors and mother, Capgrave proffers the institution of marriage itself as a force for social stability. Katherine's refusal of an earthly husband is thus affirmed because this allows her union with Christ and her participation in the institution of marriage. This narrative foretells a familiar modern impetus amongst segments of the queer community that value institutional recognition for its ability to confer existential validity and social legibility. This risks creating a hierarchy of queer lives that is determined by heteronormative delineations of worth and efficacy. For instance, the same legal systems

---

55 "'[Katherine] has no chylde, ne sche hath non ayre, | For if sche leve, sche schall love bettyr the hayre | Than any reynes aftyr that sche be drawe | Onto my servyse and to my Sones lawe'" (III, ll. 207-10).

56 'Notes' to Capgrave, *Life*, p. 299. Such a pun would not be surprising in this narrative, whose saints are hardly naïve.

57 See Kempe, *Book*, I, ll. 1158-63.

that permit same sex married couples equal recognition also maintain discrimination against trans people within medical settings.[58] Ultimately Katherine's mystical marriage and resultant martyrdom remove her from her position of political power, to instead reinscribe the transcendental power of marriage as a cultural institution. That marriage is thereby shown to be better than independence or other familial relationships is a vital development for Capgrave's contemporary communities of East Anglian women that found Katherine to be an attractive model of spiritual devotion.

From her privileged position, Capgrave's Katherine tests feminine peripheries by recasting the roles of wife and mother as genderqueer spiritual engagements. This results in her martyrdom, an outcome favourable for a saint, but not particularly desirable or institutionally advisable for fifteenth-century English readers. Capgrave navigates any problematic disjuncture between literal and figurative marriage by promoting the significance of the institution itself, regardless of the object of betrothal. Katherine is an exemplary saintly model, whose exceptionality is well established and contingent upon her marriage with Christ himself, thus rendering her status, and her refusals, unattainable for a 'common' medieval reader.[59] Capgrave's emphasis on the institution of marriage makes Katherine's position as bride of Christ ordinary, but the supernatural identity of her spouse reinforces her saintly exceptionality. By centring his narrative on Katherine's rejection of one marriage in favour of another and using the terms of biological reproduction to describe textual production, Capgrave shows that institutions endure but can be enacted otherwise.

Capgrave's text presents an ambivalent late-medieval relationship between gender and social position. The text reinforces the importance of marriage and biological reproduction as cultural cornerstones, because the viability of mystical marriage and textual production as substitutions applies only to Katherine. Her privileged position – marked by nobility, virginity, femininity, and eventually sanctity – allows her to avoid the social expectations of marriage and reproduction, and rework them to suit her desires, as well as the will of God and the salvific need of a medieval religious populace. Although Katherine transgresses cultural norms, she eventually upholds the supremacy of traditional cultural institutions, gradually securing her own sanctity.

---

58 Department of Health and Human Services, 'Nondiscrimination', pp. 37161-62.

59 For the medieval *sponsa Christi* tradition, which cast Christ as a bridegroom preferable to any other, see McNamer, *Affective Meditation*, p. 31. Katherine's nuptials represent a successful alternative to normative marriage, unrestricted by powers of the state and unconcerned with biological production.

Capgrave's Katherine evidences a history of complex genderqueer ideologies in which contradictory and competing modes of existing are enabled, and widely accepted, through access to power and homonormative praxis. Duggan theorizes homonormativity within the context of neoliberal western politics and capitalist motivation: heteronormative structures are upheld by queer individuals seeking acceptance by dominant society. Similarly, Capgrave's purpose in upholding dominant heteronormative institutions seems to be in the interest of maintaining domestic normalcy or relevancy, as exemplified by Katherine's popularity amongst a mainstream medieval public.

Afterlives

Time tends to be measured in terms of progress; a historical move 'towards modernity' signals cultural advancement, while individual 'success' relies on professional and personal advancement.[60] Queer temporality, in contrast, encompasses temporal movements deemed regressive or unsuccessful, operating 'off the designated biopolitical schedule of reproductive heterosexuality'.[61] Capgrave's Virgin Mary – a figure defined by her contradictory and remarkable status as a virgin mother – offers Katherine an alternative to reproductive heterosexuality, one that destabilizes normative biopolitical schedules. The Virgin Mary tells Adrian exactly how to court Katherine in her name: "'Say in just this way: 'The Lady both mother and maiden | Greets her well'" and identifies herself in queer terms: she is both maiden and spouse, inhabiting a sexuality unencumbered by normative modes of reproduction.[62] This link between Mary and Katherine is further reinforced by Adrian's establishment of the Virgin Mary as a model for Katherine.

When Katherine challenges Adrian's assertion that she can produce 'lineage' ('lynage') while still remaining chaste, he explains his Lord's relationship to 'his Lady', noting that Mary is both Christ's mother but also a virgin.[63] This relationship is confusing for Katherine, but Adrian reassures her:

---

60 Freeman (*Time Binds*, p. 3) explains this concept as 'chrononormativity,' whereby 'institutional forces come to seem like somatic facts'.
61 McCallum and Tuhkanen, 'Introduction', sp. 10. The authors note that 'queerness has always been marked by its untimely relation to socially shared temporal phases, whether individual (developmental) or collective (historical). More often than not, this connection remains defined in negative or hurtful ways, ways that reinforce queerness as a failure to achieve the norm' (pp. 9-10).
62 "'Sey ryght thus: 'The Lady bothe modyr and mayde Gretyth hir well'"'(III, ll. 183-84).
63 III, ll. 519-24.

> 'You shall have her Lord, who is also her Son –
> A gracious lineage that may naught fail,
> Marvellous descendants to learn of if you like:
> He is her Lord, she is His mother;
> He is her Son and she is also a maiden;
> He made her, she bore Him in her womb[.]'[64]

By referring to Jesus as Mary's 'Lord', Adrian indicates a noble bond of marriage, while Katherine's entrance into a familial relationship with the pair is suggested by the invocation of Katherine's descendants. Family, in this sense, is expansive and fluid, presenting another moment of queer recognition for modern readers.

Katherine, however, remains unconvinced that anyone could populate a lineage and remain chaste. Capgrave, intervening to narrate the scene, describes her as 'sore marred in mynde' (shocked) and details her physical reaction after hearing Adrian's promise of virginal procreation – she loses colour and finds herself in a 'trauns' (trance), unable to determine where she is and completely changed in 'kynde' (appearance).[65] Katherine's physical change is juxtaposed against a simultaneous out-of-body experience: she feels transported to another world. She abandons her present self and emerges in a future space, removed from her temporal, political, and social bindings. Capgrave explains that she finds herself '[b]etwixt two things' ('[b]etwyx too thingys'), reinforcing her liminal position.[66] Ultimately, Katherine recognizes that Adrian's offer can fulfil her desires: '[Adrian's] words have guided now full heavily her thought | That she shall have a thing long desired | […] so sore is her heart with this burning love, | It shall no more, she determined, be polluted by the world'.[67] Katherine's focus is drawn to a location outside her own worldly and polluted temporality. She chooses a future that removes her from the spatiotemporal moment she inhabits, where the possibility of producing a viable line while also remaining chaste is incomprehensible. This choice is prompted by her heart, which 'burns' with love ('with this love i-fyred'). José Esteban Muñoz conceptualizes a kind of queer futurity that

---

64 '"Ye schull have hir Lord and hir Sone eke – | A gracyous lynage that may noght mys, | A mervelyous kynrode to lerne if ye leke: | He is hir Lorde, sche His modyr is; | He is hir Sone and sche mayde iwys; | He made hir, sche bare Him in hir wombe"' (III, ll. 603-08).
65 III, ll. 610-16.
66 III, ll. 617.
67 '[Adrian's] wordes have enclyned now ful sore hir thowte | That sche schall have a thing long desyred […] so sore is hir hert with this love i-fyred, | It schall no more, sche cast, with the world be myred' (III, ll. 624-28).

takes account of the ways that '[c]ertain performances of queer citizenship contain [...] an anticipatory illumination of a queer world, a sign of an actually existing queer reality, a kernel of political possibility within a stultifying heterosexual present'.[68] Although Katherine exemplifies the homonormative valorization of marriage and reproduction, the genderqueer production of her text, involving various male hagiographers taking gestational roles as they produce her (their) textual legacies, challenges the heteronormative status quo and reveals the 'kernel' of potential for queer lives that Muñoz denotes and queer histories that I posit here. Capgrave (and others) birth the textual record of Katherine's life.

Further developing the queer temporality of lineage without procreation, the Virgin Mary assures Adrian of Katherine's divine destiny as a martyr: "'She shall have ever as glorious an end | As any woman that lived here as a human'".[69] Before Katherine has even begun her spiritual life – she is yet to actually convert – the Virgin Mary focuses on its end. That Katherine's death is to be as glorious as any other 'woman' amongst humans serves to further reinforce her narrative position as a gendered ideal, better suited to a life after death. Her desire to remove herself from the quotidian world ultimately convinces her to convert and to marry Christ. There is no real 'evidence' or persuasive material that encourages her conversion. Katherine does not even know any Church doctrine – Jesus instructs Adrian to teach her *after* she has already married him.[70] The overwhelming message surrounding the wedding of Jesus and Katherine is that it portends her death. Immediately after their wedding, Jesus tells her:

'My angels shall honour you with a service,
As a reminder that we are wedded together.
There has never been seen yet here such funeral office
Of any saint that died on earth.
This shall I do for your love dear[.]'[71]

Christ's wedding gift to Katherine is a funeral service. Capgrave's focus on death before, during, and after the mystical marriage challenges the

---

68 Muñoz, *Cruising Utopia*, p. 49
69 "'Sche schall have eke as gloryous a hende | As evyr had woman that lyved here in kende'" (III, ll. 237-38).
70 III, ll. 1324-27.
71 "'Myn aungellis schull honour yow with a servyse, | In tokne that we be wedded in fere. | There was nevyr sey yet swech funeral offyse | Of no seynt that in erde deyed here. | This schal I do for youre love dere'" (III, ll. 1338-42).

heteronormative, reproductive goals of marriage to instead inscribe alternative modes of futurity, such as queer and genderqueer textual communities.

Re-evaluation of normative modes of production that are inherently progressive is crucial to the establishment and cultivation of a queer archive and historical genealogy. Carolyn Dinshaw theorizes a 'touching across time', where, she posits, 'queers can make new relations, new identifications, new communities with past figures who elude resemblance to us but with whom we can be connected partially by virtue of shared marginality, queer positionality'.[72] Capgrave's hagiographic celebration of Katherine's non-normative modes of procreation and marriage not only speaks to the spiritual and temporal alterity of Christian medieval readers but to the future of twenty-first-century queer communities as they seek to establish a historical archive. The expansion of a (gender)queer past works to validate a (gender)queer present by establishing relevance and permanence through recognition. The close examination of the mutability and active construction of supposedly stable social and religious structures such as marriage and family disrupts modern notions of simple and automatic cultural belonging, promoting a multitude of queer temporalities, unbound by normative notions of progress. Crucially, such archive building must not only recognize queer marginality, but also the various intersectional privileges that facilitate culturally acceptable transgression throughout history. Capgrave's teleological focus in his fourteenth-century *Life of Saint Katherine* presents a kind of cultural chaos that subverts but does not ultimately destabilize conservative social institutions. Social status affords privileged access to various (gender)queer possibilities, for medieval saints as well as modern subjects.

Bibliography

Manuscripts

Oxford, Bodleian Library, MS Rawlinson poet 118.
London, British Library, MS Arundel 396.
London, British Library, MS Arundel 168.
London, British Library, MS Arundel 20.

---

72 *Getting Medieval*, p. 39. See also: Burger, 'Gender and Sexuality', p. 189.

Primary sources

Capgrave, John, *The Life of Saint Katherine of Alexandria,* ed. by Karen Winstead (Kalamazoo: Medieval Institute Publications, 1999).

Kempe, Margery, *The Book of Margery Kempe*, ed. by Lynn Staley (Kalamazoo: Medieval Institute Publications, 1996).

Middle English Dictionary, ed. by Robert E. Lewis et al. (Ann Arbor: University of Michigan, 1952-2001).

Secondary sources

Bernau, Anke, Ruth Evans, and Sarah Salih, eds., *Medieval Virginities* (Toronto: University of Toronto, 2003).

Burger, Glenn, 'Gender and Sexuality', in *Chaucer: Contemporary Approaches*, ed. by Susannah Fein and David Raybin (University Park: Penn State University, 2009), pp. 179-98.

Campbell, Emma, *Medieval Saints' Lives: The Gift, Kinship and Community in Old French Hagiography* (Cambridge: Brewer, 2008).

Coakley, John W., *Women, Men, and Spiritual Power: Female Saints and Their Male Collaborators* (New York: Columbia University, 2006).

Coon, Lynda L., *Dark Age Bodies: Gender and Monastic Practice in the Early Medieval West* (Philadelphia: University of Pennsylvania, 2011).

Crenshaw, Kimberlé, 'Demarginalizing the Intersection of Race and Sex: A Black Feminist Critique of Antidiscrimination Doctrine, Feminist Theory and Antiracist Politics', *University of Chicago Legal Forum*, 4 (1989), 139-67.

Department of Health and Human Services, 'Nondiscrimination in Health and Health Education Programs or Activities, Delegation of Authority', *Federal Register*, 85.119 (2020), 37160-248.

van Dijk, Mathilde, 'Bridgettine Virgin Martyrs', *Birgittiana*, 21 (2006), 51-82.

Dinshaw, Carolyn, *Getting Medieval: Sexualities and Communities, Pre- and Postmodern* (Durham: Duke University, 1999).

Duggan, Lisa, 'The New Homonormativity: The Sexual Politics of Neoliberalism', in *Materializing Democracy*, ed. by Dana Nelson and Russ Castranovo (Durham: Duke University, 2002), pp. 175-94.

Edelman, Lee, *No Future: Queer Theory and the Death Drive* (Durham: Duke University, 2004).

Elliot, Dyan, *Spiritual Marriage: Sexual Abstinence in Medieval Wedlock* (Princeton: Princeton University, 1993).

Freeman, Elizabeth, *Time Binds: Queer Temporalities, Queer History* (Durham: Duke University, 2010).

Halberstam, J., *Female Masculinity* (Durham: Duke University, 1998).

Karras, Ruth Mazo, *Sexuality in Medieval Europe: Doing unto Others* (London: Routledge, 2017).

Kieckhefer, Richard, *Unquiet Souls: Fourteenth-Century Saints and Their Religious Milieu* (Chicago: University of Chicago, 1984).

Lewis, Katherine J., *The Cult of Saint Katherine of Alexandria in Late Medieval England* (Suffolk: Boydell, 2000).

—, 'A King, Not a Servant: The Prose Life of St Katherine of Alexandria and Ideologies of Masculinity in Late Medieval England', in *Hagiography and the History of Latin Christendom, 500-1500*, ed. by Samantha Kahn Herrick (Leiden: Brill, 2020), pp. 397-416.

Love, Heather, *Feeling Backward: Loss and the Politics of Queer History* (Cambridge: Harvard University, 1997).

McCallum, E.L. and Mikko Tuhkanen, 'Introduction: Becoming Unbecoming, Untimely Mediations', in *Queer Times, Queer Becomings*, ed. by E.L. McCallum and Mikko Tuhkanen (Albany: State University of New York, 2011), pp. 1-19.

McNamer, Sarah, *Affective Meditation and the Invention of Medieval Compassion* (Philadelphia: University of Pennsylvania, 2010).

Muñoz, José Esteban, *Cruising Utopia: The Then and There of Queer Futurity* (New York: New York University, 2009).

Salih, Sarah, *Versions of Virginity in Late Medieval England* (Cambridge: Brewer, 2001).

Sedgwick, Eve Kosofsky, *Tendencies* (Durham: Duke University, 1993).

Williams-Krapp, Werner, *Die deutschen und niederländische Legendare des Mittelalters: Studien zu ihrer Überlierungs-, Text- und Wirkunsgeschichte* (Tübingen: M. Niemeyer, 1986).

Winstead, Karen, *Virgin Martyrs: Legends of Sainthood in Late Medieval England* (Ithaca: Cornell University Press, 1997).

About the author

CAITLYN MCLOUGHLIN received her PhD in English literature from The Ohio State University in 2019. Her dissertation examined the relationship between community, sexuality and devotional practice in late-medieval writings about holy women. She currently works in the Department of Access and Equity at the University of New South Wales, promoting literacy and university enrolment among equity students. In 2021 she will commence a postdoctoral project at the Centre for the History of Emotions at The University of Western Australia where she will continue her current research examining identity, sexuality and illness in medieval religious writing and late-twentieth-century pandemic literature.

3   Juana de la Cruz

Gender-Transcendent Prophetess

Kevin C.A. Elphick

Abstract
Interest in Mother Juana de la Cruz (1481-1534) has increased since the publication of her sermons in 1999 by Inocente García de Andrés and the re-opening of her cause for canonization by the Vatican in 2015. As a woman preaching sermons during the Inquisition, Mother Juana is a highly unusual figure, all the more so given that gender liminality pervades her thought. Gender fluidity is also a theme in her personal biography. This chapter examines gender liminality in her *Vida* and in her sermon on the Annunciation. Where gender liminality might seem novel and untraditional, Juana's use of this theme is contextualized and shown to be contiguous both with earlier hagiographic sources and with her professed Franciscan heritage.

Keywords: Franciscan, sermons, liminality, Hispanic mysticism, Mother Juana de la Cruz

Mother Juana de la Cruz (d. 1534) offers a medieval model for modern LGBTQ people, exemplifying radical authenticity to the queer and holy truth of her own identity. Juana's gender combined masculinity and femininity, and she proclaimed the presence of God she found inherent in that identity. Her sermons invited her listeners, too, to discover God in their own experiences of gender. Juana called on her audience to experience the divine through gender fluidity; gender non-conforming images of God, the saints, the Virgin and Christ are found throughout her sermons. When she told the story of her own re-gendering by God at her conception, she spoke the truth revealed to her of the gender transcendence she lived out in the authenticity of her life. Pointing to her Adam's apple as proof of this miracle, Juana also

---

Spencer-Hall, Alicia, and Blake Gutt (eds), *Trans and Genderqueer Subjects in Medieval Hagiography*. Amsterdam, Amsterdam University Press 2021
DOI: 10.5117/9789462988248_CH03

pointed to the source of her own miraculous and authentic voice, which is simultaneously both her own voice and the voice of Christ.

Juana was born in 1481 to farming parents in the village of Numancia, halfway between Madrid and Toledo. Contrary to the gender expectations of her day, she grew to fame for her sermons, whose echoes would reach the New World as her Sisters carried her relics and fame to the Americas and beyond.[1] Entering a Franciscan community of women as a teenager, she took the name Juana de la Cruz, eventually becoming the community's abbess. For centuries Mother Juana has been celebrated in Spain as 'la Santa Juana', but more recently she has gained scholarly attention due to the abundant gender theology of her sermons.[2] Published as *El Conhorte*, the seventy-two sermons evidence a theological predisposition toward gender equity that stood in marked contrast to the patriarchy of her day.[3] From the Franciscan tradition bequeathed to her community, Juana mined equality between the sexes, and spiritual transcendence of gender boundaries. Her life narrative, her Franciscan tradition, and the support of her Franciscan community all contributed to the unexpected blossoming of a full-flowering gender theology against the harsh backdrop of the Inquisition. The voices of contemporary religious women in Spain, such as Francisca Hernández and Francisca de los Apóstoles, were silenced by the Inquisition.[3] Juana's compelling sermons were instead embraced not only by her community and local parishioners, but also attended by both King Charles V and Cardinal Cisneros, Minister Provincial of the Franciscan Friars.

Undergirding the gender theology of Juana de la Cruz is her conviction that by Baptism, women and men are 'made equals in the grace and cleansing from sins'.[4] In this, her dependence upon Galatians is clear: 'For as many of you as have been baptized in Christ have put on Christ. [...] [T]here is

---

1   For a detailed treatment of her Sisters' subsequent missionary activities, see Owens, *Nuns*. See also Elphick, 'Cubas Women's Community'.
2   Foremost among scholars writing about Mother Juana are García de Andrés (*Teologia*), Surtz (*Guitar of God*; 'Privileging of the Feminine', and Boon ('Limits'; co-editor or Juana's *Visionary Sermons*).
3   The Sermons remained in manuscript form until 1999 when García de Andrés edited and published them in two volumes as *El Conhorte: Sermones de Una Mujer. La Santa Juana (1481-1534)*. The title, *El Conhorte*, is an antiquated variant of modern Spanish 'conforte' ('comfort'), and García de Andrés's full title may be translated as 'The Comfort: The Sermons of a Woman'.
3   Ahlgren, *Inquisition of Francisca*, pp. 2-3.
4   '[T]ambién como los hombres y sean iguales en las gracias y limpias de pecados'. 'Que trata de la Circuncisión de Nuestro Señor Jesucristo' ('Sermon on the Circumcision'), *El Conhorte*, 1, p. 297. Unless otherwise noted, all translations from *El Conhorte* are my own.

neither male nor female. For you are all one in Christ Jesus' (3:26-28).[5] But she also grounds this equality in the new creation of God's Incarnation: 'If then any be in Christ a new creature...' (2 Corinthians 5:17a). This new creation transcends gender. Juana explains of the Incarnate Christ: 'it has been said about you, [that you are a] new human and new law and new thing created on the earth.'[6] She then places in the mouth of God the Father this pronouncement upon Christ: 'You are a new human, making a new law and a new thing upon the earth.'[7] While 'human' is masculine in Spanish, the nouns 'law' and 'thing' (in 'new thing created' ['nueva cosa criada']) are both feminine. In Christ is a new law for this new, implicitly feminine, creation.

Not unexpectedly given her cultural context and period of history, Juana defaults to contrasting the Jewish covenant as inferior and lacking; her perspective is regrettably supersessionist. However, comprehension of this mindset is required to understand her perception that the dynamics of gender relations undergo a positive shift in salvation history. Juana's logic juxtaposes the 'Old' Law against the New Law. Contrasting circumcision and baptism as initiation rituals, Juana notes that since circumcision was solely for men, 'the blessings' of circumcision were not equally available to women.[8] In contrast, under the New Law, baptism was for both genders, and blessed both genders as equals in grace. By first establishing that in Christ, the new human is a 'nueva cosa criada en la tierra' ('a new [feminine] thing created upon the earth'), she adds to the weight of her conclusion that in this New Law, women are equal to men in grace, and a newly transcendent dynamic has been realized with regard to gender. After naming Christ the new human, the New Law, and a new thing, she has God the Father pronounce a gendered rendering of the Trinity: 'ancient God, I Myself, You [Son] and the Holy Spirit, we are one thing (*una cosa*) and one majesty (*una majestad*), and one Trinity (*una Trinidad*) and one essence (*una esencia*)'.[9] Juana's Sermons were meant to be heard, and here, her rhetorical device is the punctuated repetition of the feminine 'una' four times in rapid succession. Each of these attributes, including the Trinity itself, would thus have been

---

5   Biblical citations are from the Douay-Rheims Bible.
6   '[P]orque se ha dicho de ti nuevo hombre y nueva ley y nueva cosa criada en la tierra.' *El Conhorte*, I, p. 296.
7   'Y pues tú, *Hijo mío*, eres nuevo en cuanto hombre, haz nueva ley y nueva cosa sobre la tierra'. Ibid.
8   '[L]as bendiciones'. Ibid., p. 297.
9   '[V]iejo Dios, por cuanto Yo y Tú y el Espíritu Santo somos una cosa y una majestad, y una Trinidad y una esencia'. Ibid., p. 296.

heard by Juana's audience as feminine. God the Father then continues His self-description with a single introductory (masculine) 'un' which is used only to introduce the following two masculine adjectives, 'living' ('vivo'), and 'true' ('verdadero'), and concludes by naming and negating three grammatically masculine attributes – 'without beginning, without middle, without end'.[10] By weighting God's self-description with this litany of gendered attributes, Juana predisposes her audience to next hear highlighted as feminine the 'nueva cosa' that God is creating in Christ, and subsequently the new gender equality in this New Law and new creation. Juana thereby provides a rhetorical grounding that predisposes her audience to accept her arguments as to the radical equity between men and women in Christ, and her contention that gender can be – and even should be, for true Christians – transformed, and even transcended.

Moreover, for Juana, each gender was already encapsulated within the other. She explains:

> Man should be differentiated from woman with respect to his body; however, with respect to the soul, both are equals and compeers. Because if a woman has a soul (*anima*) which is by name female, likewise man too has a soul [...] by name female, so that every man and woman can be called female. And conversely, man and woman can be said to be male, because if man has a living and everlasting spirit (*espíritu*) likewise woman has a living and everlasting spirit.[11]

For Juana, the grammatically masculine spirit and the grammatically feminine soul transcend gender categories, each indwelling and residing in the other so that the name of each is proper to the other. Throughout her sermons and the lived example of her life, one can hear Juana's clarion call trumpeting this theme of equality between the genders, gender transcendence in God, and an ultimate human transcendence of gender in the fulfilled Reign of God.

Juana in the tradition of gender-liminal saints

The term 'liminality' is derived from the Latin word for 'threshold' (*limen, liminis*). It evokes doorways and boundaries. Gender liminality connotes

---

10   '[Y] un Dios vivo y verdadero, sin principio y sin medio y sin fin'. Ibid.
11   Surtz, *Guitar of God*, p. 25.

straddling and crossing the thresholds of gender, with movement beyond given borders. In her own life, Juana evidenced and embodied a personal gender liminality. She walked out the door of her family home dressed as a man, determined to cross the threshold into a women's community. Juana thus belongs to a well-studied category of hagiography, the 'female transvestite saint'.[12] While the term 'transvestite' is itself problematic and inadequate, it has commonly been used to describe the medieval phenomenon of saints assigned female at birth who dressed or lived as monks.[13] While Juana's adoption of male clothing was brief, her *Vida* (*Life*) recounts that as a young teenager, to escape an arranged marriage, she dressed as a man, equipped herself with a sword, and walked to the convent which would be her vocation instead of matrimony.[14] It is not unlikely that Juana would have grown up hearing the story of St Paula Barbada.[15] Paula had lived in nearby Ávila during the sixth century. Fearing the unwelcome advances of a threatening man, St Paula prayed explicitly that God transform her appearance to make her unsightly. God then miraculously caused a thick beard to grow upon her face. So complete was this gender transformation that, upon finding her hiding in a nearby chapel, the unruly man took her to be a praying hermit. St Paula remained then as a hermit, embracing this new vocation until her death. Growing up in Inquisitional Spain, it is not unlikely that young Juana would have also heard tales of the Maid of Orléans, who dressed in male attire and similarly had taken up a sword. The two women even shared the same name, 'Juana' being the Spanish translation of 'Joan'. The lives of Sts Paula and Joan evidence vocations that burst gender categories asunder, adding to the dynamically fluid Body of Christ. Juana may have been inspired by their stories.

Juana also would have had a Church calendar filled with saints assigned female at birth, whose sanctity depended upon their subsequent embrace of a male identity. Their stories of personal liberation and salvation could have helped to model her vocational flight from an arranged marriage. Among such saints are Anastasia (Anastasios), Apolinaria (Dorotheos), Athanasia, Eugenia (Eugenios), Euphrosyne (Smaragdus), Hilaria (Hilarion), Marina (Marinos), Matrona (Babylas), Pelagia (Pelagius), Susannah (John),

12 Anson, 'Female Transvestite'. See also 'Nuns Disguised as Monks' in Talbot, *Holy Women*, pp. 1-64; 'Transvestite; Transvestism' in the Appendix (p. 322).
13 See 'AFAB' entry in the Appendix: p. 286.
14 Daza wrote the earliest printed *Life* of Juana de la Cruz, published in Madrid in 1613 (*Historia*). It was translated into English by Bell (*Historie*) in 1625.
15 Cleminson and Vázquez García, *Sexo*, n. 179-183 on pp. 96-97.

and Theodora (Theodoros).[16] Stories of St Paul's associate, St Thekla, also described her donning male attire. This litany of saints places Juana's actions solidly within the canon of hagiographies which recognized passing as male as an acceptable strategy to protect virginity and gain holiness. But there were other gender non-conforming examples for Juana, closer to her own time and her own religious vocation. Juana was choosing a Franciscan life, and the Franciscan story clearly had a pull upon her vocational impulse. St Clare had fled her family on Palm Sunday to join Francis' community of men. She was then tonsured by St Francis and given a habit like that of the fellow brothers. Until later joined by her sister, the Franciscan family briefly existed as a community solely composed of Brothers and Clare. Moreover, St Francis himself was gender non-conforming, repeatedly failing at the role of warrior, and intentionally divesting himself of other male roles of his day. To his companion Leo, he wrote: 'I am speaking to you, my son, in this way as a mother'.[17] He explained that we are 'mothers' of the Messiah 'when we carry Him in our heart [...] and give birth to Him through a holy activity'.[18] Developing this theme further, Francis wrote in his first Rule that each brother should 'love and care for his brother as a mother loves and cares'.[19]

Intended as a definitive *Life* of St Francis which would provide a paradigm for all other friars, St Bonaventure's *Legenda Maior* (written c. 1260-1263) also captured this gender non-conforming aspect of Francis' personality. Bonaventure explains that through the Blessed Mother's intercession Francis 'conceived and brought to birth'.[20] He metaphorically describes the 'conception of [Francis'] first child', and his 'firstborn son' – Bernard, one of Francis' earliest followers.[21] Bonaventure then recounts Francis' own parable to the Pope in which Francis is 'a poor, but beautiful woman' who bore the great King Jesus 'children who resembled the king'.[22] Bonaventure also recounts Francis' mystical encounter with the Trinity as three poor women, an apparition unique in Christian mystical

---

16 Patlagean, 'L'histoire', p. 600. See also in this volume: Bychowski on St Marinos (pp. 245-65), Ogden (pp. 201-21) and Wright (pp. 155-76) on St Euphrosine.
17 'A Letter to Brother Leo', in Armstrong et al., *St Francis of Assisi*, p. 123.
18 'Earlier Exhortation' in Armstrong et al., *St Francis of Assisi*, p. 42.
19 'The Earlier Rule' in Armstrong et al., *St Francis of Assisi*, p. 71.
20 Bonaventure, *Life of St Francis*, in *Soul's Journey*, pp. 177-327 (p. 199). *The Life of St Francis* is the title given to the *Legenda Maior* in this volume.
21 Ibid., p. 200.
22 Ibid, p. 205.

literature.²³ And Bonaventure clearly portrays Francis as the Bride using the typology of the Song of Songs, noting that he 'followed his Beloved everywhere' and ensured that Jesus 'always rested like a bundle of myrrh in the bosom of Francis's soul'.²⁴ Bonaventure's writings were published in Spanish by the Franciscan Cardinal Cisneros (1436-1517), so Juana and her community would have had access to these and other Franciscan works. In point of fact, as a fellow Franciscan, Cisneros went out of his way to ensure that women's communities in particular had access to these formative, printed works.²⁵

From her *Vida*, we know that Juana had also been exposed to *The Little Flowers of St Francis*, a collection of stories about Francis and his followers written sometime after 1337, originally in Italian.²⁶ In its Spanish translation, she would have encountered another gender-transcending friar, John of Laverna. In his prayer, Blessed John came to know Jesus as a Mother.²⁷ While experiencing spiritual dryness, John experienced Jesus as being like a mother, temporarily withholding food: 'But He was acting like a mother with her baby when she withdraws her breast from him to make him drink the milk more eagerly'.²⁸ The author of *The Little Flowers* also uses the language of the Song of Songs to describe John's resultant pursuit of Christ: 'when his soul did not feel the presence of his Beloved, in his anguish and torment he went through the woods, running here and there, seeking and calling aloud with tears and sighs for his dear Friend'.²⁹ When Christ finally does appear to Blessed John, *The Little Flowers* uses parallels from the Song of Songs to explain the intimacy which John would enjoy:

> For he immediately threw himself down at Christ's feet, and the Savior showed him his blessed feet, over which Brother John wept [...] Now while Brother John was praying fervently, lying at Christ's feet, he received so much grace that he felt completely renewed and pacified and consoled, like Magdalene [...] he began to give thanks to God and humbly kiss the Savior's feet.³⁰

23   Ibid., p. 243. See also Elphick, 'Three Poor Women'.
24   Bonaventure, *Life of St Francis*, in *Soul's Journey*, pp. 177-327 (p. 263).
25   Pérez García, 'Communitas Christiana', pp. 107-08; Ahlgren, *Teresa of Avila*, pp. 9-11, 26.
26   Published in Spanish as the *Florento de Sant Francisco* (Seville, 1492). Juana's *Vida* records that this book was read to her (Surtz, *Guitar of God*, p. 59, footnote 18).
27   See Bynum, *Jesus as Mother*.
28   Brown, *Little Flowers*, p. 158.
29   Ibid., p. 156.
30   Ibid., p. 158.

Brother John next kisses Jesus' hands: 'Christ held out His most holy hands and opened them for him to kiss. And while He opened them, Brother John arose and kissed His hands'.[31]

However, the author of *The Little Flowers* deviates from the expected 'kiss of the mouth' of the Song of Songs, seemingly modifying this intimacy slightly for an encounter between the male Jesus and the male friar.[32] The 'kiss of the mouth' is replaced by the kissing of Christ's chest: 'And when he had kissed them [Christ's hands], he came closer and leaned against the breast of Christ, and he embraced Jesus and kissed His holy bosom. And Christ likewise embraced and kissed him'.[33] Through Bl. John of Laverna, Juana would have encountered a well-developed model of Franciscan gender liminality. John experienced Jesus both as mother and male lover. John himself was both the Maiden of the Song and a brother to Jesus. Instead of comparing him to any of the numerous available male saints, he was compared to St Mary Magdalene, with a striking emphasis on her physicality – weeping, and washing Christ's feet, even going so far as to kiss him repeatedly. It is unlikely that this early Franciscan hero would have escaped Juana's notice as she had *The Little Flowers* read to her.

Juana de la Cruz, then, inherits these traditions, and builds upon an existing Franciscan motif. God renders gender-transcendent those He calls, giving them attributes of the opposite binary gender, and ultimately recreating them to be like Him, apophatically transcending gender. It is through this background and context that we can best understand Juana's life, and her sermons.

Gender liminality in the *Life* and Incarnation Sermon of Mother Juana de la Cruz

The story of Juana de la Cruz begins not with her birth, but with God forming her upon her conception. According to her official *Vida*, God was already forming a male child when the Virgin Mary intervened.[34] Needing a woman who would eventually reform a convent dedicated to her, the Virgin persuaded God to mould the embryonic Juana into a female instead. However, as proof of the miracle, God left intact her Adam's apple as witness

---

31 Ibid.
32 Song of Songs 1:2.
33 Brown, *Little Flowers*, p. 159.
34 Surtz, *Guitar of God,* pp. 6-7.

to the divine re-gendering. Soon after her birth, she was baptized with the name Juana, the feminine version of her father's own name. And evidencing holiness even as a new-born, she fasted every Friday, nursing only once.

Her call to a religious vocation involved yet another gender transformation. Praying before a picture of St Veronica, this female saint's painted image was miraculously transformed into the face of Christ, who promised to 'espouse and bring her to religion'.[35] Gazing upon this newly male image, Juana heard his wedding proposal.[36] Having voiced his offer of marriage, 'the holy picture turned to the former likenesse'.[37] The saint, Veronica – whose name means 'true icon' – transformed to reveal the male Christ who sought to wed Juana, and having voiced his intent, reverted back to a woman's guise.[38] The gender fluidity inherent in this mystical experience would subsequently suffuse her spirituality and preaching. Inspired by this vision, and threatened with an impending arranged marriage, the teenage Juana decided to flee her hometown and join a nearby Franciscan women's community.

We can read the story of her journey in the English translation of Juana's *Vida* provided by Father Francis Bell. In 1625, Bell published an English translation of the official biography of Mother Juana de la Cruz, originally published in Spanish by Friar Antonio Daza in 1613. Published at St Omers, Bell's translation was intended for the edification of two Poor Clare nuns who had been elected Superiors of a newly erected English Monastery. Bell promises to 'faithfully [...] translate the book in a plaine and homely language',[39] but interestingly, he added a stealthy gender commentary of his own. The original Spanish and Bell's translation both explain that Juana's father and kinsfolk sought to 'remedy' her unmarried status. The original Spanish version includes a parenthetical aside noting that 'remedy' is the name given to women's marriages by the world, 'God leaving flight as the only other option'.[40] Bell instead inserts his own commentary (ignoring the theme of flight) and explains that these marriages are considered a 'remedy'

---

35 Bell, *Historie*, p. 26. 'Religion' here refers to religious life as a professed Sister. I have somewhat modernized Bell's English spelling in all citations for ease of reading.
36 Francis too hears an initial call from a painting, the San Damiano Crucifix. Bonaventure uses a quotation from Genesis 24:63 to situate this episode in parallel to Isaac's marriage to Rebekah (*The Life of St Francis*, in *Soul's Journey*, pp. 177-327 (p. 191)).
37 Bell, *Historie*, p. 26.
38 On Veronica, see: Spencer-Hall, *Medieval Saints*, pp. 243-54.
39 *Historie*, p. 3.
40 'Que este nombre pone el mundo alos casamientos delas mugeres, como sino huuiera dexado Dios otro para ellas' (Daza, *Historia*, p. 11).

for women, 'as if there were no other remedie left by God for them'.⁴¹ Clearly Bell, writing for two nuns, knowingly champions the cause that marriage and childbirth are not the only vocations available to women.

The account of Juana's fleeing an arranged marriage immediately follows her mystical experience before the image of St Veronica. Having been called to spiritual marriage and religious life by an image which transforms from female to male and back again, Juana followed this same transition in journeying to the convent. Bell's translation continues, portraying Juana's gender transformations:

> She resolved [...] to go to the happy monastery, two leagues from her town [...] not as a weak woman, but as a strong and forcible man, putting herself into the garments of one of her male cousins, and making a pack of her own, in the habit of a man; and so with a sword under her arm, alone and on foot, she took her way one morning before the rising of the sun[.]⁴²

Arriving at the Convent, Juana's first impulse was to pray:

> She came to the holy monastery, where having made her prayer in the habit of a man [...] she went and adored the holy image of the Mother of God. She turned aside to a corner of the church, and putting off that apparel, put on the woman's apparel which she brought with her. Lifting up her eyes to an image of our Blessed Lady [...] which stood over the regular door of the convent [...] and kneeling before it, [she] gave thanks to her anew [...] The image spoke unto her and said: 'My daughter, in good time you have come to my house, enter merrily, for well you may, when for the same God created you, and I give you the superiority and care over it[.]⁴³

Juana then shared her fear that the community would not receive her, but our Lady said in response: 'Fear nothing, for my Son who has brought you hither, will cause that they accept you.' Emboldened, Juana sought out the abbess and confided her intention to join, explaining that 'she had left her Father and kindred, and to take that holy habit [of St Francis] had come in the habit of a man so as not to be known.'⁴⁴ The abbess reprehended her for placing herself in such manifest peril, but still welcomed her, internally

---

41 Bell, *Historie*, p. 24.
42 Ibid., p. 27.
43 Ibid., pp. 28-29.
44 Ibid., p. 29.

thanking God 'who had infused such spirit and fortitude into so tender a damsel'.[45]

Like the miraculous image of St Veronica which had first initiated her journey, Juana had transformed from female to male appearance, and then fluidly back to the female gender that God had gifted her with in the womb. Veronica's transition had given a pattern for Juana's flight from arranged marriage to her intended homosocial vocation. Waiting above the Convent door, the statue of the Virgin approvingly greeted and welcomed her gender-fluid child. Juana then joined this community of religious women and, like them, was invested in the habit of another man, St Francis of Assisi.

Juana was eventually made Abbess of the community, and thereafter began a thirteen-year period of imitating St Francis by her preaching, a role traditionally reserved for men. As Jessica A. Boon remarks, 'it is Juana's many years as a preacher that make her unique in the history of Christianity'.[46] Her activity in preaching sermons is all the more noteworthy given that she was preaching in inquisitional Spain. These sermons were based on the liturgical year, focusing on individual feast days. In what follows, I will focus on just one, her *Sermon on the Incarnation*.[47] In this foundational sermon, Juana highlights themes which are present throughout her work: consent, gestation, and the mutability of gender roles, underpinned by her use of feminine images of God.

Juana's *Sermon on the Incarnation*

Similar to Juana's own situation, in which family members were planning an arranged marriage for her, in Juana's *Sermon on the Incarnation*, Mary is faced with the dilemma of a proposed pregnancy which seems to conflict with her vocational intent and vow of virginity. Like Juana herself, in this sermon Mary is demonstrably characterized as determined, 'strong and forcible', in advocating for her chosen vocation. In this sermon, Mother Juana presents a very different image of the Virgin Mary at the Annunciation than is found in the original account in St Luke. In this Gospel, Mary asks only:

45 Ibid.
46 Juana de la Cruz, *Visionary Sermons*, p. 5. While female preaching was otherwise known (we might think of the lay Franciscan St Rose of Viterbo (1233-1251)), the liturgical context and the ecclesial location in which Juana delivered her sermons constitute her uniqueness. For broader context, see: Muessig, 'Prophecy and Song'.
47 Juana de la Cruz, *Visionary Sermons*, pp. 40-65.

'"How will this be, since I am a virgin?"' (Luke 1: 34). Juana's rendering of the angel Gabriel's visit presents Mary as having many more questions. Mary actively challenges the archangel with eight questions, several of which are multipart inquiries. While Juana highlights the intended perpetual virginity and humility of Mary by the nature of her questions, the theme of her *willing* consent is also clearly at stake, and important to Juana. At one point the narrative comes to a standstill as the Virgin considers her options: '[T]herefore she delayed giving her consent, asking the holy angel how...?'[48] A blessed Virgin who needs all her questions answered before she consents to God's will is fully novel in the homiletic tradition up to this point.

While withholding immediate consent creates dramatic tension for her audience, it is also clear that, in her departure from the Gospel precedent of Mary's single question, Juana is intentionally crafting the image of a woman who does not give in easily and strives to understand fully before giving consent. In fact, Juana uses this dramatized example of informed consent as an opportunity to explain: 'This means that God himself never wants to use force to enter anyone's heart if they do not consent first and open it willingly'.[49] It is not until Gabriel concedes that he is telling her everything he knows about how this will affect her that Mary finally agrees with her traditional 'Fiat' of consent.[50] Juana next describes the entire Trinity entering Mary's womb and beginning the work of making the Second Person of the Trinity incarnate.[51] She highlights the Second Person as Lady Wisdom/Sophia, using the language of Proverbs 8:12: 'and then came wisdom and discretion, which are the Son, and gave birth to the Word'.[52] Uniquely, Juana herein casts the Trinity in a female guise, as being like a seamstress ('lavandera') constructing a shirt, as the Trinity weaves together divinity and the fabric of humanity in the Incarnation. She attributes the actual sewing of this fabric directly to the Holy Spirit.[53] Throughout her sermons, Juana uses these familiar domestic images again and again to convey the Divine to her audiences, counterweighing traditional male images with balancing female metaphors. Embedded

---

48 Ibid., p. 51.
49 Ibid., p. 50.
50 Ibid., p. 53.
51 The popular and widely disseminated anonymous *Meditations on the Life of Christ* imagines the Trinity present and awaiting Mary's response. However, the *Meditations* envisions only the Second Person, not the entire Trinity, entering Mary's womb (McNamer, *Meditations*, p. 11).
52 Juana de la Cruz, *Visionary Sermons*, p. 53.
53 Ibid., p. 54.

in his new dwelling place, the foetal Redeemer is delighted by this new home.[54] Juana announces: 'And he was as happy and delighted inside there in that sacred dwelling of the virginal womb (*vientre*) of Our Lady as in the bosom (*seno*) of the Father'.[55]

Ronald Surtz here translates the Spanish 'seno' as 'bosom', but 'seno' can also be readily translated as 'womb'. Juana's audience would have likely heard and envisioned both 'womb' and 'bosom'. Justification for translating 'seno' as womb is found in her *Sermon on the Trinity*. There she describes the Father pregnant with the Son: 'And for this reason it is said that the Son is enclosed in the bosom (*seno*) of the Father. And just like the woman, when the time is up, [the pregnancy] concludes, and after giving birth, they can all see and take and enjoy it, which could not be done when it was in the mother's womb (*vientre*).'[56] For Juana, a clear parallel exists between the Father's bosom and Mary's womb. In fact, Jesus does not want to leave this new home in Mary's womb. Juana tells us: '[H]e was very warm and cozy there and did not wish to leave so quickly, and said, speaking to the Father, "Oh my powerful Father! I am so happy in such a delicious dwelling! May I dwell in it a long time, for I do not want to leave this home"'.[57] Juana does not chronicle the Father's response, but her intent is clear: Jesus is equally at home in the bosom of the Father and in the womb of his Mother. It was the Church Council of Toledo in 675 CE that had declared that the Son was begotten and born 'from the womb of the Father' ('de Patris utero'), on the basis of Psalm 110:3. Juana was clearly evoking this image of the wombed and birthing Father. A less overt, but still discernible parallel is then elaborated by Juana, already alluded to by Jesus' reluctance to leave his new home. The Incarnation, the remedy for the Fall of Humanity, also occasions something akin to a 'fall' in God. Like Adam and Eve, God is depicted as enduring a temptation. Seeing generations of human perdition, Juana portrays God as stating: 'I am tempted not to go to the world [...] to redeem and ransom them'.[58] However, unlike sinful humanity, God overcomes this temptation.

---

54   The *Meditations* also describes the en-womb-ment of the Son as a homecoming: 'the Son of God, having been without a home, entered her womb at once' (McNamer, *Meditations*, p. 11). McNamer posits a female Franciscan as the author of the *Meditations* (p. xxii).

55   Juana de la Cruz, *Visionary Sermons*, p. 55.

56   'Y por esto es dicho que el hijo está encerrado en el seno del Padre. Y asi como la mujer, cuando es llegada la hora, pare el hijo y despues de parido luego le pueden todos ver y tomar y gozarse con el, lo qual no podian faser cuando estava en el vientre de la madre.' Madrid, Real Biblioteca del Monasterio de San Lorenzo de El Escorial, MS J-II-18, fol. 207v.

57   Juana de la Cruz, *Visionary Sermons*, p. 55.

58   Ibid., p. 41.

And thus God falls in another sense, downward from his throne as he descends to become flesh in the Virgin's womb.

Juana switches the perspective from the biblical account of the Annunciation on earth to what is happening in Heaven at the same time. At the moment of the Annunciation, the angels and heavenly guests are celebrating in festival. The angels' merriment occasions them to inquire of God how they could best serve and please him on this great feast. Unexpectedly, God says: '[T]ruly I feel like eating now.'[59] This statement is remarkable to the angels, who exclaim: '[A]s long as we have been in your Kingdom, we have never heard you say such a thing!'[60] Ironically, the Virgin Mary is the one who is pregnant, but it creates in God a sympathetic craving! And what God wants to eat is the fruit of a tree. Readers will no doubt recall the story of Genesis: 'And the woman saw that the tree was good to eat, and fair to the eyes, and delightful to behold: and she took of the fruit thereof, and did eat, and gave to her husband who did eat' (Genesis 3:6). However, here a pear, not an apple, is desired.[61] Yet the intended parallels are clear: tempting angels, and the fruit from a tree. God acknowledges the angels' bemusement at his request, but only reinforces it, stating: 'I do not want to have anything other than wine pears as refreshment'.[62] God's craving is very specific. After a parade of pears are brought to God by various angels, finally, only the pear offered by Gabriel is chosen. And to continue the parallels with the Fall, where Adam and Eve covered themselves in garments of fig leaves, the Lord adorns himself with the pear: '"[I]t belongs as a jewel around my neck [...]." And saying these words [...] he hung it around his sacred neck'.[63]

But in marked contrast to Adam and Eve, instead of eating this pear, 'the Lord received it with great joy and took it in his sacred hands, kissing it and embracing it and smelling it and tucking it into his womb (*seno*), greatly delighting in it'.[64] Notably, the pear is placed in the same location previously occupied by the Son, the bosom and womb of the Father. It is only after this intimate enthronement of the pear in God's centre that we learn that the pear is in fact the Virgin herself: 'And while everyone was watching, they saw that suddenly that very pear was changed into [...]

---

59 Ibid., p. 56.
60 Ibid.
61 St Ephrem the Syrian also describes God hungering for fruit: 'The Heavenly One desired the delicious fruit, the fruit that a flow of tears grew. The High One hungered very much...' (*Hymns*, p. 452).
62 Juana de la Cruz, *Visionary Sermons*, p. 56.
63 Ibid., p. 57.
64 Ibid.

Our Lady, the Virgin Mary'.[65] Juana leaves her listeners with an image of God reminiscent of nesting Russian dolls. Enclosed in God is the Virgin, and enclosed in the Virgin is the Christ. Juana has God go on to proclaim: '"You alone, my beloved, chosen among thousands. You alone, my Queen, inside whom I ruled and dwelled"'.[66] Juana's allegory of this Fall of God offers something of an antidote to the story of the Fall of Adam and Eve, in which Eve is blamed for original sin and the expulsion of humankind from paradise. Juana explains that all the pears brought before God were actually the holy women of humanity up to that point in salvation history. Juana describes them as 'the many holy and blessed women', adding that 'some were virtuous and good [...] others were holy and servants of God'.[67] In response to the ill fate which befalls all women in the Genesis account, Juana offers a feast and banquet of holy and good women, each presented before God 'because he wanted to become incarnate in a woman.' And where the Fall in Genesis occasions God to pronounce four curses – upon the serpent, the land, the woman, and the man – in Juana's revision, God instead utters four blessings upon Mary.[68]

Both stories culminate in relocation from Paradise. Adam and Eve are banished from the Garden. God falls from Heaven and comes to dwell in the womb of the Virgin on earth. Juana describes the Virgin's womb: '[T]here inside was the Redeemer himself, playing with the angels and ruling the world and judging souls'.[69] His exile is a self-imposed banishment, but a banishment from Heaven nonetheless. Where the Genesis Fall concludes with God driving Adam and Eve from the Garden, Juana's Fall concludes with God's entry into the Virgin, 'inside whom he would rule and the dwelling inside which he would live',[70] making her womb the new judgment seat of God. In both stories, women are the pivotal point upon which salvation history turns. Both stories begin with angels offering fruit. And in the parallelism set up by Juana, both God and humans find the fruit desirable. The role of women is central to each story. Taking the fruit results in dislocation for all. But Juana's is a reverse parallelism. When God takes the fruit, humanity is saved. God falls to earth. The woman is no longer the occasion of perdition, but instead, the source of salvation. Banished humanity now becomes the dwelling place of God. Instead of curses, only blessings are uttered. And

65 Ibid.
66 Ibid., p. 58.
67 Ibid.
68 Ibid., pp. 57-58.
69 Ibid., p. 55.
70 Ibid., p. 58.

woman, who was first judged and condemned by God (Eve), now becomes the judgment seat (Mary) from which God rules and judges all. By adding gender fluidity throughout her sermon, Juana's narrative further dramatizes this great salvific inversion: 'He has cast down the mighty [...] and has lifted up the lowly' (Luke 1:52). In response to the patriarchal society of her day, Juana crafts a salvation parable in which the story turns upon the actions of the otherwise 'weaker sex', and the Almighty is recast in female guise, complete with womb, bosom, and gestational cravings.

Gender fluidity – fluctuations of gender identity between and beyond the poles of binary gender – pervades her other sermons and reaches a culmination in the sermon on the Trinity where she depicts God the Father and God the Son as each pregnant with the other.[71] By unsettling the supposed fixity of gender, Juana presents a God who transcends all human boundaries and categories. This vision offers a fluid mode of *imitatio Christi*, a call to inhabit one's authentic identity in all its God-given complexity. Her own gestation having had a miraculous beginning, Juana's sermons frequently employ themes of pregnancy and fecundity, as well as gender fluidity and gender transition. In anticipation of her cause for canonization, the Vatican re-examined all her sermons and found them consistent with the Catholic faith, allowing for Pope Francis to declare her 'Venerable' in 2015.[72] Mother Juana in turn has gifted the Church with language, metaphor, tradition, and precedent to articulate new understandings of God, the human person, and gender. It is my hope that as her sermons become newly available to the English-speaking world in Boon and Surtz's translation, and her cause advances toward canonization, she can increasingly become a catalyst for dialogue and convergence on issues of faith and gender. Through her profusion of re-gendered or gender-fluid images of herself, God, and the saints, Juana effectively creates an apophatic theology of gender, a *via negativa* which denies ultimacy both to the ascendancy of one gender over the other, and to the gender binary itself. In her sermons there is a recognizable ascetical discipline at work, reverencing a transcendently-gendered mystery, as acutely nuanced as the tradition of not pronouncing G-d's Name. Repeatedly in her sermons, where the audience complacently expects to hear specific gender identifiers, Juana prophetically interjects the unexpected.

---

71   See Surtz, 'Privileging of the Feminine'; 'Genderfluid (or Gender-Fluid); Gender Fluidity' in the Appendix (pp. 298-99).
72   Pentin, 'Pope Francis'.

Juana the prophetess

Juana's life and sermons do not readily fit into preconceived notions and categories. While there is ample precedent for a female saint dressing as a man, a hagiography which begins with God re-gendering a foetus at its creation is entirely unprecedented. Her Adam's apple attests to the miracle, but it also points to gender ambiguity, which she embraced. Juana clearly identified as female, seeking out a female vocation and rising to its height as an abbess. But she also knowingly transgressed rigid gender boundaries through her homilizing, recasting salvation history and re-gendering images of God and the saints before an audience of king, cardinal, and the astounded laity. Her mystical experience of St Veronica's visage transforming into the face of Christ – this proposing Bridegroom Christ who then reappeared as the saintly woman – was seminal in her developing spirituality. This Bridegroom's call was also to an *imitatio Christi* in which gender fluidity was implicit as part of the faithful imitation. At her conception, there was gender flux, at her baptism she was named after her father and the Beloved Disciple of Christ, at her mystical espousal, gender fluidity is central, and in response to this engagement, she dresses as a man to escape heteronormative marriage. It should be of little surprise then that she realizes a call and vocation to preach, sonorously speaking with the claimed authority of Christ's voice.

But Juana's life and sermons should not be read in isolation from her Franciscan heritage. Juana was nurtured and protected by the Franciscan Cardinal Cisneros who visited her community and attended her sermons, in addition to being embraced and succoured by her Franciscan Sisters. The gender theology and spirituality in her sermons are a full and faithful flowering of her Franciscan tradition, building upon the trajectory of Clare and Francis, Bonaventure, and other early Franciscans such as Angela of Foligno and Rose of Viterbo. Juana's gender theology should not be seen as a solitary and unique aberration during the patriarchal Inquisition, but as a prophetic counter-voice, echoing otherwise drowned-out salvific refrains from the Christian tradition. Through her voice and narrative we hear hints of fully redeemed and divinized humanity, sharing in the glory of God which is beyond any gender binary. In 'la Santa Juana', we have a saint who during her life recognized the imposed limitations of a rigid gender binary and prophetically proclaimed both God and human as beyond gender categories.

In her sermons, God, the Saints, and even the Blessed Virgin herself are described in gender-fluid and gender-transgressing terms and metaphors.

To orient her audience, Juana had recourse to traditional gender categories to name and describe God, the Trinity of Persons, and the Saints. But as a poet-prophetess, she introduced unexpected gender metaphors for each, pointing her audience to a gender-transcendent reality which is proper both to the Divine and to the fully human. The cumulative effect of her liturgical year of sermons is a Divine-human pageantry in which gender is malleable and fluid, pointing to its ultimate inability to fully describe or delimit either ineffable human nature or Divinity. Barbara Newman's observations regarding the mystic Hildegard of Bingen apply equally well to Mother Juana. With regard to gendered images of God, Newman writes:

> [I]t must be a still greater folly to apply them literally to God, to understand the Transcendent One as 'merely' masculine or feminine, or even masculine *and* feminine. Here again, in our current struggles with spirituality and gender, Hildegard can be a guide. For what mystics of the *via negativa* achieve by the systematic denial of images, she accomplished by their sheer profusion.[73]

Juana also provides a profusion of gendered metaphors in her sermons, effectively communicating that no single gendered metaphor alone is adequate. Both she and Hildegard created a *via negativa* of gender, an apophatic theology of gender that points to the inadequacy of all gender categories in the final analysis, and to a Deity beyond all gender. Unique to Juana's perspective is her lived experience of the inadequacy of gender categories, a gender apophaticism present in both her body and her life experiences. Boon arrives at a similar conclusion, noting that: 'Juana's life and sermons in fact propose a new mystical language of bigender, genderqueer, trans, and intersex, culminating in a gender performance continuum that transgresses and transmutes all boundaries between heaven and earth'.[74] Juana de la Cruz was a startling and visionary voice during the Inquisition; she is all the more prophetic in our own day, giving us language and church precedent to address the gender complexities of our times. Her sermons, gender theology, and life example are a prophetic remedy and corrective for our world and faith.

---

73 Newman, *Sister of Wisdom*, p. 270.
74 Boon, 'Limits', p. 284.

Bibliography

Manuscripts

Madrid, Real Biblioteca del Monasterio de San Lorenzo de El Escorial, MS J-II-18.

Primary sources

Armstrong, Regis J., J.A. Wayne Hellmann and William J. Short, eds., *St Francis of Assisi: Early Documents*, 3 vols. (New York: New City, 1999-2001), I.
Bell, Francis, trans., *The Historie, Life, and Miracles, Extasies and Revelations of the blessed virgin, sister Joane, of the Crosse, of the Third Order of our Holy Father S. Francis by Anthonie of Aca* (St Omers, 1625).
Bonaventure, *The Soul's Journey into God, The Tree of Life, The Life of St Francis*, trans. by Ewert Cousins (Ramsey: Paulist, 1978).
—, *Commentary on the Book of Wisdom*, trans. by Campion Murray (Phoenix: Tau, 2012).
Brown, Raphael, trans., *The Little Flowers of St Francis* (New York: Doubleday Image, 1958).
Daza, Antonio, *Historia, vida y milagros, éxtasis, y revelaciones de la bienaventurada virgen Sor Juana de la Cruz* (Madrid: Luis Sánchez, 1613).
Ephrem the Syrian, *Hymns*, ed. by Kathleen E. McVey (Mahwah, NJ: Paulist, 1989).
Florento de Sant Francisco (Seville, 1492).
Juana de la Cruz, *El Conhorte: Sermones de Una Mujer. La Santa Juana (1481-1534)*, ed. by Inocente García de Andrés, 2 vols. (Madrid: Universidad Pontificia de Salamanca, 1999).
—, *Mother Juana de la Cruz, 1481-1534: Visionary Sermons*, ed. by Jessica A. Boon and Ronald E. Surtz (Tempe: Iter Academic, 2016).
McNamer, Sarah, trans., *Meditations on the Life of Christ: The Short Italian Text* (Notre Dame: University of Notre Dame, 2018).
Talbot, Alice-Mary, ed., *Holy Women of Byzantium: Ten Saints' Lives in English Translation* (Washington, DC: Dumbarton Oaks, 1996).

Secondary sources

Ahlgren, Gillian T.W., *The Inquisition of Francisca: A Sixteenth-Century Visionary on Trial* (Chicago: University of Chicago, 2005).
—, *Teresa of Avila and the Politics of Sanctity* (Ithaca: Cornell University, 1996).
Anson, John, 'The Female Transvestite in Early Monasticism: The Origin and Development of a Motif', *Viator*, 5 (1974), 1-32.

Boon, Jessica A., 'At the Limits of (Trans)Gender: Jesus, Mary, and the Angels in the Visionary Sermons of Juana de la Cruz (1481-1534)', *Journal of Medieval and Early Modern Studies*, 48.2 (2018), 261-300.

Bynum, Caroline Walker, *Jesus as Mother: Studies in the Spirituality of the High Middle Ages* (Berkeley: University of California, 1984).

Cleminson, Richard, and Francisco Vázquez García, *Sexo, identidad y hermafroditas en el mundo ibérico, 1500-1800* (Madrid: Cátedra, 2018).

Elphick, Kevin C.A., 'The Cubas Women's Community', *Franciscan Connections: The Cord – A Spiritual Review*, 68.1 (2018), 8-12.

—, 'Mother Juana de la Cruz: Faithful Daughter of St Francis and Patron Saint of Gender Inclusivity', in *Franciscan Women: Female Identities and Religious Culture, Medieval and Beyond*, ed. by Lezlie S. Knox (St Bonaventure: Franciscan Institute, 2020), pp. 175-85.

—, 'Three Poor Women Appeared', *Franciscan Connections: The Cord – A Spiritual Review*, 66.4 (2016), 15-17.

García de Andrés, Inocente, *Teología y Espiritualidad de la Santa Juana* (Madrid: Madre de Dios, 2012).

Muessig, Carolyn, 'Prophecy and Song: Teaching and Preaching by Medieval Women', in *Women Preachers and Prophets through Two Millennia of Christianity*, ed. by Beverly Mayne Kienzle and Pamela J. Walker (Berkeley: University of California, 1998), pp. 146-58.

Newman, Barbara, *Sister of Wisdom: St Hildegard's Theology of the Feminine* (Los Angeles: University of California, 1987).

Owens, Sarah E., *Nuns Navigating the Spanish Empire* (Albuquerque: University of New Mexico, 2017).

Patlagean, Evelyne, 'L'histoire de la femme déguisée en moine et l'évolution de la sainteté féminine à Byzance', *Studi Medievali*, ser. 3, 17.2 (1976), 597-623.

Pentin, Edward, 'Pope Francis Approves Canonization of St Thérèse's Parents', 18 March 2015, *National Catholic Register* <http://www.ncregister.com/blog/edward-pentin/pope-francis-approves-canonization-of-st.-thereses-parents> [accessed 19 June 2020].

Pérez García, Rafael M., 'Communitas Christiana: The Sources of Christian Tradition in the Construction of Early Castilian Spiritual Literature, ca. 1400-1540', in *Books in the Catholic World during the Early Modern Period*, ed. by Natalia Maillard Álvarez (Boston: Brill, 2014), pp. 71-113.

Spencer-Hall, Alicia, *Medieval Saints and Modern Screens: Divine Visions as Cinematic Experience* (Amsterdam: Amsterdam University, 2018).

Surtz, Ronald E., *The Guitar of God: Gender, Power, and Authority in the Visionary World of Mother Juana de la Cruz (1481-1534)* (Philadelphia: University of Pennsylvania, 1990).

—, 'The Privileging of the Feminine in the Trinity Sermon of Mother Juana de la Cruz', in *Women's Voices and the Politics of the Spanish Empire*, ed. by Jennifer Eich, Jeanne Gillespie, and Lucia Harrison (New Orleans: University of the South, 2008), pp. 87-107.

About the author

KEVIN C.A. ELPHICK earned his Masters in Franciscan Studies from St. Bonaventure University, and a Masters in Religious Studies from Loyola University, Chicago. He holds a Doctorate in Ministry from Graduate Theological Foundation in Indiana. He works fulltime for the Department of Veterans Affairs as a Supervisor on their Veterans and Military Suicide Prevention Hotline. He serves on the Charism Commission of the Franciscan Federation and previously taught at St. Bernard's Institute as an Adjunct Faculty Member. He was a contributing, subject matter expert in the development of the New York State publication, *Disaster Mental Health: A Critical Response* (2006).

4 Non-Standard Masculinity and Sainthood in Niketas David's *Life* of Patriarch Ignatios

Felix Szabo

Abstract
Eunuch saints presented Byzantine hagiographers with serious challenges. Thought to suffer from an inherent and egregious lack of self-control, how could members of this marginalized group meet the minimum requirements of good Christian behaviour, let alone aspire to sainthood? Niketas David's tenth-century *Life* of Patriarch Ignatios offers one medieval exploration of this question. In depicting his eunuch protagonist as an exemplar of specifically masculine virtues, Niketas suggests a definition of masculinity more complicated than that of the traditional eunuch/non-eunuch binary current over more than a thousand years of Byzantine history. By locating Ignatios beyond these traditional categories, the *Life* offers an unparalleled model for integrating non-conforming masculinities within the otherwise strictly gendered norms of Christian hagiography.

Keywords: eunuchs, chastity, masculinity, Byzantium, Niketas David, Patriarch Ignatios

Saintly men may act like women, and saintly women may act like men; but what about eunuchs? For the medieval West, the rarity and scarcity of eunuchs renders this question almost academic. When eunuchs do appear in Western sources, they are usually foreigners, heathens, slaves, or all three; castration in the West, whether punitive or medically indicated, was always emphatically out of the ordinary. Even in Byzantium, where castration – punitive, medical, or otherwise – was much more familiar than in the contemporary West, eunuchs occupy an uncomfortably ambiguous

---

Spencer-Hall, Alicia, and Blake Gutt (eds), *Trans and Genderqueer Subjects in Medieval Hagiography*. Amsterdam, Amsterdam University Press 2021
DOI: 10.5117/9789462988248_CH04

position. This is especially true in the context of Byzantine Christianity, where eunuchs are a subject of great concern for ecclesiastical authors: what did saintly behaviour look like for those who were, according to Byzantine understandings of the body, neither fully male nor fully female? Were eunuchs blessed with untemptable chastity, or were they cheating their way into heaven through a virtue that could never be truly tested? Did this proverbial chastity even exist – or was it merely a cover for eunuchs' innate sensuality and lack of self-control? Eunuchs could, and certainly did, achieve sainthood. Eunuch saints, especially martyrs, had existed from the earliest days of Christianity, and *Lives* of new eunuch saints – like Niketas the Patrician (761/2-836), Nikephoros of Miletos (*fl.* 965-969), and Symeon the New Theologian (949-1022) – appear throughout the Byzantine period.[1] But how did such saints fit into the broader hagiographical universe? Were they merely passive recipients of martyrdom, unable to achieve sanctity through their own initiative – or were they exceptions to the rule, whose active goodness simply cast the wickedness of their peers into sharper relief? Do the normal rules of sanctity still apply to such marginalized and contradictory individuals?

These are not anachronistic questions. Eunuch saints were a real problem for Byzantine hagiographers: eunuch saints' *Lives* generally show their subjects receiving sanctity only indirectly, a reward divinely imposed on them rather than independently achieved. Even eunuchs who successfully attain sanctity are distant, impersonal, and one-dimensional, and they are never the objects of any truly popular cults.[2] In many respects, Niketas David's early tenth-century *Life* of Patriarch Ignatios of Constantinople seems to faithfully follow this pattern.[3] At times, the author seems at least as interested in condemning his protagonist's arch-rival – the famously learned and, to Niketas, dubiously qualified Photios I (r. 858-867, 877-886) – as he is in actually relating the events of Ignatios' life; if Ignatios is the hero of the story, Photios is decidedly the villain. Yet Niketas' characterization of Ignatios is extremely unusual, even for a hagiographical hero. Niketas does

---

1   Symeon the New Theologian is not universally recognized as a eunuch by modern scholarship, but delving into the reasons behind this misidentification is beyond the scope of this chapter. Based on Symeon's promotion to the eunuch-specific position of *spatharokoubikoularios* in his *Life* (as well as his posthumous appearance as 'a graceful and dignified eunuch' to the monk Philotheos), however, the identification is clear. Stethatos, *Life*, ch. 3 (p. 6) and ch. 147 (p. 364).
2   Messis, *Les eunuques*, p. 126.
3   I rely on the Dumbarton Oaks Texts edition of the *Life of Patriarch Ignatius* (Nicetas [Niketas] David), hereafter *Life*. My citations are given to page and line numbers of the Greek text. All translations and emphases, unless otherwise indicated, are my own.

not deny that the saint he is describing is a eunuch – but, like the authors of other eunuch saints' *Lives*, he seems uninterested in paying this detail much explicit attention. Ignatios is never identified as an 'eunouchos' ('εὐνοῦχος'), and even his castration is described in a relatively oblique way.[4] The author's description of Ignatios, however, plays with and even subverts several long-lived hagiographical tropes concerning eunuchs' expected behaviour. In this chapter, I suggest that by employing this characterization, Niketas was operating under a more fluid or permeable definition of masculinity than is typically encountered in Byzantine hagiography – one that in fact reveals a much more complicated conception of masculinity than that which traditionally differentiated eunuchs and so-called 'bearded' (non-eunuch) men in the Byzantine mind. By examining the boundaries of this conception more closely, I argue that Byzantine definitions of gender – and specifically, of masculinity – were more open and accessible to non-men than the canonical historical and textual record may suggest. I conclude by exploring some implications of these expanded definitions for situating non-standard expressions of gender within broader hagiographical norms.

The path to sanctity

In writing on eunuchs and sanctity, Byzantine authors of all genres enjoyed a rich vocabulary of stereotypes, imagery, and topoi on which to draw. Much of this vocabulary, including that of the *Life* of Patriarch Ignatios, revolves around questions of sexuality – as is certainly to be expected, given the pre-eminence of chastity among the virtues of the early and medieval Christian world. At the time of Niketas' writing of the *Life*, early in the tenth century, this vocabulary had been established long enough to provide an authoritative background against which to characterize the *Life*'s protagonist.[5] As a saint, Niketas had to describe Ignatios in set, canonical

---

4   Specifically, Niketas writes that, after usurping the throne of Ignatios' father Michael I, 'the cruel [Leo V] condemned [Michael's sons] to castration and deprived them of their genitals' ('ἀφαιρεῖται δὲ τοὺς παῖδας καὶ τῶν γεννητικῶν ὁ καταδικάσας ἀμείλικτος μελῶν εὐνουχία') (*Life*, 4, 8.9-10). The terminology is strikingly periphrastic: the boys are 'deprived of their genitals' rather than simply 'castrated' or 'made eunuchs' (e.g. 'ἐκτέμνειν, εὐνουχισθῆναι'). Niketas would later be more direct in describing the fate of Leo's sons after his own deposition by Michael II: 'he [Michael] ordered [...] his [Leo's] sons *to be made eunuchs* and tonsured' ('προσέταξε [...] τοὺς αὐτοῦ δὲ υἱοὺς εὐνουχισθῆναι καὶ καρῆναι'; ibid., 10.15-16).
5   On the dating of the *Life*, see ibid., pp. xi-xiii. No manuscripts of the Life from before the fourteenth century survive; see ibid., pp. xvii-xxviii.

terminology; but Niketas' access to the standard hagiographical lexicon is complicated by a parallel body of set, canonical terminology expected in descriptions of eunuchs.

Identifying eunuchs is not always straightforward. For most modern scholars of Byzantium, a eunuch is an individual assigned male at birth and castrated before the onset of puberty, usually (though not always) for service in palace or government administration. The Byzantines themselves, however, used a number of terms broadly translatable as 'eunuch', and not always in the strict courtly or administrative sense. By Niketas' time, the usual polite term is 'eunouchos' ('εὐνοῦχος'), etymon of the English word 'eunuch'. This appears to be the most neutral term – it is used in Constantine VII's *Book of Ceremonies* to differentiate eunuch and non-eunuch courtiers of identical rank – and it is by far the most commonly used. 'Ek/tomias' ('ἐκ/τομίας', 'cut man', or 'excised man') also appears in this period, but rarely, at only a fraction of the popularity it would achieve by the time of the Crusades. Latin-derived terms, like 'spado' ('σπάδων') or 'kastratos' ('καστράτος'), are usually restricted to legal contexts, and technical terms, usually indicative of the method of castration, like 'thlibias' ('θλιβίας', 'with crushed testicles') or 'carzimasian'/'kartzimas' ('καρτζιμᾶς', usually thought to refer to eunuchs who had undergone both orchiectomy and penectomy) are similarly rare.[6] The boundaries of the designation 'eunuch' become less and less strict over time: by the early tenth century, a eunuch could even be referred to as an 'aner' ('ἀνήρ'), the generic word for 'man' that never applied to eunuchs in classical Greek. Physical castration, moreover, was not the only grounds for categorization as a eunuch, particularly in hagiographical contexts. Those castrated in dreams or visions by angels or saints, like the ninth-century patriarch Methodios, could qualify as 'eunuchs' to Byzantine audiences, and Byzantine hagiography records a number of so-called 'transvestite nuns' – saints assigned female at birth who enter and live in male monastic communities under new names, *as eunuchs*. I specifically omit consideration of these saints from this chapter as of such saints' surviving *Lives*, only that of St Mary/Marinos is spent entirely within a male monastery; although Marinos is treated (socially and grammatically) as masculine for the majority of his *Life*, including all of the acts through which his saintliness is made manifest, this is not the case for the other AFAB saints (like Matrona of Perge or Euphrosyne of Alexandria) he is usually grouped with, whose activity in

---

6   Ringrose, *Perfect Servant*, p. 15, and p. 15 n. 34. This derivation, however, is debatable: see Grabowski, 'Eunuch'.

male monasteries is usually brief.[7] Due to the predominant focus of modern scholarship on eunuchs' administrative and courtly roles, I tend to favour the modern scholarly definition. But the utility of this definition makes it all the more critical to recognize its limitations – especially as Ignatios himself was neither a courtier nor a palace servant.

For all their ambiguity, however, eunuchs were indisputably part of the Christian community from its earliest inception. From Apostolic times, eunuch imagery represented a powerful means of communicating values and lessons to the nascent community of believers. Matthew 19:12 is the quintessential example: within a broader discussion of marital practices, it distinguishes 'eunuchs, who were born so from their mother's womb [...] eunuchs, who were made so by men: and [...] eunuchs, who have made themselves eunuchs for the kingdom of heaven'. The passage goes on to apparently acknowledge the difficulties of its own interpretation, and indeed later patristic and Byzantine commentators were keen to argue that the eunuchs described here were meant to be understood metaphorically, as images of chastity, rather than as literal eunuchs. However, eunuchs were instrumental in the spread of Christianity from an early date, beginning with the Ethiopian eunuch baptized by St Philip (Acts 8:26-40). The Ethiopian eunuch is held up by Eusebius of Caesarea (260/5-339/40) as the first gentile convert, while Basil of Caesarea (329/30-379), in a sermon on baptism, instructs his audience simply: 'Imitate the eunuch'.[8] Lactantius (c. 250-c. 325) portrays Christians and eunuchs working (and being martyred) side by side in the imperial palace during the Diocletianic persecutions, and Palladius' *Lausiac History* derives its name from its dedication to Lausus, imperial chamberlain (a position reserved for eunuchs) under Theodosius II (r. 408-450).[9] Early saints' lives are full of eunuchs: from Protas and Hyacinth, companions of Eugenia of Rome (martyred 258), to Azades and Ousthazades, Persian courtiers heroically martyred by Shapur II

---

7   Ringrose, *Perfect Servant*, pp. 120-21, and p. 121 n. 51. On 'transvestite' saints, see Constas, 'Life', pp. 1-6; Bychowski (pp. 245-65), Ogden (pp. 201-21) and Wright (pp. 155-76) in this volume. See also the Appendix: 'Transvestite; Transvestism' (p. 322) and 'AFAB' (p. 286).

8   Eusebius, *Historia Ecclesiastica* 2.1, col. 137d2-4; Basil of Caesarea, *Homily XIII* (*On Baptism*), col. 437a5. The imitation Basil recommends is to seek education in Church teachings and not to postpone baptism, as the Ethiopian eunuch was baptized by Philip without delay.

9   Lactantius, *De mortibus persecutorum* 14-15. Once Diocletian is provoked to move against the Christians in the palace, eunuchs are the first to fall. The possibly spurious Prologue to Palladius' *Historia Lausiaca* calls Lausus 'the best of men (ὁ ἄριστος τῶν ἀνδρῶν), a lover of this divine and spiritual yearning [that constitutes monastic life]' (cols. 995-96). This is an unusually early instance of the word 'ἀνήρ' being used of a eunuch, and one of the earliest of which I am aware.

(r. 309-379).[10] Whether or not these figures were based on actual historical actors is a moot question. Eunuchs' inclusion in early Christian hagiography with such frequency indicates that, to early Christians, the appearance of eunuchs in the roles of saints, spiritual confidants, and martyrs was eminently believable – perhaps even to be expected.

This is not to say, however, that all early Christians were comfortable with such inclusivity. Many exegetes of Matthew 19:12, both ancient and medieval, take explicit care to argue that the verse does not endorse *literal* castration in any form. Gregory of Nazianzus (*c*. 329-390) clearly allows that eunuchs may technically be able to live a life of chastity, but is insistent that such a life is in no way meritorious:

> Do not think yourselves great, those who are eunuchs by nature. Your chastity (σωφροσύνης) may be involuntary, for it has never been put to the test, nor has your self-control (τὸ σωφρονεῖν) passed the scrutiny of a trial. A virtue that comes naturally is unsatisfactory: but one that proceeds from choice is worthy of praise.[11]

Any literal interpretation of Matthew 19:12, Gregory says, is 'cheap, exceedingly weak, and unworthy of Scripture'.[12] Such attitudes are likewise expressed by John Chrysostom (*c*. 349-407), who, like Gregory (and Basil, as we shall see below) clearly believes eunuchs to be incapable of chastity in any meaningful sense – they are merely 'deprived of enjoyment, but without reward'.[13] Instead, he explains, Matthew 19:12

> [d]oes not speak of excision of body parts – away with such thoughts! – but of the elimination of evil considerations. [...] For if [chastity] was only a gift from above, and those who remain virginal contribute no effort of

---

10 As enumerated, for example, in Lactantius, *De mortibus persecutorum* 15.2 (the general association of eunuchs and Christians); Eusebius, *Historia Ecclesiastica* 7.32 and 8.6 (Dorotheus and Gorgonius, martyred under the Tetrarchy), cols. 721b7-14, 752a13-756a12; Sozomen, *Historia Ecclesiastica* 2.9 and 2.11 (Ousthazades and Azades, martyred by Shapur II), cols. 956b1-960b10, 961c1-964a15; see also Tougher, *Society*, pp. 72-73.
11 'μὴ μέγα φρονεῖτε, οἱ ἐκ φύσεως εὐνοῦχοι. τὸ γὰρ τῆς σωφροσύνης, ἴσως ἀκούσιον. οὐ γὰρ ἦλθεν εἰς βάσανον, οὐδὲ τὸ σωφρονεῖν ἐδοκιμάσθη διὰ τῆς πείρας. τὸ μὲν γὰρ ἐκ φύσεως ἀγαθὸν, ἀδόκιμον· τὸ δ" ἐκ προαιρέσεως, ἐπαινετόν.' Gregory of Nazianzus, *Oration* 37.16-17, col. 301a6-9.
12 'τὸ μὲν γὰρ μέχρι τῶν σωματικῶν εὐνούχων στῆσαι τὸν λόγον, τυχὸν μικρόν τε καὶ λίαν ἀσθενὲς καὶ ἀνάξιον λόγου.' Ibid. 37.16-17, col. 305b4-6.
13 'τῆς ἀπολαύσεως μὲν ἐστηρημένος, μισθὸν δὲ οὐχ ἔχων.' John Chrysostom, *Oration* 62, col. 599 ln. 36-7.

their own, the kingdom of heaven was proclaimed to them, and [Christ] distinguished them from other eunuchs, for no reason.¹⁴

Due to the immense influence of these authors on the later exegetical tradition, similar interpretations would go on to become standard in patristic catenae and other Byzantine scriptural commentaries. Centuries later, Theophylact of Ochrid (c. 1055-after 1107), the famous exegete of the New Testament, and author of the work now generally known as the *Defence of Eunuchs*, could open his commentary on Matthew 19:12 by stating: 'The virtue of virginity belongs, it is said, to few'.¹⁵ Even for Theophylact, the eunuchs of Matthew 19:12 are only metaphorical.

Early Christians treated eunuchs with similar suspicion even outside of exegetical contexts. Despite competing (and concurrent) assumptions of perpetual chastity, the sexual license of eunuchs was proverbial in the ancient world. The absence of desire could render eunuchs impervious to sexual temptation, but at the same time, their deficient masculinity (and consequent effeminacy) was thought to make them particularly vulnerable to a lack of self-control – whether in food, drink, or (most dangerously) sexuality. A notoriously hostile letter by Basil of Caesarea provides a brief but thorough résumé of these stereotypes:

> The race of eunuchs [is] without honor, and utterly forsaken – and this indeed they are: unfemale, unmale, mad for women, envious, rewarded with evil, capricious, unsharing, easy, insatiable, always complaining about their dinner, quick to anger, mad for gold, cruel, effeminate, and slaves to their bellies. What else can I say? They were condemned to the knife at their very birth; how can their belief be upright when their feet are crooked? They are chaste (σωφρονοῦσι) to no reward on account of the knife, and they lust to no purpose through their characteristic filthy conduct (αἰσχρότητα).¹⁶

---

14 'ὅταν δὲ λέγῃ, ὅτι 'εὐνούχισαν ἑαυτούς,' οὐ τῶν μελῶν λέγει τὴν ἐκτομήν· ἄπαγε· ἀλλὰ τῶν πονηρῶν λογισμῶν τὴν ἀναίρεσιν.' Ibid. 62, col. 599 ln. 47-600 ln. 45.
15 'ὀλίγων, φησίν, ἐστὶ τὸ κατόρθωμα τοῦτο τῆς παρθενίας.' Theophylact of Ochrid, *Commentary on Matthew* 19:12, col. 353a3-4.
16 '[...] εὐνούχων γένος ἄτιμον καὶ πανώλεθρον· τοῦτο δὴ τοῦτο, ἄθηλυ, ἄνανδρον, γυναικομανὲς, ἐπίζηλον, κακόμισθον, εὐμετάβλητον, ἀμετάδοτον, πάνδοχον, ἀπροσκορές, κλαυσίδειπνον, ὀξύθυμον, χρυσομανές, ἀπηνές, θηλυδριῶδες, γαστρίδουλον, καὶ τί γὰρ ἔτι εἴπω; σὺν αὐτῇ τῇ γενέσει σιδηροκατάδικον. πῶς γὰρ ὀρθὴ γνώμη τούτων ὧν καὶ πόδες στρεβλοί; οὗτοι μὲν σωφρονοῦσι ἄμισθα διὰ σιδήρου, μαίνονται δὲ ἄκαρπα δι' οἰκείαν αἰσχρότητα.' Courtonne, *Saint Basile*, Letter 115.

As this compact invective reveals, much of the anxiety caused by eunuchs revolves around questions of sexual behaviour. In this sense, eunuchs were simultaneously thought to threaten the sexual propriety of both women – as affairs with eunuchs did not run the risk of being revealed by pregnancy – *and* men. The word used to conclude this passage, 'aiskhrotēs' ('αἰσχρότης'), normally means 'ugliness' or 'deformity', but was also used euphemistically from the Classical period for fellatio.[17] Thanks to the prestige of patristic voices like Basil in eastern Christianity, such descriptions of eunuchs' paradoxical state – maintaining virginity without effort, but effortlessly, pathetically sexual – would go on to be circulated and elaborated throughout the later Byzantine world. Especially in monastic contexts of Middle Byzantium, any temptation (or worse, outright assault) against the primary virtue of chastity represented a serious threat to an individual's salvation; eunuchs, without any capacity for self-control, were therefore tremendously dangerous. Their path to sanctity, then, was a treacherous road indeed.

A *Life* of spiritual struggle

Ignatios himself would have been very familiar with this scriptural and patristic substrate. According to Niketas, from the beginning of his monastic career, Ignatios had 'devoted his time with great effort to all the writings of the Holy Fathers'.[18] As a deposed prince, Ignatios was an unusual historical figure; however, he was also an unusual eunuch. Two 'bookends' of the *Life* will demonstrate the variability with which it characterizes its protagonist's masculinity: first, Niketas' initial description of Ignatios near the beginning of the *Life*, and secondly, his final eulogy for Ignatios at the conclusion of the text. The neat juxtaposition of tropes and specific vocabulary in these episodes – not, I think, an accidental one – should illustrate how flexible hagiographic gender could be, at least in Byzantium, at least for someone as unusual as Ignatios.

In many ways, the *Life* is an unexceptional example of the hagiographic genre, and its characterization of Ignatios fits well within traditional hagiographic conventions. Niketas begins the *Life* by explicitly declaring its educational agenda. 'To set out in order the *Lives* of all the saints[;] [...] to provide by such a *Life* an exhortation to future generations', he says, 'is a

17 Liddell and Scott, *Lexicon*, s.v. 'αἰσχρότης.'
18 '[...] πᾶσι δὲ λόγοις τῶν ἱερῶν Πατέρων φιλοπόνως ἐσχολακὼς' (*Life*, 12.14-15).

most noble and at the same time salvific activity'.[19] Niketas' hero, Ignatios, is the quintessential saintly figure: pious, virtuous, orthodox, and readily willing to suffer for his convictions. In youth, Ignatios shows great promise. As the young prince Niketas, he is named commander of a special division of imperial bodyguards, a post created especially for him.[20] Disaster – in this case, deposition and castration – befalls him early in life, but allows him to more completely show his saintly virtues through the extended askesis of ongoing, lifelong persecution at the hands of Iconoclastic emperors and rival patriarchal claimants alike. From the beginning of his life in monastic exile, starting at the tender age of fourteen, Niketas records Ignatios' ministry with the highest praise:

> To see him as he did this work was like seeing one of Christ's ancient disciples: he readily received those who came to him as if they were sent by Christ, teaching and advising each person to cling to the orthodox faith and to reject the perversion and madness of the heretics [i.e. Iconoclasts]; to completely sweep away all filth and defilement of the spirit and of the flesh; and to be mindful of all virtue, propriety, and self-control (σωφροσύνης).[21]

In addition to his career of literally apostolic ministry, Ignatios is also presented as a modern-day martyr. Although this martyrdom is not attained in the usual sense – Ignatios is not killed outright – the *Life* is permeated by themes of unjust persecution at the hands of those who seized power through illegitimate means, whether the violent Iconoclast Leo V, or the nefarious patriarchal usurper Photios I.

A closer examination of the *Life*'s composition, however, raises further questions. Ignatios is the only contemporary (or near-contemporary) to be memorialized in Niketas' hagiographical writing.[22] Although Niketas' typical subject – a virtuous, orthodox, Iconophile patriarch – is well-represented

---

19 'πάντων μὲν τῶν ἁγίων τοὺς βίους ἀνατάττεσθαι [...] καὶ παράκλησιν ταῖς ἐπιούσαις τῷ βίῳ παραδιδόναι γενεαῖς, κάλλιστον ὁμοῦ καὶ σωτήριον' (ibid., 2.6-8).
20 Ibid., 6.25-30.
21 'καὶ ἦν ὁρᾶν τοῦτον ὥσπερ ἕνα τῶν πρότερον Χριστοῦ μαθητῶν ἔργον τοῦτο ποιούμενον, τοὺς πρὸς αὐτὸν ἰόντας ὡς ὑπὸ Χριστοῦ πεμπομένους προθύμως καταδέχεσθαι, διδάσκειν τε καὶ νουθετεῖν πάντα ἄνθρωπον ἀντέχεσθαι μὲν τῆς ὀρθοδόξου πίστεως, ἀπέχεσθαι δὲ τῆς τῶν αἱρετικῶν δυστροπίας καὶ φρενοβλαβείας, καὶ πάσης μὲν ἑαυτοὺς ῥυπαρίας καὶ παντὸς ἀνακαθαίρειν πνεύματος μολυσμοῦ καὶ σαρκός, πάσης δὲ ἀρετῆς ἐπιμελεῖσθαι καὶ κοσμιότητος καὶ σωφροσύνης' (ibid., 16.24-32). I revisit the final word of this passage, which can also be (and is more usually) translated into English as 'chastity', below.
22 Hinterberger, 'Genres,' p. 45; 'Hagiographer and his Text,' p. 226.

in post-Iconoclastic hagiography, Ignatios' specific treatment is not: the *Life* includes, for example, the only known collection of miracles performed by a patriarch of Constantinople from the ninth and early tenth centuries.[23] Many of the *Life*'s narrative events are instigated not by Ignatios himself, but through the intervention of his political and ecclesiastical rivals – notably the *kaisar* Bardas, brother of the empress and regent for the young Michael III, and Photios I, who twice succeeded Ignatios (in Niketas' view, illegitimately) as Patriarch of Constantinople. Indeed, it seems at times that Niketas is at least as interested in condemning Photios and his supporters as he is in detailing Ignatios' saintly activity.[24]

The *Life* is also unusual as one of only a handful of surviving biographies of Byzantine eunuchs. Throughout the Byzantine period, very little is known of most eunuchs' lives. At best, it is possible to use the documented trajectories of particularly well-known individuals, like saints or high-ranking courtiers, to sketch brief, superficial outlines – outlines that cannot be applied to the eunuch population as a whole. The age at which eunuchs were usually castrated is uncertain, although most instances of (non-punitive, non-medical) castration in Byzantium took place before puberty.[25] If destined for a courtly or governmental career – as seems to have been the case for the vast majority of Byzantine eunuchs – they would have been relocated to Constantinople and introduced to the court at a young age, after which they may have been instructed either in the women's quarters or in special schools by senior eunuchs, before embarking upon the usual progression through courtly offices.[26] Once in court, they would have been clearly distinguished from non-eunuch courtiers by both distinctive prescriptions in court dress as well as by the absence of facial hair.

Ignatios, however, hardly follows this 'typical' eunuch life course. His castration was a political mutilation following the deposition of his father, meant to ensure he could pose no dynastic threat to his father's successor, Leo V (r. 813-820).[27] Until the age of about fourteen, then, Ignatios had been not a servant but an imperial prince. Within the *Life*, explicit reference to Ignatios' status as a eunuch is rare.[28] Yet the fact that Ignatios was indeed a eunuch could never have been far from the author's mind. If it were inconsequential,

23 Efthymiadis, *Companion*, p. 119.
24 Messis, *Les eunuques*, p. 142; Rydén, 'New Forms', p. 544.
25 Ringrose, *Perfect Servant*, p. 61.
26 Ibid., p. 73-77.
27 *Life*, 4.
28 It is possible that this silence is meant to keep the reader from being 'distracted' from Niketas' critiques of Photios; Tougher, 'Holy Eunuchs!', p. 102.

Figure 4.1 Mosaic portrait of Ignatios in N. tympanum of the Hagia Sophia

The Byzantine Institute, The Byzantine Institute and Dumbarton Oaks Fieldwork Records and Papers, photograph c. late 1920s-2000s, Dumbarton Oaks, Trustees for Harvard University, Washington, D.C.

why did Niketas take the time to reference Ignatios' castration in such an odd way? Ignatios is not the only eunuch in the *Life*: the kaisar Bardas' prophetic dream features two angels in the guise of eunuch courtiers, and the *praipositos* (ceremonial eunuch chamberlain) Baanes Angoures is a recurring henchman of both Bardas and Photios.[29] Even in overtly hostile texts, however, eunuchs are not usually so bluntly erased. Ignatios' status as a eunuch, moreover, would have been immediately obvious to anyone who had actually seen the patriarch in life; even his posthumous portrait in the Hagia Sophia (see Fig. 4.1) singles him out as the only beardless figure in a series of patriarchal mosaics.

Ignatios' undeniable identification as a eunuch – however understated and oblique – complicates mainstream expectations of hagiographical subjects. Ignatios shows all the virtues to be expected of a post-Iconoclastic Byzantine saint: humility, obedience, orthodoxy, and chastity. As an ascetic,

29 *Life*, 72.17; ibid., 46.10 and 80.5-8.

he passes through the trials of life – some, like Photios' scheming and opposition, imposed by others, and some, like fleshly desires, imposed by human nature – to emerge in a state of refined spiritual perfection. As abbot, he is father and model to the monks of his community; as saint, he is a faithful and capable advocate for those who call upon him. Yet as a eunuch, Ignatios' perceived effeminacy, inconstancy, and lack of self-control would have called all of these virtues into question. Does Niketas' praise of these saintly actions acquire new meaning when bestowed upon a eunuch – however unusual his circumstances? It is in the *portrayal* of these virtues that Niketas' innovation – and the variability with which his hero's masculinity is defined – become most apparent. But this innovation can only be fully appreciated in contrast to the preceding tradition against which it was originally meant to be read.

Labour and chastity

The greatest of all monastic virtues is, of course, chastity. This has been a standard attribute of saints since the earliest days of Christianity, and plays an important role in Christian hagiography since the lives of the earliest saints. In the formulaic world of Byzantine hagiography, which relied heavily on the use of clear cut, straightforward stock traits, chastity was in many ways the defining characteristic of saintly figures.[30] The monastic life, in particular, is often ideally conceptualized in the words of Matthew 19:12 – the ideal monks are those 'who have made themselves eunuchs for the sake of the kingdom of heaven'. In simple logistical terms, chastity must also have been one of the most accessible routes to sainthood: in the absence of pagan emperors by whom to be martyred, or (more recently) iconoclast emperors by whose heretical regimes to be oppressed, a life of chastity was a path of proven virtue, as well as theoretically open to all. Post-Iconoclastic hagiography, overwhelmingly dedicated to monastic subjects, seems to impose the chaste monastic ideal even on non-monastic figures. Many *Lives* of lay saints from this period show their subjects only narrowly escaping either consummation specifically, or marriage in its entirety.[31] As a monk, a patriarch, and a saint (to say nothing of being a eunuch), it might then seem that Ignatios' chastity should naturally be above suspicion.

---

30 Kazhdan, 'Byzantine Hagiography', p. 131. For the Late Antique substrate informing these attitudes, see Brown, *Body and Society*; Kuefler, *Manly Eunuch*.
31 Krausmüller, 'Chastity or Procreation?', pp. 53-54.

But the chastity of eunuch saints is problematic. On the one hand, eunuchs *were* often thought to enjoy perpetual, or at least effortless, chastity as a result of castration. It seems that this was a commonly accepted topos from the time of the Church Fathers and even of early Christian monasticism more broadly, because some of the same Fathers suggest that acquiring such virtue through castration is really a kind of cheating. We have already encountered the hostility of some prominent exemplars of this tradition above. Their objection, echoed by generations of subsequent ecclesiastical authors, is perhaps an understandable one. What, after all, is the value of a virtue that has not been, or even *cannot* be tested? On the one hand, this 'default' lack of temptation could allow eunuchs to be entrusted with safeguarding the chastity of others. This is certainly the rationale justifying their extensive employment among the empress' staff, and eunuchs may have been preferred for service in, for example, female monasteries, precisely because they were thought to be a 'safer' alternative to non-castrated priests and doctors.[32] Yet eunuchs continued to be held in suspicion, especially in male monasteries, throughout the Byzantine period: the earliest surviving *typika* from Mt. Athos, a major medieval Byzantine monastic centre, forbid the admission of eunuch novices in all circumstances, sometimes even against imperial decree, apparently for fear that the mere presence of eunuchs on the Holy Mountain would tempt the bearded monks into sin.[33]

Niketas, however, is keen to emphasize that although Ignatios is of unimpeachable virtue, this was no easy achievement. Ignatios is no pampered luxuriate, passively avoiding evil rather than actively pursuing good. Early in the *Life*, during a lengthy exposition of Ignatios' various monastic merits, Niketas explains that for his hero the preservation of chastity was – perhaps contrary to his audience's expectations – a demanding challenge:

> He [Ignatios] pursued not only *holiness* and *purity* of his own body but also *chastity* (σωφροσύνη), which from an early age he had established *through great labour and the sweat of his brow* so as to arrive at the utmost detachment from himself, or rather, to come to the absolute mortification of all

---

32 For a résumé of this tension, see Tougher, 'Holy Eunuchs!', p. 94; for eunuchs' roles in monasteries, see for example the twelfth-century typikon of the *Kekharitomene* monastery (Thomas and Hero, *Byzantine Monastic Foundation Documents* [hereafter *BMFD*] 27), 14-16, 57, 80.

33 See *Typikon* of Emperor John Tzimiskes (*BMFD* 12, 16); *Typikon* of Athanasios the Athonite for the Lavra Monastery (*BMFD* 13, 48); and *Typikon* of Emperor Constantine IX Monomachos (*BMFD* 15, 1 [Introduction]). The repetition of these bans may imply that eunuchs nevertheless continued to seek admission to the Holy Mountain; some may even have succeeded in establishing their own communities. Morris, 'Symeon the Sanctified', pp. 133-147.

fleshly thought. In this way, not only was the beauty of his own *chastity* (τῆς σωφροσύνης) defined, but he sanctified his Church with complete zeal and through the gravity and perseverance of the instruction of the Holy Spirit, and *he was so chaste* (ἐπὶ τοσοῦτον [...] ἐσωφρόνιζεν) that not even the name of fornication or of any other impurity was to be heard from those around him.[34]

This excerpt could hardly emphasize more the preoccupation of both author and subject with chastity. In this short passage, chastity is mentioned no less than five times, of which three instances specifically are forms of the word 'sōphrosynē' ('σωφροσύνη', 'moderation, chastity'). The term is used twice as a substantive, and a third time as a verb, with Ignatios as its subject. This had been a word associated with (particularly masculine) sexual self-restraint since antiquity.[35] Most importantly, this is a term which features frequently in the patristic and Late Antique traditions to which both Ignatios and Niketas were responding. It seems unlikely that Niketas would so prominently feature this term so early in the *Life*, in such a closely-coordinated cluster, if not to make a deliberate point – particularly given his simultaneous attention to the difficulty Ignatios experienced in pursuit of this virtue. The labour involved in Ignatios' renunciation of bodily desire is pointed out not once but twice, even at this relatively early point in the narrative, in both personal and interpersonal contexts; moreover, Ignatios so completely manifests the quality of chastity that it actually affects the community around him. From the very beginning of the *Life*, Niketas shows his readers that Ignatios' attention is firmly fixed on loftier things.

Nor is attention to such details limited to Ignatios' lifetime. Despite Niketas' glowing praise of Ignatios, numerous coincidences of language serve to remind the reader of Ignatios' special circumstances. This brings us to our second 'bookend' in the *Life*: Niketas' final eulogy of Ignatios after the saint's death, and particularly its characterization of Ignatios as a

---

34 'σωφροσύνη δὲ οὐ τοῦ οἰκείου σώματος μόνον ἡ ἁγνότης τε καὶ καθαρότης, ἣν ἐκ νεαρᾶς ἡλικίας οὕτω πόνοις συχνοῖς καὶ ἱδρῶσι κατωρθώσατο ὡς εἰς ἄκραν αὐτὸν ἀπάθειαν ἤτοι παντελῆ νέκρωσιν τοῦ σαρκίνου φρονήματος ἐλθεῖν. οὐ ταύτῃ γοῦν μόνον τὸ τῆς σωφροσύνης ὡρίζετο καλόν, πάσῃ δὲ σπουδῇ καὶ τὴν κατ' αὐτὸν Ἐκκλησίαν ἐπὶ τοσοῦτον ἤγνιζε καὶ τῷ ἐμβριθεῖ τε συνεχεῖ τῆς τοῦ Πνεύματος διδασκαλίας ἐσωφρόνιζεν ὡς μηδ' ὄνομα πορνείας ἢ τινος ἄλλης ἀκαθαρσίας ἐν τοῖς αὐτῷ πλησιάζουσιν ἀκούεσθαι' (*Life*, 22.28-24.6).
35 See, for example, Rademaker, *Sophrosyne*; Kuefler, *Manly Eunuch*, pp. 27-28 and 96-102. Elsewhere in the *Life*, 'σωφροσύνη' occurs strictly in relation to Ignatios or his family (*Life*, 16.32, 100.30); 'ἁγνότης' ('holiness') and 'καθαρότης' ('purity'), alternative (but conceptually similar) terms for what we might broadly translate as 'chastity', occur only in the passage cited in the previous note.

father. Of course, as *Patriarch* of Constantinople, it is possible that Ignatios was already understood as a 'father' in a certain conceptual sense. But this does not seem to be the only way the term is used within the *Life*. Niketas uses the term father ('patēr', 'πατήρ') of Ignatios on a number of occasions, the most striking of which occur in relatively close succession towards the end of the work, following Ignatios' death.[36] However, this is not its first appearance. After the death of Ignatios' father, the former Michael I, Ignatios is elected abbot of their monastic community in his place. His reputation for piety attracts so many postulants that Ignatios must found four additional monasteries – one on each of the so-called Princes' Islands (Plate, Hyatros, and Terebinthos) and one, dedicated to Michael the Archangel, on the Asiatic side of the Bosporus – to house them. They are all, of course, fully provisioned and administered to 'by their great leader and *father*'.[37] Like the initial descriptions of Ignatios' chastity, the use of this term so early in the *Life* sets the tone for the rest of the narrative. However, the term's real power is made evident only towards the end of the text, after Ignatios' death, in a close constellation of appearances that – like the parallel cluster of σωφροσύνη at the beginning of the *Life* – reveals Niketas' real flexibility towards his eunuch hero.

Throughout the *Life,* Ignatios is characterized as a 'father' on five separate occasions. Such appellation eludes easy commentary. At first glance, this is perhaps not the most immediately obvious description for even the most virtuous eunuch saint. The sterility of eunuchs is a Biblical topos, inherited and transmitted from the Hebrew Bible (Isaiah 53:3-5). While we have no records of Byzantine eunuchs' thoughts on this subject, it seems clear from the historical record that they could and did sometimes maintain contact, even quite closely, with their natal families.[38] Ignatios is in every respect an involved, pious son – after his father's death, Ignatios, his mother Prokopia,

---

36 The index to the *Life* lists an additional appearance at the very beginning of the text, in the superscription ('ΒΙΟΣ ΗΤΟΙ ΑΘΛΗΣΙΣ ΤΟΥ ΕΝ ΑΓΙΟΙΣ ΠΑΤΡΟΣ ΗΜΩΝ ΙΓΝΑΤΙΟΥ ΑΡΧΙΕΠΙΣΚΟΠΟΥ ΚΩΝΣΤΑΝΤΙΝΟΥΠΟΛΕΩΣ'; '*Life* or *Contest* of our father among the saints, Ignatios, archbishop of Constantinople') but I would hesitate to include it with the other instances internal to the text given the possibly editorial nature of such headings. See *Life*, p. 3 n. 2.
37 'ὑφ' ἐκείνῳ καθηγεμόνι καὶ πατρὶ' (*Life*, 14.20).
38 This is particularly common among high-ranking eunuchs, and is perhaps best exemplified by Basil Lekapenos (c. 915/925-after 985): the illegitimate son of Romanos I, he was the close and long-time confidant of his half-sister Helena and her husband, Constantine VII Porphyrogennetos (as senior emperor, r. 944-959), and spent much of the mid-tenth century as the protector of his great-nephews Basil II and Constantine VIII. It seems reasonable to assume similar practices among less illustrious individuals, whose familial connections would have been all the more important in the absence of loftier responsibilities.

and his sisters, Georgo and Theophano, work together to comfort the victims of Iconoclastic persecutions – but family according to the flesh is not Niketas' primary interest.[39] It is only at the moment of Ignatios' liberation from the flesh that he assumes his true role in the 'family' of believers. After the patriarch's death, Niketas writes:

> [Ignatios] was numbered with holy men as a holy man, with bishops as a great bishop, with confessors as a confessor, and with the great Fathers *as one who had laboured no less than they for the Justice and Truth of God*.[40]

This glowing eulogy is delivered in extremely specific terms. Through this series of deliberate juxtapositions, Niketas makes explicit Ignatios' simultaneous association with, and separation from, his saintly peers: he is their equal, or even their better, in every way but spiritual fatherhood. Had Niketas ended the *Life* here, this would be strange enough: the normative masculine ideal of fatherhood, secure in its place at the summit of acceptable male behaviour, has been approached by the virtuous, ascetic, yet ultimately physically defective saint, and remains, in the end, essentially unchallenged.

Yet, as in any good hagiography, mere bodily death is not the end of the story. Ignatios' death introduces a sequence of eight brief miracle narratives, of which the most intriguing are a trio of fertility miracles. In the first, not one but two women are unable to breastfeed their children due to lack of milk; both are cured after treatment with water that had been exposed to relics of Ignatios' hair.[41] Next, a barren woman is able to conceive after she anoints herself with oil from Ignatios' tomb (procured by her husband) and is subsequently 'freed from the shackles of sterility'.[42] Finally, Ignatios' intervention assures a happy ending to a dangerous instance of breech birth, in which both mother and child were in mortal danger. In gratitude, the parents name the boy Ignatios.[43] The series of miracles concludes with reassurances that such events continue to occur: 'the grace of the Spirit which operated through them [Peter and Paul] [...] is the same as that which through this apostolic *man (ἀνδρὸς)* [i.e. Ignatios], truly a new God-bearer (θεοφόρου) [...] is believed to work the same miracles

---

39 *Life*, 18.12-28.
40 'προστίθεται τοῖς ὁσίοις ὁ ὅσιος, τοῖς ἱεράρχαις ὁ μέγας ἱεράρχης, τοῖς ὁμολογηταῖς ὁ ὁμολογητὴς καὶ μεγάλοις πατράσιν ὁ ὑπὲρ δικαιοσύνης Θεοῦ καὶ ἀληθείας οὐδενὸς ἔλαττον ἐκείνων κεκοπιακώς' (ibid., 104.31-106.3).
41 Ibid., 112.15-25.
42 Ibid., 112.26-114.2.
43 Ibid., 114.15-30.

for the glory of God and the salvation of the faithful'.[44] This is the only time in the text that Niketas qualifies Ignatios as 'anēr' ('ἀνήρ'), the generic Greek word for a (non-castrated) man. This subtle, but striking, descriptive shift would seem to imply that it is only after his death, and subsequent miracles, that Ignatios falls under this categorization: Ignatios has finally surpassed the limitations of his mortal body, and taken his place among the (intact) elect.

These episodes make a serious case for Ignatios' spiritual virility, and Niketas himself concludes the argument of the *Life* in a no less emphatic way. Following the miracle accounts, at the end of a subsequent addendum on the continued wickedness of Photios and his allies (some ten sides of parchment later), Niketas returns to the subject of Ignatios' reception in heaven. Now, however, Niketas revises his earlier description of Ignatios. Rather than continuing to dwell on the evils of emperors and false patriarchs, Niketas instead exhorts his readers to praise and contemplation of God, the Virgin Mary, the angels, apostles, martyrs, and other saints: 'And to all these [I add the name] of Ignatios the younger, our *father* among the saints, archbishop of Constantinople, truly a confessor and bearer of God'.[45] This is the final sentence of the *Life*; its hero emerges from a life of saintly *athlesis* triumphant, and at last seems to have had the final word. Ignatios is not the only eunuch saint to be called a 'father', and I suspect he is not the only eunuch saint to so clearly achieve such spiritual – though hard-won – virility. But Ignatios' sainthood is hardly the divinely imposed, passively acquired reward suggested of earlier ancient and late antique eunuch saints: in the end, Ignatios might become a father, but only with qualifications, and only at the cost of a literal lifetime of struggle.

We must be careful not to interpret this characterization too broadly. Ignatios came from a uniquely privileged social background. Along with other notable eunuch saints and patriarchs of this period, he was a member first of the secular and then of the ecclesiastical elite.[46] Ignatios had once been an imperial prince – a fact he seems to have held onto even in adulthood, as he is the only patriarch since the end of Iconoclasm to use on his official seal not an image of Mary but an image of Christ, the patron of the

---

44 'ἡ γὰρ ἐν ἐκείνοις ἐνεργοῦσα χάρις τοῦ Πνεύματος [...] αὕτη καὶ νῦν διὰ τοῦ ἀποστολικοῦ τούτου ἀνδρὸς καὶ νέου ὡς ἀληθῶς θεοφόρου [...] τὰ ὅμοια πιστεύεται δρᾶν εἰς τὴν Θεοῦ δόξαν καὶ σωτηρίαν τῶν πιστῶν' (ibid., 114.32-116.7). The title of God-bearer ('θεόφορος') is an unmistakeable allusion to Ignatios' patristic namesake, Ignatios of Antioch (ibid., p. 157 n. 177).

45 'πρὸς τούτοις πᾶσι δὲ καὶ τοῦ ἐν ἁγίοις πατρὸς ἡμῶν Ἰγνατίου ἀρχιεπισκόπου Κωνσταντινουπόλεως τοῦ νέου ἀληθῶς ὁμολογητοῦ καὶ θεοφόρου [...]' (ibid., 132.1-4).

46 Messis, *Les eunuques*, p. 162.

imperial family.⁴⁷ Although castration early in life would have left him beardless, he could hardly have been mistaken for a palace eunuch, surely the largest and most visible eunuch population in Byzantium. Indeed, Niketas never treats Ignatios with the general suspicion of such eunuchs that is otherwise relatively common in Byzantine hagiography: Ignatios' admirable qualities are monastic, and emphatically manly – far from the product of any kind of 'cheating', they are the result of lifelong discipline and self-control.

Although hagiography can be a productive medium for pushing, interrogating, or even subverting behavioural norms – saints are, after all, inherently models of extraordinary behaviour – the *Life* of Ignatios, at first glance, seems to present a relatively unproblematic narrative. Ignatios initially seems to be more or less a generic hagiographical protagonist: he is a model of *manly* self-control, his tenure as patriarch is marked by *manly* prudence and leadership, and his struggle against Photios' and Bardas' schemes is one of *manly* forbearance. Yet Ignatios is not a generic male saint. The circumstances of his life – a deposed imperial prince who embraces monastic obscurity before being elevated to the Patriarchate of Constantinople not once but twice – were hardly applicable to the general population. Male saints traditionally set the standards of virtuous behaviour for other men; women and eunuchs typically achieved the same level of sanctity only by sufficiently suppressing their inner unmanly natures. If hagiography is meant to be read as a model of salutary behavior, as Niketas claims in his introduction to the *Life*, what kind of model does Ignatios provide? What might Niketas' audience for this *Life* have looked like?

Without surviving evidence for any kind of meaningful cult dedicated to Ignatios, answers to such questions remain elusive. But Niketas' portrayal of Ignatios remains an important testament to the elasticity of gender in Byzantine Christianity. Throughout the *Life*, Niketas casts Ignatios in a number of roles: the emperor's son, the obedient monastic novice, and most importantly the virtuous patriarch. A political castration in early adolescence would have made Ignatios visually (and audibly) distinct from other Byzantines, but Niketas presents him as a universal model of behaviour; yet as full of manly virtue as Ignatios was, he was unable to match the abilities of his non-castrated counterparts until after his death, through miracles. At the same time, Niketas clearly – and I argue, *deliberately* – associates Ignatios with non-eunuch virtues, specifically those of chastity and fatherhood – neither of which come easily to other eunuchs, even other

---

47   Cotsonis, 'Imagery', p. 106.

eunuch saints. Niketas' Ignatios does not fit neatly within either established paradigm. He is a eunuch, but spiritually fertile; the victim of corrupt and worldly powers, but a manly athlete of Christ. For Niketas, the boundaries between 'eunuch' and 'non-eunuch' are no longer as insurmountable as they may have seemed to his patristic antecedents. After the turmoil of the ninth century – which saw the rise and fall of at least three imperial dynasties, continued pressure from Byzantium's Balkan and Near Eastern neighbours, the ever-present danger of heresy and Iconoclasm – perhaps it is natural that hagiography should portray a world that no longer adhered to expected norms. But the *Life* is also the product of a period of Byzantine history in which eunuchs, especially in imperial contexts, were more visible than ever before. Ignatios' unusual characterization defies clear gendered categorization. The *Life*'s exceptionally fluid treatment of its hero points to the continued importance of these marginal, deeply theological texts to understanding the complexity of medieval gender expression(s).

Bibliography

Primary sources

Basil of Caesarea, *Homily XIII (On Baptism)*, in *Patrologiae cursus completus, series graeca*, ed. by Jacques Paul Migne, 161 vols. (Paris: Garnier, 1857-1891), XXXI, cols. 424-44.

Constas, Nicholas, trans., 'The Life of St Mary/Marinos', in *Holy Women of Byzantium: Ten Saints' Lives in English Translation*, ed., by Alice-Mary Talbot (Washington, DC: Dumbarton Oaks, 1996), pp. 1-12.

Courtonne, Yves, *Saint Basile: Lettres*, 3 vols. (Paris: Les Belles Lettres, 1957-1966), II.

Eusebius, *Historia Ecclesiastica*, in *Patrologiae cursus completus, series graeca*, ed. by Jacques Paul Migne, 161 vols. (Paris: Garnier, 1857-1891), XX, cols. 9-910.

Gregory of Nazianzus, *Oration 37*, in *Patrologiae cursus completus, series graeca*, ed. by Jacques Paul Migne, 161 vols. (Paris: Garnier, 1857-1891), XXXVI, cols. 281-308.

John Chrysostom, *Oration 62*, in *Patrologiae cursus completus, series graeca*, ed. by Jacques Paul Migne, 161 vols. (Paris: Garnier, 1857-1891), LVIII, cols. 595-604.

Lactantius, *De mortibus persecutorum*, in *L. Firmiani Lactanti Opera Omnia. Corpus Scriptorum Ecclesiasticorum Latinorum*, 2 vols., ed. by Samuel Brandt and George Laubmann, Corpus scriptorum ecclesiasticorum Latinorum, 27.2 (Vienna: Tempsky, 1897), II.

Liddell, Henry George, and Robert Scott, *A Greek-English Lexicon*, rev. by Sir Henry Stuart Jones (New York: Oxford University, 1996).

Nicetas [Niketas] David, *The Life of Patriarch Ignatius*, ed. and trans. by Andrew Smithies (Washington, DC: Dumbarton Oaks, 2013).

Palladius, *Historia Lausiaca* in *Patrologiae cursus completus, series graeca*, ed. by Jacques Paul Migne, 161 vols. (Paris: Garnier, 1857-1891), XXXIV, cols. 995-1260.

Sozomen, *Historia Ecclesiastica*, in *Patrologiae cursus completus, series graeca*, ed. by Jacques Paul Migne, 161 vols. (Paris: Garnier, 1857-1891), LXVII, cols. 843-1630

Stethatos, Niketas, *Life of Saint Symeon the New Theologian*, trans. by Richard Greenfield (Cambridge: Harvard University, 2013).

Theophylact of Ochrid, *Commentary on Matthew* 19:12, in *Patrologiae cursus completus, series graeca*, ed. by Jacques Paul Migne, 161 vols. (Paris: Garnier, 1857-1891), CXXIII, cols. 351-53.

Thomas, John, and Angela Constantinides Hero, eds., *Byzantine Monastic Foundation Documents: A Complete Translation of the Surviving Founders' "Typika" and Testaments* (Washington, DC: Dumbarton Oaks, 2000).

Secondary sources

Brown, Peter, *The Body and Society: Men, Women, and Sexual Renunciation in Early Christianity* (New York: Columbia University, 1988).

Cotsonis, J., 'The Imagery of Patriarch Ignatios' Lead Seals and the *Rota Fortunae* of Ninth-Century Byzantine Ecclesio-Political Policies', *Greek Orthodox Theological Review*, 56 (2011), 89-141.

Efthymiadis, Stephanos, ed., *The Ashgate Research Companion to Byzantine Hagiography*, 2 vols. (Burlington: Ashgate, 2011-2014), II.

Grabowski, Antoni, 'Eunuch Between Economy and Philology. The Case of *Carzimasium*', *Mélanges de l'École française de Rome – Moyen Âge*, 127.1 (2015). doi:10.4000/mefrm.2408.

Hinterberger, Martin, 'The Byzantine Hagiographer and his Text', in *The Ashgate Research Companion to Byzantine Hagiography*, ed. by Stephanos Efthymiadis, 2 vols. (Burlington: Ashgate, 2011-2014), II, pp. 211-46.

—, 'Byzantine Hagiography and its Literary Genres. Some Critical Observations', in *The Ashgate Research Companion to Byzantine Hagiography*, ed. by Stephanos Efthymiadis, 2 vols. (Burlington: Ashgate, 2011-2014), II, pp. 25-60.

Kazhdan, Alexander, 'Byzantine Hagiography and Sex in the Fifth to Twelfth Centuries', *Dumbarton Oaks Papers*, 44 (1990), 131-43.

Krausmüller, Dirk, 'Chastity or Procreation? Models of Sanctity for Byzantine Laymen During the Iconoclastic and Post-Iconoclastic Period', *Journal for Late Antique Religion and Culture*, 7 (2013), 51-71.

Kuefler, Mathew, *The Manly Eunuch: Masculinity, Gender Ambiguity, and Christian Ideology in Late Antiquity* (Chicago: University of Chicago, 2001).

Messis, Charis, *Les eunuques à Byzance: entre réalité et imaginaire* (Paris: Centre d'études byzantines, néo-helléniques et sud-est européennes, 2014).

Morris, Rosemary, 'Symeon the Sanctified and the re-foundation of Xenophon', *Byzantine and Modern Greek Studies*, 33.2 (2009), 133-47.

Rademaker, Adriaan, *Sophrosyne and the Rhetoric of Self-Restraint: Polysemy and Persuasive Use of an Ancient Greek Value Term* (Boston: Brill, 2005).

Ringrose, Kathryn, *The Perfect Servant: Eunuchs and the Social Construction of Gender in Byzantium* (Chicago: University of Chicago, 2003).

Rydén, Lennart, 'New Forms of Hagiography: Heroes and Saints', in *The 17th International Byzantine Congress: Major Papers* (New Rochelle: Caratzas, 1986), pp. 537-51.

Thomas, John, and Angela Constantinides Hero, eds., *Byzantine Monastic Foundation Documents: A Complete Translation of the Surviving Founders' "Typika" and Testaments* (Washington. DC: Dumbarton Oaks, 2000).

Tougher, Shaun, *The Eunuch in Byzantine History and Society* (New York: Routledge, 2008).

—, 'Holy Eunuchs! Masculinity and Eunuch Saints in Byzantium', in *Holiness and Masculinity in the Middle Ages*, ed. by P. H. Cullum and Katherine J. Lewis (Cardiff: University of Wales, 2004), pp. 93-108.

About the author

FELIX SZABO is a doctoral candidate in the Department of History at the University of Chicago (USA); his dissertation investigates the role of eunuchs in Byzantine Christianity from the end of Iconoclasm to the Fourth Crusade. His other research interests include eunuchs' kinship, agency, and embodiment; court culture, ceremony, and ritual; and Byzantium's relationship with the medieval West.

Peripheral Vision(s)

Objects, Images, and Identities

5. Gender-Querying Christ's Wounds

A Non-Binary Interpretation of Christ's Body in Late Medieval Imagery

Sophie Sexon

Abstract
This chapter argues that Christ's body can be read as a non-binary body in Late Medieval imagery through analysis of images of Christ's wounds that appear in Books of Hours and prayer rolls. Wounds opened up the gendered representation of the holy body to incorporate aspects of femininity, masculinity and aspects that signify as neither. Through a reading of Christ's wounds as potential markers of the genderqueer, I argue that an individual's identification *with* the non-binary body of Christ could result in identification *as* a non-binary body for the viewing patron. Genderqueer interpretation of Christ's body shows how non-binary visual interpretation more broadly is useful for understanding the complexity of medieval bodies and gender.

Keywords: non-binary, wounds, Christ, late medieval, Book of Hours, religion and gender

The Late Middle Ages in Europe saw a distinct shift in devotional practice from a collective to a more individual model of worship, encouraging more intimate relationships with the divine through meditative practices and the use of literary and artistic devotional aids. This period, understood as roughly 1320-1500 for the purposes of this chapter, manifested a change in Christ's representation from a purely divine body to a body that simultaneously represented humanity and divinity. Empathy with the suffering of both the Virgin Mary and Christ was increasingly emphasized in worship and encouraged among worshippers. From the middle of the eleventh century onwards a new kind of affective piety encouraged devotees to contemplate Christ's humanity and suffering as if it were their own.[1] Affective piety encouraged intense reflection on Christ's sufferings in the crucifixion and drew focus to Christ's humanity and vulnerability. Thomas Bestul characterizes affective piety 'by an ardent love for Christ in his human form, compassion for the sufferings of Christ, and intense longing for union with God'.[2] Affective piety inspired devotion that entailed use of all of the senses, in order both to imagine oneself witnessing the Passion, and to viscerally feel and identify with Christ's suffering. In particular, the image of Christ's wounds opened up the gendered representation of the holy body to incorporate aspects of femininity, masculinity and aspects that signify as neither. This diversely gendered body could have personal resonances for every viewer by displaying bodily morphology recognizable to all, irrespective of their gender. Through a reading of Christ's wounds as potential markers of the genderqueer, I argue that an individual's identification *with* the non-binary body of Christ could result in identification *as* a non-binary body for oneself.

Non-binary is an umbrella term for a range of gender identities that signify neither as wholly female nor wholly male. Non-binary people may or may not identify as trans, since they reject their assigned sex/gender in favour of their identified gender.[3] Although trans identities tend to be regarded as relatively recent, close attention to primary sources, including texts, images and objects, suggests that medieval people could – and did – have an awareness of their own gender as signifying outside the dichotomized binary of male and female, even without identifying language or discourses surrounding gender identity being present in the medieval period.[4] Below, I offer case studies of devotional objects, specifically considering the function of prayer books and prayer rolls in which Christ's wound(s) are depicted, to demonstrate that Christ's body could be, and indeed was, presented as a body which does not conform to the binarized gender distinctions of male/female. In this way, I attend to the possibility that such representations may have had resonance for people in the medieval period who did not conform to the gender binary themselves, who could see their non-binary identities reflected in Christ's holy body.

Studies of non-binary and genderqueer identities are recent phenomena; however, as Christina Richards, Walter Pierre Bouman and Meg-John Barker

---

1   On this shift, see: Beckwith, *Christ's Body*, pp. 43-73; McNamer, *Affective Meditation*.
2   Bestul, *Texts of the Passion*, p. 35.
3   See 'Assigned Sex; Assigned Gender' (p. 287), 'Identified Gender' (p. 301), and 'Non-Binary' (p. 306) in the Appendix.
4   Whittington, 'Medieval'. For a survey of medieval trans studies, see: this volume's 'Introduction', pp. 22-23.

write, 'it would be foolish to assume that non-binary gender is a purely modern phenomenon'.[5] Here I use the terms 'genderqueer' and 'non-binary' synonymously to refer to people who identify neither as male nor as female, whilst acknowledging a wealth of complexity of identification within these terms.[6] As Richards, Bouman, and Barker note:

> In general, non-binary or genderqueer refers to people's identity, rather than physicality at birth. [...] Whatever their birth physicality, there are non-binary people who identify as a single sexed gender position other than male or female. There are those who have a fluid gender. There are those who have no gender. And there are those who disagree with the very idea of gender.[7]

This definition demonstrates that non-binary gender identification has less to do with the morphology of the body and more to do with the way an individual identifies, experiences and understands their own gender irrespective of their physicality. When making reference to visual sources depicting bodies there has to be, understandably, a considerable emphasis on morphology. However, I assert that a more diverse understanding of gender emerges that is appropriate to a medieval context if we consider these bodies in a different light. Rather than focusing solely on making binary distinctions and comparisons, richer and more complex understandings of the medieval body emerge when we practice a more fluid way of seeing the body in manuscript illumination not bound by the binary categories of 'male' and 'female'.

Gendering Christ's body: From feminization to fluidity

One did not need to identify as male to feel the pains and suffering of Christ, nor did one need to identify as female to feel the sorrow and grief of the Virgin Mary.[8] Images and texts with intense devotional focus on Christ's humanity proliferated in the Late Middle Ages, with the suffering body being depicted explicitly in a range of objects both public (such as altarpieces and wall paintings) and private (such as printed woodcuts and

---

5   Richards, Bouman, and Barker, 'Introduction', p. 2.
6   See 'Genderqueer' (p. 299) and 'Non-Binary' (p. 306) in the Appendix.
7   'Introduction', p. 5.
8   On Marian devotion and gender, see Waller, *Virgin Mary*, pp. 29-107.

small ivories).⁹ However, artistic depiction of Christ's gender necessitated greater fluidity in order to have productive relevance for women who were using this body as a personal devotional focus during affective meditation. As part of this change, depictions of Jesus as a mother figure increased in popularity from the twelfth-century onward, particularly in the work of female mystics.

Since the 1980s, much attention has been paid to the feminization of Christ's body in late medieval contexts by scholars including Caroline Walker Bynum and Karma Lochrie.¹⁰ Bynum's work *Jesus as Mother*, for example, interrogates twelfth- and thirteenth-century writing to provide a history of spirituality amongst men and women of the era that was grounded in images of Christ's holy maternity. She identifies common tropes, such as Christ feeding the individual soul with blood from his side wound as a mother feeds an infant with breastmilk.¹¹ Where Bynum argues that Christ's feminization is linked to maternal functions of feeding and nurturing, Karma Lochrie develops the arguments to include queer sexuality as a central aspect of Christ's genderfluidity. In the article 'Mystical Acts, Queer Tendencies', Lochrie challenges and disrupts heteronormative historicist assumptions by engaging in a queer reading of mystical texts and manuscript images. She acknowledges the lack of organising terminology around discourses of sex and gender in medieval texts but speaks of sexuality to unsettle heterosexual bias in scholarship and to explore itinerant queer meanings and interpretations of texts and imagery concerning the feminized Christ. I propose to extend and nuance these analyses by looking at the feminization of Christ's body not as a restructuring that renders the body wholly female, but as an aspect of Christ's gender identity that lies between the bounded categories of male and female.

The marked feminization of Christ's body in medieval art does not give way to a full morphological transition of Christ's gender from male to female. Instead, both genders are incorporated into one holy body that signifies fluidly. Christ's body is characterized, through a range of biblical stories and liturgical practices, as that which is subject to change. From transfiguration (a change of form from human to divine) to transubstantiation (a change from one substance [bread] into another [body]), Christ's body is marked by impermanence, malleability, and an openness to representing contrary states

---

9   For examples of such objects, see Bynum, *Christian Materiality*.
10 Bynum, *Jesus as Mother*; Lochrie, 'Mystical Acts'.
11 For other examples of Christ's feminization with a focus on Christ as a nurturing mother figure, see Bynum, *Holy Feast*.

in parallel. This can be seen in the hypostatic union of Christ's divinity and humanity in one individual existence; Christ is both perfectly divine and perfectly human simultaneously. Conceptualizing Christ's body as capable of expressing a range of genders, not limited to signifying in binary terms to a binarized audience, offers productive insights into medieval responses to the archetypically perfect Christian body.

Christ and various saints have often been depicted as being beyond binarized gender as an aspect of their holiness.[12] Leah DeVun notes that in alchemical texts from the late medieval period Christ is often characterized as a hermaphrodite.[13] Focusing on the early fifteenth-century *Book of the Holy Trinity*, a German alchemical treatise attributed to the Franciscan Frater Ulmannus, DeVun identifies 'a new pair of images: the Jesus-Mary hermaphrodite and the Antichrist hermaphrodite.'[14] The image of the Jesus-Mary hermaphrodite highlights the inseparable nature of Christ and Mary, which leads DeVun to describe Christ as 'the ultimate hermaphrodite, a unity of contrary parts – the human and the divine, the male and the female'.[15] DeVun notes that medieval saints' lives also often reflect narratives where saints' genders appear ambiguous or change, such as in accounts of Saints Pelagius of Antioch, Marinus and Wilgefortis; the former two saints were assigned female at birth but later changed their appearances and lived as men by choice, whereas the latter was given male secondary sex characteristics in response to prayer.[16] In late medieval images of Wilgefortis, for instance, the bearded saint is depicted in *imitatio Christi*, crucified on a cross with one shoe off and one shoe on; the empty slipper playfully alludes to the vagina, as 'an indication of the saint's – and Christ's – hermaphroditic nature.'[17] These cultural and artistic artefacts align Christ's body with these saints of undetermined gender, demonstrating how holy bodies can be seen to transcend binarized gender as part of God's divine will.

---

12 For a summary of scholarship on saints' gender as beyond binaristic categories, see: Spencer-Hall, *Medieval Saints*, pp. 56-59.
13 'The Jesus Hermaphrodite', p. 209. 'Hermaphrodite' is a now antiquated term for individuals who would now be referred to as intersex. 'Intersex' is the modern term for a person whose biological characteristics do not fit neatly within cultural binary definitions of 'male' and 'female'. Intersex individuals are (almost) always assigned a binary gender at birth, and in most of the world are still subjected to non-consensual surgical or hormonal treatment. See 'Hermaphrodite' (p. 300) and 'Intersex' (p. 302) in the Appendix.
14 DeVun, 'The Jesus Hermaphrodite', p. 208.
15 Ibid., p. 209.
16 On AFAB saints, see Bychowski (pp. 245-65), Ogden (pp. 201-21) and Wright (pp. 155-76) in this volume.
17 DeVun, 'The Jesus Hermaphrodite', p. 213.

Wellcome MS 632

To show how the image of Christ's wounds could be used to signify a breakdown between binarized understandings of the medieval body, I begin by looking at the materiality of the image as used on birthing aids. Wellcome MS 632 is a parchment roll in worn condition, used as a birthing girdle in the late fifteenth century to protect women in labour.[18] It contains images of the instruments of the Passion, the *arma Christi*; the crucifix; and Christ's highly abstracted dripping side wound surrounded by Christ's pierced – and penetrated – hands and feet. The inscription on the back states that the roll's length is equal to the height of the Virgin Mary, and on the front, where there was intended to be an image of a cross, is the inscription: 'If multiplied fifteen times, this cross is the true length of our Lord.'[19] Therefore the scroll itself as a material object was positioned as an authentic measure of both the Virgin Mary's feminine body and Christ's masculine body, showing how both bodies could be tangibly realized via one object. The roll promises to protect both male and female users from sudden death, pestilence, death in battle, wrongful judgement and robbery, if the user bears the measure about their person and says certain prayers. It had a particular function for women in childbirth, who were to be granted a safe delivery, with the promise that the user would survive to be purified in church, and her child would survive to be baptized. This kind of birthing girdle was designed to be placed around the abdomen of the woman in labour. The physical juxtaposition thus makes apparent the link between Christ's wound and the vagina, as the image of Christ's bleeding wound resembles the body of the woman in labour.

Wellcome MS 632 is an example of the many kinds of objects that bore Christ's wound, and that were intended to be used in childbirth.[20] Use of these objects involved a tactile interaction with the image, in which women's bodies came into contact with an authenticating measure of the body of Christ. These two bodies touched not only for protective purposes, but also in the manner that the female user of the object was assimilated to Christ: the body in childbirth mimicked Jesus's suffering body in the Passion. In these tactile uses, the employment of the image of Christ's wound

---

18 Bühler, 'Prayers', p. 274. For a transcript and description of the roll, see Moorat, *Catalogue*, pp. 491-93.
19 Olsan ('Wellcome MS. 632') gives the original: 'Thys crosse if mette [measured] xv [15] tymes ys the trewe length of oure Lord'.
20 For more examples, see Bynum, *Christian Materiality*, pp. 197-200.

destabilizes a binary understanding of Christ's gender, demonstrating that Christ knows the pains of childbirth in his capacity as mother of the church.[21] Therefore, the user of the material object comes to recognize Christ's suffering as transcending gender, encouraging the idea that Christ's identity is a non-binary one wherein labour pains can be felt through the side wound in an otherwise masculine-coded body.

Gendering Christ's wound(s)

Central to Christ's apparent feminization is the prominence of his wounds, and the symbolic meanings ascribed to them. The iconographic isolation of Christ's wounds as foci for contemplation is an important part of late medieval religious imagery, as the wounds display Christ's capability for suffering and draw attention to his humanity. Of particular interest, both in medieval representations and in medievalist scholarship, is the side wound inflicted by the Roman soldier Longinus after the Crucifixion. This wound frequently appears, seemingly detached from Christ's body, in Books of Hours, prayer rolls, and widely disseminated woodcut prints across Britain and Europe in the fourteenth and fifteenth centuries.[22] Lucy Freeman Sandler notes that wound images start to appear after 1320, and that contemplation of the isolated wounds was characteristic of the fourteenth century, when narrative images were replaced by devotional ones to create greater emotional impact.[23]

The symbolic representation of the side wound, by its visual association with the vulva and the vagina, opens up Christ's gender to non-binary interpretations. The wound is frequently depicted in a vertical orientation, abstracted from the body; this has been analysed as symbolically representational of the vulva by scholars such as Karma Lochrie, Martha Easton and Flora Lewis.[24] Where these scholars have contended that the wound as a vulvar synecdoche entirely feminizes the body of Christ, I argue that the vulva-wound is better understood as evidence of the integral fluidity of Christ's gender, being incorporated into a body that refuses to signify as either/or within binary terms. Parts of Christ's body represent the typologically female body, showing that the feminine and the masculine

---

21 Amsler, 'Affective Literacy', p. 98.
22 For examples, see Areford, 'The Passion Measured'.
23 Sandler, 'Jean Pucelle', p. 85.
24 Easton, 'Wound'; Lewis, 'Wound'; Lochrie, 'Mystical Acts'.

are inseparably connected, and that both elements must necessarily exist within Christ's body. The icon is therefore not reducible to either gender.

Wound images often appear with an encircling inscription stating that this is the 'true measure' of Christ's wound, and that certain indulgences can be granted if the wound is touched, kissed or prayed to as instructed.[25] Bynum notes that: 'An enthusiasm for measurement and quantification was a new characteristic of fourteenth- and fifteenth-century culture [...] If made to the dimensions supposedly given in a vision or brought from the Holy Land, an image of the wound was Christ'.[26] Therefore these images held importance as supposedly authentic measurements of a holy body, with a representative verisimilitude to the wounds made in Christ's flesh. These measurements made the wound seem more realistic given the specificity of their measurement, but they also increased the likelihood that the size given could be approximate to the size of the vulva. The wound's resemblance to the vulva gave it iconographic versatility, as well as another range of protective and apotropaic functions.

Images of Christ's side wound could be rolled up and tied to the body to prevent illness, danger in childbirth, or sudden death. The veneration of wound images had a medical function, linked to the promise of preventing pain; Bynum argues that the side wound is, in medieval culture, 'explicitly connected' with birthing, measuring, or the obtaining of indulgences.'[27] These disembodied wound images were at times explicitly connected with typologically female anatomy. Not only did they resemble the vulva visually, they were used to prevent pains associated with the vagina. Birthing girdles often carried depictions of the side wound; these strips of vellum were pressed against women in labour to help ease the pain of childbirth. Depicted on the vellum could be a range of images relating to Christ's Passion (such as the *arma Christi*). Prayers to a variety of saints and holy figures would also be inscribed on them, which would grant protection to both mother and baby during childbirth if recited. The images and incantations were not only intended for use in childbirth, but also to help with period pain and other issues related to menstruation. Easton, for example, describes an amulet that purports to have the measure of the wound of Christ, that will aid problematic menstruation if the user makes an entreaty to Longinus.[28] There are multiple meanings of wound imagery, and multiple reasons why

---

25   On such measurements, see Areford, 'The Passion Measured', pp. 211-38.
26   Bynum, 'Violent Imagery', p. 20.
27   Bynum, *Christian Materiality,* p. 200.
28   Easton, 'Wound', pp. 408-09; Rudy, 'Kissing Images', p. 51.

image-makers utilized the wound. In the same moment, it could signify variously to different audiences, inflected with an overlapping plurality of gendered interpretations.

The trans haptics of Christ's wound

Contact with Christ's wound, both as image and as literal wound, is central to its devotional potency, and the ways in which it signifies genderfluidity. This includes both spiritual or meditational contact with the wound, and physical skin-to-skin intimacy, such as pressing the girdle to the abdomen or touching the image with one's fingers. Easton and Lochrie have discussed the erotic significance of images of Christ's wounds in late medieval culture, acknowledging that the wound often resembles a vulva in these various depictions, and that images of the side wound have often been venerated by rubbing or kissing the image, suggesting eroticized devotional practices.[29] For Lochrie this marks out queer contact with Christ's body, however, it is not only eroticism that is suggested by these physical contacts with the image of the wound. Another queer aspect of this contact is the manner in which physical touches of the image help one to orientate one's own body and understanding of gender.

Jack Halberstam encourages a tactile and haptic understanding of the contemporary trans body, writing that: 'The haptic offers one path around the conundrum of a binary visual plane (what is not male appears to be female, what is not female appears to be male.)'[30] For Halberstam the haptic is important as it encourages a method of knowing that goes beyond the visual and that 'names the way the mind grasps for meanings that elude it while still holding on to the partial knowledge available.'[31] In going beyond language and the visual, the haptic is a mode of perception adept at resisting binaries and useful for a trans understanding of the body.

The haptic is the mode engaged when we consider the material technology of medieval objects depicting Christ's wound. As Bynum notes, 'even where representational, medieval depictions are sometimes more tactile than visual.'[32] This aligns with medieval conceptions of optics. There is

29 Easton, 'Good for You?', passim and especially pp. 4-5; Lochrie, 'Mystical Acts'.
30 Halberstam, *Trans**, p. 90.
31 Ibid.
32 Bynum, *Christian Materiality*, p. 38.

a fundamental collapse between the categories of subject and object in medieval optical theories, such as Roger Bacon's theory of intromission and extromission, popular in the thirteenth century, wherein species (versions of the object) were either emitted from the viewer's eye to touch the object, or emitted from the object to touch the viewer.[33] Touch was therefore an integral part of sight.

In this context, Alicia Spencer-Hall presents a theory of 'coresthesia' to describe how one interacts with a medieval manuscript. Coresthesia requires responding to text and image with touches, in the sense that the body not only touches the material object, but is 'touched affectively by the text's content' and this process of touches 'are conjoined, non-hierarchical operations which shape the experience of a text.'[34] The experience of the text in a haptic sense therefore affects the reader in diverse ways, and in the case of wound imagery, shapes the terrain of the bodies both of the holy figures depicted within, and of the readers themselves. Spencer-Hall notes the non-hierarchical relation of text to image, material, and context, and how this also affects the hierarchy of subject and object within the praxis of viewing, as 'the aim of religious vision was to fuse entirely with one's object, God Himself: touching and being touched in a single glance [...]. This haptic interplay ultimately renders subject/object labels irrelevant.'[35] In this formulation, one fuses not only with God, but also with Christ as part of the Trinitarian nature of God: a body that is human and divine, and also genderfluid. There is not only the collapse of the subject/object distinction, and the collapse of binary classification through haptic understanding. There is also the collapse of the distinction between past and present, where the trans/non-binary reader of the present comes into contact with the trans/non-binary viewer of the past, in what Spencer-Hall calls a 'trans-chronological rendezvous', facilitated by the traces left by earlier readers in manuscripts.[36] To take forward trans studies in the middle ages will require sensitivity to these rendezvous and attentiveness to possibility. It is not the retroactive ascription of contemporary identity labels to those who lived in the past that brings us forward. Rather, I propose acts of affective listening with the body, allowing our bodies to become the site of trans-chronological trans and queer assembly, touching and being touched across time.

33 Spencer-Hall, *Medieval Saints*, pp. 107-18.
34 Ibid., p. 143.
35 Ibid., p. 118.
36 Ibid., p. 142.

When we read a manuscript or view a medieval object, it is not only the text and illuminations within that command our attention. What bring us into dialogue with the viewer of the past are the marginal annotations, the dirt marks on the page, the smears of painted pigment rubbed off by lips and fingers, the ghostly remnants of objects that were pressed into the manuscript that have fallen out over time. The handled object is brought to life by haptic understanding, wherein the ways bodies have used it come to tell us something about how the images were viewed and understood. When reflecting on the haptic and material uses of objects such as birthing girdles and manuscripts we also come to know the non-binary body through handling objects depicting the body and thinking about the various ways touches help us to reflect on gender through use. However, manuscript images sometimes depict themselves how we should touch an image and, in doing so, teach us how to think about the bodies that we touch – both our own and those of others.

Bonne of Luxembourg's Book of Hours

The way Christ's side wound is depicted in manuscripts demonstrates the complexity of the trope. One such example can be seen in Bonne of Luxembourg's Book of Hours (*c.* 1349), illuminated by Jean le Noir with grisaille miniatures.[37] This relatively small prayer book, measuring 13.2 by 9.7 cm, was made for the Bohemian princess Bonne of Luxembourg (d. 1349), wife of John, Duke of Normandy. The small format of this manuscript, and other similar Books of Hours, indicates the intensely personal and private relationship that the owner-user was encouraged to have with the object. The images and text within are so small as to necessitate a considered and intimate focus during use.[38] The narrative revealed by the succession of images in the book guides the user to think through the images carefully in conjunction in order to contemplate the wound fully, therefore incorporating the handling of the manuscript into the practice of devotion. Folio 328r (Fig. 5.1) depicts Bonne of Luxembourg and her husband kneeling before Christ on the cross, who draws focus to his side wound through gesture. With his elongated, phallic finger, Christ invites us to contemplate his wound by pointing at it and touching his finger to the wound.

---

37   For further discussion of this manuscript, see Bynum, *Christian Materiality*, pp. 197, 199-201; Easton, 'Wound'; Lochrie, 'Mystical Acts', pp. 190-191; Sandler, 'Jean Pucelle', pp. 86, 92, 94.
38   Clanchy, 'Images'.

Figure 5.1 Psalter and Prayer Book of Bonne of Luxembourg

New York, Metropolitan Museum of Art, The Cloisters MS. 69.86, fol. 328r. CC0 1.0 Universal

Spencer-Hall focuses on the 'agape-ic' encounter in medieval hagiographic texts, staking the claim that 'the scopic act can be an experience of complete mutuality between the individual who looks and that which is looked at.'[39] This encounter is conjoined with transcendence, a glory that is felt in the viewer's body: 'This is due to the inherently synaesthetic nature of the scopic act, in which looking opens out into multisensory experience across the viewer's entire body.'[40] Felt with many of the senses, this feeling of ecstasy is also a transitory state. The agape-ic encounter shares in Halberstam's notion of the haptic, as it brings one's self into being, where looking becomes a form of feeling. It is described as an 'act of genuinely reciprocal spectatorship' as the object exerts itself as subject and returns to us a sense of ourselves as object. In looking back at us, 'we perceive (feel and see) ourselves being seen, and thus we are looked and felt into being.'[41] By confronting us directly,

39   Spencer-Hall, *Medieval Saints*, p. 15.
40   Ibid.
41   Ibid., p. 16.

Figure 5.2   Psalter and Prayer Book of Bonne of Luxembourg

New York, Metropolitan Museum of Art, The Cloisters MS. 69.86, fol. 331r. CC0 1.0 Universal

the presence of Christ's fragmentary and divine body in Bonne's Book of Hours is what causes us to consider our own body, and our own gender. The reflection on this holy object is a reflection on ourselves as subjects, and brings us to awareness of the borders and boundaries where our own awareness of the gendered self breaks down. In Bonne's prayer book we meet the gaze of Christ and are seen not only as the patrons of the manuscript in folio 328r (Fig. 5.1), but also as part of the body of Christ when we encounter the image on folio 331r (Fig. 5.2).

Turning the pages, the move from folio 328r to folio 331r expands and dilates the image of Christ's wound. We progress from Christ on the Cross imploring the patrons of the manuscript to contemplate his wound, to a brightly coloured, elaborate image of the wound separated from Christ's body and presented alone, surrounded by the *arma Christi*. The movement between folios zooms in on the side wound, enhanced by the image of the hybrid creature in the margins positioning a ladder above the border of the image, highlighting its significance to the viewer. The ladder is not only part of the *arma Christi* removed and abstracted from the central image, but is here used as a tool to convey some more information regarding the significance of the image gestured to. The ladder is a tool that links from the previous narrative image on folio 328r, indicating that we should ourselves climb it along with the hybrid creature from the margins of the image to contemplate the wound more specifically and fully that was depicted initially on 328r. This aligns the viewer with the hybrid creature from the margins as we share its tools for viewing the side wound, and encourages us to scrutinize more carefully those tools we use for interpretive visual functions. The hybrid creature is part human and part beast, and, as Robert Mills argues in the essay 'Jesus as Monster', Christ's body too assimilates some of the hybridity of marginal figures.[42] Christ's body is structured by hybridity as our own is, and these manuscript images hint that this applicable to gender too by leading us to focus on the meaning of Christ's abstracted vaginal wound.

The ladder not only directs us to contemplate the wound more fully, but Christ points to his own wound asking that attention be paid to it. In doing so, Christ invites the reader to think of the role of touch in their devotions. Christ extends an invitation to the person handling the manuscript to contemplate the wound through touch. Sight and touch are irrevocably bound when we view these images in conjunction with one another, and the subject/object boundaries are dissolved as outlined by medieval optics. The concepts of subject and object dissolve as we move from viewing the patrons of the manuscript on folio 328r to becoming the viewing patrons ourselves on folio 331r. We become not only the patrons, but also all of the affective participants in holy meditation who have chosen to focus so intently on the wound. Our position in viewing the wound on folio 331r also situates us as the touching finger of Christ from folio 328r, our entire bodies become a sense organ. Note also the change in the orientation of the wound from horizontal to vertical in the passage from folio 328r to 331r, which encourages vulvic connotations.

Touching the wound

Tactile interaction with wound imagery is a tactic routinely utilized in devotional meditation, where touch becomes as important as sight.[43] Mark Amsler writes that we see 'the wound (*vulna*) as vagina (*vulva*), with

---

42 Mills, 'Jesus as Monster'.
43 For examples, see: Rudy, 'Kissing Images', p. 4.

a reading gesture at once sacred, erotic, scandalous, and transgressive.[44] This tactile understanding of wound imagery allows the reader to become one with the image, and to gain a more haptic understanding of Christ's body as one that resembles one's own, irrespective of gender. The reader identifies with Christ not only through *imitatio Christi* but also through viewing and recognising iconography that resembles their own body. The viewer is intended to have a personal and intimate connection with the images in the small prayer book, wherein one has the freedom to touch, to feel (literally and emotionally), to become, through meditative practices, similar to this suffering body, connected to it through touch and sight.

The Loftie prayer book, a mid-fifteenth-century Book of Hours written in Dutch, offers another example of such haptic engagements.[45] With eighteen grisaille miniatures produced by the Masters of the Delft Grisailles, the Book is relatively small, measuring 9.5 cm wide by 14.5 cm high. Most of the illustrations within the book show no traces of tactile engagement, save for folio 110v, a miniature of the five wounds of Christ next to a Prayer to the Five Wounds of Christ. In this image, the lower two wounds have been touched or kissed in a way that has resulted in abrasion of the pigment.[46] Since no other images have been rubbed away in this manuscript, it raises the question as to why the wounds have attracted such attention. Were these wounds touched with a feeling of identification, a sense of empathy, or even with erotic desire? Although there is no manner to identify the kinds of touches lavished upon the illustrations, we have the spectral remains of the adored image, and the knowledge that no other illustrations in the manuscript, including those of Christ's body and face, have been touched quite so fervently. This singles the wounds out as objects of adoration in this particular manuscript, worthy of attention that other body parts do not merit.

The birthing girdle and the manuscript image, as objects to be touched, kissed and used with full acknowledgement of their materiality, engage affective piety and encourage the utilization of all the senses in order to convey a complex theological understanding of Christ's body as that which is always similar to one's own. The haptic is evoked when viewing images in which Christ's finger points to his wound, asking the viewer to consider how that suffering body is similar to their own suffering body. The image erases the opposition between subject and object by pointing out the similarities between Christ's humanity and the humanity of the viewer. The viewer is

---

44 Amsler, 'Affective Literacy', p. 98.
45 For more information on the manuscript, see Marrow, *Passion Iconography*, p. 225 (8b).
46 Rudy, 'Kissing Images', p. 56.

an affective participant in Christ's suffering, and their body mirrors the icon irrespective of the gender of the viewing subject. Halberstam writes that hapticality is a form of knowing that exceeds the rational and intellectual, instead relying on the senses and feeling in much the same manner that late medieval affective piety encourages one to know the body of Christ. For Halberstam, 'This is a perfect frame for the trans* body, which, in the end, does not seek to be seen and known but rather wishes to throw the organization of all bodies into doubt.'[47] This frame also works well for the divine body of Christ which, in its fragmentary and multivalent state, throws the organization of all human bodies into doubt. The viewer is encouraged to use all of their senses in order to challenge their ways of knowing the fragmentary, trans/non-binary body of Christ, in order to understand a body which does not signify wholly as masculine or feminine, as it conveys a complex theological message about the roles Christ plays in Christian devotion. The manuscript images of gestures and touches, and the rubbed remains of images ardently kissed demonstrate that medieval viewers understood the body through using their senses to engage with images beyond sight alone.

The artistic depiction of Christ's genitals has been a topic of wide scholarly and theological debate. Corine Schleif shows that Gospel accounts are ambiguous about whether Christ was stripped down to the skin and notes that this matter was the subject of debates in the thirteenth century and again around 1500.[48] His nakedness during the Passion created a conundrum for medieval artists, as they dealt with an increase in demand for images of Christ's Passion across the visual arts. The tension between depicting a suffering human body and a body that was divine had to be addressed with delicacy by image-makers. One aspect of Christ's nudity to be considered in this context is the displacement of attention from the genitalia to the side wound in images of the Passion.

Wound imagery may have been used as an apt way to address ideas of humanity and generation within the Christ-icon. Christ would need to be depicted with male genitalia if he was to embody the ideal human form. However, to be depicted in this way would problematically ascribe a sexuality to the divine body. Drawing focus instead to Christ's wound resolves the problem of depicting genitalia, as evidenced in the Man of Sorrows image on folio 19r of the Rothschild Canticles. Here Christ is depicted nude at the moment of the flagellation, but the illuminator has depicted Christ's

---

47 *Trans**, p. 90.
48 Schleif, 'Christ Bared'. On this topic, see also: Steinberg, *Sexuality of Christ*.

body twisted so that his left leg covers the genital area. Instead, focus is drawn to the side wound, encircled by red pigment, to which Christ points. Christ's wound draws attention away from the genital area, while also representing genitalia. The phallic pointing finger suggests a penis, while the side wound suggests a vulva; both are present in one body, and in one image, just as in Bonne of Luxembourg's Book of Hours.[49] The wound as vulva renders Christ's body generative – he gives birth to the church through the wound – without the need to display genitalia. The central depiction of Christ's wound provides representation of female anatomy without fully feminizing Christ's physical form. His body is then understood in parts: this feminized aspect of Christ is part of the whole, a union of the feminine and the masculine that allows both men and women to see themselves reflected in a body that signifies in non-binary terms. The wound, as symbol, achieves this purpose by reflecting both Christ's humanity and his divinity, his masculinity and his femininity, through synecdoche.

Physical objects carrying the image of Christ's wound could thus be used to engage a complex, haptic understanding of Christ's body as non-binary. The abstracted vulva-like wound asks how we come to gender ourselves when we focus on the elements of our bodies. As Bonne of Luxembourg's book attests, we are not only the viewing patrons shown within the margins of folio 328r. We are also, ourselves, the body of Christ as shown on folio 331r, just as we are, too, the hybrid viewing creature in the margins of folio 331r; both human and animal in nature, capable of being both male and female, in the course of our affective meditations.

Representational images of Christ's body assimilate aspects of culturally defined masculinity and femininity into one body. I argue that medieval audiences would have understood and accepted the fluidity and flexibility of Christ's gender, particularly when reflecting on this body through affective practices such as *imitatio Christi*. By analysing a body so central to Western iconography I hope to open up the possibility for further non-binary readings of medieval imagery, both secular and sacred. Such readings help us to understand that the later Middle Ages had a refined view of gender not entirely dependent on the gender binary, and thus contribute to the project of identifying, defining, and exploring the history of non-binary identity.

This chapter shows what a non-binary hermeneutics of medieval art history might look like in the attempt to acknowledge the 'full ideological existence' of transgender identities.[50] As Robert Mills has previously stated,

49 For further interpretation of this image, see Mills, *Suspended Animation*, p. 192.
50 Spencer-Hall and Gutt, 'Introduction' to this volume, p. 11.

it is important to do this work to militate against the 'phobic underbelly [...] in which queer possibilities continue to be checked, censured and circumscribed in even the most purportedly 'liberal' contexts.'[51] To take forward transgender studies of the medieval period will require sensitivity and attentiveness to possibility. Sensitivity entailing both a literal use of the senses, and a sensibility not commonly found in proscriptive academic discourse. We do not ask for the ascription of contemporary identity labels to those who lived in the past, as it is not for us to retroactively ascribe. When one reads a medieval text or glimpses a manuscript illumination that resonates with something in you, this is the material touching something in you that is timeless and immaterial about our trans identities. Listen to your body and feel those queer touches, in order to be able to translate the medieval trans past to a modern audience. These touches tell you that your experiences and identity have always existed in some form, whether we had the language to designate or describe it, or not. And know that, through these touches, you are not alone, both historically, and among the community of trans and non-binary academics who have contributed to bring together the volume that you presently hold within your hands.

Bibliography

Manuscripts

Birthing girdle, London, Wellcome Collection, Wellcome MS 632.
Psalter and Prayer Book of Bonne of Luxembourg, New York, Metropolitan Museum of Art, The Cloisters Collection, MS 69.86.
The Loftie Hours, Baltimore, Walters Art Museum, Walters MS W.165. <http://thedigitalwalters.org/Data/WaltersManuscripts/html/W165/> [accessed 14 August 2020].
Rothschild Canticles, New Haven, Yale University Library, Beinecke MS 404.

Secondary sources

Amsler, Mark, 'Affective Literacy: Gestures of Reading in the Later Middle Ages', *Essays in Medieval Studies* 18.1 (2001), 83-110.
Areford, David S., 'The Passion Measured: A Late-Medieval Diagram of the Body of Christ', in *The Broken Body: Passion Devotion in Late-Medieval Culture,* ed.

---

51 Mills, 'Ecce Homo' p. 154.

by A. A. MacDonald, H. N. B. Ridderbos, and R. M. Schlusemann (Groningen: Egbert Forsten, 1998), pp. 211-38.

Beckwith, Sarah, *Christ's Body: Identity, Culture and Society in Late Medieval Writings* (New York: Routledge, 1993).

Bestul, Thomas H., *Texts of the Passion: Latin Devotional Literature and Medieval Society* (Philadelphia: University of Pennsylvania, 1996).

Bühler, Curt F., 'Prayers and Charms in Certain Middle English Scrolls', *Speculum*, 39.2 (April 1964), 270-278.

Burgwinkle, William, and Cary Howie, *Sanctity and Pornography in Medieval Culture: On the Verge* (Manchester: Manchester University, 2010).

Bynum, Caroline Walker, *Christian Materiality: An Essay on Religion in Late Medieval Europe* (New York: Zone, 2011).

—, *Holy Feast and Holy Fast: The Religious Significance of Food to Medieval Women* (Berkeley: University of California, 1987).

—, *Jesus As Mother: Studies in The Spirituality of The High Middle Ages* (Berkeley: University of California, 1982).

—, 'Violent Imagery in Late Medieval Piety', *Bulletin of the German Historical Institute*, 30, (Spring 2002), 3-36.

Clanchy, Michael, 'Images of Ladies with Prayer Books: What Do They Signify?' *Studies in Church History*, 38, (2004), pp. 106-122.

DeVun, Leah, 'The Jesus Hermaphrodite: Science and Sex Difference in Premodern Europe', *Journal of the History of Ideas* 69.2 (2008), 193-218.

Easton, Martha, 'Was it Good for You Too? Medieval Erotic Art and its Audiences', *Different Visions: A Journal of New Perspectives on Medieval Art*, 1 (2008), 1-30.

—, 'The Wound of Christ, the Mouth of Hell: Appropriations and Inversions of Female Anatomy in the Later Middle Ages', in *Tributes to Jonathan J. G. Alexander: Making and Meaning of Illuminated Medieval and Renaissance Manuscripts, Art and Architecture,* ed. by Susan L'Engle and Gerald B. Guest (Turnhout: Harvey Miller, 2006), pp. 395-414.

Halberstam, Jack, *Trans*: A Quick and Quirky Account of Gender Variability* (Oakland: University of California, 2018).

Lewis, Flora, 'The Wound in Christ's Side and the Instruments of the Passion: Gendered Experience and Response', in *Women and the Book: Assessing the Evidence*, ed. by Jane H. M. Taylor and Lesley Smith (Toronto: University of Toronto, 1997), pp. 204-299.

Lochrie, Karma, 'Mystical Acts, Queer Tendencies', in *Constructing Medieval Sexuality*, ed. by Karma Lochrie, Peggy McCracken, and James S. Schultz (Minneapolis: University of Minnesota, 1997), pp. 180-200.

Marrow, James H., *Passion Iconography in Northern European Art of the Late Middle Ages and Early Renaissance: A Study of the Transformation of Sacred Metaphor into Descriptive Narrative* (Kortrijk: Ars Neerlandica, 1979).

McNamer, Sarah, *Affective Meditation and the Invention of Medieval Compassion* (Philadelphia: University of Pennsylvania, 2010).

Mills, Robert, 'Ecce Homo', in *Gender and Holiness: Men, Women and Saints in Late Medieval Europe*, ed. by Samantha J. E. Riches and Sarah Salih (London: Routledge, 2002), pp. 152-173.

—, 'Jesus as Monster', in *The Monstrous Middle Ages*, ed. by Bettina Bildhauer and Robert Mills (Cardiff: University of Wales, 2003), pp. 28-54.

—, *Suspended Animation: Pain, Pleasure and Punishment in Medieval Culture* (London: Reaktion, 2005).

Moorat, Samuel A.J., *Catalogue of Western Manuscripts on Medicine and Science in The Wellcome Historical Medical Library* (London: Wellcome Historical Medical Library, 1962), pp. 491-493.

Olsan, Lea, 'Wellcome MS. 632: Heavenly Protection During Childbirth in Late Medieval England', *Wellcome Library Blog* <http://blog.wellcomelibrary.org/2015/10/wellcome-ms-632-heavenly-protection-during-childbirth-in-late-medieval-england/> [accessed 1 December 2018].

Richards, Christina, Walter Pierre Bouman, and Meg-John Barker, 'Introduction', in *Genderqueer and Non-Binary Genders*, ed. by Christina Richards, Walter Pierre Bouman, and Meg-John Barker (London: Palgrave Macmillan, 2017), pp. 1-8.

Rudy, Kathryn M., 'Kissing Images, Unfurling Rolls, Measuring Wounds, Sewing Badges and Carrying Talismans: Considering Some Harley Manuscripts through the Physical Rituals They Reveal', *Electronic British Library Journal* (2011), 1-56. <https://www.bl.uk/eblj/2011articles/pdf/ebljarticle52011.pdf> [accessed 14 August 2020].

Sandler, Lucy Freeman, 'Jean Pucelle and the Lost Miniatures of the Belleville Breviary', *The Art Bulletin*, 66.1 (1984), 73-96.

Schleif, Corine, 'Christ Bared: Problems of Viewing and Problems of Exposing', in *The Meanings of Nudity in Medieval Art*, ed. by Sherry C. M. Lindquist (Farnham: Ashgate, 2012), pp. 251-278.

Spencer-Hall, Alicia, *Medieval Saints and Modern Screens: Divine Visions as Cinematic Experience* (Amsterdam: Amsterdam University, 2018).

Steinberg, Leo, *The Sexuality of Christ in Renaissance Art and Modern Oblivion*, 2nd edn., (London: University of Chicago, 1996).

Waller, Gary, *The Virgin Mary in Late Medieval and Early Modern English Literature and Popular Culture* (Cambridge: Cambridge University, 2011).

Whittington, Karl, 'Medieval' in 'Postposttranssexual: Terms for a 21st Century Transgender Studies', *TSQ: Transgender Studies Quarterly*, 1-2 (2014), 125-29.

About the author

SOPHIE SEXON is an AHRC-funded PhD researcher at the University of Glasgow (UK). Their thesis explores queer interpretations of Christ's wounds in late medieval imagery and contemporary extreme body art. Sophie is an active performer in the UK who frequently performs as a drag king under the pseudonym 'Boris Gay'. They have performed globally and enjoy mixing drag performance with academic presentations on how to identify genderqueer subjects across time.

6. Illuminating Queer Gender Identity in the Manuscripts of the *Vie de sainte Eufrosine*

Vanessa Wright

Abstract

This chapter analyses the visual representations of the *Vie de sainte Eufrosine* in three fourteenth-century Parisian manuscripts. It questions how two medieval artists, the Maubeuge Master and the *Fauvel* Master, approached illustrating the text's protagonist St Eufrosine/Esmarade, a figure assigned female at birth who lives most of their life as a eunuch in a monastic community. This chapter examines the artists' depiction of St Eufrosine/Esmarade in three manuscript miniatures, comparing how the artists used signifiers of gender and identity in their portrayals of the saint and other figures to reveal the extent to which the artists represented the saint's queer gender visually.

Keywords: genderqueer, *Vie de sainte Eufrosine*, manuscript illuminations, eunuch, Old French literature, medieval dress

The *Vie de sainte Eufrosine* is a thirteenth-century French verse hagiography of the saint whose preferred name was Esmarade. Composed around 1200, this *Life* introduces an individual whose gender identity does not conform to a binary model. Esmarade's queer gender is inextricably linked to their devotion to God as they leave secular society for a monastery in which they spend the rest of their life living as a eunuch. In their accompanying illuminations, the manuscripts of this *Life* offer hitherto relatively unexamined visual representations of the saint and their gender expression. This chapter considers Esmarade as a genderqueer saint, since they express an identity that does not fit into a binary understanding of gender. Unlike

---

Spencer-Hall, Alicia, and Blake Gutt (eds), *Trans and Genderqueer Subjects in Medieval Hagiography*. Amsterdam, Amsterdam University Press 2021
DOI: 10.5117/9789462988248_CH06

other similar texts, Esmarade does not make an explicit statement outlining their identified gender, and the gendered language used by both protagonist and narrator is inconsistent.[1] However, the saint does present themself to others as a eunuch. This could be seen as a way for them to articulate a non-binary, genderqueer identity. Consequently, this chapter uses they/them pronouns and the saint's preferred name, Esmarade, to recognize the saint's expression(s) of gender.

The *Life* of Eufrosine/Esmarade tells the story of a saint assigned female at birth who does not wish to marry the partner chosen by their father, preferring to retain their virginity.[2] After a brief stay at a monastery with their father Pasnutius, they realize they wish to enter the religious life. Esmarade seeks the guidance of several monks, who each advise the saint to reject marriage for God; one monk cuts their hair and gives them a nun's habit so that they can join a convent.[3] At this point, the monk names the saint Esmarade, an Old French gender-neutral name meaning 'Emerald', signalling their move from secular society to the religious life. Esmarade becomes concerned that if they join a convent, their father will be able to find them and force them into marriage. Esmarade therefore decides to enter a monastery presenting as a eunuch. Many of the monks are greatly affected by the saint's beauty, to the point that they request that Esmarade be removed, leading the abbot to place Esmarade in seclusion.[4] The saint's father comes to the monastery, distressed about the loss of his child, and the abbot recommends that the saint counsel him. This continues, without Pasnutius recognizing his child, for many years until Esmarade's death at the end of the narrative. Moments before death, the saint informs Pasnutius that they are his child, and asks that he alone prepare the body for burial and that he should ensure that no one else sees them posthumously.[5]

---

1   See, for example, *Life* of Margaret-Pelagia/Pelagien (Jacobus de Voragine, *La Légende dorée*, pp. 966-68).
2   Hill, *Vie*, pp. 191-223. All quotations of the Old French text are from this edition. Translations are the author's own. Any personal pronouns referring to Esmarade that are not supplied in the Old French will be translated as singular they/them and placed in square brackets.
3   Cutting or shaving hair was a part of the ritual of becoming a nun, showing their entry into the religious life (Milliken, *Ambiguous Locks*, p. 37.).
4   The narration explicitly states that the monks desire Esmarade as a eunuch; see Hill, *Vie*, pp. 205-206, ll. 566-78. This is important to note as some previous scholarship has interpreted the monks as being attracted to the saint's femininity. See, for example: Anson, 'Female Transvestite', p. 17.
5   Although Esmarade uses their given name and feminine gendered vocabulary when explaining matters to their father, I do not consider this a 'return' to their assigned gender, but rather it has a distinct purpose as it is used to show familial connection. The use of gendered vocabulary

Although the saint does not explicitly state why they wish this, it seems likely that it is to avoid their body being viewed by the monastic community, preventing them from 'discovering' Esmarade's assigned gender. Esmarade's request, however, is not followed: their body is prepared by another monk and, as a consequence, they are venerated as female both by their fellow monks and by the narrator.[6] After death, the saint performs a miracle by restoring a monk's sight.

The religious and gendered aspects of Esmarade's identity intersect: the saint's queer gender is explicitly linked to their religious identity. The connection is first introduced when the monk gives Esmarade the tonsure and a nun's habit. At this point, the text tells the reader that the saint has been given a new name: the monk 'changed [their] name; he called [them] Emerald. | This name is common to males and females'.[7] These lines inform the reader that the name Esmarade, which the saint retains for the rest of their life, is not associated with a binary gender. This name is given as soon as the saint leaves secular society for a life devoted to God. Emma Campbell suggests that the saint's spiritual marriage to God, which is marked by their name change, removes them from secular kinship and gender systems.[8] As a consequence, the saint is no longer limited by secular understandings of gender and is able to articulate a queer gender that is closely connected with their religious identity.

The saint's queer gender identity is further highlighted when, on introducing themself at the monastery, they state that they are a eunuch. Eunuchs were a notable part of late Roman and Byzantine society, and also existed in other global contexts, often holding secular positions of power as well as monastic and ecclesiastical roles.[9] Eunuchs were assigned male at birth, but if castration occurred before the onset of puberty the development of secondary sexual characteristics would be affected. For example, castration affected skeletal and muscular development and limited the growth of facial and body hair.[10] The social gender and gender identity

---

is different at the *Life*'s conclusion as the narrator and other characters use it to reinscribe Esmarade into their assigned, binary gender.

6   It is notable that, after death, Esmarade tends to be referred to as 'le cors' ('the body') rather than by name. 'Le cors' is used seven times in ll. 1130-259 (Hill, *Vie*, pp. 219-23), which run from the saint's death to the end of the *Life* (excluding the narrator's concluding address).

7   'Se nom li at cangié; Esmarade l'apele. | Cis nons est commuaz a marle et a femele' (Hill, *Vie*, p. 202, ll. 445-46).

8   *Medieval Saints' Lives*, pp. 99-100.

9   Tougher, *Eunuch*, pp. 8-11.

10   Ringrose, 'Shadows', p. 91.

of eunuchs have been the subject of much discussion, with Kathryn M. Ringrose proposing that, in certain social contexts, eunuchs in Byzantium could be considered a third gender.[11] Shaun Tougher argues that, although some contemporary sources support Ringrose's suggestion, later Roman and Byzantine understandings of eunuchs and gender were varied.[12] Consequently, we might consider the category of eunuch to constitute a non-binary or genderqueer identity, as the lives of these individuals reveal the limitations of a binary understanding of gender. In fact, in Byzantium, the male pole of the male-female binary was itself a binary, being split between eunuchs and 'bearded' (non-eunuch) men.[13] On arriving at the monastery, Esmarade presents themself as a eunuch: 'Porter, let me talk quickly to the abbot! | Say to him that you have left a eunuch at the door'.[14] This *Life*, by showing the AFAB saint declaring themself to be a eunuch, presents a genderqueer individual whose gender disrupts and challenges binary categories.[15]

The *Life* has received significant critical attention; scholars have examined Esmarade's gender expression as well as how the text presents sexuality, family, and other related subjects.[16] There has, however, been limited consideration of the visual representation of Esmarade in manuscript illuminations.[17] Despite the number of extant manuscript witnesses of Old French hagiographic collections, there is a similar paucity of scholarship concerning the depiction in manuscript miniatures of other saints assigned

11 Ibid., pp. 85-109; Tougher, *Eunuch*, pp. 109-11.
12 Tougher, *Eunuch*, p. 111.
13 See Szabo in this volume: pp. 109-29.
14 'Portier, fai moi parler vias a dant abé! | Dis li que a la porte as laissiét un castré' (Hill, *Vie*, p. 204, ll. 514-15).
15 Amy V. Ogden argues that the saint, in these lines and in other conversations with the abbot (*Hill*, Vie, p. 204, ll. 524-25), uses ambiguous phrasing and does not declare the eunuch identity explicitly. Ogden suggests that this allows them to express their queer gender without having to lie about their assigned sex (*Hagiography*, pp. 84-85). However, this chapter argues that by introducing themself to the monastery as a eunuch, whether indirectly or not, the saint establishes their genderqueer identity. For Ogden's latest research on this *Life*, including a reassessment of her earlier arguments, see pp. 201-21 in this volume. See also 'AFAB' in the Appendix: p. 286.
16 See, for example, Gaunt, 'Straight Minds'; Hotchkiss, *Clothes*, pp. 13-31; Ogden, *Hagiography*; Campbell, *Gift*, pp. 99-100 and 'Translating Gender'.
17 Ogden (*Hagiography*, pp. 48-51) provides detailed description and analysis of the text's manuscripts and their illuminations, and Emma Campbell also includes an examination of the manuscript miniatures in her 2019 article 'Translating Gender' (pp. 240-44); this chapter will offer interpretations of these manuscript miniatures focusing on their representation of a genderqueer saint.

female at birth who enter the religious life as monks.[18] Saisha Grayson, in a study of artistic representations of Sts Marina/Marin, Pelagia/Pelagien, and Eugenia/Eugenius, argues that these saints posed a challenge for medieval artists because they destabilize categories and signifiers, such as clothing, hairstyles, and symbols of status or profession, used to depict identity.[19] Grayson states that artists avoided 'picturing transvestism', by which she means showing the saint 'in disguise' or in transition; however, I argue that presenting the saint as a monk does not obscure this aspect of their Life, but rather privileges their identified gender.[20]

The Manuscript Context of the Vie de sainte Eufrosine

The *Life* is contained in four extant manuscripts, the oldest of these being Oxford, Bodleian Library, Canonici Miscellaneous 74. This codex dates from around 1200 and includes seven saints' *Lives*, but unlike the other three manuscripts, Canon. Misc. 74 does not include any accompanying illustrations.[21] This chapter therefore examines how artists depicted Esmarade's queer gender in these other three, closely connected, Parisian manuscripts. This chapter also compares the representation of the saint with other illustrations completed by the same artist within each volume and in other codices, to facilitate a greater understanding of how each artist approached the figure of Esmarade.

The three manuscripts which are the focus of this chapter are: Paris, Bibliothèque de l'Arsenal, MS 5204; Brussels, Bibliothèque royale de Belgique, MS 9229-30; and The Hague, Koninklijke Bibliotheek, MS71 A 24.[22] KB 71 A 24 and BRB 9229-30 share the same contents, but Arsenal 5204 differs

---

18   This group of saints includes Eufrosine/Esmarade, Marina/Marin, Pelagia/Pelagien, Margaret-Pelagia/Pelagien, Theodora/Theodore, and Eugenia/Eugenius. Old French versions of these lives can be found in Clugnet, 'Vie', pp. 288-300; Jacobus de Voragine, *La Légende dorée*. Martha Easton ('Transforming', pp. 333-47) and Saisha Grayson ('Disruptive Disguises', pp. 138-74) discuss the visual representation of these and other saints. For a discussion of saintly 'transvestism', and a critique of the latter term, see: Bychowski in this volume, 245-65, especially 245-53.
19   Grayson, 'Disruptive Disguises', pp. 139-40. Grayson conflates the saints Pelagia/Pelagien and Margaret-Pelagia/Pelagien, but these are two distinct saints and there are significant differences between their *Lives*.
20   Grayson, 'Disruptive Disguises', p. 144.
21   Ogden, *Hagiography*, p. 24.
22   These manuscripts will be referred to as Arsenal 5204, BRB 9229-30, and KB 71 A 24. Arsenal 5204 is fully digitized, and KB 71 A 24 is partially digitized with only the manuscript miniatures available online.

in three ways: it does not include the *Dit de l'unicorne*, found in both BRB 9229-30 and KB 71 A 24, and it contains an additional two items, *Les enfances nostre sire Jhesu Crist* and the *Complainte Nostre Dame*.[23] These manuscripts were all altered after completion when each had its first section, containing the *Vie des saints*, removed.[24]

It has been convincingly argued by Richard H. Rouse and Mary A. Rouse that all three manuscripts were produced by Thomas de Maubeuge, a *libraire* working in Paris in the early to mid-fourteenth century.[25] *Libraires* were lay professionals who coordinated the production of manuscripts, including hiring artists and scribes, but they may have additionally worked as copyists, flourishers, or artists themselves. Although Thomas de Maubeuge would have worked with a large network of scribes, artists, and pen flourishers, there were certain artisans whom he employed frequently. For example, artists like the Maubeuge Master, the *Fauvel* Master, and the Master of BnF fr. 160 regularly worked for this *libraire*, as did the scribe Jean de Senlis and the 'long-nose' scribe.[26]

From contemporary documentary evidence, Arsenal 5204 has been provisionally identified as a manuscript purchased in January 1328 by Mahaut, Countess of Artois.[27] Thomas de Maubeuge provided a receipt to the Countess at this time recording payment for a manuscript that contained a *Vie des Saints* and the *Miracles de Nostre Dame*.[28] This identification cannot be confirmed, however, because Arsenal 5204 does not contain any marks of ownership and the details on the receipt could relate to another

---

23   At the time of completion, BRB 9229-30 and KB 71 A 24 contained *La Vie des saints*, Gautier de Coinci's *Miracles de Nostre Dame*, *La Vie des pères*, *Le Dit de l'unicorne*, *La Vie de sainte Thais*, *La Vie de sainte Eufrosine*, *Les Quinze signes du jugement dernier*, and Huon le Roi de Cambrai's *Li regres Nostre Dame*. Arsenal 5204 contains in addition to the above *Les enfances nostre sire Jhesu Crist* and the *Complainte Nostre Dame* but lacks the *Dit de l'unicorne*. (Van den Gheyn, *Catalogue*, pp. 338-44; Rouse and Rouse, *Manuscripts*, I, 189-91.)

24   In at least two cases, these removed sections were rebound as separate codices. Paris, Bibliothèque nationale de France, MS fonds français 183 was originally bound with KB 71 A 24, and Bibliothèque royale de Belgique, MS 9225 with BRB 9229-30, but unfortunately the *Vie des saints* text from Arsenal 5204 has been lost (Rouse and Rouse, *Manuscripts*, I, 189-90).

25   Rouse and Rouse argue that at least two of these manuscripts were sold by Thomas de Maubeuge and, considering their similar size, date, and contents, it is likely that he produced all three (Rouse and Rouse, *Manuscripts*, I, 189). For more information on Thomas de Maubeuge and his customers, see: ibid., 173-83.

26   For information on the scribes and artists who worked for Thomas de Maubeuge, see: ibid., II, 182-86.

27   Ibid., I, 189.

28   Ibid.

codex.[29] Although it has been concluded that Thomas de Maubeuge did produce Arsenal 5204, and produced a manuscript very like it for Mahaut, there is no way to prove that these codices are one and the same.[30] Arsenal 5204 was copied by Jean de Senlis, and the miniatures were completed by the Maubeuge Master.[31]

It has been argued that BRB 9229-30, and its detached first volume BRB 9225, were foundation gifts for a Carthusian Charterhouse near Diest, in modern-day Belgium, which was established by Gérard of Diest and Jeanne of Flanders in 1328.[32] Although there is no written evidence to link these codices with a specific bookseller, their similarity to KB 71 A 24 and Arsenal 5204 would indicate that they were produced and sold by Thomas de Maubeuge.[33] The manuscript was copied by the 'long-nose' scribe but there has been some debate regarding the artist(s) who produced this manuscript. Rouse and Rouse identify the artist as the *Fauvel* Master.[34] Rouse and Rouse, with Marie-Thérèse Gousset, compiled a list of fifty-six manuscripts that were illuminated by the artist.[35] However, due to the significant differences in the quality of the illuminations, some have concluded that the *Fauvel* Master's supposed œuvre is in fact the work of multiple artists.[36] Alison Stones states that there were two artists – the *Fauvel* and the Sub-*Fauvel* Masters – and that the Sub-*Fauvel* Master completed a large proportion of the manuscripts usually attributed to the *Fauvel* Master, often producing work of a lower quality; Stones attributes BRB 9229-30 to the Sub-*Fauvel* Master.[37] However, Rouse and Rouse argue convincingly that the standard

---

29 The records of this purchase from Mahaut's household do not match Arsenal 5204 exactly: the records state that the manuscript included an *Apocalypse*. No such text is found in the manuscript, though this might be a reference to the *Quinze signes du jugement dernier*, which does figure in its contents. The record reads 'A mestre Thomas de Malbeuge libraire pour .i. Roumant contenant la vie des sains, lez miraclez Notre Dame, la vie des sains perres, et L'Apocaliste et pluisers autres hystoires [...].' ('To monsieur Thomas de Malbeuge, *libraire*, for a book containing the *Vie des saints*, the *Miracles de Nostre Dame*, the *Vie des pères*, and the *Apocalypse* and many other stories'). Rouse and Rouse, *Manuscripts*, II, 175.
30 Ibid., I, 197.
31 Ibid., II, 184.
32 Ibid., I, 195; Hogg, 'Carthusian General Chapter', p. 367.
33 Rouse and Rouse, *Manuscripts*, I, 194.
34 Ibid., II, 184; Stones, 'Stylistic Context', p. 529. This artist was named after Paris, Bibliothèque nationale de France, MS fonds français 146, which contains the *Roman de Fauvel*.
35 Rouse and Rouse, *Manuscripts*, II, 195-200.
36 Ibid., I, 208.
37 Stones, 'Stylistic Context', pp. 530-32, p. 558. Stones refers to the Master of BnF fr. 160 as the Master of BnF fr. 1453, but these are two designations for a single artist (Morrison and Hedeman, *Imagining the Past*, p. 144).

of the *Fauvel* Master's work could vary within the same codex, and suggest that changes in quality do not always indicate multiple artists but could result from changing practices or constraints.[38] It is a matter of continuing scholarly debate whether the corpus of work attributed to the *Fauvel* Master was completed by one or multiple artists; however, this chapter follows Rouse and Rouse in the understanding that the *Fauvel* Master was a single artist.

The *Fauvel* Master's work also appears in KB 71 A 24, which was owned by King Charles IV of France. As with the other manuscripts, the details of the commission are not entirely clear, but on 30 April 1327, King Charles IV paid Thomas de Maubeuge for a manuscript of saints' *Lives* and the *Miracles de Nostre Dame*.[39] In 1373, an inventory confirms that KB 71 A 24 was housed in the French royal library.[40] Like Arsenal 5204, KB 71 A 24 was copied by Jean de Senlis, who signed the manuscript on fol. 81v, but the other two hands identified in this codex cannot be assigned to specific scribes.[41] As with BRB 9229-30, the *Fauvel* Master was solely responsible for the manuscript's programme of illumination.

Representating St Esmarade

Each of the three versions of the *Vie de sainte Eufrosine* is accompanied by a single miniature, which appears at the start of the text. These images have several functions: not only do they help the reader to locate texts within the manuscript, but they also present the content of the narrative to the reader. As such these images set up the reader's expectations of the text, as well as informing their interpretation of the saint, the saint's behaviour, and the didactic purpose of the *Life*. An examination of these images quickly reveals that there was no standard way of portraying Esmarade.

The Maubeuge Master

On folio 87v of Arsenal 5204, the miniature immediately follows the rubric: 'Here begins [the Life] of St Euphrosyne who was a monk'.[42] This rubric, which also appears in BRB 9229-30 and KB 71 A 24, foregrounds

38 Rouse and Rouse, *Manuscripts*, I, 210.
39 Ibid., I, 188.
40 Delisle, *Recherches*, II, 148; Rouse and Rouse, *Manuscripts*, I, 194.
41 Jean le Senlis copied quires 10 to 24 of KB 71 A 24 (Rouse and Rouse, *Manuscripts*, II, 183).
42 'Ci endroit coumence | De sainte euphrosyne | Qui fu moinnes' (fol. 87v).

Figure 6.1

Paris, Bibliothèque de l'Arsenal, MS 5204, fol. 87v.

Esmarade's monastic identity to the reader and signals the saint's gender non-conformance through the juxtaposition of their given name and the grammatically feminine 'sainte' with the masculine status of 'monk'.[43] The miniature does not depict a specific episode, but rather focuses the viewer's attention on the saint themself. Esmarade is presented against a gold background, standing to the left of a white building (Fig. 6.1). This building, based on its architectural style and the content of the *Life*, represents the monastery in which Esmarade lived. The saint wears a black monastic habit but is not tonsured. The figure faces to the right as if looking upon the monastery. Their left hand is open and gestures towards the monastery whilst the right holds a red book, which, alongside their clothing and position in the frame, serves as a visual signifier of the saint's monastic identity.

43   The rubric in BRB 9229-30 is found in the lower margin of fol. 61v whereas the Life starts around halfway down the first column after the miniature. In KB 71 A 24, the rubric is found in the first of the three columns of text, immediately before the miniature; the text itself begins after the miniature.

By presenting Esmarade without a tonsure, the Maubeuge Master marks them as different from the other religious and clerical figures found in this codex. Although this miniature does not include any other figures with whom we could compare the saint, the manuscript features many representations of monks, priests, and clerics, who are all shown in typical garb befitting their role. The rubrics that accompany these miniatures often identify the social role of the individual, but the images themselves also differentiate social groups by dress and other signifiers. Monks, priests, and clerics are all presented tonsured and wearing long monastic habits in mostly neutral colours. There is variety in how the hair of these figures is depicted. Clerics and priests are mostly presented with longer, curling hair to the jawline whereas, in the majority of cases, monks are depicted with a band of short hair above the ears, with no curls – but all are tonsured. Robert Mills notes that the tonsure was considered a sign of access to God as it was a visual signifier of clerical status.[44] Therefore, despite the rubric that states that Esmarade 'fu moinnes' ('was a monk'), the Maubeuge Master has explicitly differentiated the saint from cisgender male religious or clerical figures through the artist's choice of hair style or head covering.

Instead of a tonsure, the artist depicts Esmarade with what either could be shoulder-length hair or a head covering. Although the lines of paint could suggest strands of hair, a close examination of the miniatures in this manuscript reveals that, whilst cisgender male figures are often shown with longer hair, or with short hair curling back from the forehead, no one is shown with long, uncovered hair in the style shown in this miniature. It is therefore more likely that the artist decided to present Esmarade with their hair covered, and it is important to consider how this affects the representation of the saint.[45] Having compared the miniature to the seven portrayals of nuns and abbesses in this codex, it is clear that the artist has not chosen to represent Esmarade as a female religious, as the veils worn by nuns are different in shape, style and colour.[46] There are many instances of laywomen wearing headdresses; most wear their hair up, covered by a green headdress, but there are examples of individuals who wear a green headdress along with a white head covering. However, it is the Virgin Mary's head covering which most closely resembles that worn by Esmarade. The

---

44   Mills, 'Tonsure', pp. 111-13. Mills notes that although nuns were also required to cut their hair on entering a convent, their heads were then covered by the veil.
45   This is also supported by Campbell's analysis of the image: 'Translating Gender', p. 240.
46   These figures are found on fols. 48v, 54r, 56r, 72v, 124r, 140v, and 170r.

Virgin Mary is one of the most frequently depicted figures in this manuscript and her appearance is generally consistent throughout: she wears a long orange robe with a blue cloak, and her hair is covered by a white head covering – the folds of the fabric being clearly visible – and a crown.[47] By presenting Esmarade in a similar head covering, the artist associates them visually with the Virgin Mary but also with St Thais, whose *Life* immediately precedes that of Esmarade.[48]

Thais' *Life* (fols. 78r-87v) is illustrated by three miniatures, in which Thais, similarly to the Virgin Mary, wears a blue gown and orange cloak, with a white head covering. In aligning Esmarade with these saintly figures, the Maubeuge Master highlights the saint's holiness, but by presenting Esmarade using the visual signifier of the head covering, the saint is associated with their assigned gender. In using iconography related to the Virgin Mary and St Thais, as well as monastic and clerical figures, the Maubeuge Master renders visible the rubric's juxtaposition of 'sainte' ('[female] saint') and 'moinnes' ('monk'). Although this illumination includes a feminine signifier, this does not mean that assigned gender is foregrounded and the saint's queer gender is obscured entirely from view. Instead, it is through combining the typically feminine and masculine signifiers of the head covering and monastic dress that the artist is able to signal that the saint's identified gender is outside of the gender binary.

The Fauvel Master

The *Fauvel* Master completed two miniatures of Esmarade, in BRB 9229-30 (Fig. 6.2) and KB 71 A 24 (Fig. 6.3). These images present different episodes from the narrative. There are similarities in the artist's approach to these miniatures, and in the programmes of illumination in the manuscripts more generally; for example, the *Fauvel* Master makes frequent use of architectural motifs in these images and others. The most important similarity between the representations of Esmarade is that each image depicts the saint's relationship with their fellow monks. Rather than depicting the saint as a solitary figure, as occurs in Arsenal 5204, the *Fauvel* Master portrays Esmarade as part of a monastic community.

---

47   The Virgin Mary is represented in 42 of 161 miniatures contained in this manuscript.
48   St Thais' *Life* recounts that Thais was a rich, beautiful woman who, with the help of a hermit, rejected her past life and sins. After burning her clothing and possessions, she was imprisoned in penance and prayer.

Figure 6.2

Brussels, Bibliothèque royale de Belgique, MS 9229-30, fol. 61v.

In BRB 9229-30, the miniature that accompanies the *Life* of Esmarade is composed of two registers showing different scenes from the narrative (Fig. 6.2). The left-hand register illustrates a group of four monks. The second figure from the left (possibly representing the abbot) and the monk on the right, who represents Esmarade, sit in the foreground and are positioned facing towards each other. This placement and their hand gestures indicate that they are in conversation. This does not accurately reflect the narrative as Esmarade, after entering the monastery, is almost immediately placed in seclusion, but this scene functions to highlight the saint's integration into the monastic life and identity. All four are tonsured and wear monastic dress, with the monks on the extreme left and right having their heads covered. The only visual difference between them is that three of the four monks are bearded. The beardless figure, who sits on the right, has some slight damage to the lower half of their face: the line of the nose is smeared and there is a small mark where the mouth should be, but the figure's jawline and beardlessness have not been obscured. It is unlikely that this erasure was intentional or caused by readers because the damage appears to have

Figure 6.3

The Hague, Koninklijke Bibliotheek, MS 71 A 24, fol. 61v.

occurred before the paint had fully dried.[49] A lack of facial hair, which was a common visual signifier of eunuch identity, is used by the *Fauvel* Master here to distinguish the saint from the other monks, and it also serves to highlight their genderqueer identity.[50] Although one could argue that the lack of facial hair was used by the artist to present the saint as female, an examination of the right register of this miniature suggests that this is not the case. In the right register, the saint is depicted with long hair without the tonsure which serves, as will be discussed later, to illustrate the monks' discovery of the saint's assigned sex.[51] Considering that the *Fauvel* Master

---

49   Similar damage is found in the right-hand register, depicting the saint after death where the black outline of the pillow and the facial features of the monk standing to the right are also smeared.
50   Tougher, *Eunuch*, pp. 112-14.
51   Long, loose hair was typically associated with women, and had multiple symbolic meanings: it could be interpreted as a symbol of beauty, virginity, and youth, but also of unrestrained sexuality (Milliken, *Ambiguous Locks*, pp. 171-77). See Easton, 'Transforming' for more on representations on hair and gender in hagiography.

uses hair to portray the saint's assigned gender in the right register, it seems unlikely that they would not use hair to the same representative end within the same illumination. Consequently, as Esmarade is depicted with the monastic tonsure and beardless, we can understand this lack of facial hair to depict the saint as a eunuch.

The right-hand register shows the saint's death scene: Esmarade's body is laid out on a bed, behind which stand three monks. Although the saint is in the foreground, greater emphasis is placed on the monks and their reactions to the saint, which are revealed through their gestures.[52] The monk to the right gestures towards the saint's body, and the monk to the left-hand side holds his hands up, palms open, in a gesture of surprise. The gestures of the monk in the centre are noteworthy as, although he looks towards the right-hand monk, he points to the left: not towards the saint's dead body, but to the left-hand register and the figure of Esmarade. This links the two registers together and indicates to the viewer that the supine figure shown is that of the beardless monk from the other scene. Another significant element of this miniature is the additional figures painted into the architectural framework above the two registers. These three bearded figures gaze down at the scene, with the figure in the centre appearing to hold up the miniature's frame with both hands. These onlookers are both internal and external to the image, and their positioning and facial expressions serve to direct the reader's attention. The left and central figures look towards the left register as if watching the discussion between Esmarade and their fellow monks. Consequently, they emphasize this aspect of the miniature and the saint's life to the reader. The right-hand figure plays a slightly different role as they look out of the image at the reader: in doing so, their direct gaze challenges the viewer to interpret and respond to the scene displayed below.

Although the saint remains fully clothed after death, there is a change to their physical appearance. Whilst they appear with a tonsure in the left register, in the right register their hair, although covered, is longer and sweeps to either side from a central parting. Ogden argues that the representation of the saint in each register portrays the monks' perspective; the artist illustrates how the monastic community perceives Esmarade's gender at different points in the narrative.[53] The addition of longer hair therefore demonstrates that, after learning of the saint's assigned sex, they view the saint as a woman. However, we could equally argue that the artist makes

---

52 Ogden, *Hagiography*, p. 51.
53 Ibid., p. 49.

these changes to reflect the understanding of the narrator: the narrator also returns to identifying Esmarade as female by using the saint's given name as well as grammatically feminine agreements, pronouns, and other markers.[54]

In considering the change in hairstyle between the two registers, it is worth comparing this depiction of Esmarade to other illuminations by the same artist. The *Fauvel* Master portrays Esmarade with the longer hairstyle again in their representation of Esmarade in KB 71 A 24 (Fig. 6.3): the saint wears secular clothing associated with their assigned gender and has long, loose hair that falls from a centre parting. This hairstyle is also found elsewhere in KB 71 A 24: the Virgin Mary is presented with a similar hairstyle, for example, on fol. 13v. When illuminating a manuscript of the *Legenda aurea* (Munich, Bayerische Staatsbibliothek München, MS CLM 10177), the *Fauvel* Master presents the *Life* of St Pelagia/Pelagien in a similar way to Esmarade in BRB 9229-30 (Fig. 6.4).[55] Both of these scenes are set out in similar ways, with, in Figure 4, the saint, whose preferred name was Pelagien, being shown on their deathbed surrounded by monastic figures but significantly they are portrayed with long, uncovered hair.[56] From an analysis of hairstyles used in this manuscript, and others, it is clear that the *Fauvel* Master frequently used this hairstyle to represent individuals assigned female at birth. Consequently, in using this hairstyle for Esmarade and Pelagien, the artist privileges assigned over identified gender.

In each register of the miniature of Esmarade in BRB 9229-30, the *Fauvel* Master offers a different depiction of the saint. In both images, their monastic identity is stressed not only by their dress, but also through their interactions with the monastic community. Their position as a eunuch is reflected in the left-hand register, but this genderqueer expression is not found in the right-hand register, in which the saint's assigned gender is presented instead. In this way, the image accurately reflects as well as reinforces the narrative as Esmarade's genderqueer identity is shown during their life in the monastery, before being eventually obscured after death. After this

---

54 For example, in the narrator's concluding address, Hill, *Vie*, ll. 1260-79 (p. 223).

55 Busby, *Codex*, I, 33; II, 716. The *Life* states that the AFAB saint was converted to Christianity after leading a luxurious, worldly life. The saint refused the devil's attempts to tempt them and decided to leave Antioch to live as a (male) hermit; they gained renown under the name Pelagien. After their death, a visiting priest discovered the saint's assigned sex while preparing the body for burial. (Jacobus de Voragine, *La Légende dorée*, pp. 963-66.)

56 The *Fauvel* Master appears to have painted many scenes in this way, which suggests that they had a template for representing deathbed scenes as similar images; for example, a miniature on fol. 42v of KB 71 A 24 shows a monk lying on a bed being cured by the Virgin Mary, with four other monks standing behind their bed. Although this monk is presented as ill, rather than dead, the resemblance between the three images is evident.

Figure 6.4

Munich, Bayerische Staatsbibliothek München, MS Clm 10177, fol. 373v.

point, the saint's gender identity is reinscribed by their father and monastic community, their genderqueer identity is ignored, and they are celebrated as female. This therefore leads to the erasure, or at least minimization, of the saint's non-normative gender identity and expression.

The miniature of Esmarade in KB 71 A 24 offers a different perspective from those previously discussed. Over half of the miniature is taken up by the monastery and the pair of monks who stand in its doorway (Fig. 6.3). The two monastic figures are shown tonsured and wearing black/brown habits. One of the monks remains in the doorway whilst the other steps out towards the saint, who is depicted on the left. Esmarade stands with their head inclined and hands together in prayer as the first monk dresses them in a habit. The saint's move from a secular to religious identity is marked by the exchange of a light pink robe with dark blue sleeves for a habit. This pink and blue robe appears in thirteen other miniatures in this manuscript.[57] In each of these cases it is worn by cisgender laywomen, both married and

57 On fols. 43v, 53r, 61v, 79r, 88v, 93v, 112v, 121r, 127r, 160r, 168r, 176r, and 180r.

unmarried, which thus emphasizes both Esmarade's move from a secular to a religious identity, and a change in their gender expression.[58] As discussed earlier, the saint's hair is worn long and loose.

It is possible that the miniature in KB 71 A 24 illustrates not the saint's entry into the monastery, but rather their earlier decision to join a convent. At this point in the narrative, a monk advises Esmarade to avoid marriage, and to dedicate their life to God instead. The monk addresses the question of lay clothing directly, stating: '"It is necessary for you to change your secular clothing"'.[59] It is arranged for someone to come and help the saint cut their hair, and to provide clothing suitable for a nun. The clothing scene is described as follows: 'The clothing was prepared, the shears were brought; | [They] had themself tonsured and clothed in the manner of a nun'.[60] The narrative stresses the monk's involvement in this process, commenting that he tonsured and blessed the saint. The miniature could therefore reflect this scene, especially considering the monk's active role in dressing the saint. However, a similar scene takes place when Esmarade joins the monastery: the abbot gives the saint the tonsure and dresses them in their monastic habit. It is possible that this is a conflation of the two scenes but, given the space taken up in the miniature by the monastery building, it seems more likely that this image was intended to represent the later scene.[61] If this is the case, it is important to note that the illustration does not accurately reflect the events of the narrative, in which Esmarade changes from their nun's habit to clothing typical of a nobleman, and approaches the monastery presenting as a eunuch. Ogden argues that, by not showing Esmarade putting on secular male dress, this scene minimizes the saint's queer gender and focuses instead on them being given monastic dress by a religious authority.[62] Although the *Fauvel* Master does not depict the saint as a noble eunuch, they do present Esmarade in the process of transition. By illustrating the saint putting on monastic clothing, the artist foregrounds the moment when, on entering the monastery, Esmarade is able to fully articulate their queer gender and religious identity. However, by portraying the saint using clothing and

---

58 The Virgin Mary is shown wearing this robe on fol. 43v, which is different from her usual attire in this codex. Given the relative consistency with which she is depicted elsewhere in the codex, I do not consider this garment to be typical of the Virgin Mary.
59 'Ton abit seculer toi covient a cangier' (Hill, *Vie*, p. 199, l. 329).
60 'Les dras ot aprestez, les forces fait venir; | A guise de nonain se fait tondre et vestir' (ibid., p. 202, ll. 437-38).
61 Campbell also suggests that the habit Esmarade is given by the monks may be a conflation of the nun's and monk's habits that the saint receives in the text ('Translating Gender', p. 240).
62 Ogden, *Hagiography*, p. 50.

visual signifiers associated with their assigned gender, the artist obscures Esmarade's identification as a eunuch; consequently, this miniature does not fully represent their gender identity. This image has significance in a wider context because it is one of the few examples in which the process of transition is represented visually, with most manuscript illuminations presenting the saint either in their assigned gender or after transition.[63]

There has been some damage to the saint's face meaning that we can no longer see their facial features and expression. The rest of the miniature, including the monks' faces, remains intact, which indicates that one or more readers paid specific attention to this portrayal of Esmarade. Unlike in the miniature from BRB 9229-30, this damage occurred after the illustration was complete. However, it is not clear whether the damage is the result of intentional erasure, or the result of readers touching the saint's face, which, over time, would have removed the paint. Kathryn Rudy suggests that kissing and touching of manuscripts and images were part of individual devotional practices and provides many examples of such behaviour and its effects.[64] No other miniatures in this codex display this kind of erasure, suggesting that at least one of the readers had a strong response, be it one of acceptance, rejection, or another type of reaction, to this *Life* or this representation. The reader's intervention is likely to have affected, and will continue to affect, later readers in their reading and understanding of the saint. The erasure may have drawn later reader's attention to the miniature and the figure of the saint specifically, causing them to spend more time examining and interpreting the image as well comparing its portrayal to the narrative.

It is relevant to consider why the *Fauvel* Master represented different scenes in these two versions of Esmarade's *Life*. We should remember that artists would produce large numbers of illuminations, and it is unlikely that they would be able to recreate images at a later date without using templates or having an exemplar to follow.[65] Another factor that might affect representation was the type of instruction provided. Artists would not necessarily have a detailed knowledge of the texts; rather, they generally worked from instructions or the rubrics to create interpretations. Rouse and Rouse note that some instructions to artists have survived in these

---

63 Another example is discussed by Mills (*Seeing Sodomy*, pp. 200-208), Grayson ('Disruptive Disguises', pp. 144; 155-65), and Ambrose ('Two Cases', pp. 8-11): a sculpture of St Eugenia/Eugenius at a monastic church in Vézelay in which the saint, in monastic dress, is presented at the moment at which they are required to bear their breasts to prove their innocence of rape. Mills (*Seeing Sodomy*, p. 204) interprets this sculpture as reflecting a moment of transition.
64 Rudy, 'Kissing Images'.
65 Rouse and Rouse, *Manuscripts*, I, 201.

manuscripts, generally written in plummet in the lower margins.[66] Such notes are often difficult to read as they have been partially erased or worn over time, but can be seen on fols. 197r and 152r of Arsenal 5204; fols. 127r and 158r of KB 71 A 24; and on fols. 5r and 32v of BRB 9229-30.[67] It is not generally possible to identify the hand in which such notes are written; it could be that of the artist, the *libraire* or other people involved in the codex's production. If these instructions were given by the *libraire*, it is possible that they reflect the interests of or requests from the commissioner. The *libraire* may have had the commissioners in mind and adapted any instructions accordingly. BRB 9229-30 was first owned by a group of Carthusians whereas KB 71 A 24 was owned by Charles IV of France. This may explain why the illumination in BRB 9229-30 focuses on the saint as part of a monastic community; however, this remains speculation as no marginal instructions related to Esmarade's *Life* are visible in any of the three manuscripts.

Conclusion

To conclude, our extensive knowledge surrounding the production of Arsenal 5204, BRB 9229-30, and KB 71 A 24, and the artists who worked on them, provides a rare opportunity to analyse representations of a single figure across multiple codices. The Maubeuge and *Fauvel* Masters illuminated a significant number of manuscripts, meaning that it is possible to compare iconographic details across their work to uncover patterns of representation. Their depictions of Esmarade, although different in style, size, and design, share some significant features. Most importantly, each miniature highlights the saint's religious identity and the important role of the monastery in their *Life*. The images completed by the *Fauvel* Master in particular emphasize the saint's engagement with the monastic community and integration into the religious life. Although their religious identity is highlighted by each artist, Esmarade's queer gender expression and eunuch identity are illustrated less consistently. Nevertheless, their non-normative gender is at no point entirely ignored or obscured from view. The visual signifiers of gender and social position chosen by the Maubeuge and *Fauvel* Masters, and the combinations in which they are used, reveal how these artists approached expressions of gender that challenged binary understandings and categories. Whereas much scholarship has been centred on literary

66   Ibid., I, 200.
67   Ibid.

portrayals of genderqueer and transgender saints, attention to manuscript illumination and production provides valuable additional insight into understandings and representations of non-normative gender, genderqueer identities, and their expression in late medieval culture.

Acknowledgments

I would like to thank Blake Gutt, Alicia Spencer-Hall, and Charles Whalley for their comments on an earlier version of this chapter. Support for a research trip to consult the manuscripts was provided by the Society for the Study of Medieval Languages and Literature and the Royal Historical Society.

Bibliography

Manuscripts

Brussels, Bibliothèque royale de Belgique, MS 9225.
Brussels, Bibliothèque royale de Belgique, MS 9229-30.
Munich, Bayerische Staatsbibliothek München, MS Clm 10177.
Oxford, Bodleian Library, MS Canonici Miscellaneous 74.
Paris, Bibliothèque de l'Arsenal, MS 5204.
The Hague, Koninklijke Bibliotheek, MS 71 A 24.

Primary sources

Clugnet, Léon, ed., 'Vie de Sainte Marine', *Revue de L'Orient Chrétien*, 8 (1903), 288-300.
Hill, Raymond T., ed., '*La Vie de Sainte Euphrosine*', *The Romantic Review*, 10.3 (1919), 191-223.
Jacobus de Voragine, *La Légende dorée*, ed. by Jean Batallier and Brenda Dunn-Lardeau, trans. by Jean de Vignay (Paris: Champion, 1997).

Secondary sources

Ambrose, Kirk, 'Two Cases of Female Cross-Undressing in Medieval Art and Literature', *Source: Notes in the History of Art*, 23.3 (2004), 7-14.
Anson, John, 'The Female Transvestite in Early Monasticism: The Origin and Development of a Motif', *Viator*, 5 (1975), 1-35.

Busby, Keith, *Codex and Context*, 2 vols. (Amsterdam: Rodopi, 2002).
Campbell, Emma, *Medieval Saints' Lives: The Gift, Kinship and Community in Old French Hagiography* (Cambridge: Brewer, 2008).
—, 'Translating Gender in Thirteenth-Century French Cross-Dressing Narratives: *La Vie de Sainte Euphrosine* and *Le Roman de Silence*', *Journal of Medieval and Early Modern Studies*, 49.2 (2019), 233-64.
Delisle, Léopold, *Recherches sur la libraire de Charles V*, 2 vols. (Paris: Champion, 1907), II.
Easton, Martha, '"Why Can't a Woman Be More like a Man?" Transforming and Transcending Gender in the Lives of Female Saints', in *The Four Modes of Seeing: Approaches to Medieval Imagery in Honor of Madeline Harrison Caviness*, ed. by Evelyn Staudinger Lane, Elizabeth Carson Pastan, and Ellen M. Shortell (Farnham: Ashgate, 2009), pp. 333-47.
Gaunt, Simon, 'Straight Minds/"Queer" Wishes in Old French Hagiography: *La Vie de Sainte Euphrosine*', *GLQ*, 1.4 (1995), 439-57.
van den Gheyn, J., *Catalogue des manuscripts de la Bibliothèque royale de belgique*, 10 vols. (Brussels: Henri Lamertin, 1905), V.
Grayson, Saisha, 'Disruptive Disguises: The Problem of Transvestite Saints for Medieval Art, Identity, and Identification', *Medieval Feminist Forum*, 45 (2009), 138-74.
Hogg, James, 'The Carthusian General Chapter and the Charterhouse of Diest', *Studia Cartusiana*, 1 (2012), 345-70.
Hotchkiss, Valerie, *Clothes Make the Man: Female Cross-Dressing in Medieval Europe* (New York: Garland, 1996).
Milliken, Roberta, *Ambiguous Locks: An Iconology of Hair in Medieval Art and Literature* (Jefferson: McFarland, 2012).
Mills, Robert, *Seeing Sodomy in the Middle Ages* (Chicago: University of Chicago, 2015).
—, 'The Signification of the Tonsure', in *Holiness and Masculinity in the Middle Ages*, ed. by P. H. Cullum and Katherine J. Lewis (Cardiff: University of Wales, 2005), pp. 109-26.
Morrison, Elizabeth, and Anne D. Hedeman, *Imagining the Past in France: History in Manuscript Painting, 1250-1500* (Los Angeles: J. Paul Getty Museum, 2010).
Ogden, Amy V., *Hagiography, Romance, and the Vie de Sainte Eufrosine* (Princeton: Edward C. Armstrong, 2003).
Ringrose, Kathryn M., 'Living in the Shadows: Eunuchs and Gender in Byzantium', in *Third Sex, Third Gender: Beyond Sexual Dimorphism in Culture and History*, ed. by Gilbert H. Herdt (New York: Zone, 1996), pp. 85-109.
Rouse, Richard H., and Mary A. Rouse, *Manuscripts and Their Makers: Commercial Book Producers in Medieval Paris, 1200-1500*, 2 vols. (Turnhout: Miller, 2000).

Rudy, Kathryn M., 'Kissing Images, Unfurling Rolls, Measuring Wounds, Sewing Badges and Carrying Talismans: Considering Some Harley Manuscripts through the Physical Rituals They Reveal', *The Electronic British Library Journal*, 2011 <http://www.bl.uk/eblj/2011articles/articles.html> [accessed 25 February 2017].

Stones, Alison, 'The Stylistic Context of the Roman de Fauvel, with a Note on *Fauvain*', in *Fauvel Studies: Allegory, Chronicle, Music, and Image in Paris, Bibliothèque Nationale de France, MS Français 146*, ed. by Margaret Bent and Andrew Wathey (Oxford: Clarendon, 1997), pp. 529-67.

Tougher, Shaun, *The Eunuch in Byzantine History and Society* (New York: Routledge, 2008).

About the author

VANESSA WRIGHT holds a PhD in Medieval Studies from the Institute for Medieval Studies at the University of Leeds (UK). Her research focusses on gender in medieval French literature, literary engagement with canon law, and medieval book culture. She is the co-editor of the special issue of *Medieval Feminist Forum*, 'New Approaches to Medieval Romance, Materiality, and Gender' (forthcoming).

7 The Queerly Departed

Narratives of Veneration in the Burials of Late Iron Age Scandinavia

Lee Colwill

Abstract
This chapter explores four remarkable burials in Late Iron Age Scandinavia, looking beyond the static scene uncovered at the point of excavation to the funerary processes that created the sites. The majority of the graves discussed here have been associated with the magico-religious practice of *seiðr*; the chapter therefore also explores the evidence for connecting this practice with transgressive gender performances, taking into account the problematic literary evidence as well as the difficulty in interpreting the archaeological material. Based on an analysis of these burials, the chapter argues that an approach to gender archaeology which moves beyond assumptions of a fixed binary inherent to the physical body can only enrich our understanding of the past.

Keywords: gender archaeology, Late Iron Age Scandinavia, mortuary archaeology, *seiðr*

Appropriation of the medieval period – and especially the history of pre-Christian Scandinavia – for white supremacist ends is well attested.[1] Modern völkisch groups (nationalist and ethnocentric Norse neo-pagans) have also used their own idealized views of the early history of Scandinavia to justify cis- and heteronormative approaches to gender roles in the modern day.[2]

---

1 See, for example, the inclusion of Thor's hammer and the 'valknut' (a set of three interlocking triangles of uncertain meaning seen on some of the Gotlandic picture stones) on lists of hate symbols (Anti-Defamation League, 'Database').
2 Southern Poverty Law Center, 'Neo-Volkisch'.

Spencer-Hall, Alicia, and Blake Gutt (eds), *Trans and Genderqueer Subjects in Medieval Hagiography*. Amsterdam, Amsterdam University Press 2021
DOI: 10.5117/9789462988248_CH07

Ideas about white supremacy and gender essentialism often go hand-in-hand. One way of disrupting this paradigm is to emphasize the ways in which gender in pre-Christian Scandinavia was far queerer (in all senses of the word) than the traditional narrative acknowledges.

This chapter seeks to challenge the ahistorical idea, still widespread in the popular imagination, that Late Iron Age Scandinavia – the area of modern-day Denmark, Norway and Sweden, in approximately the eighth to the tenth century CE – was a homogenous place where white men lived lives defined by hypermasculine aggression, white women were confined to the domestic sphere, and queer people and people of colour were nowhere to be seen. In recent decades, a number of scholars have attempted to counteract this view, exploring, among other topics, the construction of race in Icelandic sagas, the potential for queer readings of Norse mythology, and the varied forms of masculinity and femininity seen in the written sources.[3]

Focusing on the question of how gender was negotiated in the Late Iron Age, this chapter draws on evidence from four burials from across continental Scandinavia, dated to the ninth and tenth centuries. Burials can be interpreted as narratives of veneration, with the procedures of the funerary rite forming a 'text' that can be read.[4] It is in this context that the ship burials at Oseberg and Kaupang, the chamber grave Bj. 581 at Birka, and the cremations at Klinta are discussed. The sites explored here have been chosen in part because their complexity lends itself well to this kind of interpretation, but also because their comparatively good preservation and detailed documentation make it possible to conduct in-depth analysis in a way that is not often the case with Scandinavian burials. All of these graves raise questions about the applicability of a strict gender binary to the communities which produced them. In particular, individuals from the majority of these graves have been connected with the practice of *seiðr*, a form of magic which, it is often argued, involved transgressive gender performances as part of its rituals.

---

[3] On race in the sagas see Cole, 'Racial Thinking'; Heng, *Invention of Race*. On the queerness of Norse cosmology see Mayburd, 'Reassessment'; Normann, 'Woman or Warrior?'; Solli, *Seid*; and 'Queering the Cosmology of the Vikings'. On masculinities and femininities see Bandlien, *Man or Monster?*; Evans, *Men and Masculinities*; Jóhanna Katrín Friðriksdóttir, *Women*; Phelpstead, 'Hair Today'.

[4] On archaeological remains as a meaningful text that can be interpreted, see, for example, Hodder and Hutson, *Reading the Past*; Hodder, 'Not an Article'; Patrik, 'Record?'.

Transgender archaeology

The past gains meaning for modern interpreters through its connections to the present. This chapter therefore uses the terms 'transgender' and 'genderqueer' in their modern senses to refer to individuals who today would likely be perceived as belonging to these categories.[5] This is not to say that all such figures would have recognized themselves, or been recognized by their communities, as crossing from one gender category to another. Rather, our understanding of gender roles in the Late Iron Age may require significant revision in the light of recent discoveries such as the genomic sexing of Birka grave Bj. 581, a 'warrior' grave previously assumed to be that of a man, whose occupant proved to have XX chromosomes.[6] This example is a particularly well-publicized one, but is far from the only case where identities read into grave goods seem incongruous with identities read into the sexed body.[7] In such cases, a transgender reading is one possibility, though seldom the one adopted.

Archaeological sexing is far from a fail-safe tool, particularly for exploring the often-intangible concept of identities. Remains are sexed osteologically (by examining the size and shape of the bones) or on the basis of genomic analysis ('genomic' or 'chromosomal sexing'), and assigned to a particular sex, most frequently a binary male/female one, on this basis. The inaccuracy of such an approach has been criticized by numerous gender archaeologists for its frequent disregard of the possibility of intersex remains, not to mention its essentialist focus on the physical body over social identity.[8] Moreover, it is virtually impossible to accurately assign sex to children and adolescents based on osteological sexing alone, calling into further doubt the value of dividing remains into strict binary categories to begin with. Genomic sexing is likewise not the magic bullet it is often presented as, offering a ratio of X and Y chromosomes from which a chromosomal arrangement

---

5   Transgender: adjective referring to someone whose gender identity differs from the gender they were assigned at birth. Genderqueer: adjective describing an experience of gender outside the male/female binary. See the entries for 'Trans(gender)' (pp. 316-17) and 'Genderqueer' (p. 299) in the Appendix.
6   Hedenstierna-Jonson et al., 'Female Viking Warrior'.
7   Several such examples (from outside the period and region under discussion here) are explored in Weismantel ('Transgender Archaeology') and Joyce (*Ancient Bodies*), both of which make a strong case for the validity of transgender readings of the past, and the possibilities such approaches offer for expanding our understanding in the present.
8   See Ghisleni, Jordan, and Fioccoprile, 'Introduction'; Joyce, *Ancient Bodies*; Nordbladh and Yates, 'Perfect Body'; Weismantel, 'Transgender Archaeology'.

is extrapolated. As Skoglund et al. point out, chromosomal arrangements other than XY and XX are difficult to detect by this method.[9]

Throughout this chapter, the term 'sex' is used in reference to the characteristics of the physical body that Western medicine has deemed to be either 'male' or 'female'. Given that questions of internal identity can only ever be speculative when it comes to burials, 'gender' here is used in the sense of 'social gender' – a role produced in social contexts, requiring both performance and interpretation.[10]

Mortuary narratives

Burials are not static; rather, what is excavated are the remains of the 'final scene' in a lengthy process which draws together many actors – human, animal and object – in order to stage the drama of the funerary ritual.[11] As a general rule, items found in graves did not arrive there by chance, but were chosen and arranged for a reason by those who buried the deceased. Though it is impossible to be sure what motivations lay behind any given burial, the intentionality of funerary practices makes them a form of narrative through which to approach the mentalities of the society which created them. As Howard Williams has noted, the burial process creates a time and space in which identities are in flux as the living determine how they will remember the dead.[12] Actions taken during the funeral can therefore cement certain identities while obscuring others. Moreover, the objects in play during these rituals are not merely passive things to be acted upon; rather, they work in dialogue with human actors in much the same way as has been argued for oral and written narratives, to express and negotiate identities and ideologies.[13] It is this context that grave goods should be interpreted.

The best-documented graves from pre-Christian Scandinavia are frequently those of high-status individuals. This is due to the nature of find preservation: an unmarked grave consisting only of organic material subject to decay is much more difficult to trace a thousand years later than an

---

9   Skoglund et al., 'Accurate Sex Identification', pp. 4479-80.
10 'Social gender' as a concept overlaps somewhat with Butler's description of gender as an iterative performance (*Gender Trouble*, p. 177), but owes a greater debt to the multifaceted model of gender presented by Serano (*Whipping Girl*, p. xvi).
11 Price, 'Passing into Poetry', pp. 123-56; Williams and Sayer, 'Death and Identity', p. 3.
12 Williams, *Death and Memory*, p. 4.
13 The importance of recognizing non-human agency in the archaeological record has been argued by, among others, Latour (*Reassembling the Social*, p. 16).

elaborate burial in a mound with plenty of metal grave goods. Burials of slaves and children are therefore only known in this period in Scandinavia from their inclusion in multiple-person graves.[14] The burials discussed below all fall into the category of high-status burials, and the majority of their occupants seem to have been figures of religious significance. Their funerary procedures therefore form a type of hagiographic narrative: a text of veneration, testifying to their singular status and the respect – sometimes tinged with fear – that they were accorded as a result.

When it comes to exploring gender identity through grave goods, it is difficult to avoid the sort of circular reasoning which declares, for example: 'oval brooches are items of female dress, so graves containing them must be women's graves; we know oval brooches are items of female dress because we find them in women's graves'. A partial solution to the problem is offered by increasingly accurate methods of osteological sexing, although, as noted above, such methods are often inadequate when it comes to recognizing intersex remains. However, when gender is decoupled from sex, as many archaeologists argue it should be in order to more fully understand past societies, approaches that rely on the physical body do not suffice.[15] Here the idea of normative domains can be useful: if we have grave goods which, in the vast majority of cases, are found with remains of one particular osteological sex, it is reasonable to conclude that this society associated these items with a particular gender – and that they viewed this gender as largely linked to the sexed body. Unfortunately, when it comes to material from the Iron Age, many graves excavated in the nineteenth and early twentieth centuries have only been 'sexed' on the basis of grave goods, rather than through osteological analysis, making it extremely difficult to build an accurate picture of which grave goods should be associated with a given sex.[16]

As the recent results from the Birka chamber grave Bj. 581 show, this sort of grave good-based 'sexing' is far from sound. Bj. 581 was initially sexed as male when it was excavated in the late nineteenth century on the grounds that the burial was a typical 'warrior' grave, complete with a full set of weapons.[17] However, genomic sexing of the remains revealed

---

14 See Price, 'Dying and the Dead', p. 259, for a discussion of underrepresented population groups in the Scandinavian burial record.
15 Joyce, *Ancient Bodies*; Sørensen, *Gender Archaeology*, pp. 54-59; Weismantel, 'Transgender Archaeology'.
16 Moen, 'Gendered Landscape', p. 10; Stylegar, 'Kaupang Cemeteries', p. 83.
17 Arbman, *Birka*, p. 188.

that the person buried in Bj. 581 almost certainly had XX chromosomes.[18] Given the poor preservation of human remains in Scandinavian burials, and the relative newness of the technology to perform genomic sexing, very few graves have been sexed in this way, and it is therefore impossible to say how many more graves may have similar 'incongruities' between grave goods and remains.

Seiðr: A queer sort of magic?

As three of the graves discussed below have been interpreted as those of *seiðr* practitioners, it is worth pausing here to give a brief overview of what is meant by the term *seiðr*. In written sources from medieval Scandinavia, all of which significantly post-date the region's conversion to Christianity, this word is used to mean 'magic', frequently in a pejorative sense, and is often found in accounts of magic performed in Scandinavia before the Conversion. There are only a handful of detailed accounts of what *seiðr* might have involved. The most in-depth of these are *Ynglinga saga* (The Saga of the Ynglings), an account of the legendary kings of Scandinavian pre-history, and *Eiríks saga rauða* (The Saga of Eirik the Red), which features an episode of magic and counter-magic in the Norse settlement in Greenland. Both of these accounts present *seiðr* practitioners as occupying respected positions in society, with the Odin of *Ynglinga saga* presented as a human warrior, ruler, and powerful sorcerer, while Thorbjorg 'little-witch' in *Eiríks saga* is the possessor of many fine objects, treated as an honoured guest wherever she visits. However, both sagas evince a certain amount of discomfort with these figures' magical practices. When Thorbjorg requests the assistance of a woman who knows chants conducive to her magic, the only such woman present tells her that she is unwilling to take part because she is a good Christian.[19] In *Ynglinga saga*, the author's distaste for *seiðr* is more apparent. Here, Odin's magical talents include the malicious ability to cause sickness and madness in men. We are then told that *seiðr* was taught to Odin by Freyja (usually considered a goddess, but here called a 'blótgyðja' [sacrificial priestess]) and that the practice 'brought with it so much perversity that it was thought shameful for men to practise it'.[20] This does not appear to

---

18   Hedenstierna-Jonson et al., 'Female Viking Warrior', p. 857.
19   Einar Ól. Sveinsson and Matthías Þórðarson, *Eyrbyggja Saga*, pp. 206-09.
20   'Fylgir svá mikil ergi, at eigi þótti karlmǫnnum skammlaust við at fara'. Bjarni Aðalbjarnarson, *Heimskringla*, p. 19.

have dissuaded Odin, and other sources attest to his *seiðr*-working. In the mythological poem *Lokasenna* (Loki's Flyting), for example, the troublesome god Loki accuses Odin of having performed magic chants and 'beaten a drum like a witch [...] and that I thought a mark of perversity'.[21]

Since all written accounts of *seiðr* date from several centuries after Scandinavia's conversion to Christianity, their relationship to any historical reality of magico-religious practices is highly debatable.[22] In the *Ynglinga saga* account of Odin's shapeshifting and use of companion animals, such as the two ravens who bring him news, scholars have seen a connection to shamanic practices of the circumpolar region, such as those documented by eighteenth- and nineteenth-century ethnographers among the Saami and the native peoples of Siberia. Clive Tolley's comparative study of shamanic traditions and the Norse written material concludes that, though there may be shamanic elements in the later accounts of *seiðr*, there is insufficient evidence to interpret the pre-Christian practice as a shamanic one.[23] However, a number of archaeologists point to the presence of objects such as the cannabis seeds and rattles found in the Oseberg ship burial as evidence that ritual practitioners of the Late Iron Age sought to induce shamanic trances.[24] One outcome of this association between *seiðr* and shamanism has been the interpretation of *seiðr* as an intrinsically queer practice, drawing (unfortunately, often unnuanced) parallels with indigenous American gender systems to posit the idea of a 'third gender' for *seiðr* practitioners.[25]

While the inherent queerness of *seiðr* has been overstated, its portrayal in later written sources, combined with evidence from the archaeological record, does suggest that at least some of its practitioners inhabited a gender outside of a male/female binary. This has often been conceptualized by scholars as a practitioner gaining power for the duration of a *seiðr* ritual by 'transgressing' binary gender categories, though Miriam Mayburd has argued that power was instead gained through more continuous occupation of a liminal gender position.[26] Though later written narratives treat the practice of *seiðr* as despicable for its association with improper gendered behaviour, this does not accord with the archaeological record. The graves of those

---

21   '[D]raptu á vétt sem vǫlur [...] ok hugða ek þat args aðal'. Jónas Kristjánsson and Vésteinn Ólason, *Eddukvæði*, p. 413.
22   Tolley, *Shamanism*, pp. 487-88.
23   Ibid., pp. 581-89.
24   See, for example, Price, *Viking Way*, pp. 205-06; Solli, *Seid*, pp. 159-62.
25   Such interpretations tend to take a somewhat simplistic approach to gender, often conflating it with sexuality. See especially Solli, *Seid*, pp. 151-52. See 'Two-spirit' in the Appendix: p. 324.
26   Mayburd, 'Reassessment', p. 148.

suspected to be *seiðr* practitioners are often highly elaborate, deliberately emphasizing their inhabitants' magical prowess, rather than seeking to hide it as a shameful secret. The written sources thus appear to demonstrate an attempt by writers in a Christian context to reconcile their understanding of their forebears' magico-religious practices with changing ideas about acceptable gender performance. It is therefore probable that *seiðr* in the Iron Age *did* involve some sort of queer gender performance, not necessarily practised by all *seiðr* specialists, and perhaps only performed as part of short-term rituals in other cases, but nonetheless sufficiently present to be memorialized as part of the mortuary process.

The queerly departed

Oseberg ship burial, Vestfold, Norway (c. 834)

Death is a profound moment of change for those who knew the deceased. In this time of flux, the rituals of the funeral help to structure the ways in which the surviving community remembers the deceased. One example of mortuary behaviour as an ongoing process rather than a single, self-contained action can be seen in the ship burial from Oseberg, in the Vestfold region of Norway. This spectacular monument consisted of a ship, 21.6m in length, with a tent-like chamber on its deck in which two bodies were placed, surrounded by a huge variety of grave goods. On the foredeck, wooden items seem to have been heaped somewhat haphazardly, accompanied by a large number of animal sacrifices.[27] The ship was then enclosed in a turf mound. These arrangements were made around 834 CE, based on dendrochronological analysis of the burial chamber.

The grandeur of the burial originally led it to be identified as that of a queen, perhaps the legendary Queen Ása, mentioned in *Ynglinga saga* as ruling part of southern Norway in the ninth century. However, more recent studies of the grave have rejected this identification. Instead, it is generally accepted that this is the grave of at least one magic-worker, and perhaps two. This interpretation is based on the presence of a number of items in the grave, perhaps most obviously a wooden rod or staff of the kind often associated with *seiðr*.[28] The fact that this was accompanied by cannabis

---

27 Price, 'Passing into Poetry', pp. 135, 139.
28 Price, *Viking Way*, p. 206. Leszek Gardeła notes the similarity of many of these rods to distaffs; those made of iron would have been too heavy for use in spinning but are plausibly

seeds, potentially used to induce a trance-like state, and metal rattles, which may have played a part in the ritual performance of *seiðr*, suggests that the community at Oseberg wished to remember these people as ritual specialists.[29] This view is also supported by the fragments of tapestry which survive from the burial, which show figures in long robes, some with the heads of animals, apparently directing human sacrifice.

Considering the sense of supernatural significance evoked by this burial, the time it took to create is particularly relevant to the narrative underlying the grave. There has been considerable debate on this matter, with some archaeologists arguing that the differences between the fore and aft halves of the mound indicate that the aft half of the ship was covered first, while the foredeck, along with access to the burial chamber, was left exposed for many months, or even years.[30] Terje Gansum argues that this would have allowed the local community to continue to visit their dead.[31] This idea is supported by the 'anchoring' of the ship to a large rock as part of the burial process, suggesting that, despite their burial on a means of transportation, it was hoped that these two people would continue to be a presence in their community after death. However, evocative as this interpretation is, Sæbjørg Walaker Nordeide's re-examination of the original excavation reports concludes that this supposed visitation period could not have taken place, as all botanical evidence from the turf, as well as the contents of the sacrificial animals' stomachs, points to the entire construction taking place in autumn.[32]

Even proponents of the idea of a months-long ritual acknowledge that when the time came to seal up the burial, this was done with almost unseemly haste. In contrast to the careful construction of the ship itself, the entry to the central chamber was boarded up with mismatched pieces of wood, in some cases hammered in with such rapidity that the nails broke and were left in the wood.[33] Moreover, the offerings on the foredeck seem to have been piled up in a careless fashion, with no effort made to protect the more delicate items from the heavier ones thrown on top. This stands in sharp contrast to the level of care and respect needed to offer up a spectacular ship, numerous animals, and many rare and valuable items,

---

skeuomorphic representations of distaffs ((*Magic*) *Staffs*, pp. 176-84).

29   Price, *Viking Way*, p. 160.
30   Gansum, *Hauger som Konstruksjoner*, pp. 172-74; Price, 'Passing into Poetry', pp. 138-39.
31   Gansum, *Hauger som Konstruksjoner*, p. 174.
32   Holmboe, 'Oseberghaugens torv', p. 205; Holmboe, 'Nytteplanter', pp. 3-80; Nordeide, 'Death in Abundance', p. 12.
33   Price, 'Passing into Poetry', p. 139.

not to mention the investment of time and labour needed to construct a mound to cover a 21.6 m ship. The rock the Oseberg ship was anchored to also takes on a more ambiguous meaning: did the people who constructed the burial want to keep these two individuals in the community, or did they more specifically want to ensure that they remained *inside the mound*? The speed with which the bodies were sealed away under multiple layers of wood and turf points towards the latter.

The sumptuous components of the burial set against the hasty, almost slapdash actions taken apparently as the conclusion of the initial funerary rites tells a narrative of both veneration and fear. At Oseberg, we see both a deliberate deconstruction of the natural order and a breaking down of categories: a hill raised by human hands; a ship on land, tethered and immobile; two figures whose dead bodies command both immense respect and terrible fear. The narrative told here is therefore not one of straightforward admiration, but rather of the powerful mix of emotions that can come from interaction with the supernatural.

I have so far avoided gendering the two people interred at Oseberg because it is my contention that the older of these individuals could plausibly be read as transgender, in modern terms at least. Although the recovered remains are incomplete, both skeletons have been osteologically sexed as female. From his examination of the older individual's remains, the osteologist Per Holck has suggested that this person may have had Morgagni-Stewart-Morel syndrome.[34] This syndrome is characterized in skeletal remains by a thickening of the front of the skull, and can result in more body hair – including facial hair – and a deeper voice than is typical for cis women. It is therefore possible that this person was not perceived as a woman by the society in which they lived, and that their social gender was male, or a gender not recognized under a modern Western binary. Such an interpretation may also help to explain the apparently 'masculine' grave goods present in the burial, such as the harness mounts and belt fittings, which Fedir Androshchuk has interpreted as evidence for a man's body being removed during the 'break-in' that occurred soon after the construction of the mound.[35] As discussed above, the practice of *seiðr* could have involved the negotiation of trans identities, either lifelong, or temporally limited

---

34 Holck, *Skjelettene*, p. 60.
35 Androshchuk, 'En Man', pp. 124-6, although see above for caveats regarding the gendering of grave goods. The break-in has been dated to the late tenth century based on the remnants of a wooden spade found abandoned in the grave. Many valuable items were left untouched, but the bodies were disturbed; it has been argued that this was a deliberate, if delayed, part of the funeral. See Bill and Daly, 'Plundering', pp. 808-24.

in a ritual framework. This, combined with the archaeological evidence, suggests that in the Oseberg burial we are seeing mortuary practices which acknowledge and memorialize a transgender life.

Kaupang boat burial, Vestfold, Norway (ninth to tenth centuries)

The Kaupang boat burial Ka. 294-296 (the numbers refer to the adult bodies in this burial), also from the Vestfold area, is another example of the funeral process as an ongoing narrative. Here the site extends from the ninth century into the tenth, with the first interment being that of a single man (though it should be noted that most identifications at Kaupang have been made on the basis of grave goods, rather than through osteological sexing) buried there in the ninth century.[36] In the following century, a ship was placed on the same site, with its keel aligned with the body underneath. Such an arrangement speaks to the power of memorialization through burial: the original resting place was clearly still alive in the memory of the local community after a considerable period of time, perhaps even after those present at the original funeral were themselves dead, although the dating is too imprecise to be certain of this.[37] The tenth-century boat burial contains the bodies of what appears to be a small family: an adult woman at the prow with the remains of an infant laid to rest in her lap, and a man's body placed in the middle of the boat with his head close to that of the woman. These three individuals were surrounded by a range of grave goods, including silver arm rings, several axes, a sword, and multiple shield bosses. It is the fourth person in the group, however, an individual buried in the stern of the boat, that carries most significance for the present discussion.

Judging by the position of two oval brooches associated with this person, they were buried seated at the steering oar, separated from the other bodies in the grave by the body of a horse. Frans-Arne Stylegar has argued that this person should therefore be viewed as a ritual specialist, given the task of guiding the others in the burial to the afterlife.[38] In support of this interpretation is the suggestive positioning of the body: placed in the same burial, but deliberately marked out as separate; connected to the family, but not a part of it. Then there is the position at the steering oar. Unlike the Oseberg ship, the boat at Kaupang was not anchored, lending weight to the idea that, although entombed in earth, it was expected to journey

---

36 Stylegar, 'Kaupang Cemeteries', p. 82.
37 Ibid., p. 95.
38 Ibid., p. 99.

elsewhere on a course set by the person in charge of the steering oar. In addition to this, Neil Price has pointed out that although seated burial is not particularly common in Scandinavian cemeteries, it does occur with relatively high frequency in the graves he identifies as those of potential *seiðr* practitioners.[39]

Further evidence comes from the assemblage of grave goods associated with this fourth person, which included a number of unusual items. Perhaps the most obvious of these is an iron staff with a 'basket handle'. Price identifies staffs of this type as being indicative of the graves of *seiðr* workers, and Leszek Gardeła concurs that 'its placement under a stone strongly suggests that it may have been used in magic practices'.[40] The twisted prongs of its 'handle' together with its symbolic crushing under a stone suggest the ritual 'killing' enacted on other metal objects (especially weapons) in the Iron Age, but also recall the treatment of a woman – also frequently identified as a *seiðr* practitioner – buried at Gerdrup in Denmark, whose body was pinioned under a large rock.[41] As with the Oseberg ship, this is a funeral narrative which combines respect and fear.

Evidence for a transgender reading of this burial is less pronounced than at Oseberg. Nevertheless, there are several indicators that this person occupied a highly unusual social position and therefore may have been perceived as being so utterly outside the norms of society that conventional gender identities did not apply. As discussed above, this seems to have been a distinct possibility for *seiðr* practitioners. In addition to this person's probable role as a *seiðr* specialist, several other items in the grave help to create a narrative that tells of a social identity beyond the binary. One of these is the person's outfit. Though the find of two oval brooches suggests conventional female attire, fragments of animal hide preserved by proximity to the metal of the brooches point to a highly unusual leather costume, perhaps reminiscent of the strange array of catskin and lambskin worn by Thorbjorg, the female *seiðr* practitioner seen in *Eiríks saga rauða*.

The separation of the body from the rest of the burial by the body of a horse leaves little doubt that the axe head and shield boss found in the stern should be connected with the figure seated there, rather than with the adult man placed in the middle of the boat. Women's

---

39 Price, *Viking Way*, pp. 127-40. It should be noted that Price's examples come from the Birka cemeteries, where a number of graves apparently unconnected with *seiðr* workers also feature seated burial (e.g. Bj. 581, discussed below).
40 Gardeła, *(Magic) Staffs*, p. 312; Price, *Viking Way*, p. 203.
41 Gardeła, 'Buried with Honour', p. 342; and *(Magic) Staffs*, p. 217.

graves containing axes are not common, though they are also hardly unknown.[42] However, the inclusion of a shield boss (presumably once a whole shield, with the wooden part rotted away) is more unusual; such armaments are virtually unknown in female graves. In combination, these two items and the peculiar leather outfit suggest that this burial was deliberately designed to evoke a sense of this person inhabiting a social role outside that of conventional femininity. Other burials in the Kaupang cemetery feature similar objects to those found with the seated figure, but in these other burials, object types in the male and female burials have almost no overlap.[43] This lack of overlap suggests that the community who created this grave made a conscious effort to construct distinct memorial narratives for the man and woman buried in Ka. 294-295, perhaps divided down gendered lines. In light of this, then, the presence of oval brooches, metal rods and an iron sword beater (all also found with Ka. 294, the woman in the prow) in combination with an axe head and shield boss (also found with Ka. 295, the man amidships) argues in favour of a memorial narrative for this *seiðr* practitioner that incorporated elements of masculinity and femininity, but which was also in some ways outside both.[44]

Klinta double cremation, Öland, Sweden (tenth century)

Another grave combining material culture conventionally associated with both masculine and feminine identities is the Klinta double cremation, 59:2 and 59:3, from the island of Öland, off the south-east coast of Sweden. These have been dated to the early tenth century.[45] Once again, the level of care that went into this grave represents a significant investment of time and resources from the local community. Again, we see that the funerary process was a long one, consisting of several clear stages, each one contributing to fix the memory of these individuals in the minds of the participants. The two people cremated at Klinta were burnt together, along with a number of

---

42 See Gardeła, 'Warrior Women', pp. 273-339 for a survey of Scandinavian women's graves with weapons – although, as Gardeła points out, a number of the graves he discusses were gendered through their grave goods, rather than through any osteological sexing, raising further doubts about what precisely makes these 'women's' graves.

43 See Stylegar, 'Kaupang Cemeteries', pp. 122-23, for a complete survey of the finds from this burial.

44 Gardeła argues that these objects represent an ability to cross gender lines rather than exist outside them: 'Warrior Women', p. 290.

45 Price, *Viking Way*, p. 142.

grave goods, on a boat overlaid with bearskins that doubled as their pyre.[46] Once the flames had died, the human remains were washed and placed into separate small pottery containers, each placed in its own grave-pit and surrounded by an array of objects. The act of washing was presumably not a perfunctory hosing-down of the remains, but instead a careful and intimate process, bringing the living into direct physical contact with the dead.

The two cremations appear to deliberately blur the boundaries between the two individuals, whose remains have been osteologically sexed as being those of a man (59:2) and a woman (59:3). This is most apparent in the distribution of grave goods between each grave-pit, where items not conventionally associated with the sexed remains are present in each. In the male grave (59:2), these include a single oval brooch, a bone needle, and sixteen beads.[47] In the female grave (59:3), these consist of an axe head – described by Price as a 'battle-axe' – and an iron tool for woodworking.[48] Early interpretations of the graves concluded that this was an accident, but as Price argues, none of these items are small enough, nor badly damaged enough, to have escaped notice during what was clearly a carefully orchestrated process of separating the pyre into two graves.[49] Moreover, if the oval brooch found in 59:2 really was intended for 59:3 instead, this would suggest that the latter grave was meant to contain three oval brooches, in itself unusual for an object usually worn in pairs.

The ceramic pot in 59:3, which contained mostly female remains, also contained a small quantity of male remains, presumably those also found in 59:2. Though this has usually been interpreted as an accidental result of the two bodies being burnt together, in light of the 'mixing' of graves seen here, it was potentially a deliberate outcome, further mingling these two people in death. In contrast to 59:3, the remains in 59:2 were present in much smaller quantities, which Price argues suggests that the man only needed representing at the grave in a symbolic fashion.[50] Rather than viewing these burials as riddled with mistakes – an interpretation that does not do much credit to people at whose depths of ritual knowledge we can only guess – I concur with Price that what we are seeing here is the careful construction of ambiguous gender symbolism in both of these graves.[51]

46 Petersson, 'Ett Gravfynd', pp. 139-41.
47 Beads are not unknown in other male graves, however. For example, Ka. 295, the man in the Kaupang boat burial discussed above, was also buried with a number of beads.
48 Price, *Viking Way*, p. 144.
49 Petersson, 'Ett Gravfynd', p. 139; Price, *Viking Way*, p. 149.
50 Price, *Viking Way*, p. 147.
51 Ibid.

Birka chamber grave, Björkö, Sweden (tenth century)

From the above, it is tempting to conclude that only those deemed supernaturally 'other' in some way were able to live transgender or genderqueer lives during the Late Iron Age. However, the tenth-century chamber grave Bj. 581, from the trading site of Birka, provides a counterexample, showing no signs of being the grave of a *seiðr* practitioner, but nonetheless plausibly being the burial of an individual whose social identity was atypical for their sex. This grave lay near the building often called Birka's 'garrison', which saw violent combat at least once in its life, when it was destroyed by attackers in the late tenth century.[52]

In addition to its connection with this military building, Bj. 581 is a prototypical 'warrior' grave, complete with an array of weapons and riding equipment, even down to the bodies of two horses. Such graves have consistently been gendered as male by excavators, usually in the absence of osteological sexing. This makes it difficult to say how heavily gendered a warrior social identity really was – and by 'warrior social identity', I mean that the role of 'warrior' was not just a job title, but also a social rank, one that could be held by people who were not involved in combat on a regular basis. Such an interpretation is supported by the large number of 'warrior' graves whose occupants do not ever appear to have suffered a severe injury, as well as evidence from early medieval England, where very young children were accorded 'warrior' burials, compete with weapons they could never have wielded in life.[53] A true picture of the gender balance among 'warriors' of this period would require far more extensive osteological or genomic sexing of the remains in weapons-graves than has thus far been carried out, and would still leave the problem that sexed remains cannot tell us anything about an individual's gender.

Holger Arbman's report on the material from Bj. 581, the first published work on the grave, confidently declares its occupant to be a man – one of few occasions where this is explicitly noted in his accounts – and subsequent researchers working on the Birka material have largely followed his lead.[54] However, over the years several osteologists have raised doubts about the sexing of the bones from Bj. 581, and in 2017 a team of researchers genomically tested the remains and discovered that the deceased almost certainly had XX

---

52 Hedenstierna-Jonson, 'Birka Warrior', p. 69.
53 Härke, 'Warrior Graves?', pp. 22-43; Pedersen, *Dead Warriors*, p. 240.
54 Arbman, *Birka*, p. 188; Gräslund, *Birka*, pp. 10-11.

chromosomes.[55] Though the media – and indeed the researchers themselves – were quick to label this individual a 'female warrior' and connect them with the shieldmaiden figures popular in later literature, the obvious point should be made that chromosomal analysis cannot tell us anything about a person's social gender.[56] Indeed, without an understanding of gender which recognizes trans identities, advancements in sexing techniques such as those used on the Birka grave run the risk of reinforcing essentialist ideas of the physical body as ultimate arbiter of identity, obscuring the potential complexity of lived experiences in the Iron Age.

There has been considerable debate over the meaning of the so-called 'warrior' graves at Birka, but it seems likely, given the violent destruction of Birka's garrison building, that the person buried in Bj. 581 did have experience using weapons similar to those with which they were buried. Yet the gendering of the warrior role remains in doubt. As noted above, so few graves have been osteologically sexed, as opposed to having gender assigned based on grave goods, that it is impossible to derive a meaningful picture of the assigned-sex-based distribution of weapons in graves, let alone the implications of this for our understanding of Late Iron Age Scandinavian social gender. However, at our current state of knowledge, unambiguous weapons (as opposed to knives and axes, which have non-combat uses) are vanishingly rare in 'female' graves in Scandinavia.[57] In the absence of a fuller re-examination of weapons-graves across Scandinavia, such objects can be plausibly interpreted as part of a funerary narrative that sought to construct an image of masculine social identity, an identity which, as in the case of Bj. 581, was not always in alignment with modern, binary sexing of the body.

Conclusion

The archaeological material from Iron Age Scandinavia is perhaps most notable for its complexity and diversity. Though individual elements may recur, such as the basket-handled staffs in the *seiðr* graves discussed above, it is always in combination with new motifs. As such, no two burials are identical in the stories they tell and the way in which they tell them. In the examples given above, humans, animals and objects interact to create

---

55 Hedenstierna-Jonson et al., 'Female Viking Warrior', pp. 855, 857.
56 On this, see Price et al., 'Viking Warrior Women?', p. 191.
57 Gardeła, 'Warrior Women', p. 300.

narratives, both of the funerary proceedings themselves, and of the surviving community's memory of the deceased. A deliberate result of these actions was the creation of physical monuments, often on a large scale, which served as a visual trigger for memories of these narratives embedded in the landscape. The narratives presented by the burials discussed here share a common feature: the evocation of a gender system that was more complicated than a simple male/female binary, reliant on anatomy. Our understanding of this system is still limited by the nature of the evidence, which is often fragmentary and subject to a variety of interpretations. In many cases, we are still working within the constraints laid down by archaeologists of the nineteenth century. It is only by bringing a wider range of perspectives to bear on the matter, including approaches which take account of trans identities, that we can begin to overcome the limitations of a binary approach. In this way, we can appreciate more clearly the complexity of gender in the Iron Age, and begin to understand gender in this historical moment – as well as in our own – with greater contextual insight.

Bibliography

Primary sources

Bjarni Aðalbjarnarson, ed., *Heimskringla*, 3 vols., Íslenzk Fornrit, 26-28 (Reykjavik: Hið íslenzka fornritafélag, 1941-1951), I.

Einar Ól. Sveinsson and Matthías Þórðarson, eds., *Eyrbyggja Saga. Grœnlendinga Sǫgur*, Íslenzk Fornrit, 4 (Reykjavik: Hið íslenzka fornritafélag, 1935).

Jónas Kristjánsson and Vésteinn Ólason, eds., *Eddukvæði*, 2 vols., Íslenzk Fornrit (Reykjavik: Hið íslenzka fornritafélag, 2014), I.

Secondary sources

Androshchuk, Fedir, 'En Man i Osebergsgraven?', *Fornvännen*, 100 (2005), 115-28.

Anti-Defamation League, 'Hate on Display™ Hate Symbols Database', <https://www.adl.org/hatesymbolsdatabase> [accessed 10 July 2019].

Arbman, Holger, *Birka. Untersuchungen und Studien. I. Die Gräber. Text* (Uppsala: Almqvist & Wiksell, 1943).

Bandlien, Bjørn, *Man or Monster? Negotiations of Masculinity in Old Norse Society* (Oslo: Faculty of Humanities, University of Oslo, 2005).

Bill, Jan, and Aoife Daly, 'The Plundering of the Ship Graves from Oseberg and Gokstad: An Example of Power Politics?', *Antiquity*, 86.333 (2012), 808-24.

Brink, Stefan, 'How Uniform Was the Old Norse Religion?', in *Learning and Understanding in the Old Norse World: Essays in Honour of Margaret Clunies Ross*, ed. by Judy Quinn, Kate Heslop, and Tarrin Wills (Turnhout: Brepols, 2007), pp. 105-36.

Butler, Judith, *Gender Trouble: Feminism and the Subversion of Identity* (London: Routledge, 1990).

Cole, Richard, 'Racial Thinking in Old Norse Literature: The Case of the *Blámaðr*', *Saga-Book* 39 (2015), 5-24.

Evans, Gareth Lloyd, *Men and Masculinities in the Sagas of Icelanders* (Oxford: Oxford University, 2019).

Gansum, Terje, *Hauger som Konstruksjoner: Arkeologie forventninger gjennom 200 År* (Göteborg: Department of Archaeology, Göteborg University, 2004).

Gardeła, Leszek, 'Buried with Honour and Stoned to Death? The Ambivalence of Viking Age Magic in the Light of Archaeology', *Analecta Archaeologica Ressoviensia*, 4 (2009), 339-75.

—, '"Warrior-Women" in Viking Age Scandinavia? A Preliminary Archaeological Study', *Analecta Archaeologica Ressoviensia*, 8 (2013), 273-339.

—, *(Magic) Staffs in the Viking Age* (Vienna: Fassbaender, 2016).

Ghisleni, Lara, Alexis M. Jordan, and Emily Fioccoprile, 'Introduction to "Binary Binds": Deconstructing Sex and Gender Dichotomies in Archaeological Practice', *Journal of Archaeological Method and Theory*, 23 (2016), 765-87.

Gräslund, Anne-Sofie, *Birka. Untersuchungen und Studien. IV. The Burial Customs* (Stockholm: Almqvist & Wiksell, 1980).

Härke, Heinrich, 'Warrior Graves? The Background of the Anglo-Saxon Weapon Burial Rite', *Past and Present*, 126 (1990), 22-43.

Hedenstierna-Jonson, Charlotte, 'The Birka Warrior: The Material Culture of a Martial Society' (unpublished doctoral thesis, Stockholm University, 2006).

Hedenstierna-Jonson, Charlotte, Anna Kjellström, Thorun Zachrisson, Maja Krzewińska, Veronica Sobrado, Neil Price, Torsten Günther, Mattias Jakobsson, Anders Götherström, and Jan Storå, 'A Female Viking Warrior Confirmed by Genomics', *American Journal of Physical Anthropology*, 164.4 (2017), 853-60.

Heng, Geraldine, *The Invention of Race in the European Middle Ages* (Cambridge: Cambridge University, 2018).

Hodder, Ian. 'This is Not an Article about Material Culture as Text.' *Journal of Anthropological Archaeology*, 8.3 (1989), 250-69.

Hodder, Ian, and Scott Hutson, *Reading the Past: Current Approaches to Interpretation in Archaeology*, 3rd edn (Cambridge: Cambridge University, 2003).

Holck, Per, *Skjelettene fra Gokstad- og Osebergskipet* (Oslo: University of Oslo, 2009).

Holmboe, Jens, 'Nytteplanter og Ugræs i Osebergfundet', in *Osebergfundet*, ed. by A.W. Brøgger and Haakon Shetelig, 5 vols. (Oslo: Universitetets Oldsaksamling, 1927), V, 3-80.

—, 'Oseberghaugens Torv', in *Osebergfundet*, ed. by A.W. Brøgger, Hj. Falk, and Haakon Shetelig, 5 vols. (Oslo: Universitetets Oldsaksamling, 1917), I, 201-05.

Jóhanna Katrín Friðriksdóttir, *Women in Old Norse Literature: Bodies, Words, and Power*, New Middle Ages (New York: Palgrave Macmillan, 2013).

Joyce, Rosemary A., *Ancient Bodies, Ancient Lives: Sex, Gender, and Archaeology* (New York: Thames & Hudson, 2008).

Latour, Bruno, *Reassembling the Social: An Introduction to Actor-Network Theory* (New York: Oxford University, 2007).

Mayburd, Miriam, '"Helzt þóttumk nú heima í millim...": A Reassessment of Hervör in Light of *Seiðr*'s Supernatural Gender Dynamics', *Arkiv för Nordisk Filologi*, 129 (2014), 121-64.

Moen, Marianne, 'The Gendered Landscape. A Discussion on Gender, Status and Power Expressed in the Viking Age Mortuary Landscape' (unpublished master's thesis, University of Oslo, 2010).

Nordbladh, Jarl, and Timothy Yates, 'This Perfect Body, This Virgin Text', in *Archaeology After Structuralism: Post-Structuralism and the Practice of Archaeology*, ed. by Ian Bapty and Timothy Yates (London: Routledge, 1990), pp. 221-37.

Nordeide, Sæbjørg Walaker, 'Death in Abundance – Quickly! The Oseberg Ship Burial in Norway', *Acta Archaeologica*, 8.1 (2011), 8-15.

Normann, Lena, 'Woman or Warrior? The Construction of Gender in Old Norse Myth', in *Old Norse Myths, Literature and Society. Proceedings of the 11th International Saga Conference, 2-7 July 2000, University of Sydney*, ed. by Geraldine Barnes and Margaret Clunies Ross (Sydney: Centre for Medieval Studies, 2000), pp. 375-85.

Patrik, Linda E., 'Is There an Archaeological Record?', *Advances in Archaeological Method and Theory*, 8 (1985), 27-62.

Pedersen, Anne, *Dead Warriors in Living Memory. A Study of Weapon and Equestrian Burials in Viking-Age Denmark, AD 800-1000* (Copenhagen: University of Southern Denmark and the National Museum of Denmark, 2014).

Petersson, K.G., 'Ett Gravfynd fran Klinta, Kopings sn., Oland', *Tor*, 4 (1958), 134-50.

Phelpstead, Carl, 'Hair Today, Gone Tomorrow: Hair Loss, the Tonsure and Medieval Iceland', *Scandinavian Studies*, 85.1 (2013), 1-19.

Price, Neil, Charlotte Hedenstierna-Jonson, Thorun Zachrisson, Anna Kjellström, Jan Storå, Maja Krzewińska, Torsten Günther, Verónica Sobrado), Mattias Jakobsson, and Anders Götherström, 'Viking Warrior Women? Reassessing Birka Chamber Grave Bj. 581', *Antiquity*, 93.367 (2019), 181-98. <https://doi.org/10.15184/aqy.2018.258> [accessed 11 August 2020].

Price, Neil S., 'Dying and the Dead: Viking Age Mortuary Behaviour', in *The Viking World*, ed. by Stefan Brink and Neil S. Price (London: Routledge, 2008), pp. 257-73.

—, 'Passing into Poetry: Viking-Age Mortuary Drama and the Origins of Norse Mythology', *Medieval Archaeology*, 54 (2010), 123-56.

—, *The Viking Way. Religion and War in Late Iron Age Scandinavia* (Uppsala: Department of Archaeology and Ancient History, Uppsala University, 2002).

Serano, Julia, *Whipping Girl: A Transsexual Woman on Sexism and the Scapegoating of Femininity*, 2nd edn (New York: Seal, 2016).

Skoglund, P., J. Storå, A. Götherström, and M. Jakobsson, 'Accurate Sex Identification of Ancient Human Remains Using DNA Shotgun Sequencing', *Journal of Archaeological Science*, 40 (2013), 4477-82.

Solli, Brit, 'Queering the Cosmology of the Vikings: A Queer Analysis of the Cult of Odin and "Holy White Stones"', *Journal of Homosexuality*, 54.1/2 (2008), 192-208.

—, *Seid: Myter, sjamanisme og kjønn i vikingenes tid* (Oslo: Pax, 2002).

Sørensen, Marie Louise Stig, *Gender Archaeology* (Cambridge: Polity, 2000).

Southern Poverty Law Center, 'Neo-Volkisch' <https://www.splcenter.org/fighting-hate/extremist-files/ideology/neo-volkisch> [accessed 10 July 2019].

Stylegar, F.-A., 'The Kaupang Cemeteries Revisited', in *Kaupang in Skiringssal*, ed. by Dagfinn Skre, Norske Oldfunn, 22 (Aarhus: Aarhus University, 2007), pp. 65-128.

Tolley, Clive, *Shamanism in Norse Myth and Magic*, 2 vols. (Helsinki: Academia Scientiarum Fennica, 2009), I.

Weismantel, Mary, 'Towards a Transgender Archaeology. A Queer Rampage Through Prehistory', in *The Transgender Studies Reader 2*, ed. by Susan Stryker and Aren Z. Aizura (New York: Routledge, 2013), pp. 319-34.

Williams, Howard, *Death and Memory in Early Medieval Britain* (Cambridge: Cambridge University, 2006).

Williams, Howard, and Duncan Sayer, '"Halls of Mirrors": Death and Identity in Medieval Archaeology', in *Mortuary Practices and Social Identities in the Middle Ages. Essays in Burial Archaeology in Honour of Heinrich Härke*, ed. by Howard Williams and Duncan Sayer (Exeter: University of Exeter, 2009), pp. 1-22.

About the author

LEE COLWILL is a PhD student at the University of Cambridge, working on constructions of gender in medieval Icelandic *rímur* poetry. Their MA thesis examined the motif of women disguised as male warriors in medieval Icelandic literature, focusing on the poem *Snjáskvæði*. Their research interests include the construction of identity – particularly gendered identity – in Viking Age and medieval Scandinavia. As a transgender researcher of historical attitudes to gender, they are also interested in how the present informs our perceptions of the past, and vice versa.

Genre, Gender, and Trans Textualities

8. *St Eufrosine*'s Invitation to Gender Transgression

Amy V. Ogden

Abstract

In the Old French *Vie de sainte Eufrosine* (c. 1200), gender transgression is central to the poet's pedagogical techniques. The fusion of masculine and feminine elements in Panuze's lamentations and in the roles he assumes demonstrates the depth of his virtuous love for his daughter. The poet imitates Panuze, both showing the audience how to cultivate virtuous love and involving them in the transgression of gender to do so. Throughout, the poem presents masculine and feminine traits as equal. *Eufrosine*'s transgressive models offer modern readers the opportunity to rethink medieval orthodoxy and, consequently, the history behind modern identities and inequities.

Keywords: St Euphrosine, St Alexis, gender, exemplarity, hagiography, medieval, Old French

What if the queerness of medieval saints was meant to be imitated, and not just by those called to a saintly or celibate life? In the medieval French and English traditions, we have long recognized that St George's submission to tortures that penetrate his body, St Catherine's bold and effective preaching, and St Margaret's violent slaying of a dragon (to name only a few) all reflect behaviours that transgress modern ideas of pre-modern gender ideologies.[1] The last few decades of scholarship on gender identities and roles among the clergy, monks, nuns, and others have suggested that such transgressions are, in fact, simply extreme forms of not uncommon ideals

---

1   George: Riches, 'St George', pp. 65-85; Catherine: Vitz, 'Gender', pp. 79-99; Margaret: Mills, *Suspended Animation*, p. 124. See also Ogden, 'Centrality'.

Spencer-Hall, Alicia, and Blake Gutt (eds), *Trans and Genderqueer Subjects in Medieval Hagiography.* Amsterdam, Amsterdam University Press 2021
DOI: 10.5117/9789462988248_CH08

among the celibate, and perhaps even among the merely chaste.[2] However, even as we recognize a broader circle of potentially transgressive imitators of the saints, the belief endures that, in medieval European cultures, gender ideologies were essentially hierarchical and normative.[3]

The tension between the atypical gender behaviour of the saints and modern conceptions of medieval gender ideologies is perhaps most noticeable in scholarship on the group of legends about holy people designated as 'transvestite' or 'cross-dressing' saints or as *monachoparthenoi* (monk-virgins). Surviving in many languages and composed from Late Antiquity through the Middle Ages, these narratives, many of which lack a verifiable historical basis, tell of a pious young person who grows up female for a time and later dresses in masculine clothing to pursue a religious calling; other characters then perceive the protagonist as a man until they or the saint eventually identify the saint as female, generally close to the saint's death.[4] These works present an intriguing paradox that has attracted significant scholarly attention: although they are apparently orthodox expressions of faith, they focus on the unorthodox motif of cross-dressing.[5] With regard to the different versions of the Life of St Euphrosyne ('Eufrosine' in Old French [OF]), scholars have put particular emphasis on the fact that the saint is isolated in a solitary cell and that she dies as a woman; they see these elements as efforts to 'restore the social order'.[6] Evidence suggesting that the Lives' authors found the ambiguities of gender and desire 'fascinating' and 'enticing', they argue, either reflects anxieties or subconscious yearnings, or serves to entice audiences towards a transcendent ideal defined in opposition to earthly realities.[7]

Among many scholars working on these narratives, there lingers, then, a 'tendency [...] to view the Middle Ages as somehow having had a single interpretive stance, one shaped by a single ecclesiastical discourse of misogyny', as Jacqueline Murray argued about medievalists in the 1990s. Murray counters this tendency by showing the value of looking at how

---

2   See, among others, Murray, 'One Flesh', especially pp. 42-43, 50-51; Lewis, 'Male Saints', pp. 112-33.
3   See, for example, Phillips, 'Gender', pp. 309-10.
4   For a list of these saints, see Hotchkiss, *Clothes*, pp. 131-41. See Bychowski in this volume on 'transvestite saints' (pp. 245-65, especially 245-53), and Schäfer-Althaus, *Gendered Body*, pp. 156-57.
5   Bernau, 'Translation', pp. 12-14, summarizes the prohibitions against cross-dressing.
6   Schäfer-Althaus, *Gendered Body*, pp. 108, 168. See also Gaunt, 'Straight Minds', p. 168-69; Lowerre, 'To Rise', p. 71.
7   Clark, *Medieval Men*, p. 199-200 (but see also p. 209); Gaunt, 'Straight Minds', pp. 167-69. For a highly nuanced reading, see Campbell, *Gift*, especially pp. 16, 116, 214.

individual texts address similar topics from different viewpoints and towards different ends.⁸ For their part, Louise Fradenburg and Carla Freccero have suggested that 'in studying the specificity of a particular "moment," it might, precisely, be more pleasurable *and* ethically resonant with our experience of the instabilities of identity-formation to figure that "moment" as itself fractured, layered, indeed, historical', allowing ourselves to see multiple perspectives at work at any moment in history, and appreciating both alterity and 'desirous identifications' in our relationship to the Middle Ages.⁹ Before we decide how to categorize perspectives (dominant, subversive, orthodox, subconscious, etc.), and whether to enjoy a 'desirous identification' shared across time or to maintain a firm alterism in our reading of the seemingly familiar gender ambiguities in the Lives, shouldn't we collect as much evidence from as many diverse sources as we can?

The following analysis focuses on the OF *Vie de sainte Eufrosine*, which conveys a significantly different perspective to those described by scholars working on the Latin and Old English (OE) versions.¹⁰ An anonymous 1,276-line poem in alexandrine epic stanzas, the work survives in four manuscripts, the oldest from around 1200 and a later group made for wealthy aristocrats in the early fourteenth century (studied elsewhere in this volume by Vanessa Wright).¹¹ In the discussion that follows, I use an edition of the Life based on the earliest manuscript, retaining the OF forms of most of the characters' names to insist on their particularity to this version of the legend (as opposed, for example, to 'Euphrosyne', the saint whose life is recounted in many languages). I make an exception for the name that Eufrosine goes by during most of the work: 'Emerald', a common noun that captures the character's gender ambiguity. In addition to its poetic form, merging romance and epic elements, a certain number of features distinguish this version of the Life. For example, when the protagonist secretly takes vows, she receives a name ('Esmerade') that 'both men and women have'.¹² Pronouns and names hereafter will vary by context following the poet and the saint, who sometimes identify Eufrosine-Emerald as

---

8   Murray, 'Thinking', p. 2.
9   Fradenburg and Freccero, 'Introduction', p. xix. See also Mills on visual representations of the *monachoparthenoi* ('Visibly Trans?').
10   Regarding variations among the main Latin (*Bibliotheca hagiographica latina* no. 2723), OE, and OF versions of Euphrosyne's Life, see Ogden, 'Centrality', pp. 4-5.
11   Ogden, *Hagiography* (hereafter *HRVE*), pp. 24-39.
12   'Esmerade', l. 445; 'Cis nons est comunaz a marle et a femele', l. 446. Quotations (OF and translations) are from my forthcoming edition of the *Life of St Eufrosine* (referred to as *E*) as it appears in Oxford, Bodleian Library, Canon. Misc. 74.

female, sometimes male, and sometimes neither. A vision from St Sophia inspires Eufrosine-Emerald to don knightly clothing and flee to a monastery. When his beauty inspires 'evil thoughts' among the other monks, Emerald, sent off to a solitary cell, pronounces a long prayer of thanksgiving that she 'will be put in a chamber with [her] lover', God.[13] Lengthy passages of direct discourse relate Eufrosine-Emerald's struggles over how to honour conflicting loyalties to God, father, and abbot; her father Panuze's despair over the loss of his beloved daughter; and Emerald's advice that comforts Panuze, who does not recognize his counsellor as Eufrosine.[14] The poem ends with an eloquent, affectionate epilogue that is unique to this version of Euphrosyne's Life and, indeed, to the earliest copy of *Eufrosine*, and that evokes an intended audience unskilled in Latin.[15]

As we might suspect from these features, *Eufrosine* expresses a strong interest in love and in the obstacles to it that result from gender roles: essentially, the Life tells of an individual who abandons a clearly feminine identity to pursue love for God. In approaching union with God, Eufrosine-Emerald moves from gender transgression (dressing a female body in masculine clothing) to gender transcendence (inhabiting an identity without gender).[16] I have argued elsewhere that such extreme gender fluidity conveys saints' exceptional heroism.[17] Here, I examine how Eufrosine's father and the poet themselves engage in gender transgression in ways that translate the saint's extraordinary virtue and actions into less perfect but more imitable forms.[18] I use 'gender transgression' to denote behaviour and perspectives that do not conform to the binary gender roles that are typical in *Eufrosine* and, indeed, in much contemporary literature; 'transgression' acknowledges that this unusual behaviour contravenes common expectations – both medieval and modern. I do not mean, however, that *Eufrosine* suggests this transgressive

---

13 'Cogitasïon male', *E*, l. 570; 'Or serai mise en canbre ensenble mon amant', ibid., l. 645.
14 The OE and Latin versions contain variations of some of these speeches.
15 The intended and real audiences remain anonymous. Campbell (*Gift*, pp. 205-22) and I (*HRVE*, pp. 26-33) present different interpretations of who they may have been. Lifschitz (*Religious Women*, pp. 166-70) and Grossel ('Quand l'enfant', p. 82, n. 1) offer evidence for female audiences (monastic and secular) of other versions of Euphrosyne's Life.
16 See *HRVE*, especially 81-94. Cf. Campbell, 'Epistemology', pp. 214-15.
17 'Centrality', pp. 13-14.
18 See *HRVE*, pp. 94-95, 205, regarding Panuze's and the poet's persona's roles in *Eufrosine*'s didactic strategies. For the OE, cf. Stallcup, 'Old English Life', pp. 18-19, and Norris, 'Genre Trouble', pp. 138-39. Like me, Campbell studies how *Eufrosine* juxtaposes gender identities to convey ideas that exceed articulation, but, whilst Campbell emphasizes the ultimate untranslatability of these ideas, my argument here focuses on how the translation of virtue can succeed, albeit imperfectly ('Translating', pp. 236-45, 256-57).

behaviour is reprehensible. The Life does not present either expectations of distinct gender roles or their disruption as inherently good or bad: context and intentions define their morality. This is where distinguishing between 'common' and 'normal' becomes highly important. As Karma Lochrie shows, 'normal', an invention of the nineteenth and twentieth centuries, attributes positive value to (and even idealizes) the average, but, to medieval thinkers, the common state after the Fall was always a corruption of the ideal.[19] By setting aside the concepts of 'normal' and 'norms' as alien to medieval perspectives, we perceive more easily the varying moral judgements that medieval authors pass (and refrain from passing) on behaviour they see as typical as well as that which they present as transgressive.

In *Eufrosine*, the poet deploys common expectations regarding binary gender to show the limitations of worldly life, and by reconfiguring gendered behaviours and concerns, they convey the possibility of escaping those constraints.[20] Using Panuze, themselves, and even the audience, the poet teaches that gender transgression can express an otherwise ineffable form of love, and that this love is an inherent quality of the soul that can be cultivated through transgressive action. Rather than reinforcing or even accepting gender hierarchies, the *Eufrosine* poet argues that active gender transgression – both within the cloister and beyond – offers salvation.

Modelling transgression in perspective

Through Panuze's lamentations and actions, the poet invites the audience to scrutinize the baron's love for his child, transgressions of gender roles, and exemplarity: Panuze is by no means a clearly positive example of virtue. In part, his complexity reflects the poet's meditation on the OF *Life of St Alexis* (c. 1080) and its troubling perspective on familial love as incompatible with virtue in this world. Like *Eufrosine*, *Alexis* tells of a young person who flees his wealthy home to serve God; he then returns to live there, unrecognized, for seventeen years.[21] In both poems, discovery

---

19   Lochrie, *Heterosyncrasies*, pp. xxii-xxxiii. Lochrie's discussion of the multiple senses of 'natural' is also extremely useful.
20   As argued below, the singular 'they' is the appropriate way to refer to the poet, who uses various techniques to avoid a binary gender identity.
21   The relationship between *Eufrosine* and the Alexis Lives remains unclear, but since *Eufrosine* may have influenced the later Alexis texts, including one in the same manuscript as *Eufrosine*, I use the earlier Hildesheim version. For the relationship between the Lives, see Storey, 'Reminder', pp. 385-93, and McCulloch, 'Saint Euphrosine', pp. 181-85.

of the child's flight and later death prompt lengthy lamentations by the family. In *Alexis*, the values and concerns of these laments reflect gender roles consistent with the findings of modern studies of medieval gender: while Alexis's father's sense of honour and justice are quite pronounced, the women's lamentations emphasize bodily connections and hyperbolic emotions.[22] By contrast, in *Eufrosine*, direct repetitions of phrases as well as rewordings of prominent themes from *Alexis* lend Panuze a gender-transgressive perspective.

All of the echoes of *Alexis* in Panuze's lamentations emphasize worldly concerns. For example, borrowing from Alexis's father, Eufemien, the *Eufrosine* poet conveys Panuze's sense of the futility of all his work to establish the honour of his child. Panuze laments, "'Daughter, for five years *I have toiled for you*, | [...] Had *rich houses and manors* constructed | *So you would be honoured* as long as you lived'", while Alexis's father exclaims, "'Oh, son, to whom will go my large inheritance, | [...] | *My great palaces* in the city of Rome? | *For you I laboured* for them, | *So that you would be honoured* because of them after my death'".[23] From Alexis's mother, the *Eufrosine* poet takes a deep physical connection that is grounded in the past dependence of child on parent. In an *ubi sunt* passage, Panuze asks, "'My daughter, where is the *flesh* that I nourished?'"; Alexis's mother exclaims, "'My son Alexis, your tender *flesh*! | [...] Why did you flee from me? I carried you in my womb'".[24] The connection is so deep that the parents cannot understand how they can continue to exist without their children.[25] In a similar vein, Alexis's bride declares that she would be better off dead.[26] Deprived of their loved one, Panuze and Alexis's mother – and Alexis's bride, too – are each incapable of seeing any future happiness: 'I will nevermore be happy' echoes from one poem to the other.[27] As for Alexis's bride, she also shares with Panuze

---

22 See, for example, Bynum, *Jesus as Mother*, p. 148; Bouchard, *Discourse*, p. 122; Phillips, 'Gender and Sexuality', pp. 310-11.

23 "'Filhe, mut sui por vos, cinc ans at, *travilhiez*, [...] | Faites *riches maisons, manoirs* edefiiez, | *Por vos metre a honor* en tant ke vos viviez'" (*E*, ll. 690-93); "'O filz, qui erent mes granz ereditez, [...] | Mes *granz paleis* de Rome la cité? | Ed *enpur tei* m'en esteie *penét*, | Puis mun decés *en fusses enorét*'" (*A*, ll. 401-05). Emphasis added. I use Storey's edition of *Alexis*, referred to as *A*; translations are mine.

24 "'Ma filhe, u est la cars que j'avoie norrie?'" (*E*, l. 1160; cf. 705, 1154); "'Filz Alexis, de la tue carn tendra! | [...] Pur quem fuïs? Jat portai en men ventre'" (*A*, ll. 451, 453; cf. 131, 437, 442, 444, 453, and 456-58).

25 *E*, ll. 1145-47; *A* l. 445. Cf. Kelly, *Place*, p. 107.

26 *A*, l. 485.

27 "'Jor mais ne serai liez'" (*E*, l. 687); "'Ja mais n'ierc lede'" (*A*, l. 135); "'Ja mais ledece n'avrai'" (*A*, l. 492). Cf. Panuze's initial emotionality, contrasted to his wife's wisdom (*E*, ll. 27-29).

a keen awareness of the saint's loss of physical beauty: they exclaim over the disappearance of their loved one's beautiful face and mouth.[28] Whether or not the *Eufrosine* audiences recognized the allusions to *Alexis*, it seems highly likely that Panuze's perspective combined identifiably masculine and feminine traits.

This fusion of gendered concerns could well mark Panuze's grief as especially sinful.[29] Combining the perspectives of all three of Alexis's family members, Panuze's lamentations condense into one character the grief that emphasizes Alexis's father's, mother's, and bride's profound incomprehension of the saint – an incomprehension that Eufemien ascribes to his identity as a sinner.[30] Similarly, material wealth, worldly honour, and particular love prevent Panuze from recognizing God's will. Moreover, the inclusion of the bride's perspective in Panuze's lament lends the latter certain undertones of incest: the father who speaks longingly of the lost physical beauty of his daughter – her laughing eyes, pale face, and beautiful mouth – and regrets not having cared for her sounds rather more like a lover than a parent.[31] Is the poet deploying the hagiographical motif of the (usually pagan) father who desires and persecutes his saintly daughter – 'a way of signalling the inherently corrupt nature of human relationships', as Emma Campbell argues for other Lives?[32]

It is perhaps in this very troubling emotion, however, that we also begin to see how the combination of perspectives may indicate that in *Eufrosine*, more clearly than in *Alexis*, terrestrial love – with all its limitations – turns out to be the primary path to spiritual progress rather than an impediment. In studying the uses of incest in various Lives, Campbell distinguishes between the corrupt form, just cited, and the transcendent: in certain Lives, the intensity of the spiritual love between characters can only be expressed through the image of incest – that is, by exceeding the limits of acceptable worldly relationships.[33] The concluding stanza of Panuze's final lament – his last words in the Life – strongly suggests such an intensely spiritual love. His words echo, in quick succession, certain ideas of Alexis's parents and then, with a final parallel to the bride's lament, express a sudden faith in

---

28 *E*, ll. 1162-63; *A*, l. 481.
29 Norris convincingly argues that in the OE, the father's lamentations provide the occasion for his daughter to save him miraculously from the sin of excessive sorrow ('Genre Trouble', pp. 130-37).
30 Kelly, *Place*, pp. 94, 104; *A*, l. 394.
31 *E*, ll. 1164-66. See, too, ll. 919-21 and 1135.
32 Campbell, *Gift*, p. 89.
33 Campbell, *Gift*, p. 95. On the incestuous holy kinship, see ibid., p. 89.

Eufrosine's saintly ability to intercede with God on his behalf.[34] Although the abrupt shift from incomprehension to faith is paradoxical and may seem illogical, Panuze's change in perspective indicates that after deeply human love inevitably leads to profound grief, this grief can serve as a catalyst to faith and perhaps spiritual understanding. This is, after all, the premise of Christ's incarnation.[35]

The baron's spiritual understanding is clear in his request to his now-dead 'filhe Eüfrosine' ('daughter Eufrosine') to maintain the relationship Panuze had with Emerald by continuing to serve as the baron's spiritual guide.[36] He thus shows full recognition that Eufrosine and Emerald are the same person, and that Eufrosine is now an intercessor to whom he can still speak and who can continue to help him beyond death. His faith in his child seems to depend equally on their loving familial relationship (with all the joy and pain that it has entailed) and the spiritual friendship that developed between them as men.[37]

The blending of spiritual love, faith, grief, and terrestrial attachments evident in the ending shows that Panuze's combination of gendered perspectives reflects both his spiritual imperceptiveness (in the particular concerns) and his transcendent spiritual love (in their combination). It is important to note that all these concerns and emotions – masculine and feminine – function as obstacles to and as expressions of love alike, and that there is no hierarchy among them. Moreover, Panuze demonstrates this combination of gendered perspectives throughout his lamentations, before he has encountered Emerald as well as after. It would thus appear to be an inherent part of his character rather than an imitation of the gender transgressions of his child. The combination is, however, more pronounced in the final lines as he realizes the depth of his loss, sorrow, and anger and then expresses his faith; the ability to move from imperceptiveness and resistance to faith would suggest that he has learned, from his interactions with Emerald, to cultivate this inherent trait. For Panuze, as for Eufrosine-Emerald, gender transgression is not in itself a sin or a virtue, but rather an expression of the human soul's highest nature as genderless.[38] As the poet comments, 'Panuze laments for his daughter, as nature demands.'[39] The

---

34 *E*, ll. 1166-68; *A*, ll. 458-59, 455 (Mother). *E*, ll. 1169-70; *A*, l. 410 (Eufemien). *E*, ll. 1171-75; *A*, ll. 486, 490, 492-95 (Bride).
35 *HRVE*, pp. 93, 113-30.
36 *E*, l. 1166.
37 Cf. Campbell, *Gift*, p. 100.
38 Cf. Elliott, 'Rubber Soul', pp. 92-93.
39 'Panuzes plaint sa filhe, si que requiert nature' (*E*, l. 1230).

baron's grief for Eufrosine – in its queer combination of paternal, maternal, and spousal aspects – is natural, acceptable, and even virtuous because it stems from deep spiritual love.

Cultivating virtue through transgressive action

If Panuze's lamentation expresses his innate virtue, then the poet's comment that the baron's grieving is natural suggests that this virtue is shared (to a greater or lesser extent) by all people: the *imago Dei* obscured by sin but nonetheless enduring in all human beings.[40] The following line of the Life, however, indicates that this natural virtue is insufficient in some way. The poet notes, 'But Abbot Teodose is happy about the event'.[41] The contrast between the two men's reactions, emphasized through the direct juxtaposition, reminds the audience that one of the main problems of the story has been Panuze's rebellious grief against God's will. By recalling this problem, the poet suggests that Panuze's verbal acknowledgment of conversion is not sufficient. As Alison More has noted, patristic and medieval theologians saw conversion not as a momentary experience, but as 'a journey towards holiness and ultimately towards God'.[42] The final sixteen lines of the narrative provide a resolution focused entirely on the actions that demonstrate the baron's developing conversion – we have no further access to his thoughts. The fact that these actions lead to a sense of resolution reinforces the earlier suggestion that natural virtue needs to be cultivated, and shows the audience that actions are an effective means of perfecting virtue.[43]

In their fusion of masculine and feminine aspects, Panuze's actions indicate that exemplary virtue for men, as for women, involves active abandonment of their typical gender roles.[44] Panuze's explicit imitation of Eufrosine-Emerald in the concluding episode of the Life translates the saint's extraordinary actions into a potentially realizable paradigm. From one perspective, Panuze's final actions seem unexceptional: moved by sorrow for his daughter, he retires to a monastery to devote his life to serving God.

---

40 Cf. Peter Lombard, *Sentences*, 1.iii.2 (tr. Silano 1:21-22).
41 'Mais l'abes Teodoses est lies de l'aventure' (*E*, l. 1231).
42 More, 'Convergence', p. 34 and p. 45, n. 2.
43 'Alain de Lille, who [...] had declared that the virtues started from nature, had also taken the position that virtue was something people acquired with practice, a *habitus*' (Cadden, 'Trouble', p. 218).
44 Cf. note 2 above and More, 'Convergence', especially p. 33.

Certainly, the Life does not directly identify Panuze's actions as transgressive in any way, merely suggesting that they are exceptionally pious.[45] Within the context of the social systems set up in *Eufrosine*, however, his behaviour looks quite different: he submissively follows his daughter's directions about money, makes himself completely dependent on and obedient to men, and occupies an enclosed space identified as a woman's.

From the beginning, the *Life of St Eufrosine* establishes the ability to pursue, control, and dispense riches in the acquisition and assertion of power as a defining characteristic of secular masculinity. Not surprisingly, women serve as instruments for transferring wealth from man to man.[46] Thus, the young men of Alexandria desire Eufrosine and her father's wealth equally.[47] Panuze himself refers to Eufrosine as his 'treasure' ('tresor') and 'gem' ('gemme'), showing that he, too, sees her as closely linked to his wealth.[48] Even if his almsgiving to churches and to the poor shows his inherent piety, its very public nature also contributes to his power and status.[49] Part of Eufrosine's own gender transgression involves participation in the masculine control of money when the saint asserts a feminine identity as Panuze's daughter in order to claim the masculine power of determining what will happen to the family inheritance.[50]

Within the narrative logic of the text, the direction that Eufrosine gives Panuze does not necessitate any gender transgressions on the latter's part, but the baron chooses actions that place him in both masculine and feminine roles. To fulfil the saint's request that the inheritance be given to the monastery, Panuze could simply occupy the role of Eufrosine's son, waiting until his own death to donate the money. In fact, his first financial actions after her death are perfectly in keeping with his masculine relationship to wealth: he builds an expensive sepulchre for his daughter, as he did for her mother, and then gives generous alms to churches and paupers.[51] In the very next line, however, he takes the remainder of his wealth and gives it all to Abbot Teodose.[52] Completely absent from this scene is any indication that Panuze has patriarchal/baronial responsibilities. Although we earlier learned that the baron and

---

45   *E*, ll. 1244-48.
46   Cf. Campbell, *Gift*, p. 52.
47   *E*, ll. 142-44.
48   Ibid., ll. 208, 928.
49   See, for example, ibid., ll. 104-06, 908-12.
50   Ibid., ll. 1119-23. *HRVE*, pp. 92-93; 199.
51   *E*, ll. 1226-29; 107, 118; 1237-39.
52   Ibid., ll. 1240-41.

his wife 'all their days [...] maintained a very wealthy household', there is now no mention of any dependents.[53] The poet thus removes Panuze from his masculine roles when he chooses the feminine role of inheriting wealth only to transfer it immediately to a new source of support.[54] The gender transgression here – and the poet's lack of concern about it – is striking when we look at how other OF Lives deal with similar situations: there is no question in *Alexis* of Eufemien abandoning his wealth and position, while in Guillaume de Berneville's *Vie de saint Gilles*, the protagonist's household expresses eloquent, troubling, and ultimately unresolved objections to Gilles's excessive charity.[55]

The particularities of Panuze's life in the monastery further reveal both his gender transgression and his virtue. Rather than simply becoming one of the community, Panuze apparently inherits 'his daughter's cell', where he then lives, lying 'there [...] on the mat where he had found her'.[56] The poet thus defines the space Panuze occupies very explicitly as that of a woman, an association heightened earlier when the poet and the saint characterized the cell as a chamber where the nun Emerald would be with her lover (God).[57] However, the cell is also the space that allows Emerald to become part of a community of men, and to speak to Panuze as an equal. The poet makes no explanation for why Panuze might need this special accommodation. Given these circumstances, the baron's occupation of the cell, like his use of money, seems not only to imitate his child's actions but also to re-enact the gender transgressions of those actions. In this 'physical and spiritual [...] *imitatio*', as Campbell cogently argues, Panuze 'both literally and metaphorically inhabits his daughter's cell as an indication of a crucial shift in perspective that promises more intimate knowledge of the saint and the spiritual viewpoint with which she is identified'.[58] Panuze's actions within the cell demonstrate the deep understanding of his daughter that he gains from inhabiting this space: the poet mentions no further grief but instead recounts how the baron's extreme asceticism wins renown for the abbey, remarking on Panuze's complete obedience before invoking him as

---

53 'Demenerent lor tens a mut riche barnage' (ibid., l. 25).
54 Finding that the somewhat later *Golden Legend* defines feminine charity as excessive, Cullum characterizes St Francis's 'feminised form of piety and charity' as consistent with larger trends of saints' 'transgendered behaviour' that serves 'to destabilise normative expectations and thus to highlight the call of God' ('Gendering Charity', pp. 148-49).
55 *Gilles*, ll. 281-340.
56 'la cele sa filhe' (*E*, l. 1242); 'Illuc [...] sor la nate u il l'avoit trovee' (ibid., l. 1243).
57 Ibid., ll. 595-98, 645.
58 'Epistemology', p. 216.

a 'good petitione[r] toward God on our behalf'.[59] In the end, although still a secondary character, Panuze attains the role of saintly intercessor.

As a model for a worldly but devout audience, Panuze's actions might seem, in their broadest sense, to demonstrate more imitable forms of Eufrosine's extraordinary virtue, and, in their specificity, to show that ideal virtue, associated with gender transgression, is unattainable in this world. Like Panuze, some audience members could seek solace from grief by giving up wealth to join a monastery and cultivating obedience through the actions of monastic life. Those with more responsibilities could still give charitably and submit to God's will. Audience members cannot, however, imitate the specific behaviours that involve Panuze in gender transgression: it is only in response to Eufrosine-Emerald's actions of disposing of the family wealth and inhabiting an unusual space in an unusual way that Panuze chooses actions pertaining to both masculine and feminine roles. Given Panuze's final exceptional position, the baron's extreme virtue might seem to mark him, like his daughter, as liminal: his gender transgressions cannot continue in the world and need to be excluded from society, contained within the cell and within a celibate life. It would seem that the divisions of humanity in gendered roles are an inevitable characteristic of the corrupt world after all.

Translating transgression into daily practice

The idea that *Eufrosine* reinforces gender hierarchies within the world and holds up gender transcendence as an ideal only for exceptional celibates, however, becomes much harder to maintain when we see which aspects of Panuze's exemplarity the poet amplifies in the epilogue. In fact, the epilogue ignores monasticism as a path to salvation and instead emphasizes virtuous love. Here, the poet adopts gender transgressive roles to express love for the saint, much as Panuze did in his lamentations, and then proceeds to transgress the boundaries between composer and audience, drawing readers into the same transgressions and inviting them to perform acts of love and faith.

In part, the poet uses the same technique as we have seen in Panuze's lamentations, weaving together language (and here, sounds) from different characters' prayers in the Life, both male and female. While Abbot Teodose addresses the saint as "'*Lady Eufrosine, friend of* our Lord *God*'", the poet

---

59 *E*, ll. 1244-46, 1248; 'Tu nos soies o lui a Deu bons plaidoïs' (ibid., l. 1252).

apostrophizes Eufrosine as '*Lady Eufrosine, God's* bride and *friend*'.[60] The echoes emphasize the poet's authority and respectful attitude towards the saint, and reaffirm institutional approval of Eufrosine's status. Since Teodose's lines open his public eulogy of the saint, the poet's repetition of them endows the poet with a particularly clerical masculinity. From Panuze, the poet borrows not only an expression of faith in Eufrosine as an intercessor at the Last Judgement.[61] He even – in the rhymes – adopts the sounds in which Panuze expresses his grief and his faith. Both passages conclude with a stanza of lines ending in the sound -*ie* followed by another in -*or*/-*ort*: the rhyme sounds of Panuze's speech – "'amie/... vie/... deport/... confort/... resort/ ... port'" – echo in the poet's 'envie/ ... compagnie/ ... amor/... dolçor/ ... flor/ ... labor'.[62] Although the sounds are immaterial, their existence of course depends entirely on the use of bodies. Consequently, the repetition of the sounds here, combined with the expression of faith in the saint as an intercessor, suggests an optimistic view of terrestrial existence: even if embodiment and relationships sometimes create obstacles to faith, they are also essential to the pursuit and expression of virtue. In addition, by repeating the sounds used by the saint's nearest relative, the poet proclaims a deep attachment to the saint and demonstrates that anyone can follow Panuze – loving the saint is not confined to those who knew her in life. Finally, from Eufrosine herself, the poet borrows a supplication that their work be well received: Eufrosine-Emerald says to God, "'Accept *my humble service* in this life'" while the poet prays to the saint, 'Receive with *love my humble service*'.[63] The poet imitates both the saint's humility and active devotion. By selecting words that the saint speaks at the moment she offers her love to God, when she characterizes herself in extremely feminine language, as female beloved ('amie'), handmaiden ('ancele'), and sinful woman ('pecheris'), the poet emphasizes the feminine roles they borrow with the saint's words.[64] Just as Panuze's lamentations draw on the words and ideas of Alexis's family to show the extent and depth of his grief – and therefore of his love for Eufrosine – the poet's borrowings from Eufrosine,

60 "'Eüfrosine dame, amie Damledé'" (ibid., l. 1206); 'Eüfrosine dame, Deu espose et amie' (ibid., l. 1257). Emphasis added.
61 Ibid., 1174-75, 1269-74.
62 Ibid., ll. 1164-67, 1173, 1175, 1265-68, 1275-76. Stanzas CVII-CVIII: -ie /-or; stanzas XCVII-XCVIII, -ie /-ort. Cf. McCulloch, 'Saint Euphrosine', p. 177.
63 "'Recuel le mien petit servise en ceste vie'" (*E*, l. 635); 'Le mien petit servise recivez par amor' (ibid., l. 1267). Emphasis added.
64 Ibid., ll. 637, 638, 641.

Panuze, and Teodose allow the poet to express forms of love that exceed individual subjectivities and identities.[65]

Some of these echoes have previously caught the attention of critics, leading to discussion about the author's sex. When Florence McCulloch noticed the repetition of the phrase 'my humble service' in the saint's prayer and in the epilogue, she proposed that the poet might be a woman.[66] Christopher Storey dismissed the hypothesis as having 'no convincing reason', Simon Gaunt determined that it was 'not [...] persuasive', and I myself have previously argued that the poet, who explicitly describes themself with masculine nouns, should be treated as male.[67] However, both the poet's claim to a masculine identity and their troubling of that identity deserve equal respect. It is particularly interesting that the poet combines the words of male and female characters to speak of the poem's genesis: the poet echoes Teodose's words as a preface to describing the discovery of the story in a library book, while 'my humble service', borrowed from the self-feminizing saint, refers to the composition of the poem. The poet thus associates the scholarly work of finding the Life and translating it into romans (vernacular French) with a male cleric, and the devotional work of composing the Life 'with tenderness' with a female saint.[68] Clearly defined and even stereotypical roles here combine to evoke the poet's gender fluidity.

The conclusion to the epilogue deepens the gender indeterminacy of the poet. Just after repeating Emerald's phrase, 'my humble service', the poet claims the identity of a 'wretched [masculine] sinner' ('chaitif pecheor') – in the rhyme position no less – and then curiously that of a 'boiseor', a '[masculine] deceiver'.[69] Why would the poet, at a key moment of establishing authority, declare themself a deceiver? 'Boiseor' may simply be paired with 'pecheor' to emphasize the poet's humble recognition of their sinfulness. Nonetheless, the word also evokes Panuze's multiple denunciations of his daughter's deceit: in his opinion, she has deceived, misled, confounded, and tricked him.[70] At the same time, the poet's use of 'pecheor' echoes Emerald's self-identification as a 'pecheris' (feminine sinner) just after she offers her 'humble service', like the poet.[71] The context of the saint's words – a prayer that explores the

---

65   Cf. *HRVE* 129-30.
66   McCulloch, 'Saint Euphrosine', p. 185.
67   Storey, *Annotated*, p. 50; Gaunt, 'Straight Minds', p. 171, n. 19; *HRVE*, pp. 13, 95.
68   '[P]ar dolçor' (*E*, l. 1268).
69   Ibid., ll. 1270, 1272. See 'boiseor' in *Tobler-Lommatzsch*, col. 1033-34.
70   "'deceü'" (*E*, l. 1150), "'malemens sui menez'" (l. 1153), "'confondu'" (l. 1153), "'tricherie'" (l. 1159). He utters these accusations in the midst of his grief before he regains faith in his daughter.
71   Ibid., ll. 641-42.

intricacies of chosen identity, power, truth, deception, and sin – allows the possibility that Eufrosine-Emerald's gender transformation is in some way sinful, but it in no way defines how. Instead, it emphasizes the responsibility of witnesses to recognize truths that depend on multiple sources of meaning: God's assumption of true fleshly 'clothing', says Emerald, allowed the apostles to recognize him but deceived Leviathan into thinking God was just a man.[72] Might the epilogue's elliptic allusion to these themes establish the poet's authority as a transgender imitator of a transgender saint – a messenger whose ability to convey an ineffable truth depends, as Eufrosine's does, on inhabiting an identity that people confounded by sin see as deceitful? It is impossible to say: the saint's sin and the poet's deception remain obscure. Nonetheless, all of these elements indicate that we should take the anonymity of *this* poet, at least, as a conscious choice to avoid a single gendered identity.[73]

Engaging the audience in transgression

The poet models for the audience, then, a love for the saint and a transformation of that love into the action of composing *Eufrosine*, both using language that transcends gendered identities. This model leaves little room for a merely passive understanding, since the poet explicitly invites the audience to participate, through reading the Life and voicing its words, in this same active love:

> Now, as soon as I read it, I received your protection.
> Inspired by love for you I have rewritten [the Life] in French,
> Not in order to improve it with greater refinement
> But because I want it to be heard by more people.
> If someone else joins me in loving you, I will not be in the least jealous.
> I would like to have the whole world in my company.[74]

---

72 Emerald notes twice that Leviathan was deceived ('deceüs', ibid., ll. 609, 613) when God '"received, through a virgin, real flesh and a real soul"' ('"Voire car et voire arme de virgene receüs"', l. 603) and came to earth '"clothed in human form"' ('"d'umanité vestus"', l. 617). She contrasts Leviathan's imperceptiveness to the disciples' recognition ('reconeüs', l. 621).

73 I am belatedly beholden to Karl D. Uitti for challenging me to take McCulloch's suggestion seriously and for his unwavering refusal to be convinced by my earlier arguments against the poet's female identity.

74 'Ore cant je l'ou liute, reçui t'avourie. | Por t'amor ai ta vie en romans recoilhie, | Non por li amender par maior cortesie, | Mais par ce ke je vulh qu'ele plus soit oïe. | S'atres t'aimet o moi, je n'en ai nule envie. | Tot le siecle en voroie avoir a compagnie' (*E*, ll. 1261-66).

Although the final line of the stanza – 'Tot le siecle en voroie avoir a compagnie' – might seem at first like a coy suggestion rather than a direct invitation, it eliminates the distinction between poet and audience. If we read it, especially aloud, *we* are saying that we want others to join us in loving Eufrosine, and we are therefore already participating in the poet's project to spread that love to the whole world. We should note the all-inclusive use of 'the whole world', too. Rather than addressing the listeners as 'Sagnors' (Lords), and thereby defining the primary audience as masculine and distinct from the speaking voice, as the later copies of *Eufrosine* and many OF Lives do, the poet dissolves all boundaries among devotees of the saint.[75]

Since the very next line of the poem echoes the saint's offering of 'servise' (service), the final stanza, with its continuing use of the first person singular, implicates the audience further in both the production of the poem and the imitation of the saint's devotion:

> Receive with love my humble service.
> If I have not done it well, I have at least done it with tenderness.
> Call on God, our dear Redeemer, for me,
> That he have mercy on me, the wretched sinner,
> That he never think my grave misdeeds come from animosity,
> That he make settlement with this his deceiver while I still live,
> And allow me to come, through fasting and weeping
> For the sins I have committed, before my judge.
> And you, holy maiden, noble one, sweet flower,
> Reward me now for my intent and my labour. Amen.[76]

As we have seen, the poet here merges the words of the saint, Panuze's expression of faith in the saint as intercessor at the Last Judgement, the masculine subject position of the 'chaitif pecheor', and the ambiguous identity of 'boiseor'; the reader voicing these perspectives joins the poet in occupying multiple identities. In discussing the nature of the poet's love for the saint, Gaunt, while rejecting McCulloch's supposition that the poet

---

75 See *HRVE*, p. 46, for a discussion of how the later copyist changes the relationship between narrative voice and audience; pp. 220-21 address other aspects of how the poet engages the audience's virtue.

76 'Le mien petit servise recivez par amor. | Se je ne l'ai fait bien, je l'ai fait par dolçor. | Apele Deu por moi, nostre chier redemptor, | Qu'il ait de moi mercit, le chaitif pecheor, | Ne les mie{n}s grans forfais ne mes toz a iror, | Prende droit en cest siecle d'icest sien boiseor | Et me laist parvenir, et o june et o plor | Des pechiez que j'ai fais, devant me jugeor. | Et tu, sainte pucele, franque rien, dulce flor, | En itant moi meris m'entente et me labor. Amen' (*E*, ll. 1267-76).

is female, notes that 'were we to assume the text was written by a woman, this would have interesting implications for a "queer" reading, given the eroticism of the narrator's relationship with the saint'.[77] If we agree that the poet transcends any singular gendered identity, then their love for the saint is undoubtedly queer. Consequently, the audience who reads the epilogue lovingly participates in this same queer love, exceeding the boundaries of individual worldly relationships, just as we have seen in Panuze's love for Eufrosine. The virtuous, salvific value of this excessive love should not be underestimated. The love and its expression in devotional acts like composing or reading *Eufrosine* are the offerings that the poet-audience makes to the saint to convince her to argue for the poet-audience's salvation at the Last Judgement; rather than sinful, this love is what may compensate for grave misdeeds.[78] Although fasting and weeping for one's sins are necessary here, too, the structure of the stanza lays the emphasis on love, tenderness, and labour. The poem as a whole amplifies this emphasis, showing penitential actions as one form of devotion, but teaching love as the primary path to virtue and salvation.

Conclusion

As models, Panuze and the poet contribute to the growing body of evidence that some medieval thinkers, writing as clerics, saw fixed gender roles as a limitation connected to sin that could be overcome through the cultivation of virtue. How should we situate this anti-hierarchical perspective in relation to the extensively documented misogynist literature? Yes, Eufrosine dies a woman, Panuze a man, and the poet self-identifies using masculine pronouns, but how they inhabit those identities matters: Eufrosine dies a female monk recognized for her power, Panuze dies an enclosed, silent, obedient, and dependent monk, and the poet constructs a voice and perspective out of a variety of subjectivities. For the characters, the transgressions do take place at the edge of secular society and within monastic life, but they are also the key dramatic elements of a story; the poet's invitation in the epilogue opens the possibility of cultivating virtue and transgressing gender in daily activities such as reading and responding to literature. Combined with Eufrosine's and Panuze's examples, those activities might involve relations to authority figures, money, and space in worldly life. If

---

77 Gaunt, 'Straight Minds', p. 171, n. 19.
78 L. 1271.

we decide to subordinate *Eufrosine*'s transgressive pedagogy – along with *Catherine*'s and *George*'s and the rest – as unorthodox or subconscious, then we buttress a monolithic idea of the Middle Ages as the antithesis of what we 'moderns' hope to be. Consequently, we fortify the historical foundations for attitudes like misogyny or transphobia, thereby legitimizing these attitudes, at least for some people. Enjoying *Eufrosine*'s transgressive ideals does not demand a naïve refusal of medieval 'realities'. Sharing with *Eufrosine* the pleasure of the transgressions demands questioning our understanding of those realities and recognizing that people across time have seen gender inequities as constructed and changeable.[79] If we allow ourselves to read *Eufrosine*'s invitation to gender transgression as intentional and orthodox, we destabilize – even if only a little – the foundations of current inequities, demonstrate the value of medieval literature for rethinking modern problems, and contribute to revealing the deep history of people now recognized as trans or genderqueer.

Bibliography

Primary sources

Guillaume de Berneville, *La Vie de saint Gilles*, ed. and trans. by Françoise Laurent (Paris: Champion, 2003).

Ogden, Amy V., ed. and trans., *La Vie de sainte Euphrosine*, MLA Texts and Translations (New York: Modern Language Association, forthcoming 2021).

Peter Lombard, *The Sentences*, trans. by Giulio Silano (Toronto: PIMS, 2007).

Storey, Christopher, ed., *La Vie de saint Alexis: Texte du Manuscrit de Hildesheim* (Geneva: Droz, 1968).

Secondary sources

Bernau, Anke, 'The Translation of Purity in the Old English Lives of St Eugenia and St Euphrosyne', *Bulletin of the John Rylands University Library of Manchester*, 86.2 (2004), 11-37.

Bouchard, Constance Brittain, *"Every Valley Shall be Exalted": The Discourse of Opposites in Twelfth-Century Thought* (Ithaca: Cornell University, 2003).

---

79   See also Gutt, 'Transgender Genealogy', p. 130; Mills, 'Visibly', pp. 541, 553-56; Campbell, 'Hagiography', pp. 394-95; Bychowski, in this volume (pp. 245-65, especially 247-50, 258, 261-63).

Bynum, Caroline Walker, *Jesus as Mother: Studies in the Spirituality of the High Middle Ages* (Berkeley: University of California, 1982).

Cadden, Joan, 'Trouble in the Earthly Paradise: The Regime of Nature in Late Medieval Christian Culture', in *The Moral Authority of Nature*, ed. by Lorraine Daston and Fernando Vidal (Chicago: University of Chicago, 2010), pp. 207-31.

Campbell, Emma, 'Epistemology of the Cloister: Knowledge, Identity, and Place in Old French Saints' Lives', *Journal of Medieval Religious Cultures*, 36.2 (2010), 205-32.

—, 'Hagiography, Gender, and the Power of Social Norms', in *Hagiography and the History of Latin Christendom, 500-1500*, ed. by Samantha Kahn Herrick (Leiden: Brill, 2019), pp. 375-96.

—, *Medieval Saints' Lives: The Gift, Kinship and Community in Old French Hagiography* (Woodbridge: Brewer, 2008).

—, 'Translating Gender in Thirteenth-Century French Cross-dressing Narratives: *Le Roman de Silence* and *La Vie de Sainte Euphrosine*', *Journal of Medieval and Early Modern Studies*, 49.2 (2019), 233-64.

Clark, David, *Between Medieval Men: Male Friendship and Desire in Early Medieval English Literature* (Oxford: Oxford University, 2009).

Cullum, P.H., 'Gendering Charity in Medieval Hagiography', in *Gender and Holiness: Men, Women and Saints in Late Medieval Europe*, ed. by Samantha J.E. Riches and Sarah Salih (London: Routledge, 2002), pp. 135-51.

Elliott, Dyan, 'Rubber Soul: Theology, Hagiography, and the Spirit World of the High Middle Ages', in *From Beasts to Souls: Gender and Embodiment in Medieval Europe*, ed. by E. Jane Burns and Peggy McCracken (Notre Dame: University of Notre Dame, 2013), pp. 89-120.

Fradenburg, Louise, and Carla Freccero, 'Introduction: Caxton, Foucault, and the Pleasures of History', in *Premodern Sexualities*, ed. by Louise Fradenburg and Carla Freccero (New York: Routledge, 1996), pp. xiii-xxiv.

Gaunt, Simon, 'Straight Minds/"Queer" Wishes in Old French Hagiography', in *Premodern Sexualities*, ed. by Louise Fradenburg and Carla Freccero (New York: Routledge, 1996), pp. 155-73.

Grossel, Marie-Geneviève, 'Quand l'enfant se convertit: Vies des saintes Euphrosine et Cristine, Barlaam et Josaphat ....', in *Pouvoir, liens de parenté et structures épiques : actes du deuxième colloque international du REARE (Réseau Eur-Africain de recherche sur les épopées): Amiens (17-19 septembre 2002)* (Amiens: Centre d'Études Médiévales, 2003), pp. 82-93.

Gutt, Blake, 'Transgender Genealogy in *Tristan de Nanteuil*', *Exemplaria*, 30.2 (2018), 129-46.

Hotchkiss, Valerie R., *Clothes Make the Man: Female Cross Dressing in Medieval Europe* (New York: Garland, 1996).

Kelly, Molly Robinson, *The Hero's Place: Medieval Literary Traditions of Space and Belonging* (Washington, DC: Catholic University of America, 2009).

Lewis, Katherine J., 'Male Saints and Devotional Masculinity in Late Medieval England', *Gender and History*, 24.1 (2012), 112-33.

Lifshitz, Felice, *Religious Women in Early Carolingian Francia: A Study of Manuscript Transmission and Monastic Culture* (New York: Fordham University, 2014).

Lochrie, Karma, *Heterosyncrasies: Female Sexuality When Normal Wasn't* (Minneapolis: University of Minnesota, 2005).

Lowerre, Sandra, 'To Rise beyond their Sex: The Representation of Female Cross-Dressing Saints in Caxton's *Vitas Patrum*', in *Riddles, Knights and Cross-Dressing Saints. Essays on Medieval English Language and Literature*, ed. by Thomas Honegger (Bern: Peter Lang, 2004), pp. 55-94.

McCulloch, Florence, 'Saint Euphrosine, Saint Alexis, and the Turtledove', *Romania*, 98 (1977), 168-85.

Mills, Robert, *Suspended Animation: Pain, Pleasure and Punishment in Medieval Culture* (London: Reaktion, 2005).

—, 'Visibly Trans? Picturing Saint Eugenia in Medieval Art', *TSQ: Transgender Studies Quarterly*, 5.4 (2018), 540-64.

More, Alison, 'Convergence, Conversion, and Transformation: Gender and Sanctity in 13th-c. Liège', in *Representing Medieval Genders and Sexualities in Europe: Construction, Transformation, and Subversion, 600-1530*, ed. by Elizabeth L'Estrange and Alison More (London: Routledge, 2016), pp. 33-48.

Murray, Jacqueline, 'One Flesh, Two Sexes, Three Genders?', in *Gender and Christianity in Medieval Europe: New Perspectives*, ed. by Lisa M. Bitel (Philadelphia: University of Pennsylvania, 2008), pp. 34-51, 110-113.

—, 'Thinking about Gender: The Diversity of Medieval Perspectives', in *Power of the Weak: Studies on Medieval Women*, ed. by Jennifer Carpenter and Sally-Beth MacLean (Urbana: University of Illinois, 1995), pp. 1-26.

Norris, Robin, 'Genre Trouble: Reading the Old English *Vita* of Saint Euphrosyne', in *Writing Women Saints in Anglo-Saxon England*, ed. by Paul E. Szarmach (Toronto: University of Toronto, 2013), pp. 121-39.

Ogden, Amy V., 'The Centrality of Margins: Medieval French Genders and Genres Reconfigured', *French Forum*, 30.1 (2005), 1-23.

—, *Hagiography, Romance and the* Vie de sainte Eufrosine (Princeton: Edward C. Armstrong, 2003).

Phillips, Kim M., 'Gender and Sexuality', in *The Routledge History of Medieval Christianity, 1050-1500*, ed. by R.N. Swanson (London: Routledge, 2015), pp. 309-21.

Riches, Samantha J.E., 'St George as a Male Virgin Martyr', in *Gender and Holiness: Men, Women and Saints in Late Medieval Europe*, ed. by Samantha J.E. Riches and Sarah Salih (London: Routledge, 2002), pp. 65-85.

Schäfer-Althaus, Sarah, *The Gendered Body: Female Sanctity, Gender Hybridity and the Body in Women's Hagiography* (Heidelberg: Universitätsverlag Winter, 2016).

Stallcup, Stephen, 'The Old English Life of Saint Euphrosyne and the Economics of Sanctity', in *Anonymous Interpolations in Ælfric's Lives of Saints*, ed. by Robin Norris (Kalamazoo: Medieval Institute, 2011), pp. 13-28.

Storey, Christopher, *An Annotated Bibliography and Guide to Alexis Studies (la Vie de Saint Alexis)* (Geneva: Droz, 1987).

—, 'La Vie de sainte Euphrosine: A Reminder of a Neglected Thirteenth-Century Poem', *French Studies*, 31.4 (1977), 385-93.

Tobler-Lommatzsch Altfranzösisches Wörterbuch (Berlin: Weidmann, 1925).

Vitz, Evelyn Birge, 'Gender and Martyrdom', *Medievalia et Humanistica*, 26 (1999), 79-99.

About the author

AMY V. OGDEN, Associate Professor at the University of Virginia (USA), studies saints' Lives written in the French vernaculars and their manuscript and social contexts. In addition to publications on *Eufrosine* (*Hagiography, Romance and the Vie de sainte Eufrosine*, 2003; *The Life of Saint Eufrosine in Old French Verse, with English Translation*, 2021), she is the director of the web-based 'Lives of the Saints: The Medieval French Hagiography Project' (http://www.frenchsaintslives.org/). Other relevant publications include 'The Centrality of Margins: Medieval French Genders and Genres Reconfigured', *French Forum*, 2005 and *Wace, The Hagiographical Works*, 2013, with Jean Blacker and Glyn Burgess.

9 Holy Queer and Holy Cure

Sanctity, Disability, and Transgender Embodiment in *Tristan de Nanteuil*

Blake Gutt

Abstract
This chapter explores the ways that sacred, physically impaired, and transgender embodiment(s) are all structured by reference to notions of wholeness, perfection, and cure. Focussing on the character of Blanchandin·e in the fourteenth-century French narrative, *Tristan de Nanteuil*, the analysis considers how disability, cure, and gender transformation are employed to modify a body according to the exigencies of the surrounding hagiographic narrative. Blanchandin·e's physical form is repeatedly altered in response to the needs of their son, St Gilles. The chapter traces the shared effects and affects of the social formation – and disassembly – of trans-ness, sanctity, and physical impairment through the related, connected, and leaky bodies of Blanchandin·e and St Gilles.

Keywords: sanctity, disability, transgender, medieval, narrative prosthesis, cripistemologies

Saints are not truly saints until they are dead. As Brigitte Cazelles writes, 'the death of the saint is [...] the first stage of the hagiographic phenomenon [...]. Interest in the dead person ignites the desire to know more about their life'.[1] A saintly death simultaneously produces and confirms saintly identity. The perfection associated with sanctity thus draws on a notion of completeness: the saint's life is over; we can tell the whole story. We can be

---

1 Cazelles, *Le Corps*, p. 48: 'La mort du saint est [...] l'étape initiale du phénomène hagiographique [...]. L'intérêt pour le mort a ainsi suscité le désir d'en savoir plus sur sa vie.' All English translations in the main body of the text are my own.

Spencer-Hall, Alicia, and Blake Gutt (eds), *Trans and Genderqueer Subjects in Medieval Hagiography*. Amsterdam, Amsterdam University Press 2021
DOI: 10.5117/9789462988248_CH09

sure that this individual is a saint, since they are not alive to fall from grace through a human act. We can possess them completely – in memory, in narrative, and in relic form. Yet the phenomenon of sanctity simultaneously troubles any notion of completeness. Saints do not only exist in the past: their continued presence, bridging earth and heaven, is what makes them valuable as intercessors.[2] The narratives that relate their lives are multiple and variable, and fluid enough to cross generic boundaries. And holy relics, in the words of Caroline Walker Bynum, offer completeness 'either through reunion of parts into a whole or through assertion of part *as part* to *be* the whole'.[3] This equivocal and protean relationship to completeness marks and shapes saints' embodiment, as well as their *dis*embodiment.[4]

In this chapter, I explore the ways that perceptions of sacred, disabled, and transgender embodiment(s) are structured by reference to similar notions of wholeness, perfection, and cure. 'Disability', of course, is a broad umbrella term. In this analysis I specifically address physical impairment, as I examine how disability and gender transformation are employed to modify the body of a literary character (*Tristan de Nanteuil*'s Blanchandin·e) according to the exigencies of the surrounding hagiographic narrative. I use the terms 'impairment' and 'disability' interchangeably, following Alison Kafer's political/relational model of disability. Kafer's model undoes the rigid distinction that the social model draws between 'impairment' and 'disability', recognizing that both of these categories – the 'physical or mental limitation[s]' that the social model refers to as 'impairments', and 'the social exclusions based on, and social meanings attributed to' those impairments (which the social model defines as 'disability') – are in fact social constructs, dependent upon 'economic and geographic [and, I would add, temporal] context'.[5] My case study, the character of Blanchandin·e in the anonymous fourteenth-century French text *Tristan de Nanteuil*, vividly demonstrates the imbrications of sacred, transgender, and disabled embodiments. Blanchandin·e's body is transformed from female to male, and impaired by the loss of a limb before being cured through a miracle. These physical changes chart the entwined bodily destinies of Blanchandin·e and their son, St Gilles. To fully analyse the patterning of this narrative, it is necessary first to consider the interwoven theoretical constructions of these embodiments.

2   On saints and time, see: Spencer-Hall, *Medieval Saints*, pp. 65-105.
3   Bynum, *Fragmentation*, p. 13.
4   See Spencer-Hall, 'Wounds', pp. 399-400; p. 405.
5   Kafer, *Feminist, Queer, Crip*, p. 7.

Sacred, disabled, and transgender bodyminds

'Disability' is only comprehensible through reference to the supposed norm of 'ability'. Thus, the disabled bodymind is frequently perceived as doubled, haunted by the 'perfect' or 'complete' bodymind which is deemed to be absent when the disabled bodymind is present.[6] Likewise, transgender embodiment is perpetually at risk of being read either as an incomplete or imperfect imitation of cisgender embodiment (i.e. a trans man can never access the authentic masculinity of a cis man), or as a degraded form of a previously perfect embodiment (i.e. a trans man has corrupted his embodiment by 'refusing' to conform to the norms of cis womanhood). Such flickering doubles of trans and disabled subjects lurk in the mind's eye of the beholder. The social order dreams of cure for both disabled subjects ('repairing' or replacing the bodymind) and trans subjects (a becoming-cis which is either curative or violently 'restorative'). Both transgender and physically impaired embodiments are non-normative, according to social rules, patterns and structures. As such, these embodiments are never free of context; transgender identity and disability are community effects, and produce community affects. Sacred embodiment, too, is a collective embodiment, since it represents salvation not only for the saint but for those who surround them.[7] Sacred embodiment is a paradoxical notion, since to be a saint is progressively to abandon materiality, including the body itself, in a translation into the spiritual that is completed by death. Yet it is always *through* and *by* the body that sanctity is achieved. A body is required, so that it can be disdained – its flesh chastised, nourishment refused – or so that it can be inhabited with an intensity that expands bodily possibilities. Excessive saintly forms display uncanny abilities such as levitation, or the miraculous healing of other bodies. The discarding of the body at the moment of death figures a transition beyond the material, yet even post mortem the body of a saint has work to do: remaining incorrupt, emitting sweet odours and, in the form of relics, performing intercessory and healing functions. Thus, although the metaphysical existence of saints is what ultimately affirms their sanctity, sacred bodies remain essential. The varied meanings of these bodies are determined though social interactions.

All bodies are subject to intense and complex socio-cultural mediation. For the unmarked subject, this mediation is smooth and silent, enabling the

---

6   The term 'bodymind' reflects 'the imbrication (not just the combination) of the entities usually called "body" and "mind"': Price, 'Bodymind Problem', p. 270.

7   See Spencer-Hall, 'Wounds', p. 396; pp. 408-09.

fantasy of direct, automatic, and natural being-in-the-world. For marked subjects, such as trans people and physically impaired people, these processes of mediation are rendered painfully clear through socio-cultural discourse(s) that invoke normative modes and models of existence. Disabled and transgender individuals' own relationships to and understanding of their bodies are afforded less significance and validity than dominant notions of physical (ab)normality. Whereas saints' bodies are frequently de-emphasized, the bodies of trans and physically impaired people are typically over-emphasized. Both of the latter groups are routinely reduced to their bodily topography, and specifically to its differences from the (cis, able-bodyminded) norm; the effect is multiplied for individuals who are both disabled and trans.[8] Similarly, the meaning of the saintly body is produced by, and shared out among, a community, since the saintly body signifies through and for others. Alicia Spencer-Hall describes this function of sacred embodiment in the case of the thirteenth-century Cistercian nun known as Alice the Leper as follows:

> Alice's leprosy is a boon for her community, and a means for them to expurgate sin: She bears their spiritual wounds in somatized form, and there is little space for Alice's own experiences. Alice is a gap – or wound – in the tissue of her community, rather than a subject proper.[9]

Alice's sanctity and her disability signify simultaneously: the illness that progressively impairs her body is both a mark of divine love and a mechanism for taking on the sins of her peers. Through each of these aspects of her leprous embodiment, her piety and her spiritual status are enhanced.[10]

Linking bodyminds

Alice's example demonstrates how sacred embodiment functions both to reinforce normative embodiment (the holy body marks the boundaries of physical normativity), and to indicate the potential for transcendence (the boundaries are marked by means of their transgression). Thus, sacred embodiments constitute what I refer to as an 'included outside': a section of a system which marks the edges of that system; which, while nominally

---

8   On the term 'able-bodyminded(ness)', see Sheppard, 'Using Pain', pp. 55-56.
9   Spencer-Hall, 'Wounds', p. 396.
10 Ibid., p. 390.

included, makes manifest what is beyond and outside the system's scope. Holy bodies are at once alluring and terrifying. This contradiction, I suggest, is part of the mechanism that ensures that saints remain rare, extraordinary. Normate subjects inhabit the centre of the system, and the abjection of the included outside delineates borders which cannot safely be crossed. For non-normate subjects, however, the logic of sanctity reveals liberating individual, spiritual, and social relationships to the body, relationships that resist mainstream cultural expectations. The model of sacred embodiment offers a way of understanding and experiencing bodies that defy norms not as abject but as productive – both of metaphysical signification and of earthly community ties. I argue that medieval literature depicts sacred, impaired, and transgender embodiments in similar ways. Modern ableism casts disability as 'inherently negative, ontologically intolerable and in the end, a dispensable remnant'.[11] Medieval texts, however, offer myriad ways to read disability of all kinds – physical, intellectual and sensory; acquired and congenital; chronic illness and chronic pain – as meaningful, productive, valuable, and above all, connective, linking earthbound bodies to each other, but also to the divine.[12] These readings resonate profoundly with modern crip theory, whose structures in turn draw on queer theory. As Robert McRuer argues, able-bodied identity is a fantasized state which, like cisheterosexuality in Judith Butler's analysis, must be repeatedly imitated in order to give the impression that it exists as a stable referent.[13]

McRuer indicates that compulsory cisheterosexuality and compulsory able-bodymindedness are fundamentally intertwined. He writes:

> Able-bodied identity and heterosexual identity are linked in their mutual impossibility and in their mutual incomprehensibility – they are incomprehensible in that each is an identity that is simultaneously the ground on which all identities supposedly rest and an impressive achievement that is always deferred and thus never really guaranteed.[14]

The very impossibility and unknowability of both able-bodyminded embodiment and cisheterosexual embodiment reveals them as socio-cultural imaginings. Thus, the cultural production of both disabled and transgender bodies fortifies the supremacy of normate embodiment. Non-normate

---

11   Campbell, *Contours of Ableism*, p. 12.
12   See Spencer-Hall, 'Chronic Pain'.
13   McRuer, *Crip Theory*; Butler, 'Imitation', p. 21.
14   McRuer, *Crip Theory*, p. 9.

embodiment is always constructed through socio-cultural norms, such that even the individuals who inhabit these bodies are constrained to an indirect relation to their physical selves, a contact refracted through ambient concepts of 'correct' and normative embodiment. The force of this knowledge regime is intensified via the inevitable internalization of ableism and transphobia. As a result, trans and disabled individuals' knowledge of and authority over our own bodies is delegitimized. However, the sharing of bodily effects and affects among individuals indicates a pathway for another kind of communal production of meaning, and the construction of networks centred on the reclaiming of non-normate embodiments and identities.

The link between sacred bodies and trans bodies is well attested in medieval Western Christianity. From the writings of major figures in the church, to hagiography, mysticism, and extra-canonical genres such as hagiographic romance, non-normatively gendered embodiments frequently signify a privileged relationship to the divine. Better-known examples include the corpus of 'transvestite monk' narratives, in which individuals assigned female at birth live as monks and ultimately become saints, and the popularity of maternal imagery in descriptions of God and Christ among twelfth-century Cistercian monks.[15] Many medieval hagiographic texts also assume that disability needs sanctity, so that miracles can be performed, and impairments can be removed. This in turn means that sanctity needs disability as its object, or its substrate: a saint cannot demonstrate sanctity through miraculous healings if there is no one to heal.[16] Saints, too, frequently experience illness, pain, or impairment. These events are presented as establishing or affirming contact with the divine, and as giving rise to specific kinds of embodied and situated knowledge, dependent on and produced through disability: cripistemologies.[17] I argue that this constellation of bodies and social formations – transgender, physically impaired and sacred embodiments – coheres because of the similarity of the structuring logics, meaning that the individual elements will often be found in conjunction.

---

15   See Bynum, *Jesus as Mother*, pp. 110-169; Gutt, 'Transgender Genealogy' and 'Medieval Trans Lives'; and in this volume, 'Introduction' (pp. 24-27), Newman (pp. 43-63, especially 47, 54, 59), Wright (pp. 155-76), Ogden (pp. 201-21), Bychowski (pp. 245-65).
16   There are also saints who inflict 'miracles' of injury or impairment; see relevant chapters in Spencer-Hall, Grace-Petinos, and Pope-Parker.
17   See, for example, Spencer-Hall, 'Chronic Pain'; Spencer-Hall, Grace-Petinos and Pope-Parker. On cripistemologies, see Patsavas, 'Recovering'; Johnson and McRuer, 'Introduction'.

Blanchandin·e's bodymind

I now turn to my case study, the character of Blanchandin·e in *Tristan de Nanteuil*, an anonymous fourteenth-century French *chanson d'aventures*.[18] The text, which is preserved in a single manuscript, is made up of 480 monorhyming *laisses*, or variable-length stanzas, comprising a total of 23,361 lines.[19] The complex narrative of this vast work incorporates a version of the life of St Gilles, the patron saint of people living with permanent physical impairments, such as absent limbs or limited mobility, and of beggars.[20] The body of Blanchandin·e, Gilles' parent, is demonstrably malleable, and can be altered to serve Gilles' needs. Blanchandin·e, who might be considered a quasi-saint themself, experiences a complex trajectory of physical transformation in the course of the narrative. They are first known as Blanchandine, and later as Blanchandin (the feminine and masculine forms, respectively, of the same name). The original French employs the pronouns 'she' ('elle') for Blanchandine, and 'he' ('il') for Blanchandin. I follow this usage when discussing specific moments in the character's life; however, I also strategically refer to the character using the compound form 'Blanchandin·e', and singular they/them pronouns, in order to emphasize the unity of the character's identity despite changes to their embodiment.

When we first meet Blanchandine, she is a Muslim princess; she subsequently converts to Christianity, and becomes the first wife of the eponymous Tristan de Nanteuil. The couple have a son, Raimon, and three years later Blanchandine encounters an angel who transforms her into a man. The transformation follows a period of male disguise intended to protect her identity while Tristan and Blanchandine are in hiding from the latter's vengeful father. Though it may be tempting to read the time Blanchandine spends in male dress, and using the name Blanchandin, as a social transition, I have argued elsewhere that this interpretation of the text does not withstand scrutiny.[21] The 'Blanchandin' disguise is just that; it is not until the moment of physical transformation that Blanchandine

---

18 *Chanson d'aventures* is the name given to some later examples of the *chanson de geste* genre, in which the focus shifts from battles to marvellous adventures.
19 Paris, France, Bibliothèque nationale de France, MS Français 1478. The critical edition is Sinclair, *Tristan de Nanteuil*.
20 Gilles, also known as St Giles or St Aegidius, appears in the *Golden Legend*, and is the subject of a twelfth-century Anglo-Norman Life, *La Vie de saint Gilles*, based on the Latin *Vita sancti Aegidii*, dated to the tenth century (Guillaume de Berneville, *Vie*, pp. xvii-xviii). *Tristan de Nanteuil* rewrites the saint's story, retaining only a few key motifs.
21 See Gutt, 'Transgender Genealogy', pp. 140-41.

becomes Blanchandin. For this reason, my focus in this chapter is on embodiment rather than identity. Modern discussion of 'identifying as' and 'identified gender' often seems to separate *being* from *identifying (as)*.[22] Thus transness is held at a remove from *being*; an apparently structured (or constructed) transgender existence is opposed to the supposed immediacy and naturalness of cisgender existence. An exploration of the depiction of transgender embodiment in *Tristan de Nanteuil* allows consideration of transgender status as a reality produced by sociocultural interactions in the same way as cisgender status. My analysis returns to the physicality of trans embodiment not to reinscribe shallow notions of the 'wrong' body, but rather to consider how transgender being, like cisgender being, is always produced through the body, its affects, and its relations and orientations to other bodies. This is true in the case of transformation narratives such as *Tristan de Nanteuil*, but also in cases where trans embodiment is produced through and by bodily techniques and technologies ranging from medical interventions and prostheses, to dress and grooming choices, to social performances and interactions.

When Blanchandine meets the angel, she is presented with a choice. The angel says:

> Jesus, who made the world, now asks you which you would prefer – speak honestly: to remain a woman, as he created you, or to become a man? The choice is yours. You will be a man, if you wish, because he will change you, and give you everything that belongs to a man. Now speak your desire, because it will be according to your wish.[23]

According to Butler's analysis of the functioning of gender, this framing is paradoxical. We are shown the impossible instant in which the pre-gendered subject is free to decide on their own gender – impossible because it is only *through* gender that subjectivity can be achieved.[24] However, as in Butler's theorization, the notion of freedom to define the terms of one's own subjectivity is revealed to be an illusion. Blanchandine decides to become a man because she believes that her husband, Tristan, is dead, and wishes to

---

22 See 'Identified Gender' in the Appendix: p. 301.

23 "'Or te mande Jhesus qui le monde estora, | Lequel tu aymes mieulx, or ne me celles ja : | Ou adés estre femme ainsy qu'i te crea, | Ou devenir ungs homs? A ton vouloir sera. | Homs sera, se tu veulx, car il te changera | Et te donrra tout ce qu'a home appertendra. | Or en di ton vouloir, car ainsy il sera | Selon ta voulenté.'" Sinclair, *Tristan de Nanteuil*, ll. 16142-49.

24 Butler, *Bodies that Matter*, pp. xvi-xvii. For further analysis of this moment in *Tristan de Nanteuil*, see Gutt, 'Transgender Genealogy', p. 141.

avenge him. Yet soon after the transformation has taken place, Blanchandine learns that Tristan is in fact alive. Far from avenging Tristan's death, the newly transformed Blanchandin is now separated from his husband by his own altered embodiment, since, as he states: "'God certainly does not wish that a man should ever have another man in this mortal life'".[25] Thus it is clear that the transformation does not serve Blanchandin·e's desires, but rather God's plan: Blanchandin·e and their cousin Clarinde must conceive St Gilles.[26] Attention to patterns of desire is crucial in trans readings, as interpretations of this affect can flatten transgender embodiment to a number of simplistic paradigms in which, for example, wanting is equated directly to being (one wants, therefore one is), or transgender *desiring to be* is construed as the imperfect analogue of cisgender *being*. Rhetorics of desire also permeate modern, ableist perceptions of disability. Disabled people, particularly those with chronic illness or chronic pain, are often subject to suspicion, assumed to lack sufficient desire – or sufficient willpower – to transcend their impairments.[27] Here, the circumstances of Blanchandin·e's transformation demonstrate that transgender embodiment is not something that the individual can control; it is not a question of desiring, but a question of being.

The angel describes God's genealogical plan to Blanchandin·e as follows:

> Lie with [Clarinde] as often as you please, for the first night that your body lies with hers, you will be able to engender [...] an heir whom it will please God to crown richly for the good works that he will do. He will be called St Gilles.[28]

Metonymic use of 'your body' ('ton corps') for 'you', 'my body' ('mon corps') for 'me', etc, occurs throughout *Tristan de Nanteuil*. This insistence on embodiment *as* being, embodiment *as* identity, supports and informs my analysis of the primacy of the body in this text. Following his transformation, Blanchandin and Clarinde conceive St Gilles, as the

---

25 "'Dieu ne le veult mye | C'oncques homs ne fist aultre en celle mortel vie'". Sinclair, *Tristan de Nanteuil*, ll. 16283-84.
26 On Blanchandin·e and Clarinde's relationship, and the steps taken to ensure the legitimacy of their union, see Gutt, 'Transgender Genealogy', pp. 137-38.
27 On chronic illness, see Wendell, 'Unhealthy Disabled', p. 29; on chronic pain, see Patsavas, 'Recovering', pp. 210-11.
28 "'couches o lui tant quë il te plaira, | Car la premiere nuyt que ton corps y gerra, | [...] pourras engendrer ung hoir que Dieu vourra | Haultement couronner pour le bien qu'i fera ; | Saint Gilles yert clamés'". Sinclair, *Tristan de Nanteuil*, ll. 16187-91.

angel had prophesied. Soon after Gilles' birth, however, the new family is separated when their home is attacked in revenge by 'pagan' Greeks whom Blanchandin had forcibly converted. Blanchandin's left arm is cut off, and he spends the next thirty years searching for his son, the only one who will be able to reattach the amputated limb. In this way, Blanchandin's body itself becomes a shibboleth that facilitates both a family reunion and the recognition of Gilles' sanctity. Blanchandin·e's body is not Gilles' body, yet transformation, impairment, and cure are successively imposed upon it to serve Gilles' needs; without Blanchandin·e, Gilles could not be the saint that he is in this text. After the amputation of his arm, Blanchandin spends fifteen years begging, followed by fifteen years restored to the rank of knight, using an iron prosthetic arm to hold his shield. Thus, during his thirty-year search for his son, Blanchandin embodies two of the categories of individuals of whom Gilles is the patron saint: beggars, and people with physical impairments.[29] By the end of the narrative, Blanchandin's disabled trans body has been restored to wholeness by Gilles' holy body. This wholeness is shared between the two physical forms. According to the logic of the text, both are rendered more 'perfect' (Blanchandin is cured, and Gilles is demonstrated to be a saint) by this interaction. We do not hear Blanchandin speak in the aftermath of the miracle. The cripistemologies to which Blanchandin had access in his disabled embodiment disappear silently with the reattachment of his arm. Following the miracle, the attention of the text is refocused on Gilles; it is he who is demonstrated to possess unique and valuable embodied knowledge. But are cripistemologies lost, or rather transformed? Gilles takes Blanchandin's narrative place as the connective node around whom the rest of the characters coalesce, and one type of specific, situated knowledge is transfigured into another through the transformative moment of cure.

Notions of cure

Kafer's political/relational model of disability '[sees] "disability" as a potential site for collective reimagining', producing activist community solidarity.[30] The political/relational model is radically inclusive, making space for anyone who is not fully able-bodyminded, whether temporarily or permanently. This intrinsic openness empties the notion that able-bodymindedness

---

29 On disability and begging in the Middle Ages, see Metzler, *Social History*, pp. 154-98.
30 Kafer, *Feminist, Queer, Crip*, p. 9

can be a concrete or enduring form of embodiment. Simultaneously, work by Kafer, McRuer and others indicates the pervasive cultural bracketing of queerness and disability as 'abnormal' or 'unnatural' embodiments. Disabled and transgender embodiments, as disruptions to the fantasized states of automatic cisheterosexuality and automatic able-bodymindedness, are structurally constituted. Thus each exists as part of a fluid, relational nexus; as McRuer's analysis demonstrates, neither able-bodiedness nor cisheterosexuality is ever more than a fantasy of completeness. Kafer argues that 'disability is experienced in and through relationships; it does not occur in isolation'; and I propose that the same is true of transgender embodiment.[31] Each comes into signification and comprehension only through relation to the abilities, sensations, and physical experiences of other bodyminds – and each is stigmatized through comparison to bodyminds recognized as more socio-culturally normate.

Alyson Patsavas describes pain as: '[A] fluid, relational, and [...] leaky experience that flows through, across, and between always-already connected bodies'.[32] We might think of transgender embodiment in a similar manner. Gender itself is social and situational, and produced through relationships. Sanctity, as we have seen, operates relationally, orienting communities around the saintly body. Cure, too, is relational; its technologies and performances are typically prescribed to a patient by an authority. Many disabled people oppose rhetorics of cure, rejecting the medical model that situates disability within the individual. The medical model seeks to remove disability even at the cost of removing disabled human beings from society via institutionalization, euthanasia, eugenics, and selective abortion. Alternative models, such as the social model and Kafer's political/relational model, locate disability within the (built) environment, and the social structures and discourses that limit the participation of impaired bodyminds. As Eli Clare writes: 'At the center of cure lies eradication and the many kinds of violence that accompany it'.[33] The eradication of disability constitutes the eradication not only of bodyminds, but of cripistemologies: human ways of being, and of knowing, which have intrinsic value.[34] Similarly, trans people typically do not see themselves as requiring a 'cure' because the trans bodymind is not a defective version of a cis bodymind, but a facet of human diversity. Trans embodiments

---

31 Ibid., p. 8.
32 Patsavas, 'Recovering', p. 213.
33 Clare, *Brilliant Imperfection*, p. 26.
34 Wendell, 'Unhealthy Disabled', pp. 31-32.

generate trans epistemologies, distinct forms of embodied knowledge and knowledge production which, like cripistemologies, are often unknown to or devalued by normative discourse. Their disappearance, if disabled and/or trans lives were somehow to cease to exist, would constitute a significant loss to the sum of human expertise. Cripistemologies and trans epistemologies not only carve out space for marginalized existences in the present, but render disabled and trans futures thinkable, and therefore possible.[35] When medieval cure operates in a sacred perspective, it does not enact eradication, but rather relationality, proximity, and futurity. Pain or impairment is transferred or transformed, and functions to forge bonds both human and divine.

The reader of *Tristan de Nanteuil* is taught to envision impairment in a relational mode. In the passage preceding Blanchandine's transformation into Blanchandin, this secular text takes a turn for the hagiographic, declaring itself worthy of being preached as a sermon before offering its own theorization of the meaning of disability:

> If a good person experiences any obstacle (*encombrier*), they should realize that God has sent it to them; and the one who is most afflicted owes the most thanks to God. This is how God demonstrates his love and welcomes one to the glory of heaven; this [affliction] is the payment.[36]

Physical impairment is thus located within the extremely broad category of 'obstacle' ('encombrier'); anything that interrupts expected or anticipated patterns of experience is essentially rendered equivalent in both effect and signification. Notably, for Blanchandin·e this category includes both becoming trans and becoming impaired. Yet at the same time that this theorization relies upon the undesirability of the 'obstacle' – for how else is it to be identified as such? – the model seamlessly reframes what is supposedly inherently undesirable as precisely *that which should be desired*. Disability is revealed to be not only relational (it is sent by God), but also transactional: it constitutes the necessary payment for a paradisiac future in which the notion of disability – along with the notion of ability – ceases to exist. This structure enables the apparently radical proposal of desiring

---

35   On trans epistemologies see Ridley, 'Imagining Otherly'; Radi, 'Políticas'; McKinnon, 'Allies', pp. 170-71.

36   '[S]e bonne persone a aucun encombrier, | Il doit penser que Dieu lui a fait envoier ; | Et qui plus a d'anoy, plus le doit gracïer ; | Ensement l'ayme Dieu et le fait heberger | En la gloire des cieulx et la le fait paier.' Sinclair, *Tristan de Nanteuil*, ll. 15781-85.

disability, yet the desire is always predicated on the certain eradication of the supposedly desired state. That is: one may aspire to impairment, since such experience connotes contact with the divine. However, impairments are always and only ever temporal, and therefore temporary. Whether in this life or the next, a cure will be enacted, and the bodymind will be 'returned' to the fantasized state of wholeness. This promise of perfection reveals that, when disability is desired in this context, what is truly desired is the radically non-disabled state which can be accessed by means of earthly impairment.

Narrative prostheses

The paradigm described above resonates with David T. Mitchell and Sharon L. Snyder's analysis of the function of disability within narrative, which demonstrates that a fundamental operation of narrative is to rehabilitate or fix deviance. Mitchell and Snyder's theory of narrative prosthesis reveals how disability frequently serves as a plot mechanism, driving and shaping the narrative until its own elimination can be achieved.[37] Blanchandin's amputated arm functions in this manner. It serves as a device to ensure the eventual reunion of parent and child, as well as to dramatically and conclusively demonstrate Gilles' saintly status through the miraculous healing. Both the text's own structure, and Mitchell and Snyder's theorization, are predicated on the ultimate effacing of impairment, which is what appears to happen when Blanchandin's arm is reattached. But when disability is understood through a relational model, can it ever really disappear? Or is it simply reoriented or relocated, as an integral aspect of a network of vulnerable bodies? As Spencer-Hall notes in relation to another medieval tale of miraculous healing: 'Disability can never be annihilated; instead, it is forever reconstituted along relational pathways'.[38]

In the course of the text, Blanchandin·e welcomes physical events ranging from thorn pricks, to transformation from female to male, to the loss of a limb, since each is an expression of God's will. When she encounters the angel who transforms her into a man, Blanchandine is fleeing through the forest. She prays as she runs, believing that her husband, Tristan, is dead. The text casts this journey as a process of abjection in the model of saintly

37 Mitchell and Snyder, *Narrative Prosthesis*, pp. 6-8.
38 Spencer-Hall, 'Chronic Pain', p. 62.

mortification; we are told that she willingly takes the path where she sees most thorns. The narrative continues:

> She weeps and sighs very piteously; her legs and feet are bloody, and as soon as a thorn causes her heart to suffer, she throws herself to her bare knees with admirable desire and says: 'God, I worship you and fervently thank you for whatever you send me; my body gratefully accepts it. I want to endure this torment in your name, and in honour of Tristan and his salvation. The penance that I will have to perform for a long time, I perform in his name, so that on the Day of Judgement he may dwell with you on high'.[39]

Here, pain and physical change are demonstrated to exist not only in relation to God, but also in relation to another person – someone that Blanchandine believes is dead, and on whose behalf she wishes to intercede. The relational web that produces disabled embodiment is thus shown to encompass at least three categories of beings: God, living people, and dead people. While in much of modern culture – particularly medical(ized) discourses – pain is framed as 'an isolating, devastating experience', for Blanchandine, pain is a sign that she is not alone.[40] The sensation affirms that she is accompanied by God, and is held in relation both to him and to other mortal beings, including Tristan. God is the source of embodied experience, which must be rendered meaningful through its active interpretation as part of a transactional relationship with him. Blanchandine's pain also connects her to her husband: she can bargain with God to transform the meaning of her suffering, such that its result, the obliteration of suffering, is transferred to Tristan. Thus, all

---

[39] 'Elle pleure et souspire assés piteusement ; | Les jambes et les piés lui estoient senglant, | Et sy tost c'une espine lui fait au ceur tourment, | A nuz genoulx se gette d'amourable tallant | Et dit : "Dieu, je t'aoure et te graci granment | De quanques que m'envoyes ; mon corps en gré le prent. | Je veul ou non de toy endurer le tourment | En l'onneur de Tristan et de son sauvement. | La penance qu'aray a fere longuement, | Je le fais en son non, par quoy au Jugement | Puist avoir avec toy lassus hebergement."' Sinclair, *Tristan de Nanteuil*, ll. 16085-95.

[40] Patsavas, 'Recovering', p. 204. Scarry's foundational discussion of pain contends that 'pain comes unsharably into our midst as at once that which cannot be denied and that which cannot be confirmed' (p. 4). Although this view is still widespread, Scarry's analysis has been extensively challenged and productively nuanced by work including: van Ommen, Cromby, and Yen, 'New Perspectives'; and Gonzalez-Polledo and Tarr, *Painscapes* (see especially pp. 5-10). Patsavas emphasizes that 'we never experience pain in isolation' ('Recovering', p. 209). Work such as Patsavas's is inherently political, revealing and subverting ableist medical discourses that view pain as insupportable, and thus the lives of those with chronic pain as less valuable (even eradicable, if this is the only way that the pain can be 'cured').

three are linked by the relational network. The metonymic use of 'my body' ('mon corps') instead of 'I' once again demonstrates that the text operates on a logic of embodiment, rather than a logic of identity.

The next section of the text sees Blanchandine transformed into Blanchandin; the text states that: '[W]hen he saw himself transformed, he praised Jesus Christ'.[41] It is notable that the changes to Blanchandine's body are presented as straightforwardly additive, and focused on the genitals. Much is made of Blanchandin's new penis, the literalized narrative prosthesis that permits the continuation of God's plan, Blanchandin's lineage, and the text itself. When he meets Tristan's half-brother, Doon, Blanchandin has to display 'his flesh, which was completely changed below the belt' in order to convince Doon that he is now a man.[42] Blanchandin's penis is soon displayed to all and sundry at court as he takes a bath. The ability that a penis implicitly demonstrates, of course, is the ability to engender a child; the narrative again underscores that it is for the sake of the yet-to-be-born St Gilles that Blanchandin·e's body has been transformed. This casts the pre-transformation, female Blanchandine both as lacking in ability, and as physically lacking, or incomplete; both these 'lacks' are 'cured' by the angel. This transformative 'cure' reflects the misogynistic moral hierarchy expounded by early church fathers such as St Jerome, who wrote that a devout woman 'will cease to be a woman and will be called man' ('mulier esse cessabit, et dicetur vir').[43] Blanchandin's altered body both reflects and enacts his altered relationship to God, as well to the saintly future son he is required to engender. This divinely ordained reproductive futurism calls normative modern understandings of queer and crip futures into question.[44] According to certain pervasive modern discourses, queer people *cannot* reproduce (since reproductive sex is equated to cisheteronormativity), whereas disabled people *should not* reproduce (because they 'risk' reproducing disability). Blanchandin's reproductive future, however, is not only possible, but essential.[45] The transformation of his body enables the conception of St Gilles, while the loss of his arm produces the cripistemologies that shape Gilles' embodiment as he 'comes out' as a saint. Thus, the network of embodied relations is shown to link not only God, the living, and the dead, but also angels, saints, and the unborn.

41 'Quant se vit transmué, Jhesus Crist en loa'. Sinclair, *Tristan de Nanteuil*, l. 16204.
42 '[S]a char qui toute estoit changie | Par dessoubz le braiel'. Ibid., ll. 16240-41.
43 See Mills, *Seeing Sodomy*, pp. 205-06.
44 On the logics of reproductive futurism, see Edelman, *No Future*; and McLoughlin in this volume (pp. 65-85).
45 See Gutt, 'Transgender Genealogy'.

Fragmentation and reassembly

When Blanchandin's arm is severed, he responds by praising and thanking God; he interprets the impairment as a direct reflection of his moral status:

> Lord God who, from death, returned to life, I know well that through some foolish action I have deserved the great torment that I am in, and the great suffering, and I accept it willingly.[46]

Blanchandin relates the injury to God not only as its source, but also as a model for how to live this experience. God himself has experienced greater physical disability; thus, mortal impairments are at once trivial (because they cannot compare to Christ's suffering) and significant (because they replicate this suffering, however faintly). Here I use the term 'suffering' to reflect Blanchandin's statements about his experience, yet in medieval Western Christianity, pain and impairment were frequently conceptualized as both positive and productive.[47] Similarly, modern crip theory challenges the ableist assumption that pain and impairment can only be experienced as suffering.[48] Yet in the central paradox of Christian redemption, as presented in *Tristan de Nanteuil*, disability is to be desired and welcomed in the knowledge that impairment exists only to be erased. If God is the paradigm of total ability, which humans, though made in his image, can never approximate, then Jesus is the model of 'perfect' disability, which is only ever transitory, and always ennobling. Christ therefore fits Sami Schalk's archetype of the 'superpowered supercrip': 'a character who has abilities or "powers" that operate in direct relationship with or contrast to their disability'.[49] The *imitatio Christi* practiced by disabled saints, in turn, reveals them as 'glorified supercrips', disabled characters who achieve dramatic feats through hard work. Yet Schalk notes that such characters benefit not only from their own 'extraordinary and compensating qualities', but also from significant socio-cultural privilege.[50] The privilege of saints is their relationship with God which, in a circular and paradoxical paradigm, provides and affirms the sanctity that their actions perform and declare.

---

46 "'Beaus sire Dieu qui de mort vins a vie, | Bien sçay, j'ay desservy par aucune folie | Le gref tourment que j'ay et la grant maladie ; | Et je le prens en gré.'" Sinclair, *Tristan de Nanteuil*, ll. 17965-68.
47 Spencer-Hall, 'Chronic Pain', pp. 52-53.
48 Patsavas, 'Recovering', pp. 203-04.
49 Schalk, 'Supercrip', p. 81.
50 Ibid., p. 80.

The promise of paradise is that this complex relational network will collapse into oneness with God; notions of ability and disability, along with the concept of bodymindedness itself, will no longer be relevant. The apparent wholeness and completion of resurrection, however, will be composed – figuratively, but also perhaps literally – of the wounds and fractures that earned and marked fitness for heaven.[51] Cure cannot, therefore, eradicate impairment, because lived experiences of disability constitute complex and valuable ways of being human. These experiences produce the cripistemologies that multiply links between community members, but also link the entire community to the divine. Similarly, transgender embodiment, as a way of sensing, experiencing, and relating to the body *otherwise*, produces trans epistemologies with communal effects.[52]

Following Blanchandin's injury, his status as quasi-saint is solidified as he becomes a kind of living relic; he is informed by an angel that he must carry his severed arm with him as he searches for his son, since Gilles alone can cure him. When Blanchandin is finally reunited with his son, the saint receives the arm as if it is a cross between a long-lost relative and a holy relic, which is in fact the case. He marvels to find it incorrupt after thirty years: 'When Gilles holds the arm, straight away he begins to kiss it; he hugs it in his arms and squeezes it tightly. He is astonished that it is so rosy.'[53] This transfer of the arm from Blanchandin to Gilles once again literalizes narrative prosthesis. This prosthesis is transformed throughout the text from Blanchandine's phantasmatic phallus, to Blanchandin's 'large and thick' penis ('gros et quarrés'), to Blanchandin's severed arm, to Gilles' sanctity.[54] Each in turn serves as the focal point that structures the relational web linking the text's characters. The moment when Gilles receives the arm figures the fusion of Blanchandin's trans cripistemology with Gilles' sacred epistemology. This is not an erasure, but a cumulative process of knowledge development, shared between intimately connected yet differently situated bodies. The passing of the arm also reconfigures the relationship between father and son, impaired subject and healer. The shibboleth of the arm affirms that Gilles is Blanchandin's son at the same time that it asserts Gilles' place in another genealogy, the lineage of saints

---

51   On medieval Western Christian conceptions of bodily resurrection, see Bynum, *Fragmentation*, pp. 227-31. On this and modern technologies, see: Spencer-Hall, *Medieval Saints*, pp. 77-102.
52   See Ridley, 'Imagining Otherly', pp. 485-86.
53   'Quant Gilles tint le bras, adonc le va baisant, | Entre ses bras l'acolle et l'alla estraignant, | De ce qu'est sy vermeil se va esbahissant.' Sinclair, *Tristan de Nanteuil*, ll. 22790-92.
54   Ibid., l. 16357.

ordained by God. Their relationships revolve and transform around the locus of the theoretical narrative prosthesis, as well as the text's literal prostheses.

St Gilles prays, and is empowered to reattach his father's arm to his shoulder: 'In front of twenty thousand Armenians, and in front of King Tristan, [Gilles] reattaches the severed arm to the stump, one flesh against the other, just as it was before'.[55] The relational network in this moment of cure encompasses not only God, Gilles, and Blanchandin, but also the twenty thousand observers who are sutured into the system as witnesses to the miracle. Their presence transforms the healing into a highly charged symbolic event, designed not only to restore Blanchandin's ability but to employ this spectacle as a means of bringing the observers closer to God. Similarly, the miracle of Blanchandin·e's transformation serves as a catalyst for Gilles' own piety. When, as a boy, he hears his mother speak of his father's transformation, the narrative affects him profoundly:

> [W]hen the child hears this, he thanks God and His sweet mother with all his heart. His father's miracle enlightens him so greatly that he places his desire and his heart and all his certainty in Jesus, the all-powerful father.[56]

Once again, transgender embodiment is revealed not as a dereliction of divine order, as many branches of twenty-first century Christianity declare, but rather as a radiant expression of God's will. Although both Blanchandin and Christ are undoubtedly male, each was formed from female flesh: Blanchandin from Blanchandine, and Christ from Mary.[57]

Throughout the text, physical changes are enacted upon the quasi-saint Blanchandin·e for the sake of St Gilles. The narrative trajectory of the pair demonstrates the paradoxically conjoined-yet-separated embodiments of parent and child, impaired person and sacred healer. It is Gilles who is marked as holy, who is demonstrated to possess a hyper-able saintly body whose non-normative abilities include the power to reattach amputated limbs. Yet Blanchandin·e's body, too, manifests hyper-ability: his incorrupt severed arm proves that he has non-normative physical aptitudes. So, too, does the transformation from female to male. God's will is always

---

55 'Devant .xx. mille Ermins et devant roy Tristan | Va la brace tranchee au mongnon resoudant, | L'une char contre l'aultre aussy fut que devant'. Ibid., ll. 22814-16.
56 '[Q]uant ly enffes va celle chose escoutant, | Dieu et sa doulce mere va de ceur graciant. | Le miracle son pere le va enluminant | Tellement qu'a Jhesus, le pere tout poissant, | Mist entente et courage et tout son essïent.' Ibid., ll. 19766-70.
57 See Bynum, *Fragmentation*, p. 172, and Sexon in this volume (pp. 133-53, especially 135-41).

required in order for these abilities to be exhibited, but then God's will is similarly implicated in impairments and cures.[58] The necessity for divine involvement does not negate the part played by human bodies in these depictions of non-normative ability; rather, it affirms the relational aspect of these shifting embodiments. Blanchandin·e's malleable body made Gilles' existence possible. In addition to being a quasi-saint, Blanchandin·e, too, can be figured as supercrip. It is doubly *through* Blanchandin·e that Gilles' sacred identity emerges; the pair are locked in a mutually dependent, mutually defining kinship. Sacred, impaired, and transgender embodiments, as they are presented in *Tristan de Nanteuil*, can be conceptualized in similar ways. The nexus of embodiment, impairment, and cure flows through, across, and between St Gilles and Blanchandin·e; their physical forms are altered through their embodied relations to each other, and to the divine.

Acknowledgements

I am very grateful to Catherine Brown for her transformative comments on an earlier version of this chapter, and to Alicia Spencer-Hall for her ever-incisive editorial advice.

Bibliography

Manuscripts

Paris, France, Bibliothèque nationale de France, MS Français 1478 <http://gallica.bnf.fr/ark:/12148/btv1b90589112/f1.image.r=guy%20de%20nanteul> [accessed 14 August 2020].

Primary sources

Guillaume de Berneville, *La Vie de saint Gilles*, ed. by Françoise Laurent (Paris: Honoré Champion, 2003).
Sinclair, K.V., ed., *Tristan de Nanteuil: Chanson de geste inédite* (Assen: Van Gorcum, 1971).

---

58 See also Elphick in this volume (pp. 87-107, especially 87, 91, 94-95).

Secondary sources

Butler, Judith, *Bodies That Matter: On the Discursive Limits of "Sex"* (London: Routledge, 2011 [1993]).

—, 'Imitation and Gender Insubordination', in *Inside/Out: Lesbian Theories, Gay Theories*, ed. by Diana Fuss (London: Routledge, 1991), pp. 13-31.

Bynum, Caroline Walker, *Fragmentation and Redemption: Essays on Gender and the Human Body in Medieval Religion* (New York: Zone, 1991).

—, *Jesus as Mother: Studies in the Spirituality of the High Middle Ages* (Berkeley: University of California, 1982).

Campbell, Fiona Kumari, *Contours of Ableism: The Production of Disability and Abledness* (Basingstoke: Palgrave Macmillan, 2009).

Cazelles, Brigitte, *Le Corps de sainteté, d'après Jehan Bouche d'Or, Jehan Paulus et quelques vies des XIIe et XIIIe siècles* (Geneva: Droz, 1982).

Clare, Eli, *Brilliant Imperfection: Grappling with Cure* (Durham: Duke University, 2017).

Edelman, Lee, *No Future: Queer Theory and the Death Drive* (Durham: Duke University, 2004).

Gonzalez-Polledo, EJ, and Jen Tarr, eds., *Painscapes: Communicating Pain* (London: Palgrave McMillan, 2018).

Gutt, Blake, 'Medieval Trans Lives in Anamorphosis: Looking Back and Seeing Differently (Pregnant Men and Backwards Birth)', *Medieval Feminist Forum*, 55.1 (2019), 174-206.

—, 'Transgender Genealogy in *Tristan de Nanteuil*', *Exemplaria*, 30.2 (2018), 129-46.

Johnson, Merri Lisa, and Robert McRuer, 'Cripistemologies: Introduction', *Journal of Literary & Cultural Disability Studies*, 8.2 (2014), 127-47.

Kafer, Alison, *Feminist, Queer, Crip* (Bloomington: Indiana University, 2013).

McKinnon, Rachel, 'Allies Behaving Badly: Gaslighting as Epistemic Injustice', in *The Routledge Handbook of Epistemic Injustice*, ed. by Ian James Kidd, José Medina, and Gaile Pohlhaus, Jr. (New York: Routledge, 2017), pp. 167-74.

McRuer, Robert, *Crip Theory: Cultural Signs of Queerness and Disability* (New York: New York University, 2006).

Metzler, Irina, *A Social History of Disability in the Middle Ages: Cultural Considerations of Physical Impairment* (New York: Routledge, 2013).

Mills, Robert, *Seeing Sodomy in the Middle Ages* (Chicago: University of Chicago, 2015).

Mitchell, David T., and Sharon L. Snyder, *Narrative Prosthesis: Disability and the Dependencies of Discourse* (Ann Arbor: University of Michigan, 2001).

van Ommen, Clifford, John Cromby, and Jeffery Yen, eds., 'Elaine Scarry's *The Body in Pain*: New Perspectives', *Subjectivity*, 9.4 (Special Issue:) (2016).

Patsavas, Alyson, 'Recovering a Cripistemology of Pain: Leaky Bodies, Connective Tissue, and Feeling Discourse', *Journal of Literary & Cultural Disability Studies*, 8.2 (2014), 203-18.

Price, Margaret, 'The Bodymind Problem and the Possibilities of Pain', *Hypatia*, 30.1 (2015), 268-84.

Radi, Blas, 'Políticas del conocimiento: hacía una epistemología trans*', in *Los mil pequeños sexos: Intervenciones críticas sobre políticas de género y sexualidades*, ed. by Mariano López Seoane (Sáenz Peña, Argentina: Eduntref, 2018), pp. 27-42.

Ridley, LaVelle, 'Imagining Otherly: Performing Possible Black Trans Futures in *Tangerine*', *TSQ: Transgender Studies Quarterly*, 6.4 (2019), 481-90.

Scarry, Elaine, *The Body in Pain: The Making and Unmaking of the World* (New York: Oxford University, 1985).

Schalk, Sami, 'Reevaluating the Supercrip', *Journal of Literary & Cultural Disability Studies*, 10.1 (2016), 71-86.

Sheppard, Emma, 'Using Pain, Living with Pain', *Feminist Review*, 120 (2018), 54-69.

Spencer-Hall, Alicia, 'Christ's Suppurating Wounds: Leprosy in the *Vita* of Alice of Schaerbeek (†1250)', in *"His brest tobrosten": Wounds and Wound Repair in Medieval Culture*, ed. by Kelly DeVries and Larissa Tracy (Leiden: Brill, 2015), pp. 389-416.

—, 'Chronic Pain and Illness: Reinstating Crip-Chronic Histories to Forge Affirmative Disability Futures', in *A Cultural History of Disability in the Middle Ages*, ed. by Jonathan Hsy, Joshua Eyler, and Tory Pearman (London: Bloomsbury, 2020), pp. 51-66.

—, *Medieval Saints and Modern Screens: Divine Visions as Cinematic Experience* (Amsterdam: Amsterdam University, 2018).

Spencer-Hall, Alicia, Stephanie Grace-Petinos and Leah Pope-Parker, eds., *Disability and Sanctity in the Middle Ages*, 2 vols. (Amsterdam: Amsterdam University, forthcoming 2022/2023).

Wendell, Susan, 'Unhealthy Disabled: Treating Chronic Illnesses as Disabilities', *Hypatia*, 16.4 (2001), 17-33.

About the author

BLAKE GUTT is a postdoctoral scholar with the Michigan Society of Fellows (University of Michigan, USA). He specializes in thirteenth- and fourteenth-century French, Occitan and Catalan literature, and modern queer and trans theory. Blake's current research project examines representations of gender transition and transformation in medieval

European literary texts. He has published on the trans Middle Ages in *Exemplaria* (2018), *Medieval Feminist Forum* (2019), and most recently in *postmedieval*'s 10th Anniversary Special Issue on Race, Revulsion, and Revolution (11.4, 2020). He is working on a monograph on medieval and modern epistemological systems, developed from his doctoral thesis (University of Cambridge, 2018).

10 The Authentic Lives of Transgender Saints

Imago Dei and *imitatio Christi* in the *Life* of St Marinos the Monk

M.W. Bychowski

Abstract
In this chapter, the author unpacks an entry in Magnus Hirschfeld's *Transvestites* (1910) on the *Life* of St Marinos the Monk to argue that his theories of the soul may be useful to flip the understanding of medieval trans saints from a frame of cisgender artifice, fears and desires to the frame of authenticity. In the process, the tradition of describing the subjects of these hagiographies as 'transvestite' saints is thoroughly critiqued by critically historicizing and reclaiming the term. *Imago transvesti* and *imitatio transvesti* are proposed as theoretical lenses that combine the medieval discourses of *imago Dei* and *imitatio Christi* with insights from trans studies in order to improve our understanding of medieval transgender saints.

Keywords: transgender, saints, transvestites, hagiography, medieval, monks

From the beginning, trans studies has invoked the lives of medieval saints. In a foundational 'trans' text, *Transvestites (Die Transvestiten)* (1910), Magnus Hirschfeld drew from medieval hagiography to historicize the phenomenon he calls 'transvestitism'. In current usage, 'transvestite' is synonymous with 'cross-dresser' – someone who wears clothing associated with another gender – and has largely diminished in usage as it is considered out of date or derogatory.[59] Yet in 1910, the word 'transvestite' was new, and had not yet developed its more narrow or negative connotations. Indeed, the word was intended to combat confusing associations with other traits or populations. In his book-length study, Hirschfeld describes a distinct population of people that differ from the homosexuals, narcissists, and schizophrenics with whom they were too often lumped: transvestites. While focusing on clothing as a key marker of trans-ness in defining his term 'transvestite', Hirschfeld seems to use the term more broadly to refer to a wider group of people, akin to how 'trans' or 'transgender' is used today. Based on his articulation of trans theory to examine pre-modern saints, Hirschfeld may be considered not only one of the founders of transgender studies in general, but also of medieval transgender studies specifically.

Among the lives he examines from the ancient to the modern world to define his term for trans-ness, Hirschfeld considers the case of St Marinos the Monk:

> There was a widespread legend during the Middle Ages about Saint Marina. When her father Eugenius became a monk, she put on men's clothing herself, so that she could become a monk and go with him. She changed her name to Marius [or, in other versions of the text, to Marinos]. As such she was supposed to have produced a child and was cast out. She did not defend herself but took the child as her own. Only after her death did her sex come to light.[60]

The story that Hirschfeld gives is concise but hits many of the main points which medieval versions of the *Life* of St Marinos (also known as St Mary, Marina, and/or Marius) expand. The story begins with the father, Eugenius, who leaves his child to join a monastery. The child advocates to become a

---

59 See 'Cross-Dress; Cross-Dressing; Cross-Dresser' and 'Transvestite; Transvestism' in the Appendix: pp. 291-92, 322.

60 While Hirschfeld acknowledges that transvestites should be allowed to transition and be affirmed in their identified gender, in case studies he regularly chooses not to use the preferred pronouns of the trans person. For instance, while using Marinos as an example of trans masculinity, Hirschfeld uses she/her pronouns and identifies the saint as female. Various reasons might be cited for Hirschfeld's decision not to use the preferred pronouns (or: pronouns reflecting the individual's identified gender), including his audience. Because Hirschfeld was among the first to define a 'trans' condition within modern medicine, he was addressing an audience that would likely be sceptical, unfamiliar with trans persons, and easily confused. Thus, while he used terms that would have been more familiar with his audience in 1910, I will use the preferred pronouns of the trans person or character under consideration, following current standards in the wake of transgender studies. Hirschfeld, *Transvestites*, pp. 307-08; *Die Transvestiten*, p. 404.

monk as well, despite having been assigned female at birth. Subsequently, the child, who takes the name Marinos, lives as an exceptional monk until he is expelled from the monastery for a time, after being accused by a woman of impregnating her, a charge upheld by the woman's father and the Superior of the monastery. After some time waiting outside the monastery, Marinos's conviction convinces the Superior to let him back into the brotherhood, where he raises the child born to the woman until the end of his life. After his death, Marinos's genitals are revealed – demonstrating his inability to impregnate a woman – and the slander against him proven false.

In the brief Hirschfeld version, Marinos is invoked as evidence in an argument for 'transvestitism' as a distinct and authentic state of being, an argument which posits transition (especially by means of clothing) as key to revealing the deep-seated gender of the trans soul.[61] While later studies of medieval trans saints invoke the term 'transvestite' without sufficient attention to Hirschfeld's analysis, the *Life* of St Marinos reveals how trans hagiography can ground and expand key elements in the affirmative conceptualization of 'transvestitism'.[62] The use and connotation of the terms 'transvestism' or 'transvestitism' in medieval studies largely seems to fall into the problems outlined in this volume's Usage Guide, functioning as a synonym for 'cross-dresser', 'founded upon the perception that trans individuals wear clothing associated with the 'opposite' assigned sex/gender, when they are in fact wearing clothing associated with their identified gender'.[63] Thus, although *Transvestites* is more a work of early psychology than of history or theology, I argue that Hirschfeld's framing of St Marinos is helpful in re-theorizing and reclaiming 'transvestitism' in ways that further our understanding of medieval transgender saints as figures embodying and inspiring authentic lives.

Authenticity is a core characteristic of a healthy psyche claims *Character Strengths and Virtues*, a text designed by psychologists Christopher Peterson and Martin Seligman to be a positive companion and antithesis to the 'Bible' of psychology, the *Diagnostic and Statistical Manual of Mental Disorders* (DSM).[64] The DSM has been used as a weapon to pathologize, hospitalize, and exclude trans people from society by marking them as disordered. Yet

---

61   Hirschfeld, *Transvestites*, p. 274.
62   Examples of such scholarship is legion but a few examples that use the word 'transvestite' without interrogating the term (especially in relation to Hirschfeld's own analysis of medieval saints) include: Constas, 'Life', pp. 1-12; Hotchkiss, *Clothes*, p. 15, p. 131; Daston and Park, 'The Hermaphrodite', p. 133; Margolis, 'Mortal Body', p. 18.
63   Appendix, p. 322.
64   Peterson and Seligman, *Character Strengths*, pp. 249-73.

it has also been instrumental in facilitating both medical transition, such as hormone replacement therapy, and legal transition, such as correcting one's birth certificate. By theorizing trans saints through the lens of authenticity rather than fantasy or disguise, we flip historical associations of trans life from a sin to a virtue, and from a disorder to a strength. The term 'authentic lives' is shared (sometimes with trepidation) as a critical phrase in both contemporary transgender and psychological parlance.[65] Stephan Joseph defines the concept this way: 'Authentic people know themselves. They are able to listen to their inner voice – their gut – and to understand the complexities of their feelings and hear their own inner wisdom. The authentic person will not let others blind them to their own truth'.[66] In key ways, the goal of Hirschfeld's *Transvestites* was to help people live authentic lives. He noticed that the gendered images and impacts of the world were harming a group of people (whom he called transvestites) whose authentic lives would require them to live differently. In citing Marinos, Hirschfeld recognizes how saints – especially trans saints – strive to live authentically, and the fact that this internal drive for authenticity calls them to also live differently.

Indeed, medieval hagiography is a genre regularly discussed in scholarly conversations about the work of authenticity. As Amy V. Ogden explains, a broad analysis of medieval hagiography demonstrates how the genre appeals to a wide range of audiences by using a wide range of lives whose stories are told using a wide range of styles.[67] This means that a saint whose *Life* seems relatively obscure and marginal, such as a trans saint, serves the wider goals of hagiography because their story speaks to the authenticity of people whose way of being might likewise be considered obscure or marginal. Whereas the authenticity of cisgender saints is readily recognized as a feature of hagiography by cisgender readers, the authenticity of trans saints might be missed or misrecognized as a problematic deception by cisgender readers of trans hagiography. By considering trans saints as authentically trans within contexts in which this authenticity is challenged by cisgender social norms, trans hagiography may be taken as exemplary of the genre's proclivity for advocating authenticity as a value for all people, whether cis or trans. Medieval trans saints, just like medieval cis saints, listened to what Joseph calls 'inner wisdom' (or what both Hirschfeld and medieval religious writers would call the 'soul') as they took steps to embody their

---

65 See Hagel, 'Alternative Authenticity'.
66 Joseph, 'Three Steps'.
67 Ogden, 'Centrality', pp. 2-3.

authentic lives. The authenticity of trans saints led them to be affected by and to impact others, through inspiration or imitation.

Additionally, by focusing on, and moving beyond, the case study of St Marinos presented in Hirschfeld's *Transvestites*, this chapter responds to a tradition in medieval studies of describing pre-modern persons as 'transvestites' or 'cross-dressers'.[68] A touchstone example at the intersection of early-/pre-modern studies and 'transvestitism' studies is Marjorie Garber's *Vested Interests: Cross-Dressing and Cultural Anxiety* (1992). While the understanding of 'transvestitism' in such works varies, the trans-ness of saints is generally regarded as somehow important both to medieval studies and medieval people. As Stephen J. Davis asserts, 'transvestitism [...] is the unmistakable "sign" or image that links this group of hagiographical narratives.'[69] For medieval studies, transvestitism has been useful in linking a host of texts, literary characters, and historical persons. Furthermore, citing around a dozen trans hagiographies that blossomed from the ninth to eleventh century in a 'revival of the genre', Davis argues that awareness of transvestitism seems more than a modern imposition, 'suggest[ing] that the hagiographers actually presumed that their ancient readers were already acquainted with other "texts" – other discourses – that would have helped make sense of the trans motif within these saints' lives.'[70] While Davis does not fully specify what 'other texts' were available, this collection, and medieval trans studies in general, works to fill out the range of trans discourses and lives present to pre-modern people. Nonetheless, there is a variation in the familiarity with, and affirmation of, trans-ness evident in both medieval texts and modern medieval studies through inconsistencies in pronoun choice, or the willingness to retain the expressed gender identity of the trans figure in one respect but not in others. To make this inconsistency in medieval texts and modern translations legible, I have not corrected the passages on Marinos cited in this chapter which acknowledge that he lived as a man from transition until death and yet use female pronouns for him. In medieval studies, variation in familiarity with trans theory is evident in the persistent and regular use of the word 'transvestite', a term that has been considered outdated in trans studies for some time. The term is often used while eschewing the historical trans person's identified gender in favour of that ascribed by cis-essentialist scribes or scholars. For instance,

---

68 See also Garber, *Vested Interests*; Bullough and Bullough, *Cross Dressing*; Bullough, 'Cross Dressing and Gender Role Change', pp. 223-42.
69 Davis, 'Crossed Texts', p. 15.
70 Ibid., p. 16.

Marinos is frequently dead-named as 'Mary' or 'Marina' despite the fact that he personally chose the name 'Marinos', and is referred to with she/her pronouns, despite that fact that he lived as a 'he/him'-using man for most of his life.[71] Furthermore, the conventional use of the early twentieth-century diagnostic category of 'transvestite' is ironic, since use of the term 'transgender' to describe pre-modern people is decried as anachronistic because this word did not exist in the Middle Ages.[72] Cis scholars seem at times to prefer their own anachronisms to the supposed anachronisms of trans scholarship.

Yet my point is not simply to say, 'don't use that word' – although the uninformed and unexplained use of the word 'transvestite' should be discouraged – nor to regard the pre-modern silence on medieval transness as disallowing any words ('transvestite' or 'transgender') which help articulate the unarticulated.[73] Rather, I contend that when medieval studies' scholars describe 'transvestites', they may tap into an unrecognized well of potential knowledge about trans life and history. We must understand the past in its own terms but we must also recognize that we can know the past better in some respects through the insights gained after later experience and reflection[74] To this end, I propose two ways of theorizing medieval transvestite saints: *imago transvesti* and *imitatio transvesti*. In coining these phrases, I purposefully blend two traditions of Latin: the language of the medieval church (represented by Marinos), and the language of modern medicine (represented by Hirschfeld). This medieval and modern trans amalgam emphasizes an intentional theoretical and critical use of terms like 'transvestite', in contrast to the word's inaccurate and uncritical application elsewhere in medieval studies. In other works, including a forthcoming piece on the 'transgender turn', I offer a more in depth critique of what I identify as 'the cisgender turn' to medieval studies and transvestite history, characterized by cisgender scholars enacting compulsory cisgender identity assignment and framing trans-ness primarily as a product of or disruption to cis culture.[75] In this current piece, however, my goal is to locate within the early end of the Middle Ages and the early end of modern trans studies a generative and distinctly trans contribution to our reading of sainthood, authenticity, and the soul.

71 See 'Dead Name; Dead-Naming; Dead Name' in the Appendix: p. 292.
72 See Whittington, 'Medieval', p. 126; Karras and Linkinen, 'Revisited', p. 113.
73 See 'Transvestite; Transvestism' in the Appendix: p. 322.
74 See Žižek, 'History'.
75 Bychowski, 'Transgender Turn'.

To provide a more complex historical examination of the intersection of Hirschfeld's conceptions of transvestitism and the *Life* of St Marinos, I will consider different parts of the *Life* from a tenth-century Athonite manuscript, believed to be closest in style and content to the earliest versions of the hagiography.[76] While the Marinos hagiographic tradition can be traced to between the fifth and ninth centuries, the exact dates and locations of the saint's life are unknown.[77] It has been suggested that Marinos lived in fifth-century Syria, possibly near Tripoli.[78] The text examined here is a Greek-language version of the *Life* found in a tenth-century text preserved in three Athonite manuscripts (Mount Athos being a significant center of monastic life), later published and named the *vita antiqua* by M. Richard.[79] The English translation of the *vita antiqua* used here is by Nicholas Constas. The introduction to Constas's translation repeats the argument that the *vita antiqua* is the closest to the original version of the *Life* of St Marinos.[80] I have selected this early version since it contains elements that later versions often abridge. Later versions tend to remove much of the dialogue, including the debate between Marinos and his father as to the theological grounding for his transition into monkhood. This conversation, present in the *vita antiqua*, may be considered a fiction, yet it attests to the ways early hagiographers imagined Marinos's relation to God and his understanding of his place in Creation, providing details of *imago transvesti*.[81] This *vita* also gives more detail on crucial steps in the plot than later abridged versions, allowing a closer reading of habits that would provide *imitatio transvesti* for later trans hagiographies – inspiring trans saints, or at least trans narratives.

In the next section, I will approach the *imago transvesti* of St Marinos as reflecting a form of *imago Dei*, a tradition in Christianity that states that each person is made in God's image and which is identifiable in medieval trans hagiography. This tradition becomes clearer by understanding Hirschfeld's transvestite principle of the 'unconscious projection of the soul' ('unbewusste Projektion der Seele').[82] In a chapter from *Transvestites* entitled 'Clothing

---

76   Constas, 'Life', pp. 1-2.
77   For dates, and a list of edited versions, see: ibid., pp. 1-3.
78   Nau, 'Histoire', pp. 276-77.
79   Richard's 'Vie Ancienne' will thus be cited in instances where the Greek is helpful in clarifying the meaning of phrases. Special thanks to Roland Betancourt for his assistance in contextualizing the text's Greek origins.
80   Constas, 'Life', p. 1.
81   These conversations point to a literary tradition and theological discourse around why and how trans lives could be justified. See Davis, 'Crossed Texts', p. 2.
82   Hirschfeld, *Transvestites*, p. 214; *Die Transvestiten*, p. 274.

as a Form of Expression of Mental Conditions', Hirschfeld argues that the clothing which the trans person wears as part of their transition may not be – as others would misidentify it – a disguise or facsimile of a foreign gender, but rather may be a revelation of the gender experienced by the transgender soul. He calls on readers to ask 'to what extent we recognize [...] the essence of the clothing as symbol, as unconscious projection of the soul'.[83] The notion of the 'unconscious projection of the soul' may thus be considered analogous to the pre-modern conception of the *imago Dei* which would have been active during the life of many trans saints, and during the reception of their hagiographies in the medieval period. Thus, reflecting pre-modern theory and medieval faith, *imago transvesti* names trans figures responding to the model of the *imago Dei*, whose authentic lives seem to arise from projections of an internal source.

Subsequently, *imitatio transvesti* is explored as the way in which trans saints enact a specific kind of *imitatio Christi*, and the way in which they inspire others to bring forth truths that are otherwise obscured, punished, or marginalized by the images of the world, *imagines mundi*. In my usage of the term, *imagines mundi* critically name the socially assigned images of the self which contrast with those made by God, associated with the *imago Dei*. This characteristic of trans saints may be recognized through an understanding of Hirschfeld's notion of transvestite 'soul-impact' or 'soul affect' ('Seelen-Einschlag').[84] In his chapter 'Women as Soldiers', Hirschfeld considers the potential case of trans men in the military, driven by 'der männliche Seelen-Einschlag', translated by Michael A. Lombardi-Nash as the 'very substantial admixture of the manly soul'.[85] This phrase may be translated more directly as 'male soul-impact'. The conjunction of 'Seele' (soul) with 'Einschlag' (impact/admixture) suggests that the soul may be affected by and may affect others. In the case of medieval trans saints, particularly those who embody the *imago transvesti*, one may see how living out the authentic truth of *imago Dei* in the community may inspire others to imitate their choices, bringing forth their own submerged truths. This willingness to live out a God-given truth, one's *imago Dei*, and suffer the punishments of a misunderstanding or prejudiced world becomes a way in which trans saints enact *imitatio Christi*, or imitation of Christ. As various saints live out the *imitatio Christi* in different ways, it is worth acknowledging that trans saints have specific habits – such as the living out

83   Hirschfeld, *Transvestites*, p. 214; *Die Transvestiten*, p. 274.
84   Hirschfeld, *Transvestites*, p. 415; *Die Transvestiten*, p. 549.
85   Hirschfeld, *Die Transvestiten*, p. 549; *Transvestites*, p. 415.

of denied authentic truths – that others (transgender and cisgender alike) may imitate or feel the impact of as *imitatio transvesti*, or trans 'soul-impact'.

Imago Transvesti: Images of the trans soul

The *imago Dei* of transgender saints

To begin, it must be acknowledged that the concepts of authenticity and the *imago Dei* have been used to undermine trans lives. For many trans, intersex, and non-binary persons, the Book of Genesis is experienced as a weapon wielded by those who insist that divine intention is reflected only in the symmetry of a biologically essentialist gender binary. In the introduction to *Transvestites*, Hirschfeld provides a list of binaries which people consider essential and which he intends to trouble, beginning with 'God and nature, one and all, body and soul', and arriving at last at one of the divisions that he believes people hold on to most firmly, 'the masculine and the feminine'.[86] Significantly, all of these dichotomies have a cultural origin, still understood by many as spiritual, in Genesis 1.27: 'God created man to his own image: to the image of God he created him: male and female he created them'.[87] This statement of resemblance, the *imago Dei*, confirms – yet also disrupts – the binaries previously established. In light of the preceding litany of divisions in Genesis 1, the *imago Dei* seems to break down the binary between Creator and creation, the One and the many. The man and woman in Genesis 1 and 2 embody the *imago Dei* in distinct ways, while sharing traits which reflect on each other and on God. Could this mean that trans, intersex, and non-binary people also distinctly embody the *imago Dei*? Or is one (male or female, cis or trans) the embodiment of God's truth (*imago Dei*), and the other the embodiment of the world's lies (*imago mundi*)?

Into this general spiritual mystery arrive the saints, including trans saints, who are held up in the medieval tradition as images of Christ, set apart from humanity and yet human enough to provide glimpses of something beyond. Embodying the intersections between seemingly fundamental divisions (God and nature, one and all, body and soul, man and woman), trans saints embody social as well as theological mysteries. As Davis argues, medieval trans saints resemble the image of God, and specifically the unique *imago Dei* of Christ, promoting 'the intertextual presentation of Christ as a mimetic

---

86   Hirschfeld, *Transvestites*, p. 17; *Die Transvestiten*, p. 4
87   All references are to the Douay-Rheims Bible.

model' for transgender saints.[88] In this respect, Davis has done significant work, along with Valerie R. Hotchkiss, in moving the study of trans saints away from analysis in terms of abstracted semiotic cultural projections, such as studies of the binaries listed above, to initiate focus on their embodiments of Christian materiality.[89] Medieval scholarship has tended to try to solve this mystery by representing trans saints as problems of inauthenticity in the *imago mundi*. Davis presents two typical approaches to trans saints from the mid-1970s, both of which flatten transgender saints into projections of cisgender fears and desires. The first example, epitomized by John Anson, views stories of trans saints as manifesting both monks' desires for women's bodies, and the patriarchal denial of femininity. Anson declares: '[t]he transvestite female saint is understood as the literary product of this tension'.[90] A second example comes from Evelyne Patlagean, who argues that the trans monk embodies the opposite, an anti-patriarchal image of a woman with the autonomy of a man.[91]

The issue with reading transitioning primarily as a problem with and for cis authenticity is that this problem and its resolutions usually end up returning focus to the cisnormative binary.[92] In short, such readings risk reducing a trans *imago Dei* to the fantasy of a cis *imago mundi*, thereby turning internal trans truths into fictions projected from an external, cisnormative world. This leads to the dangerous conclusion that trans people may not exist beyond the tensions and wish-fulfilment fantasies of cis people. Thus, the high stakes for the *imago transvesti* of trans saints become evident. On the one hand, trans saints' genders are framed as artificial fantasies or fictions projected from the outside by a conflicted cisgender *imago mundi*. On the other, these saints are trans people with a deep-seated *imago Dei* which projects their gender as an expression of their authentic internal truths.

An early treatise on *imago Dei* is found in Augustine's fifth-century *De Trinitate (On the Trinity)*; this text was still in circulation when Marinos's hagiography was written and read. Augustine argues that creation begins as a seed within each soul. '[I]f [life]', Augustine writes, 'is made after the image of God [...] then from the moment when that nature so marvelous and so great began to be, whether this image be so worn out as to be almost

---

88 Davis, 'Crossed Texts', p. 34.
89 See Hotchkiss, *Clothes*, pp. 1-12.
90 Anson, 'Female Transvestite', p. 5.
91 Patlagean, 'L'histoire', pp. 610-16.
92 Bychowski, 'The Transgender Turn'.

none at all, or whether it be obscure and defaced, or bright and beautiful, certainly [life] always is [made in the image of God].'[93] Often one's *imago Dei* is hidden, yet as a person grows it is revealed. The process of constructing the self authentically, then, can be a co-creative act of affirming the *imago Dei*. Initially present only as a seed, this *imago Dei* is revealed as each person affirms the internal logic of their creation. The *imago transvesti*, figuring the work of transitioning and transvestitism, is thus co-creative work towards an authentic life. And Hirschfeld's concept of the 'unconscious projection of the soul' becomes revelatory in framing trans saints as marking the living out of authentic truths, trans *imago Dei*, over and against the artifice of the world, the cisnormative *imago mundi*. It would seem that hagiographies are not advocating strictly cisgender lives, which would have been inauthentic for trans saints.

The trans imago Dei of St Marinos the Monk

Turning to the example of St Marinos, one sees how the *imago transvesti* functions as a medieval prefiguration of Hirschfeld's transvestite 'unconscious projection of the soul'. This is particularly evident in a key passage in the *vita antiqua*, the moment of transition that accompanies the saint's entrance into the monastery. After Marinos's father announces that he will leave his child to join the monastery, Marinos reveals his own desires to become a monk. The father resists his child's request but Marinos persists in arguing his case. Drawing on a theology of mimesis wherein Christians are to imitate Christ as Saviour and also God as Creator, Marinos instructs his father: '"The one who saves the soul is like the one who created it."'[94] This statement forms part of Marinos's argument to persuade his father to help him transition, and may function as the thesis for Marinos's vita, framing the *imago mundi*, culturally assigned gender, as a threat to the soul (and *imago Dei*) of trans persons.

What is the nature of this threat? While operating without terminology such as gender dysphoria, Marinos's *vita* evidences a dysphoric condition caused by the *imago mundi* that permits certain cis persons to live authentically in *imago Dei*, but denies this expression to trans persons. Even

---

93 '[A]c per hoc si secundum hoc facta est ad imaginem dei quod uti ratione atque intellectu ad intellegendum et conspiciendum deum potest, profecto ab initio quo esse coepit ista tam magna et mira natura, siue ita obsoleta sit haec imago ut pene nulla sit siue obscura atque deformis siue clara et pulchra sit, semper est', Augustine, 'On the Trinity, XIV.iv'.

94 Constas, 'Life', p. 7. 'ψυχὴν ὁ σώσας ὡς ὁ κτίσας', Richard, 'Vie Ancienne', pp. 87-88.

before transition makes his identification as a monk visible, the impulse to reject the *imago mundi* and express the invisible *imago Dei* is evident in Marinos's strivings to become a monk, and his persuasive understanding of Christian *imago Dei* and *imitatio Christi*. Julia Serano calls this strong but often suppressed identification with a gender, even one as specific as monkhood, 'subconscious sex'.[95] Alternatively, the fifth edition of the DSM (DSM-5) calls the rejection of assigned gender for another expressed or identified gender, 'gender dysphoria'.[96] In his analysis of a case study for *Transvestites*, that of the author of a book on forced feminization, Hirschfeld uses the term 'Seelenregungen' to describe the trans impulses that the author seems to share with characters of the book.[97] Whilst Lombardi-Nash simply translates 'Seelenregungen' as 'soul', it might also be translated as 'soul-movement' or 'soul-stirring,' perhaps even 'soul-striving'.[98] Without psychological or DSM-5 language at his disposal, Marinos too speaks of the soul. Thus, Hirschfeld's trans-soul language may again be useful in linking or connecting the concepts of medieval essentialism with the dysphoric modern psyche. The rejection of assigned gender roles that cause dysphoria prompts the projection of the soul's desire to transition.

This soul-striving seems to arise in Marinos when his father leaves to become a monk. Marinos begins to express the strong desire to transition, and the strong rejection of his socially assigned gender. "'Father,' says Marinos, 'do you wish to save your own soul and see mine destroyed?'"[99] The phrase 'save your own soul' marks Eugenius as a participant in his own salvation. He is eschewing worldly gender for a new gender, crossing not only a gender binary of man and monk but also a religious binary of secular and sacred life.[100] Marinos likewise wants to eschew the gender the world assigned for a more sanctified gender. This complicates the claim: 'The one who saves the soul is like the one who created it.' It is the father who is initially responsible for Marinos's birth into the world, yet he is also complacent enough to let his child inherit the *imago mundi* he now rejects. Thus, it is Marinos who fights to save his own soul, to transition and become a monk. The soul in this case is the seed of the *imago transvesti*, the monk which Marinos will become, which at this point may be said to already

95 Serano, *Whipping Girl*, p. 78.
96 'Gender Dysphoria: Fact Sheet', pp. 1-2.
97 Hirshfeld analyses a novel by Fraumann (*"Weiberleute"*).
98 Hirschfeld, *Transvestites*, p. 137; *Die Transvestiten*, p. 175.
99 'Πάτερ, σὺ τὴν ψυχήν σου θέλεις σῶσαι καὶ τὴν ἐμὴν ἀπολέσαι', Richard, 'Vie Ancienne', p. 87.
100 On monkhood and holy orders as distinct gender identities in the Middle Ages, see Newman, 'Crucified by the Virtues'; and More, 'Convergence'.

exist in a subconscious (or semiconscious), undeveloped form. If transition is denied, then the seed of Marinos the Monk will not fully come to be. Stuck as 'Mary', this trans soul will atrophy, or worse, be destroyed utterly or killed ('ἀπολέσαι') by the dysphoria of the *imago mundi*. By fighting to live an authentic trans life, the doing of the trans saint saves his soul and thus resembles God who created the authentic self into being ('κτίσας': to create, lay foundations, establish).

Marinos's transition allows him to begin to live his authentic life, yet the process of making the invisible subconscious sex visible must overcome the conflict between how society assigns sex according to the *imago mundi*, and the gender embedded in the 'unconscious projection of the soul'. The *imago mundi* fixates to a great degree on sex, reflected in the father's warning: '"it is through the members of your sex that the devil wages war on the servants of God"'.[101] The sexual potential of Marinos (e.g. his genitals) becomes a location of signification that generates conflict between Marinos's soul-striving, his body, and his socially assigned sex, causing dysphoria. Yet without women's clothes, Marinos's genitals and reproductive ability would no longer be advertised on the market of visible gender. The change to men's clothes, and then the monk's habit, would reorient how society reads his body, removing the focus on his genitals, since he is supposed to be celibate and effectively non-reproductive.[102] The image of celibacy that is written in Marinos's soul-striving is now authentically projected and revealed, eschewing the markers of female reproduction that prompted his dysphoria. The changes reveal the trans soul – the image of Marinos the Monk which had its seed in the youth before his transition began – which remains fundamentally the same, but is now free to authentically express itself.

Evidence that Marinos's transition allows an authentic living-out of his soul's striving is provided by his success as a monk. The *vita* emphasizes how close Marinos already was to embodying a form of manhood. 'After she lived thus for a few years in the monastery', records the text, '[they] considered her to be a eunuch, for she was beardless and of delicate voice.'[103] Beyond physical similarities between eunuchs, trans men, and female virgins in medieval literature, monks and eunuchs are not masculinities into which

---

101 Constas, 'Life', p. 7; 'ὅτι ὁ διάβολος δι' ὑμῶν πολεμεῖ τοὺς δούλους τοῦ θεοῦ', Richard, 'Vie Ancienne', p. 88.
102 For more on the role of clothing in defining medieval gender, see Crane, *Performance*. On early modern gender and clothing, see: Dekker and van de Pol, *Tradition*.
103 Constas, 'Life', p. 8; 'Ποιήσασα δέ τινας χρόνους ἐν τῷ μοναστηρίῳ, ἐνόμιζον ὅτι εὐνοῦχός ἐστιν, διὰ τὸ ἀγένειον καὶ τὸ λεπτὸν τῆς φωνῆς αὐτῆς', Richard, 'Vie Ancienne', p. 88.

one is generally born.[104] A trans monk knows, perhaps more than most, that one is not born a monk but becomes a monk. Indeed, many of Marinos's brothers compare his virtues to those of a eunuch.[105] This underlines an association between being a eunuch and being an exceptional monk.[106] One can see that Marinos succeeds because he is able to live his authentic life. Marinos the Monk is not a mere construction of external signifiers (hair, clothes, name), but the projection of an image that already existed within Marinos before his transition began, that image which medieval theologians might have called the *imago Dei* and which Hirschfeld calls the trans soul.

Imitatio Transvesti: Impacts of the trans soul

The imitatio Christi of transgender saints

Medieval scholarship displays a tension between the insistence that hagiography functions to inspire *imitatio Christi*, and the insistence (perhaps more modern than medieval) that trans-ness is a negligible or negative trait for holiness to overcome. One factor in the inability to see authentic transvestitism as more than social artifice may be that a trans life would be artificial for cisgender people, the assumed writers and audiences of both medieval literature and medieval studies. Yet others challenge the assumption that cis folx cannot learn from the specifically trans parts of trans saints's lives. As Hotchkiss asks: 'If disruptions of gender hierarchy were not encouraged, why then do so many hagiographers write about women disguised as men?'[107] For those discounting *imago transvesti*, the positive impact that these saints have poses a problem. If, as Sebastian P. Brock and Susan Ashbrook Harvey argue, 'all early Christian hagiography [...] was motivated by an ethic of imitation,' one might wonder, as does Davis: 'Were ancient readers called to seek out the example of Christ in the lives of transvestite saints?'[108] The answer, strange as it may seem, is that the authenticity of trans saints can have a positive impact on the souls of others, whether trans or cis.

---

104 See Bychowski, 'Reconstructing the Pardoner'.
105 Constas, 'Life', p. 8; Richard, 'Vie Ancienne', p. 88.
106 On eunuchs and sanctity, see Szabo in this volume: pp. 109-29.
107 Hotchkiss, *Clothes*, p. 19.
108 Brock and Harvey, *Holy Women*, p. 17; Davis, 'Crossed Texts', p. 32.

The trans imitatio Christi of St Marinos the Monk

In the last part of the *Life* of St Marinos, one sees how the impact of his truth occurs after his death, when others are inspired by the *imago transvesti* to live more authentic lives. The inclusion of these reconciliations, truth-tellings, and exorcisms is not accidental, but key to the hagiographic function of inspiring imitation of these saints as part of *imitatio Christi*. Just as the story of Jesus continues after his death through the ongoing actions of the Church, so too the imitation of the saint through shared impact is not separate from the saint's *Life* but part of its ongoing spirit. Thus, one can learn something of a saint by considering the impact and the imitation they inspire. In the case of St Marinos, I argue that the series of persons who eschew falsity and/or inauthentic lives due to the impact of the trans saint signifies his *imitatio transvesti* as the living out of an authentic life, rather than – as has been supposed in much scholarship – through the enactment of artifice. For a time, Marinos is forced to leave the monastery because of accusations begun by an innkeeper's daughter, spread by the innkeeper, and believed by the monastery's Superior. Despite these accusations of breaking his vows of chastity by impregnating the innkeeper's daughter, and despite losing his place within the monastery, Marinos remains faithful to his expression of identity as a chaste man and monk, remaining close to the monastery even during his expulsion. When Marinos's genitalia and inability to impregnate the woman are revealed after his death, the truth of his authenticity and the falsehood of the accusations against him inspire change and transformation in his community.

The first incitement to authenticity after the saint's death comes from the Superior. Upon learning the truth about Marinos's body and his suffering, he asks: "'[I]n what state did his wretched soul depart?'"[109] The Superior then realizes the unblemished state of the saint's soul, and that he himself had enacted falsehood by punishing Marinos for another's crime. The Superior falls before the body and cries: "'Forgive me, for I have sinned against you. I shall lie dead here at your holy feet until such time as I hear forgiveness for all the wrongs that I have done you.'"[110] Now more accurately perceiving the state of Marinos's soul, the Superior can glean the soul-striving that Marinos experienced in life because of the dysphoria and untruth that the leader himself had helped to inspire. The result is that the 'soul-impact' of Marinos's

---

109 Constas, 'Life', p. 11; 'Ἆρα πῶς ἀπῆλθεν ἡ ἀθλία ψυχὴ αὐτοῦ', Richard, 'Vie Ancienne', p. 93.
110 Constas, 'Life', p. 11; 'Συγχώρησόν μοι ὅτι ἥμαρτον εἰς σέ· ὧδε ἀποθνήσκω εἰς τοὺς ἁγίους σου πόδας ἕως οὗ ἀκούσω συγχώρησιν ὧν ἐπλημμέλησα εἰς σέ', Richard, 'Vie Ancienne', p. 93.

life and death will be replicated within himself, the Superior claims, until he can be reconciled to live a life that affirms truth and authenticity.

The sharing of pain encourages the Superior to reconcile with the trans monk by becoming an advocate for his truth after death. '"You must repent, brother"', the Superior tells the innkeeper.[111] Untruths can inspire others to imitate the habits of untruth, and thus the Superior blames the innkeeper for having 'incited' him to sin, 'by [his] words'.[112] The Superior and the innkeeper did not invent the untruths of the *imago mundi*, but both participated in them and inspired others to unwittingly imitate them. The revelation of Marinos's lived truth now acts as a baptism or transition for others, by which deception can die. Others can participate in the pain and death of the saint, allowing them to be reborn into more authentic truths and selves.

By the 'soul-impact' of *imitatio transvesti*, the Superior and the innkeeper realize that not only did they not see the truth of Marinos's *imago Dei*, but their perspectives were clouded by *imago mundi*. Marinos tried to share his authentic life but the Superior could not receive it; his worldview excluded trans souls. Thus when Marinos confesses: '"Forgive me, father, for I have sinned as a man"', the Superior hears him say that 'as a man' he sinned ('ἐπλανήθην': caused to wander, led astray) by impregnating the woman, while Marinos means that he has sinned (been caused to wander) by not being authentic in the way in which he exists 'as a man'.[113] The specific word, 'ἐπλανήθην' which is usually translated as 'sin' also signifies the impact and experiences of being made to wander away from his fully recognized authentic self as a trans man, and specifically a trans monk. Yet because of worldly exclusion and incomprehension of trans-ness, he would either be rejected (thus caused to wander) from the monastery for impregnating the woman, or else would have been rejected (caused to wander) from the monastery for not being able to impregnate her. This double bind may be seen as the effect of sinful *imagines mundi* that prompt untruths. The sin that Marinos confesses may not be that he lived as a *man*, but that he did not and could not live authentically as a *trans man*. Marinos was denied the power to be seen as a trans saint until after death when his community was ready to repent, to see him and their own mistakes.[114]

---

111   Constas, 'Life', p. 11; 'Μετανόησον, ἀδελφέ', Richard, 'Vie Ancienne', p. 94.
112   Constas, 'Life', p. 11; 'Κἀμὲ γὰρ τοῖς λόγοις σου συνεπῆρες', Richard, 'Vie Ancienne', p. 94.
113   Constas, 'Life', p. 9; 'Συγχώρησόν μοι, πάτερ, ὅτι ὡς ἄνθρωπος ἐπλανήθην', Richard, 'Vie Ancienne', p. 90.
114   Hotchkiss, *Clothes*, p. 16.

Beyond worldly prejudices, perhaps the greatest 'soul-impact' of Marinos comes in the form of healing and liberation of the soul. Shortly after Marinos's father dies, the saint receives from God 'the gift of healing those who were troubled by demons'.[115] The touch of the trans saint heals the possessed and further emphasizes how *imitatio transvesti* empowers the possessed to live more authentically according to their *imago Dei*. After contact with Marinos's hands, people were able to be reborn into their authentic lives. For many, trans embodiment is a liberation from the demons of living falsely in a gender misassigned at birth. Indeed, it is only after living an authentic life as a man that Marinos finds himself able to empower others to return to their authentic selves. After 'confessing the truth', that the saint did not (indeed, could not) impregnate her, and being brought to stand before the maligned body of the trans monk, the innkeeper's daughter 'was immediately healed' of her demonic possession.[116] Being brought to witness the 'unconscious projection of the soul' embodied by the trans saint empowers the woman to dispel the constructed artifice she herself has devised, and instead to live an authentic truth. In the end, even if Marinos did not live to see it, the authentic life of the trans saint is affirmed by the authentic presenting of self he inspires in others.

Conclusion: The authenticity of trans lives

In arguing for the consideration of transgender saints through the frame of authenticity, my goal has been to offer an alternative to trends in scholarship that reduce trans life to the traps and trappings of cultural fears and desires projected onto transgender bodies. In short, I am tired of transgender life merely being understood negatively, by how we disturb other people's theories and histories. In its place, I seek to root medieval trans studies in positive claims. As I tell my students, do not let yourself become someone else's worst version of you. Authenticity is one way we tell our own stories and tell our own histories.

Authenticity has been one part of the theoretical thesis of transgender lives for years. In *Whipping Girl* (2007), Serano articulates that the unconscious yearning to express oneself through transitioning is critical to understanding

---

115 Constas, 'Life', p. 8; 'χαρίσματα αὐτὴν ἰαμάτων λαβεῖν παρὰ θεοῦ κατὰ δαιμόνων', Richard, 'Vie Ancienne', pp. 88-89.
116 Constas, 'Life', p. 12; 'Καὶ παραχρῆμα ἰάθη', Richard, 'Vie Ancienne', p. 94.

her story, and the stories of many others.[117] A decade prior, in the seminal text for transgender studies, 'The Empire Strikes Back: A Posttranssexual Manifesto', Sandy Stone argues that trans people need to refuse the call to 'pass', and rather live authentically as their varied trans selves.[118] Even further back, in *Transvestites*, Hirschfeld calls on psychologists to allow trans people to live authentically according to their unconscious soul. And Hirschfeld in turn roots his theory in the medieval *Life* of St Marinos, which views authentic transvestitism as saving the God-given transgender soul. This is what I mean when I say that trans studies has been, from its beginning, interested in the authenticity of medieval transgender saints.

Today, beyond academic discourses of trans and medieval studies, being able to reclaim trans lives as authentic from the imagined traps invoked by cisgender cultural desires and anxieties is a matter of life and death. With civil rights protections requiring transgender to be categorized as a discrete insular community with immutable traits, both law and medicine hold authentic truths as necessary prerequisites to determining judgments, rights, coverage, and care. And the trans community has also seen the impact of the authenticity of transgender being denied. In the USA and elsewhere, trans students have been denied access to bathrooms on the grounds that they might be sexual predators disguising themselves to assault victims while they pee. At the same time, US states set diverse and often difficult-to-meet standards for determining the authenticity of trans adults' claims when they move to change gender markers on government-issued identity documents. In public discourse, the slur 'trap' has seen a spike, including online through hashtags (#trap), used to mark trans people (especially trans women and trans feminine people) as sexual predators disguising themselves in order to fool or 'trap' cis people into sexual encounters.[119] By defining trans people as inauthentic 'traps', transphobes also excuse 'trans panic' wherein their anger, abuse, and even deadly violence against trans people are presented as a 'natural' defensive response to someone trying to fool and trap them; this legal defence is still considered valid today, only banned within a small minority of courts in the United States.[120] Whether or not one regards transgender as essential or rooted in the subconscious soul, one should not undervalue the life-saving power that narratives of trans authenticity offer.

---

117 Serano, *Whipping Girl*, p. 78.
118 Stone, 'Empire Strikes Back', pp. 221-35.
119 See also 'Trap' in the Appendix, p. 323.
120 Woods, Sears and Mallory, 'Defense'.

In the end, this chapter is an expression of my own exhaustion with the insistence that trans lives are signifiers of artifice, fantasies, false lifestyles, and socio-sexual traps. Yet this chapter also has broader goals: to reclaim the authenticity of transvestitism and trans saints. There is more to the internal life of trans people than an amalgam of the fears and desires projected onto them. The authenticity of transgender saints was then and is now an important element and impact to consider, both for the ongoing work of current trans politics, and for medieval trans history. Authenticity is one way we escape the traps we have been made to embody for far too long.

Bibliography

Primary sources

Augustine of Hippo, 'On the Trinity, XIV.iv.', *The Latin Library*, <https://www.thelatinlibrary.com/augustine/trin14.shtml> [accessed 19 August 2019].

Constas, Nicholas, trans., 'The Life of St Mary/Marinos', in *Holy Women of Byzantium: Ten Saints' Lives in English Translation*, ed. by Alice-Mary Talbot (Washington DC: Dumbarton Oaks, 1996), pp. 1-12.

Fraumann, Luz, *"Weiberleute": Ein merkwürdiger Roman* (Budapest: M.W. Schneider, 1906).

Hirschfeld, Magnus, *Transvestites: The Erotic Drive to Cross-Dress*, trans. by Michael A. Lombardi-Nash (Amherst: Prometheus, 1991).

—, *Die Transvestiten: Eine Untersuchung über den erotischen Verkleidungstrieb* (Berlin: Pulvermacher, 1910).

Richard, M., ed., 'La Vie Ancienne de Sainte Marie surnommée Marinos', in *Corona Gratiarum. Miscellanea patristica, historica et liturgica Eligio Dekkers O.S.B. XII Lustra complenti oblata*, 2 vols. (Bruges: Sint Pietersabdij, 1975), I, pp. 83-115.

Secondary sources

Anson, John, 'The Female Transvestite in Early Monasticism: The Origin and Development of a Motif', *Viator*, 5 (1974), 1-32.

Bychowski, M.W., 'Reconstructing the Pardoner: Transgender Skin Operations in Fragment VI', in *Writing on Skin in the Age of Chaucer*, ed. by Katrin Rupp and Nicole Nyffenegger (Berlin: de Gruyter, 2018), pp. 221-50.

—, 'The Transgender Turn: Eleanor Rykener Speaks Back', *Trans Historical: Gender Plurality Before the Modern*, ed. by Masha Raskolnikov, Greta LaFleur, and Anna Kłosowska (Ithaca: Cornell University, forthcoming 2021).

Brock, Sebastian P. and Susan Ashbrook Harvey, *Holy Women of the Syrian Orient* (Berkeley: University of California, 1998).

Bullough, Vern L., and Bonnie Bullough, *Cross Dressing, Sex, and Gender* (Philadelphia: University of Pennsylvania, 1993).

Bullough, Vern L., 'Cross Dressing and Gender Role Change in the Middle Ages' in *Handbook of Medieval Sexuality*, ed. by Vern L. Bullough and James Brundage (New York: Routledge, 2000), pp. 223-42.

Crane, Susan, *The Performance of Self: Ritual, Clothing and Identity in the Hundred Years War* (Philadelphia: University of Pennsylvania, 2002).

Daston, Lorraine and Katharine Park, 'The Hermaphrodite and the Orders of Nature: Sexual Ambiguity in Early Modern France', in *Premodern Sexualities*, ed. by Louise Fradenburg and Carla Freccero (New York: Routledge, 1996), pp. 117-36.

Davis, Stephen J., 'Crossed Texts, Crossed Sex: Intertextuality and Gender in Early Christian Legends of Holy Women Disguised as Men', *Journal of Early Christian Studies*, 10.1 (2002), 1-36.

Dekker, Rudolf M. and Lotte C. van de Pol, *The Tradition of Female Transvestism in Early Modern Europe* (London: Palgrave Macmillan, 1989).

Garber, Marjorie B., *Vested Interests: Cross-dressing and Cultural Anxiety*, (New York: Routledge, 1992).

'Gender Dysphoria: Fact Sheet', *Diagnostic and Statistical Manual of Mental Disorders, Fifth Edition* (Arlington: American Psychiatric Association, 2013), pp. 1-2.

Hagel, Nina, 'Alternative Authenticity: Thinking Transgender Without Essence', *Theory & Event*, 20.3 (2017), 599-628.

Hotchkiss, Valerie R., *Clothes Make the Man: Female Cross-Dressing in Medieval Europe*, (New York: Garland, 1996).

Joseph, Stephan, 'What Are the Three Steps to an Authentic Life?', *Psychology Today* [online] (November 2017) <psychologytoday.com/us/blog/what-doesnt-kill-us/201711/what-are-the-three-steps-authentic-life> [accessed 10 August 2018].

Karras, Ruth Mazo, and Tom Linkinen, 'John/Eleanor Rykener Revisited', in *Founding Feminisms in Medieval Studies: Essays in Honor of E. Jane Burns*, ed. by Laine E. Doggett and Daniel E. O'Sullivan (Cambridge: Brewer, 2016), pp. 111-22.

Margolis, Nadia, 'The Mortal Body as Divine Proof: A Spiritual-Physical Blazon of Joan of Arc', in *Joan of Arc and Spirituality*, ed. by Ann W Astell and Bonnie Wheeler (New York: Palgrave Macmillan, 2003), pp. 9-36.

More, Alison, 'Convergence, Conversion, and Transformation: Gender and Sanctity in Thirteenth-Century Liège', in *Representing Medieval Genders and Sexualities in Europe: Construction, Transformation, and Subversion, 600-1530*, ed. by Elizabeth L'Estrange and Alison More (Farnham: Ashgate, 2011), pp. 33-48.

Nau, F., 'Histoire de sainte Marine', *Revue de l'Orient Chrétien*, 6 (1901), 276-82.

Newman, M. G., 'Crucified by the Virtues: Monks, Lay Brothers, and Women in Thirteenth-Century Cistercian Saints' Lives' in *Gender and Difference in the Middle Ages*, ed. by Sharon Farmer and Carol Braun Pasternack (Minneapolis: University of Minnesota, 2003), pp. 182-209.

Ogden, Amy V., 'The Centrality of Margins: Medieval French Genders and Genres Reconfigured', *French Forum*, 30.1 (2005), 1-23.

Patlagean, Evelyne, 'L'histoire de la femme déguisée en moine et l'évolution de la sainteté féminine à Byzance', *Studi Medievali*, 17 (1976), 598-623.

Peterson, Christopher and Martin Seligman, *Character Strengths and Virtues* (Oxford: Oxford University and the American Psychological Association, 2004).

Serano, Julia, *Whipping Girl: A Transsexual Woman on Sexism and the Scapegoating of Femininity*, (Berkeley: Seal, 2007).

Stone, Sandy, 'The Empire Strikes Back: A Posttranssexual Manifesto', in *The Transgender Studies Reader*, ed. by Susan Stryker and Stephen Whittle (New York: Routledge, 2006), pp. 221-35.

Whittington, Karl, 'Medieval', *Transgender Studies Quarterly: Postposttranssexual: Key Concepts for a Twenty-First Century Transgender Studies*, 1.1-2. (2014), 125-29.

Woods, Jordan Blair, Brad Sears and Christy Mallory, 'Gay and Trans Panic Defense', *The Williams Institute: UCLA School of Law*, (Sept 2016), <https://williamsinstitute.law.ucla.edu/research/model-legislation/> [accessed 19 August 2019].

Žižek, Slavoj, 'History Against Historicism', *European Journal of English Studies*, 4.2 (2000), 101-10.

About the author

M.W. Bychowski is the Anisfield-Wolf SAGES Fellow at Case Western Reserve University (USA) and a scholar with peer-reviewed articles on transgender, disability, and critical race studies in *TSQ, postmedieval, Medieval Feminist Forum, The Medieval Disability Sourcebook*, and *A Cultural History of Race in the Renaissance and Early Modern Age*, as well as a co-editor of *Medieval Trans Feminisms* (2019). She is a well-known, much respected blogger on equity pedagogy, disability, and trans studies (http://www.thingstransform.com). She received her Doctorate from the George Washington University in English Literature. She is currently developing book projects on trans literary theory and medieval transgender history.

Epilogue

Beyond Binaries: A Reflection on the (Trans) Gender(s) of Saints

Mathilde van Dijk

Abstract
In this epilogue, I discuss the productivity of trans and genderqueer readings of medieval hagiography in three contexts: the development of hagiographical studies since the 1960s, of gender studies since Simone de Beauvoir's seminal work *Le deuxième sexe* (1949-1950), and, finally, of historical studies, since the publication of Pierre Nora's *Les Lieux de mémoire* (1984-1992). It should be clear that this afterword is not intended as anything like a final conclusion to this volume, claiming to neatly resolve all of the questions raised. Instead, it is an invitation to further explore gender and saints, to reflect on both categories as well as on methods of trans and genderqueer reading, and, finally, on the societal meaning of such studies today.

Keywords: gender, saints, trans theory, gender studies, topicality of the Middle Ages

In this epilogue, I would like to discuss the productivity of trans and genderqueer readings of medieval hagiography in three contexts: the development of hagiographical studies since the 1960s, of gender studies since Simone de Beauvoir's seminal work *Le deuxième sexe* (1949-1950), and, finally, of historical studies since the publication of Pierre Nora's multi-volume edited collection, *Les Lieux de mémoire* (1984-1992). It should be clear that this afterword is not intended as anything like a final conclusion to this volume, claiming to neatly resolve all of the questions raised. Instead, it is an invitation to further explore gender and saints, to reflect on both categories as well as on methods of trans and genderqueer reading, and, finally, on the societal meaning of such studies today.

Scholarly contexts

Hagiographical studies have boomed since the 1960s, when historians of ideas discovered that tales about saints were among the richest sources for cultural change. Ever since the French historian Jacques Le Goff held up hagiography as a source 'par excellence', medievalists have shown how saints reflected the ideas, practices and feelings of their contexts and, indeed, how such phenomena changed over time, as well as between geographic and cultural domains.[1]

De Beauvoir arguably invented gender, although she does not use the term: the idea that, although biological sex may exist, the categories 'man' and 'woman' are constructed differently in different cultures. Lawyer Kimberlé Crenshaw developed the concept of intersectionality, drawing a connection between gender and other characteristics such as disability, race, class, age, and sexuality, which prove to be just as constructed as the difference between men and women. Philosopher Judith Butler developed de Beauvoir's suggestion that gender is not necessarily linked to bodies. For Butler, gender is constructed and reinforced through repeated social performance, leading to the ultimate conclusion that one does not need a specific body to perform femininity or masculinity.[2] Moreover, she points to the constructed nature of sex itself, as a concept created through language. Therefore, like any word or phrase, its meaning is flexible.[3]

Thus far, in historical studies, these constructivist approaches have been more influential than the theories of sexual difference advocated by a younger generation of Paris-based philosophers, including Luce Irigaray. Like de Beauvoir, Irigaray did some work on female mystics. Her interest is more in construing these women as models for a new, or as she asserts, renewed, specifically feminine form of subjectivity.[4] Philosophically inspiring with its aim of liberating women as subjects, Irigaray's theory is less useful for historical research as she is not searching for what gender or sex may have meant in the Middle Ages, nor is she interested in disrupting binary constructions of gender. The Bulgarian-French Julia Kristeva, who was often criticized for her supposed lack of feminist credentials, may be more helpful here, in terms of her theoretical stance of rejecting fixed categories.[5]

1 Le Goff, 'Les mentalités', p. 86.
2 Butler, *Gender Trouble*.
3 Butler, *Bodies That Matter*, pp. 5-6.
4 Irigaray, *Speculum*, pp. 238-52.
5 Schippers, *Julia Kristeva*, p. 21. Cf. Cohen, *Machines*, pp. 188-89.

This volume also connects to the politicized attitude towards the past, and the study of the past, promoted by French historian Nora and his team in the three volumes of *Lieux de mémoire*, in which history is studied as constructed memory. They show how certain sites, events, concepts, objects, and people from the past were appropriated by different groups in France to symbolize, and summarize, their identities. St Joan of Arc is just one example: she can be a left-wing working-class hero, a right-wing nationalist, or whatever else is useful to bolster one's sense of self.[6] Thus, Nora and his collaborators show the relevance of history for today, as well as its rootedness in our contemporary power structures and present-day concerns, ultimately highlighting history's dialogic quality.

Later, Dutch historian Willem Frijhoff stressed that appropriation of the past as an identity marker always involves expropriation, by which non-dominant groups are marginalized in the grand narrative of 'our past'.[7] The current discussion about statues of historical 'heroes', catalysed by the global Black Lives Matter movement, is a case in point.[8] For example, General Robert E. Lee was the slave-owning commander of the Confederate States Army in the American Civil War, a war fought by the South for the right to retain chattel slavery and profit from Black suffering.[9] Sculptural homages to Lee in American cities send a clear message about who determines who 'we' are, what counts as 'our' past or, even more fundamentally, what this past actually was. Aware of the occasionally toxic topicality of the past, Blake Gutt and Alicia Spencer-Hall use their privilege as editors to identify their collection of essays as 'a call to arms', an invitation to conduct historical research with an aim of generating knowledge about the past, and to reconsider one's role in producing a past that intervenes in the present – as it inevitably does.

All of this is a far cry from the ideology of the past's radical alterity, an intellectual tradition in which I was raised as a historian, and which, in itself, was a reaction against nationalists' all-too-easy appropriations of the past for their own ends, with historians as happy collaborators.[10] The consciousness of history's connection to present-day power structures is a more realist account of what actually happens in historical studies: how present-day interests inspire particular narratives of the past, and

---

6   On Joan in *Lieux de mémoire*, see Winock, 'Jeanne d'Arc'; on the saint more generally, see this volume's 'Introduction', pp. 12-13.
7   Frijhoff, 'Modes', pp. 103-08; 'Toeëigening: van bezitsdrang'; 'Toe-eigening als vorm'.
8   Grovier, 'Protests'.
9   Marcus, 'Last Confederate Statue'.
10 Cf. Frijhoff, 'Modes', pp. 94-95.

how scholarly assessments are informed by the researchers' contexts.[11] For instance, before the rise of women's or gender studies, no medievalist thought of focusing on the societal functions of female visionaries as spiritual leaders, or the political power some of these women could exert, rather than the literary or theological value of their writings, or their psychopathology. These aspects only came to the fore in the context of feminism, and the larger presence of women in the public sphere from the 1960s onwards. The same is true for trans and genderqueer readings as proposed in this volume: such readings only became possible in the context of the current challenges to a binary model of gender, both in biology and in the humanities. Genetic research has revealed that biological sex is more complex than one half of humanity having XX and the other half having XY chromosomes. Instead, there is a variety of combinations: some men have an extra X-chromosome (XXY) or an extra Y (XYY); some women are missing part of the second X-chromosome (known as X, 45), and so on. In this volume, Lee Colwill shows the effect of disregarding transgender, non-binary or non-normative possibilities. Archaeologists automatically assumed that the presence of weapons or a certain kind of jewellery in a grave indicated that the deceased was a cis man, whilst 'contrary' signs, such as 'feminine' jewellery combined with 'masculine' swords, were disregarded. Osteological evidence and DNA research have revealed that, in some cases, buried individuals who were previously assumed to be cis men had XX chromosomes. The question of their social gender remains open.

The chapters in this volume show how dialogical awareness does not necessarily entail a presentist view of the past: rigorous research on sources in their medieval contexts reveals their enduring cultural impact. Several contributors, including Kevin C.A. Elphick, Amy V. Ogden, and M.W. Bychowski, explicitly connect their medievalist research to the current struggles of marginalized people.

A third window

When it comes to saints, their most striking characteristic is that they are different, even the opposite of the people around them. Inspired by the grace of God, they imitate Christ's perfection and become like Him. This means that they relinquish all human desires, such as lust, or longings for

---

11   Donna Haraway earlier argued that this is true for all scholarly practices – see 'Situated Knowledges'.

wealth or high office, and focus on God instead. This was seen as a return to authenticity, to humankind as it was originally intended to be. Following St Augustine, medieval authors believed that the Fall had caused humanity to lose its likeness to God, at least in part, and to become infected with an almost irrepressible desire for carnality.[12] Saints had risen above this predicament and become quasi-divine, becoming humans as He intended them to be. What, however, did this mean for their gendered performances as described by their hagiographers or rendered in images, especially when their function as models for imitation is taken into account? What did it mean for the way(s) in which their bodies were represented, their stories told?

A passage in a fifteenth-century Middle Dutch *Life* of St Barbara of Nicomedia may help to explain the very special gender of saints. Barbara's original Latin *Life* is traditionally ascribed to the Augustinian hermit Johannes of Wackerzele, writing before the end of the fourteenth century. The *Life* is included in the *Compilatio de Sancta Barbara*, which contains hagiographical texts in many genres, and which was hugely popular in the late Middle Ages, not only in its original Latin, but also in translations in several vernaculars: alongside the Middle Dutch version under discussion here, there are extant editions in Middle English, Middle High German, and Middle Low German.[13]

According to the *Life* in the *Compilatio*, Barbara's father, Dioscorus, was a persecutor of Christians. Wishing to keep his daughter's beauty to himself, he locked her in a tower. A loving father, Dioscorus was careful to have it fitted with two windows, one in the North and one in the South, to ensure that the rising sun would not wake her up too early in the morning, and that she would not lie awake too long due to the evening sun. When construction was well underway, he left on a journey, only to return to an unpleasant surprise:

> Much later, her father, King Dyoscrius [*sic*], returned, and much admired the beautiful building. And when he noted that the tower had been fitted out with three windows, he remembered his orders and asked: 'Who made you build a third window, overriding my orders that there should be only two?' A builder replied: 'Sire, your daughter, my lady, pressed the masters to build it'. Instantly, he had his daughter brought before him. After he had kissed her, he asked whether she had ordered a third window to be constructed. And she replied: 'Yes, father, because three windows

---

12 As St Augustine knew to his cost; see Augustine of Hippo, *Confessions*, I, pp. 88-102.
13 For an overview of the impact of this *Compilatio*, see de Gaiffier, 'La légende', pp. 8-12.

enlighten all humankind but two engender darkness. Humankind is born divided into only two sexes, that is, man and woman. Therefore, as far as we are concerned, two windows suffice, but in the threefold number of these windows, father, a greater mystery is hidden. Please be patient and hear me out. These are the Father, the Son and the Holy Ghost, who are not three gods but one true God, the Creator of all[.]"[14]

Dioscorus realizes that his daughter has converted to Christianity, after which a long sequence of torments and discussions between the saint, her father and the local judge begins, punctuated by Dioscorus's fits of rage. Eventually, he executes her himself, and is struck by lightning as a result.

For our purposes, Barbara's message about the three windows is the most important aspect; according to the saint, they symbolize the Trinity. Should we conclude that God has three genders? This would not be in accordance with theological ideas about the nature of God. The main characteristic of God is that He is different from everything in creation. This is also why it is virtually impossible to talk about Him, as Pseudo-Dionysius the Areopagite (c. 500) so famously argued in *De mystica theologia*. His apophatic theology was embraced by scholastics and mystics alike. God was not to be encapsulated in the concepts that humankind could invent. If Barbara represents Him as being threefold, her point is that He is different. The same applied to saints, who were as close to God as any human could hope to be. Like Him, they are beyond gender. As Caitlyn McLoughlin argues in her chapter on Capgrave's rendition of the legend of Katherine of Alexandria, it is Katherine's very non-normativity as a queen who chose scholarship and virginity over marriage and reign that showed her saintliness. Bychowski and Ogden suggest that the same is true for the saints assigned female at

---

14 The Hague, Royal Library MS 73 H 13 (Maeseyck, Regular Canonesses, Saint Agnes), fols. 24r-25r: 'Na langher tijt quam haer vader weder – Dyoscrius den coninc – ende verwonderde seer vander schoenheyt des wercs. Ende doe hy sach drie vensteren gheset in den toren, waert hij ghedenckende sijnre bevelinghen ende vraechde: "Wye heeft doen maken dat derde venster daer boven dat ic gheboden hadde datmen niet dan twe vensteren maken en soude?" Doen antwoerde hem een wercman: "Here, u dochter, mijn vrouwe, heeft dat met groter ernsticheit vercreghen vanden meesters". Ter stont dede hy sijn dochter comen voer hem. Ende na dat hyse ghecust hadde, vraechde hy hoer of sy dat derde venster hadde doen maken. Sy antwoerde: "Ja ic vader, want drie vensteren verlichten alle menschen met twe vensteren verdonckeren. Die mensche en wort niet gheboren dan van twe kunnen als van manne ende van wijve. Hieromme alsoe vele als ons aen gaet so sijn twe vensteren goet, mer inden drievoldighen ghetale der vensteren, vader, is verborghen een meerder misterie, eest dat ghijt verduldichlijc horen wilt. Dat is die vader ende die sone ende die heylighe gheest, niet drie goden, mer een ghewarigher God, scepper alre dinghen". The English translation is my own.

birth, who lived in monasteries as monks. Their transcendence of gendered categories proved their saintliness.

The thought that variation in gender could happen was reinforced by biological theories. Sex, like everything else in the human body, was determined by the proportion of the humours. This is why Aristotle regarded woman as a failed man: during gestation fire and heat had developed insufficiently, which caused her to be cold and humid. In medieval thought, this had consequences for capacities and morals: women were supposed to be less suited to intellectual labour and more inclined to sin. Medieval natural scientists and theologians acknowledged that the actual division of the humours was different for each individual. Thus, sex was not seen in terms of a stark contrast between men on one side and women on the other. Depending on the balance of heat and cold, individual men or women could be closer or further away from the opposite sex, with the hermaphrodite in the middle of the scale, viewed alternately as a magical or a monstrous being.[15] The humours could be manipulated: an ascetic lifestyle was supposed to increase the proportion of fire and therefore made both men and

Figure E.1 The Lamentation of Christ

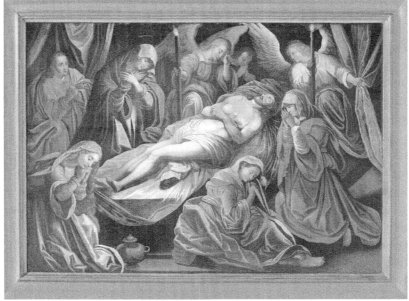

Courtesy of the Hôpital Notre Dame à La Rose, Lessen, Belgium

15 See 'Hermaphrodite' in the Appendix: p. 300.

women more manly.[16] Fire was connected to God; becoming more fiery meant that one had come closer to him.

Elphick's portrayal of Juana de la Cruz offers a perspective in which theology and biology come to the fore. According to her own testimony, Juana was initially formed in the womb as male, and was reassigned female by God himself, in response to a request from the Virgin Mary. Her sermons stress how Jesus took on characteristics from his mother and his Father alike. Thus, both in her own person and in her work, Juana challenged gender binaries – she developed an apophatic gender theology, in which gender is never fixed. The same is true for characters such as Martha Newman's Joseph, Bychowski's Marinos, and Ogden's Eufrosine. The fluidity of gender allows people assigned female at birth to live as monks, their gender unquestioned until their bodies are laid out for burial. Here, it is important to acknowledge the internal logic of these narratives, in which it is significant to show that the supposed brother was 'actually' a sister, thus undermining and enhancing the flexibility of gender simultaneously. The fact that these holy individuals could live not only as men (rising above their 'real', i.e. assigned, female sex and gender), but also as exemplary monks (rising above the commonplace of their identified male gender), is intended to put the less perfect, ordinary men, who read or heard their *vitae* to shame. Female audiences might be alerted to what spiritual perfection could bring. Felix Szabo's chapter on the eunuch Ignatios shows how his ascesis allows him to rise above his limitations. As a castrated man, he had no part in normative masculinity. It was commonly believed that the removal of their sexual parts caused eunuchs to become less manly and therefore more like females. As a result, they were presumed to become licentious as far as sex, luxury and food were concerned. Rejecting all of this, Ignatios was able to become perfect.

Vanessa Wright's chapter on the illuminations in three fourteenth-century manuscripts of the legend of Eufrosine shows artists' struggles to depict such non-normative genders, as does Szabo's chapter. According to the narrative, Eufrosine's fellow monks did not read the new arrival as female (the sex that Eufrosine was assigned at birth), or as normatively male, instead identifying this brother as a eunuch; however, showing this in an image is a challenge. Spectators must be able to recognize Eufrosine's difference by visible markers, if only to identify the protagonist. Thus, the illuminator plays with gendered performances such as wearing longer or shorter hair, or feminine-coded robes. The same is true of a mosaic depicting Ignatios, who, in the company of customarily bearded patriarchs, is shown without a beard.

---

16 See: Murray, 'One Flesh'; Cadden, *Meanings*.

Saints are special, not the least because they are capable of transgressing seemingly fixed gender categories, as is their model, Christ, who was God and human at the same time. As God, He would be beyond gender, but as Caroline Walker Bynum and other researchers have argued, the same is true as far as His body is concerned. Flexible, suffering and emitting liquids such as blood, it was similar to a woman's body, despite Christ's traditional assignment as a man. In her seminal monograph *Holy Feast and Holy Fast*, Bynum stressed the motherly capacity of His body to provide food, thus enhancing the connection to women, who can also provide food through their bodies. A spectacular sixteenth-century image, the *Lamentation of Christ* (Fig. E.1), forcefully depicts his multiple genders, his motherliness and his agonies all at once.[17] From a hospital in Lessen led by Augustinian canonesses, it connects the latter to the patients' own suffering, presumably offering them comfort.[18]

Sophie Sexon's analyses in the present collection strengthen Bynum's arguments considerably. Not only do Christ's wounds, specifically the side wound, appear similar to female genitals, but these and other images were also used to help in women's ordeals such as childbirth or menstruation. The birthing girdles that were laid across the bodies of women in labour are Sexon's most striking example: the suffering of Christ and the suffering of women were connected. They also examine the haptic practices around manuscripts, in which readers would touch and kiss texts and miniatures. Direct contact with the wound would draw the readers closer to Christ, even into him, thus dissolving the boundaries between him and the believer, who would come to share his gender fluidity, as did the saints.

It is a matter for debate whether such capacity – and preference – for gender fluidity applies to saints alone. Gutt's study of gender in the romance of *Tristan de Nanteuil*, along with Colwill's sepulchral case studies, indicates that fluidity could apply to anyone, not only canonized Christian saints. Gutt's study expands the discussion into a study of disability and the healing power of saints. Colwill discusses several graves which belonged to practitioners of *seiðr*, a form of magic which is thought to have involved ritual disruptions of normative gender practices. Indeterminate social gender belongs to these practitioners, but the same can be true for other individuals. Apparently, there was a difference between social and biological gender, as Colwill convincingly shows.

17 Bynum, *Fragmentation*, pp. 181-238.
18 It became widely known after being included in a Brussels exhibition on female mysticism; for the catalogue, see Vandenbroeck, *Hooglied*, p. 61, cat. 19.

The final words in this section are about love. In the lives of saints, there is often a contrast between the natural love of parents for their children, and the love of God and humankind that a saint practises. As Ogden describes, parental or familial love is the wrong kind, keeping the saint entrenched in worldly pursuits such as marriage. St Barbara's father is even worse than Eufrosine's, as he uncharitably strives to hide a beautiful part of creation from his fellow human beings, rather than sharing it. His rages and eventual execution of his daughter show that his love lacks measure. Saints offer an alternative by the measured love of their charity, which aims to lead their fellow human beings towards God rather than to carnal pleasures, as Eufrosine did for her father. Moreover, whilst earthly parents may not always be able to accept trans saints on their own terms, God's love embraces trans saints entirely, not in spite of their transness but perhaps because of it.

In dialogue

Living and working in a European city's downtown, passing two medieval churches every day, walking the town's medieval street plan, it is hard to imagine the Middle Ages as being irrelevant. Recently, it has become even more topical. TV series and games set in medieval contexts, such as *Game of Thrones* and *Assassin's Creed*, have become big hits. Moreover, white supremacists refer to the Middle Ages as they seek historical support for their Islamophobia, fantasizing as they do about an ethnically unified Europe, where men were men and women knew their places.[19] The essays in this volume challenge such notions.

This volume shows the fluidity of gender in saints' – and others' – lives, how gender norms could be, and were, manipulated in the Middle Ages, and how identified gender is not necessarily synonymous with sex/gender assigned at birth. In addition, it shows the co-existence of several formats for leading one's life, technically in contrast with each other, in practice intermingled. Finally, this volume bears witness to the presence of trans and non-binary people in the Middle Ages. Joan of Arc's cross-dressing might be a matter of expedience, but it might also be that she just felt more like her (or him)self when wearing men's clothes and engaging in the masculine practice of war. Beyond the Middle Ages,

---

19 For an analysis of the contemporary political appeal of the Middle Ages, see: Elliott, *Medievalism*.

history offers several well-documented examples of trans identity, such as the Chevalier d'Éon (1728-1810).[20] Recent genetic research has revealed that the differences between the sexes are structured as a continuum, rather than there being a stark contrast between male and female. The concept of a continuum is also present in medieval perceptions of the differences between the sexes, albeit on very different grounds. In any case, it seems that binaries do not work: we need messiness rather than fixed categories.[21]

From a medieval perspective, this messiness may seem less radical than it does to us. It was understood that gender, like any other category which could be applied to Creation, could not be used to define God except symbolically. Moreover, as far as human beings were concerned, it was clear that sex operated on a scale and, by manipulation, could slide either way. Therefore, describing God as a mother, or a virgin saint as a man, would not be as shocking as it may seem to some of us.

Troubling supposedly fixed categories such as male and female will challenge the usual ways of assessing gender and sex. *Frappez toujours*: eventually, this may have an effect. Only decades ago, it was a radical thought that women had very important roles in the budding movement around Christ; today this is commonplace. Only recently, women as a species were considered unfit to rule: today Christine Lagarde (Head of the European Central Bank) and Angela Merkel, the German Chancellor (*Bundeskanzlerin*) are just two examples to the contrary. Vigilance remains necessary, as this is no shining narrative of glorious progress: whereas in many countries gay and trans rights have become a matter of course, others return to persecution of non-heterosexual and non-cis individuals.

At the very least, tales of saints' gender fluidity show that medieval authors were as fascinated by the difference between sexes – and between genders – as we are. Their conclusion was to view the saints as being close to God, who was also beyond gender, and, as far as creatures were concerned, to regard gender as unstable in any individual, dependent as it was on the proportion of the humours. Trans and genderqueer readings of the sources offer an extra lens for understanding gender in the Middle Ages, and possibly in our day too. New understanding of our contemporary moment is generated in dialogue with the paradigm offered by medieval sources: a fundamental openness to instability, to gender beyond binaries.

20 Rose, 'Trans in Translation'.
21 Cf. Kristeva, *Speculum*; see also Schippers, *Julia Kristeva*, pp. 21-53.

Bibliography

Manuscripts

Johannes of Wackerzele, *Compilatio de Sancta Barbara*, The Hague, Royal Library MS 73 H 13, fols. 1r-88v.

Primary sources

Augustine of Hippo, *Confessions*, ed. by James J. O'Donnell, 3 vols. (Oxford: Clarendon Press, 1992).
Pseudo-Dionysius the Areopagite, 'De mystica theologia', in *Corpus Dionysiacum*, ed. by Günther Heil and Adam M. Ritter (Berlin: De Gruyter, 1991), pp. 141-50.

Secondary sources

de Beauvoir, Simone, *Le deuxième sexe* (Paris: Gallimard, 1949-1950).
Butler, Judith, *Bodies That Matter: On the Discursive Limits of "Sex"* (New York: Routledge, 1993).
—, *Gender Trouble: Feminism and the Subversion of Identity* (New York: Routledge, 1990).
Bynum, Caroline Walker, *Fragmentation and Redemption: Essays on Gender and the Human Body in Medieval Religion* (New York: Zone, 1991).
—, *Holy Feast and Holy Fast: The Religious Significance of Food to Medieval Women* (Berkeley: University of California Press, 1987).
Cadden, Joan, *Meanings of Sex Difference in the Middle Ages: Medicine, Science, and Culture* (Cambridge: Cambridge University Press, 1993).
Cohen, Jeffrey J., *Medieval Identity Machines* (Minneapolis: University of Minnesota Press, 2003).
Crenshaw, Kimberlé, 'Demarginalizing the Intersection of Race and Sex: A Black Feminist Critique of Antidiscrimination Doctrine, Feminist Theory and Antiracist Politics', *Chicago Legal Forum*, 1 (1989), 139-67.
van Dijk, Mathilde, 'Travelling-Companion in the Journey of Life: Saint Barbara of Nicomedia in a *Devotio Moderna* Context', in *Death and Dying in the Middle Ages*, ed. by Edelgard DuBruck and Barbara Gusick (New York: Lang, 1999), pp. 221-37.
Elliott, Andrew B.R., *Medievalism, Politics and Mass Media: Appropriating the Middle Ages in the Twenty-First Century* (Cambridge: D.S. Brewer, 2017).
Frijhoff, Willem, 'Modes of Doing Cultural History – Foucault Reformed by Certeau: Historical Strategies of Discipline and Appropriation', *Arcadia*, 33 (1998), 92-108.
—, 'Toe-eigening als vorm van culturele dynamiek', *Volkskunde*, 104 (2003), 1-17.

—, 'Toeëigening: van bezitsdrang naar betekenisgeving', *Trajecta*, 6 (1997), 99-118.
de Gaiffier, Baudouin, 'La légende latine de Saint Barbe de Jean de Wackerzele', *Analecta Bollandiana*, 77 (1959), 5-41.
Le Goff, Jacques, 'Les mentalités : une histoire ambiguë', in *Faire de l'histoire, Tome 3: Nouveaux objets*, ed. by Jacques Le Goff and Pierre Nora (Paris: Gallimard, 1974), pp. 76-94.
Grovier, Kelly, 'Black Lives Matter Protests: Why are Statues so Powerful?', *BBC* [online], 12 June 2020 <https://www.bbc.com/culture/article/20200612-black-lives-matter-protests-why-are-statues-so-powerful> [accessed 21 July 2020].
Haraway, Donna, 'Situated Knowledges: The Science Question in Feminism and the Privilege of Partial Perspective', *Feminist Studies*, 14.3 (1988), 575-99.
Irigaray, Luce, *Speculum de l'autre femme* (Paris: Minuit, 1974).
Kristeva, Julia, *Pouvoirs de l'horreur. Essai sur l'abjection* (Paris: Seuil, 1980).
Marcus, Ezra, 'Will the Last Confederate Statue Standing Turn Off the Lights?', *New York Times* [online], 23 June 2020. <https://www.nytimes.com/2020/06/23/style/statue-richmond-lee.html> [accessed 21 July 2020].
Murray, Jacqueline, 'One Flesh, Two Sexes, Three Genders', in *Gender and Christianity in Medieval Europe: New Perspectives*, ed. by Lisa M. Bitel and Felice Lifshitz (Philadelphia: University of Pennsylvania Press, 2008), pp. 34-51.
Nora, Pierre, ed., *Les Lieux de mémoire*, 3 vols. (Paris: Gallimard, 1984-1992).
Rose, Emily, 'Keeping the Trans in Translation: Queering Early Modern Transgender Memoirs', *TSQ: Transgender Studies Quarterly*, 3.3-4 (2016), 485-505.
Schippers, Birgit, *Julia Kristeva and Feminist Thought* (Edinburgh: Edinburgh University Press, 2011).
Vandenbroeck, Paul, ed., *Hooglied: de beeldwereld van religieuze vrouwen in de Zuidelijke Nederlanden, vanaf de 13e eeuw* (Brussels: Snoeck-Ducaju & Zoon, 1994).
Winock, Michel, 'Jeanne d'Arc', in *Les Lieux de mémoire*, 3 vols., ed. by Pierre Nora (Paris: Gallimard, 1984-1992), III, pp. 675-733.

About the author

MATHILDE VAN DIJK is a university lecturer in the History of Christianity and Gender Studies at the University of Groningen (The Netherlands). She is a specialist in the history of late medieval reform, with special interest in the appropriation of Early Church saints and the Church Fathers in the Late Middle Ages, and the appropriation of the Middle Ages in current popular culture. In 2019, she was awarded the Royal Holland Society of Sciences and Humanities and the NRC Newspaper's Essay Prize for her essay, 'Drink eens thee met een Alien'.

Appendix

Trans and Genderqueer Studies Terminology, Language, and Usage Guide

Abstract
The Language Guide is a resource offering succinct suggestions as to the usage of respectful, inclusive, and non-violent terminology when talking about the trans, genderqueer, and intersex communities, on a personal or group level. Designed as a reference guide for a target audience of medievalist scholars engaged in cross-temporal analyses, it offers an overview of modern terminology for use in research outputs. The Guide was conceived and assembled by trans and genderqueer medievalists and their allies.

Keywords: trans studies, gender studies, gender theory, genderqueer, glossary, terminology, usage guide

Introduction

Language matters, both in terms of what we say and how we say it. Our words can do real violence to those about whom we speak. This violence reflects the broader socio-cultural oppressions which marginalized communities face as a daily reality. Simultaneously, hateful language supports such oppressions, as a vehicle by which bigoted ideologies re-circulate and gain ever more traction in the public imagination. A considerable amount of violence has been done, and is being done, to the trans, genderqueer, and intersex communities by disrespectful, othering, and offensive language. This violence is routinely perpetuated at a group level (comments about the community in general) and at an individual level (comments about specific individuals).

Spencer-Hall, Alicia, and Blake Gutt (eds), *Trans and Genderqueer Subjects in Medieval Hagiography*. Amsterdam, Amsterdam University Press 2021
DOI: 10.5117/9789462988248_APPEN

Some wield discriminatory language knowingly, using their words as dog whistles for transphobia and queerphobia. Others, however, use disrespectful language unknowingly – due to ignorance of the offensive nature of certain terminology. Nevertheless, language is always political, and linguistic choices serve to reinscribe, consciously or not, certain paradigms. The gender binary is a cultural construct, supported by normalized language which serves simultaneously to obscure alternative possibilities whilst reinforcing existing hegemonies. We provide this language guide as a resource, offering succinct suggestions as to the usage of respectful, inclusive, and non-violent terminology when talking about the trans, genderqueer, and intersex communities, be that on a personal or group level.

This document is absolutely not intended to operate as lexical doctrine. Our guidance can be only that: *guidance*. What constitutes respectful language shifts and evolves over time, dependant on myriad intersectional factors. Slurs are reclaimed, for instance, and new – better, or at least more expressive – coinage gains traction, reframing previously affirmative terminology in problematic lights. Language is both political *and* personal, and context is key. This guide has been produced by members of the medievalist trans and genderqueer community and their allies. It thus reflects the consensus of a group of engaged scholars. However, we, quite obviously, do not speak for all trans, genderqueer, and intersex individuals. Preferences will vary for the usage, or avoidance, of certain terms – words which may even appear in this guide as acceptable vocabulary. Above all else, listen to individuals, learn their preferences, and defer to them.

Allies can never speak for, or speak as, the community itself. Trans, genderqueer, and intersex scholars, those with lived experience of the material which we study, may formulate different kinds of analyses than allies, drawing different conclusions. The job of allyship is to amplify the voices of those whose contributions may otherwise be suppressed from the record, to trust in our colleagues who may know more – and know differently – from us.

When compiling this guide, we have been particularly concerned to make evident the granularity of language and identities. By 'granularity', we mean in particular the ways in which identity categories can be endlessly subdivided, into more and more personal(ized) descriptors: zooming in on any given label reveals the multiplicity of nuance within all group-level categories. For example, 'trans' can be subdivided into binary and non-binary identities; non-binary identities may include 'agender', and some agender identities may be more minutely described by a term such as 'gendervoid'. Gender identity is intensely personal. Thus, the same terminology can be understood and applied differently by different people, and the unfolding of categories can only end when a description precisely encompasses a single individual's identity. Language is slippery here, answering imperfectly to the desire to name and communicate lived experiences which operate outside certain assumptions which govern cis-heterosexual culture. Crucially, gender and its systems are inextricable from racialization. Awareness of this is essential for substantive engagement with the field/s of trans/gender studies. White supremacy imposes white Eurocentric gender norms, and refuses to acknowledge non-white identities on their own terms. Non-white bodies are policed more strictly, including in terms of gender (non)conformity. Within the broader community, for example, trans women of colour face the highest levels of often deadly systemic violence. The two principal architects of this guide are white and British, thus the guide is fundamentally structured by a white, Western (and, indeed, Eurocentric) viewpoint. We recognize this as a significant limitation, and encourage our readers to strive to decolonize their thinking, as we strive to ourselves.

It is important not to elide complex identifications on the supposed grounds that they are too complicated to be understood, expressed, or respected. Some trans and genderqueer people may use language in ways other than those suggested here – this is their prerogative. For example, certain adjectives which we would not recommend using as nouns may be used in this way by those who have direct lived experience(s) of trans and genderqueer identities. In this context, individuals assigned female at birth may describe themselves as 'AFABs', although this usage would be disrespectful if deployed by other individuals. If you do not have such lived experience(s), it is best to avoid potentially offensive usages and terminology with especially fraught histories. Furthermore, appropriate usage may differ when referring to real historical figures versus literary characters. We believe that literary representations of lives, particularly those marked by supernatural occurrences such as divine physical transformation, often function as a means for thinking about and through the complexities of gender and its significations. As such, it may be productive to analyse these metonymic portrayals in ways which would not be appropriate or respectful when referring to lived experiences, even if those lives now seem distant or inaccessible. It is vital to attend to textual evidence concerning the character or figure's relationship to their own gendered existence.

A note on shifting terminology is necessary. The vocabulary used to describe trans, genderqueer, and gender non-conforming identities changes relatively quickly. This terminological impermanence can result in an unwillingness to employ a transgender optic in criticism. This may be due to concerns about stability and comprehensibility as regards the terms themselves, or to the suspicion that unsettled vocabulary implies a shifting frame of reference unconducive to the stable production of meaning. In establishing this guide, we therefore acknowledge that to write about a community whose terminology is in flux implies risks: future reception of the analysis may be affected by rejection of the vocabulary in which it is couched. Nevertheless, we do not believe that this is a valid reason to abandon fruitful inquiry which has the potential to increase comprehension of marginalized groups, in addition to introducing a source of productive comparative material for the analysis of literary texts.

Excessive emphasis on recent shifts in vocabulary also gives the inaccurate impression that non-normative gender is a new phenomenon which is yet to establish a consistent phraseology and thereby gain legitimacy. It also suggests that critics have only to wait until this is established, at which point non-normative gender will suddenly become a more easily accessible concept. This perspective dismisses the consistent presence of non-normative gender, which is attested throughout history and literature. Moreover, this compounds the problem that non-normatively gendered identities have always been rendered harder to see and to discuss as a result of inadequate or reductive descriptive terminology. Only engagement with these identities will allow the development of more apt vocabulary, and the disentangling of non-normative gender from the normative sex/gender system. If we wait for the opportune moment to do so, we may well wait forever. In this spirit, then, we anticipate – and welcome the fact – that this language guide will become outdated as affirmative cultural understanding of non-normative gender develops.

This guide is an artefact of work and thought undertaken between 2017 and 2019, necessarily influenced by our personal perspectives, subject positions, experiences, and scholarly backgrounds. Medievalist scholars have been at the forefront of developing queer critical frameworks for at least a quarter of a century. This guide, then, is grounded in the seminal work of scholars such as John Boswell, Bill Burgwinkle, Joan Cadden, Carolyn Dinshaw, Karma Lochrie, Robert Mills, to name only a few – that is, we write with a particularly medievalist approach to nuancing and critiquing modernist theories of gender and sex. Nevertheless, this guide does not address specifically medieval terminology and usage. Instead, it provides an overview of modern terminology and usage, which may be particularly useful to medievalist scholars – and our colleagues working on premodern materials more broadly – engaging in cross-temporal analysis. Finally, this guide is anglocentric and thus inherently limited in its cross-cultural and cross-linguistic reach. As we write, Clovis Maillet and colleagues are preparing a French-language counterpart to this guide. We look forward to seeing similar work emerge across languages, with guides produced by native-language trans scholars and their allies.

The guide is grounded in theories of sex and gender, especially the work of Judith Butler who remains a touchstone for entry into the critical field for many scholars, including the editors of this volume. Our approach is nuanced by the work of numerous trans scholars, including Susan Stryker, Julia Serano, and C. Riley Snorton, alongside the lived experiences and observations of the trans and genderqueer medievalist community. In order to grasp more fully the points set out in the guide, we strongly recommend consulting core texts in this area. These are the entries marked by an asterisk in the Bibliography below. What comes to the fore in reading such literature is the immense complexity, and contingent cultural determination, of the terms 'sex' and 'gender'. Broadly speaking, our usage of 'sex' refers to assigned sex, based on biological essentialism, whereas we use 'gender' to refer to an individual's innate sense of their own identity. We also recommend Alex Kapitan's 'Radical Copyeditor's Style Guide for Writing About Transgender People' which offers a thorough overview of best practice in writing about trans and genderqueer individuals, including suggestions for rewording. Another especially helpful resource is the online glossary created by M.W. Bychowski.

There will always be exceptions to the indications we set out below – prescriptivism can only go so far. However, if you are not trans or genderqueer yourself, be wary of potentially offensive usages; our aim in the guide below is to offer an accessible grounding in relevant terminology. The most important point we can make about these usages is that, above all, it is necessary to think carefully and critically about your word choices, and how your choices may integrally affect textual interpretations – and do real harm to readers. Aim for precision and transparency: tell your readers what choices you are making, and why.

This guide was immeasurably improved thanks to the unpaid labour of members of the trans and genderqueer medievalist community. We owe an enormous debt of thanks to folx for sharing their knowledge with us and spending their time and energy on this document. Any errors or omissions are absolutely and entirely our own.

Blake Gutt (Ann Arbor, Michigan, USA)
Alicia Spencer-Hall (London, UK)
August 2020

AFAB (adjective)
Assigned Female At Birth. Reference to birth assignment is a way to acknowledge the particular constellation of experiences which individuals may share due to gendered socio-cultural practices, without making assumptions about individuals' experiences of gender or gender identity. 'AFAB' is an adjective, not a noun.
See also: **AMAB, Assigned Sex; Assigned Gender, CAFAB, CAMAB, Identified Gender**

Agender (adjective)
An agender individual has no gender. Some agender people consider their identity to fall under the genderqueer and/or the non-binary umbrellas. Others consider their identity to be distinct from genderqueer and/or non-binary identities, since genderqueer and non-binary people may experience a gender(ed) identity, although this identity is not recognized by the gender binary. By contrast, agender individuals experience a *lack* of gender (and thus, a lack of gender(ed) identity). Agender people may use any pronouns, and may present in feminine, masculine, or androgynous ways. Specific terms for agender identities may include: genderfree, genderless, gendervoid, **Neutrois**, and non-gendered.
See also: **Androgynous; Androgyny, Genderqueer, Neutrois, Non-Binary, Pronouns**

Androgynous; Androgyny (adjective; noun)
The term 'androgynous' describes a person who appears neither female nor male. Its origins lie in a myth recounted by Aristophanes in Plato's *Symposium*, in which he posited three types of human beings: male, female, and androgynous. Originally a slur for a man perceived as feminine or a woman perceived as masculine, the word has taken on neutral or positive connotations since the mid-twentieth century. It is important to note, however, that androgyny (the state of being or appearing androgynous) is highly culturally contingent: what is read as androgynous is defined in relation to cultural norms of masculinity and femininity. Furthermore, androgynous appearance is a facet of gender expression, which, although it is an aspect of gender identity, does not predict or denote whether a person is transgender or cisgender.
See also: **Gender, Gender Non-Conformity; Gender Non-Conforming**

APPENDIX

AMAB (adjective)
Assigned Male At Birth. Reference to birth assignment is a way to acknowledge the particular constellation of experiences which individuals may share due to gendered socio-cultural practices, without making assumptions about individuals' experiences of gender or gender identity. 'AMAB' is an adjective, not a noun.
See also: *AFAB, Assigned Sex; Assigned Gender, CAFAB, CAMAB, Eunuch, Identified Gender*

Assigned Sex; Assigned Gender (nouns)
'Assigned sex' is the binary sex to which an individual is declared to belong at birth, typically with the declaration by a medical professional: 'It's a girl!' or 'it's a boy!'. 'Assigned gender' is the binary gender classification assumed to 'match' the assigned sex: those assigned boys are assumed to be male, and those assigned girls are assumed to be female. Everyone has both an assigned sex and gender, and an identified gender. Cisgender individuals' identified gender matches their assigned sex/gender, whereas transgender individuals' identified gender is different from their assigned sex/gender.

'Identified sex' is not a useful term, since awareness of the socially constructed nature of assigned sex/gender reveals the fact that sex itself is a gendered category. By this, we mean: a category produced through and by means of gender, rather than, as the cultural narrative often presents it, the ground and *cause* of gender. Gender, whether assigned or identified, is always the key signifier, and 'identified sex' is therefore meaningless. (For more on this see Butler, *Gender Trouble*.)

Intersex individuals are almost always assigned a binary sex at birth, although a few countries now allow an 'X' gender marker instead of the binary 'M' or 'F' categorizations. Note, however, that the 'X' gender marker may also designate an individual's gender as non-binary; practices vary between countries. Intersex individuals often undergo medically unnecessary surgery to make their genitals and/or internal reproductive organs more closely resemble binary categories of sex.

Be aware that 'assigned' language always implies the presence of an assigning entity, be that a cultural authority or an individual. Therefore, be circumspect in describing literary characters, for example, as having been assigned female or male if it is you, the critic, who is in fact doing the assigning. Such usage effectively reduces assignment to concrete identity rather than social imposition.
See also: *AFAB, AMAB, CAFAB, CAMAB, Intersex, Identified Gender*

Asterisk (*)
See: *Trans(gender)*

Binary (adjective and noun)
There are several cultural binaries relating to sex, gender, and sexuality.

The notion of binary *sex* claims that people are either men or women, depending on narrow definitions of their genitals and/or reproductive organs. When cursory visual categorization fails, reference to hormone profile and chromosome configuration is presumed to stabilize the categories of 'man' and 'woman'. This binary erases intersex bodies, understanding them only as aberrant, and results in cultural inability to conceptualize transgender identities. The notion of binary *gender* claims that there are only two genders, male and female. Binary gender is usually already heterosexualized (conceived of in order to fit in with the norm of heterosexuality, or to make heterosexuality appear inevitable). Thus, the notion of binary gender is typically subordinate to the notion of binary sex, and claims that men are/should be masculine, and women are/should be feminine. This binary erases non-binary and agender gender identities.

The notion of binary *sexualities* dictates that there are two forms of sexuality, heterosexuality and homosexuality. This binary results in erasure of bisexual, asexual, and pansexual sexualities, which are construed as non-existent, or as a transitional phase between the heterosexual norm and coming out as homosexual.

See: Barker and Iantaffi, *Life Isn't Binary*.
See also: *Assigned Sex; Assigned Gender, Cis(gender), Gender, Gender Non-Conformity; Gender Non-Conforming*

Bind; Binding; Binder (verb; present participle; noun)
Some transmasculine, non-binary, or agender people flatten their chests by binding, in order to appear more normatively masculine and reduce dysphoria. Binding can be done with tape or bandages, but these methods are dangerous as they may restrict breathing or cause damage to the ribs. Commercially made binders are typically vest-like garments, made of nylon and spandex. People who bind may do so intermittently, or on certain occasions and not on others.

Note: 'bind', as used by the transgender community, is an intransitive verb. Do not use the older expression 'X binds her breasts': people who are dysphoric about their chests are likely also to be dysphoric about the use of gendered terms such as 'breasts'. Instead, use 'chest' as a gender-neutral alternative if you need to reference body parts. Similarly, a person who

APPENDIX   289

binds may use pronouns other than 'she/her' – make sure you know what *Pronouns* a person uses. If referring to a literary character or historical figure who cannot be asked, the key is to be sensitive to the individual's intention, and the identity they are displaying. If in doubt, use singular *'They/Them'* pronouns.
See also: Gender Dysphoria; Gender Dysphoric, Pack; Packing; Packer, Pad; Padding, Pass; Passing, Tuck; Tucking

Butch (noun; adjective)
Butch is a gender non-conforming presentation and/or gender identity, most frequently associated with masculine *AFAB* individuals, and often with lesbian identity. Precise definitions of butchness are temporally and culturally contingent, but butch identity is typically contrasted to *Femme* identity. For *AMAB* individuals, butchness is a particular type of masculinity, often associated with gay men. Prevailing stereotypes within dominant cis-heterosexual culture associate butch women with masculine behaviour, activities, appearance, and so on, and assume the pairing of a butch lesbian with a femme partner.

See: Bergman, *Butch is a Noun*; Halberstam, *Female Masculinity*. For a case study of butch and femme identities in the queer ballroom scene in Detroit (Michigan, USA), see: Marlon M. Bailey, *Butch Queens*, pp. 29-76.
See also: AFAB, AMAB, Femme, Gender Non-Conformity; Gender Non-Conforming

CAFAB (adjective)
Coercively Assigned Female At Birth. The term 'CAFAB' is used as an alternative to *AFAB* to emphasize the individual's lack of agency in their own sexing/gendering, which was externally imposed by society. CAFAB is particularly used by intersex individuals to reflect the violence of surgical interventions and/or enforced hormone treatments which are often used to 'normalize' intersex bodies by attempting to fit them into a binary sex category.
See also: AFAB, AMAB, Assigned Sex; Assigned Gender, CAMAB, Intersex

CAMAB (adjective)
Coercively Assigned Male At Birth. The term 'CAMAB' is used as an alternative to *AMAB* to emphasize the individual's lack of agency in their own sexing/gendering, which was externally imposed by society. CAFAB is particularly used by intersex individuals to reflect the violence of surgical interventions and/or enforced hormone treatments which are often used

to 'normalize' intersex bodies by attempting to fit them into a binary sex category.
See also: *AFAB, AMAB, Assigned Sex; Assigned Gender, CAFAB, Intersex*

Cis(gender) (adjective)
A cisgender, or simply cis (note: not CIS – it is not an acronym) individual is someone whose identified gender matches their assigned gender. It is a description of a state, rather than a process. For this reason, avoid the term 'cisgendered'. 'Cisgender', or 'cis', is the neutral antonym of 'transgender' or 'trans'. The Latin prefixes 'trans' and 'cis' mean, respectively: 'across, over' (i.e. crossing from one gender (the gender assigned at birth) to another (the identified gender)); and 'on this side of' (i.e. not crossing over, but remaining in the gender assigned at birth).

Terms such as 'biological', 'natal', 'natural-born', or 'real' are offensive, suggesting that trans people are deceitful, disguised, constructed, and/or 'really' the gender/sex they were assigned at birth. On this, see: *Trap*. Use 'cis' or 'cisgender' instead of these problematic descriptors.

'*Cissexism*' (adjective: 'cissexist') is a form of essentialist bigotry which assumes all individuals are defined by their assigned sex/gender. '*Cisgenderism*' (adjective: 'cisgenderist') is sometimes used as a synonym for 'cissexism', though can also carry a nuanced meaning, relating to gender as opposed to sex.
See also: *Cis-het(erosexual), Trans(gender)*

Cisgenderism; Cisgenderist (noun; adjective)
See: *Cis(gender)*

Cis-het(erosexual) (adjective)
'Cis-het' refers to individuals who are both cisgender and heterosexual. Cis-het individuals do not face oppression on either of the axes which, combined, constitute the category of 'queer'. In this way, cis-het individuals occupy a place of cultural normativity. Obviously a cisgender, heterosexual individual may nevertheless face oppression on other axes: sexism, racism, ableism, classism, and so on.
See also: *Cis(gender), Trans(gender)*

Cisnormativity; Cisnormative (noun; adjective)
Cisnormativity is the cultural discourse which presents and promotes the 'congruence' of sex and gender as the primary and normative state of existence. In this context, cis is the default, and any non-cis identity is aberrant and unnatural. The discourse of cisnormativity is supported and maintained

by transphobia and cissexism. Cisnormativity is reinforced by the use of binaristic and cisnormative language which assumes that trans, genderqueer, and intersex individuals do not exist. This is the case, for example, in supposedly neutral assertions such as 'women have periods' or 'men should attend prostate cancer screenings', which reinforce biological essentialism and ignore the diversity of human experience. Some trans women have a prostate, whereas some cis men do not. Similarly, some cis women do not have periods, whereas some trans men do. Thus, in order to preserve the cultural regime of cisnormativity, cisnormative assumptions work to disguise the fact that neither prostates nor periods, nor the lack thereof, are indicative of gender.
See also: Binary; Cis(gender)

Cissexism; Cissexist (noun; adjective)
See: Cis(gender)

Closet (In The); Closeted (noun; adjective and past participle)
As with non-straight sexualities, a non-cis individual who has not revealed this fact, and who presents as their assigned gender, is referred to as being 'closeted' or 'in the closet'. A non-cis individual who presents as their identified gender, but who does not disclose their trans-ness, may describe themself, and be described within their community, as being *'Stealth'*.
See also: Out; Outing, Pass; Passing, Transition; Transitioning, Trap

Come Out; Coming Out (verb; present participle)
See: Out; Outing

Cross-Dress; Cross-Dressing; Cross-Dresser (verb; present participle; noun)
The term 'cross-dressing' carries a complex history. Whilst it has long been used derogatorily and inaccurately to refer to trans individuals, it also has a precise, useful meaning when deployed in other contexts.

Using the term 'cross-dressing' (or 'cross-dresser', etc.) in relation to trans individuals demonstrates a fundamental misunderstanding of trans identity. This misunderstanding is founded upon the perception that trans individuals wear clothing associated with the 'opposite' *Assigned Sex/Gender*, when they are in fact wearing clothing associated with their *Identified Gender*. Describing a transgender individual as a cross-dresser reduces their identity to an 'incorrect' application of cultural norms regarding clothing, and implies that they are 'really' their assigned sex/gender, but masquerading as the 'opposite' sex/gender.

However, individuals who identify as cisgender may engage in cross-dressing (wearing clothes of another gender) for a variety of reasons ranging from personal preference, performance, sexual role-play, or participation in community events. Cross-dressing may be seen to uphold the *Binary*, or to fracture it. This partly depends upon context, as well as the intention of the cross-dresser. A cis man who wears a dress for a Halloween fancy-dress party may intend to parody femininity, whereas a cis man who wears a dress to express his gender identity is more readily visible as challenging binary gender norms.

Drag is a particular iteration of cross-dressing, though the two terms are not interchangeable.

See also: *Assigned Sex; Assigned Gender, Cis(gender), Drag, Trans(gender)*

Dead Name; Dead-Naming; Dead Name (verb; present participle; noun)
See: *Names*

DFAB (adjective)
Designated Female at Birth.
See: *AFAB*

DMAB (adjective)
Designated Male at Birth.
See: *AMAB*

Drag (noun and adjective)
Drag is a culturally specific form of cross-dressing for purposes of entertainment. Individuals whose drag persona is female are referred to as drag queens, whereas individuals whose drag persona is male are referred to as drag kings. Drag performers may use a different name and pronouns when in character. Drag performers may be cis or trans.

For more on this, see in particular: Rupp, Taylor, and Shapiro, 'Drag Queens and Drag Kings'; Taylor and Rupp, 'Chicks with Dicks, Men in Dresses'.
See also: *Cross-Dress; Cross-Dressing; Cross-Dresser*

Dysphoria; Dysphoric (noun; adjective)
See: *Gender Dysphoria; Gender Dysphoric*

Essentialism; Essentializing; Essentialist (noun; present participle; adjective)
Essentialism is the socio-cultural, often pseudo-scientific, framework which claims that certain 'essential', typically biological, characteristics – such as genital configuration at birth; hormone profile; chromosomal configuration – reflect a definitive and unalterable truth. In this essentialist context,

'biological' *Sex* 'is' *Gender*, full stop. Essentialist beliefs lead people to dismiss or reject trans and genderqueer people's lived experience, as well as their accounts of their own identity, as impossible, deluded or the result of mental illness. *Intersex* individuals are relegated to the status of 'rare' instances of aberrance, of deviance from the binaristic, essentialist 'norm'. In this worldview, intersex individuals are 'really' and 'essentially' men or women. Thus, for essentialist thinkers, the sex/gender binary (i.e. gender's origin in sex, and the deterministic relation between the two) remains primordial and all-encompassing.

Other types of essentialism include those relating to hierarchical gender roles (men and women are innately different, and naturally suited to different work, activities, levels of responsibility, etc) and to race (racialization is not a socio-cultural phenomenon, but reflects real and unalterable biological characteristics; racial groups have specific and unalterable natures, resulting in differing levels of aggression, intelligence, libido, etc.).

See also: **Binary, Cisnormativity; Cisnormative, Gender, Intersex, Sex**

Eunuch (noun)
A historical term for an *AMAB* individual who has undergone surgical and social transitions (often against their will) from one form of masculinity to another. The surgery involved took on many forms but traditionally involved the removal of the testes, although not necessarily the penis. These surgeries and transitions were often enacted on slaves and/or criminals but were not always levied against lower-class individuals or as a form of punishment. Cases of self-castration and becoming-eunuch are reported. Eunuchs tended to have distinct social/religious roles and legal status in societies, marking them as a non-binary gender in addition to men and women but existing within the spectrum of masculinity.

For relevant analyses, see: Szabo, 'Non-Standard Masculinity'; Tougher, 'Holy Eunuchs!'.

See also: **AMAB, Transition; Transitioning**

Ey/Em (pronouns)
An example of gender neutral or non-binary pronouns, to replace 'he/him' and 'she/her'. This pronoun set, formed by removing the 'th' from 'they', 'them', and so on, seems to have been invented several times, with slight variations, by a number of different individuals. This pronoun set is often referred to as Spivak pronouns, after mathematician Michael Spivak, who used these pronouns in an AMS-TeX manual, *The Joy of TeX*, in 1983. The subject pronoun 'ey' is sometimes seen as 'e', and all Spivak pronouns may be capitalized.

See also: **Pronouns**

Femme (adjective and noun)

Femme is often seen as a counterpart to, or the opposite of, **Butch**. Femme *AFAB* individuals are generally considered to be gender-conforming, which erases the fact that being femme is as much a specific presentation and/or gender identity as being butch is. Femme identity is significantly associated with lesbian and bisexual identity. For *AMAB* individuals, being femme is a gender non-conforming presentation and/or gender identity, and is often associated with being gay. Precise definitions of femme-ness are temporally and culturally contingent. The prevailing stereotype of the femme woman within dominant cis-heterosexual culture is the 'lipstick lesbian'.

On this, see: Burke, *Visible*; Harris and Crocker, *Femme*. For a case study of butch and femme identities in the queer ballroom scene in Detroit (Michigan, USA), see: Marlon M. Bailey, *Butch Queens*, pp. 29-76.

See also: *AFAB, AMAB, Butch, Gender Non-Conformity; Gender Non-Conforming*

FTM (adjective and noun)

The acronym 'FTM' stands for 'Female to Male'. The term is used by many trans men to describe themselves affirmatively. Other trans men find 'FTM' problematic for a number of reasons, chiefly because the term foregrounds transition over identity, which many feel is inaccurate both practically and conceptually.

The practical issue is the following: a trans man may transition, then live for decades in his identified gender. Fifty years after the process of transitioning is over, the term 'FTM' may seem to define him by a stage in his life which is long past and of little relative importance. For many trans men, **Transition** is a finite process, a ring-fenced, relatively brief period compared to the rest of an individual's life, marking a 'before' and an 'after'. In contrast, many other individuals (both trans and cis) feel that their identity is more accurately represented by a process of constant becoming. As a rule, transition is a personal process which is both irrelevant and inaccessible to external parties. Thus, identifications made on the basis of an individual's transition status are based on invasive assumptions and should be avoided.

The conceptual issue is that the term 'FTM' presents both female and male gender identities as valid and important parts of the trans man's identity. Yet many trans people experience recognizing and coming to understand their identified gender as a process of realizing that they have always been this gender, although they may not have been able to understand their gender in this way previously due to social conditioning and the effects of *Essentialist* assumptions in the cultural climate. Thus, *Transition* is experienced as a process of understanding and expressing their innate gender. By transitioning, they are moving to live and present in ways which are (socially coded as, or innately felt to be) congruent with that identity, rather than (as the term 'FTM' may be considered to suggest) undertaking a process which *produces* or *enacts* a new gender.

The foregrounding of 'F' in 'FTM', for some, suggests that trans men are 'really' or 'naturally' women, and that their male identity is either an 'unnatural' replacement for their innate femaleness or an accretion layered on top of it. This plays into dangerous stereotypes of trans identities as 'disguises' intended to *Trap* and deceive others. This perspective is not shared by all, however. Some consider the positioning of 'F' in 'FTM' to signify the way in which an individual has left the 'F' behind, and thus constitutes the full recognition of their gender identity, while others consider that they were never 'F' in the first place, but were incorrectly assigned this identity due to essentialist socio-cultural assumptions. These individuals may prefer the acronym 'MTM' ('Male to Male'), which acknowledges their trans identity and their transition, whilst affirming the fact that they were always men.

Whilst plenty of trans men still use the term 'FTM', it is a complicated and contested designation. For this reason, do not use unless you know that this is an individual's preferred term.
See also: *Essentialism; Essentializing; Essentialist, FTN/FT*, MTF, MTN/MT*, TERF, Transition; Transitioning, Transphobia; Transphobic, Trap*

FTN/FT* (adjective and noun)
The acronyms 'FTN' and 'FT*' signify 'Female to *Neutrois*' and 'Female to [other gender]'. 'FTX' is another variant of these acronyms, for 'Female to X-gender', with 'X-gender' referring, broadly speaking, to agender or *Non-Binary* identities. The terms follow the same logic as *'FTM'*, whilst acknowledging that not every *AFAB* person who transitions is a binary trans man.
See also: *AFAB, Essentialism; Essentializing; Essentialist, FTM, MTF, MTN/MT*, Neutrois, TERF, Transition; Transitioning. Transphobia; Transphobic, Trap*

Gender (noun and adjective)
Gender is deeply important to many people's sense of their own identity, yet incredibly difficult to define. The most fundamental aspect of gender is identification: who one feels and understands oneself to be. This identification may be affected or influenced by cultural gender norms. The

dominant paradigm of gender connects binary genders to the binary sexes from which they supposedly derive. This amounts to a cultural system in which male or female gender is ascribed to an individual on the basis of the appearance of their body at birth. The assumption is that everyone has a fixed gender, which can be discerned through observation of their body. However, this assumption is faulty, or at best ineluctably culturally and temporally contingent. Throughout history, individuals have experienced and demonstrated non-normative gender, including trans (and thus non-binary), genderqueer, and gender non-conforming identities.

Although assigned gender is a cultural imposition, individuals have choices (circumscribed to a greater or lesser degree depending upon cultural and temporal context) as to how they inhabit their gender, including presentation and expression, and the social roles undertaken.

'Gender' is often used as an umbrella term covering a lot of ground, incorporating meanings such as 'gender identity' and 'socialized gender roles', amongst other things. This rhetorical manoeuvre suggests that all these gendered experiences can be assumed to be monolithic, that is, there is no room for variety or divergence within an individual's lived gender (which is already itself assumed to correlate to assigned gender).

As the multitude of lived experiences demonstrates, gender is a vast and variable array of possible identifications, which is not necessarily static. The phrase 'opposite gender' should be avoided, since it implies that gender is binary and oppositional: that is, the genders are two poles, defined by their separateness from each other. Thus, one is male *because one is not female*, and vice versa.

For more in-depth exploration of gender, see in particular: Bornstein, *Gender Workbook*; Butler, *Gender Trouble*; 'Imitation and Gender Insubordination'. *See also: **Assigned Sex; Assigned Gender, Identified Gender, Sex***

Gender-Affirming Surgery; Gender Confirmation Surgery (noun)
*See: **Transition; Transitioning***

Gender-Creative (adjective)
'Gender-creative' is a term popularized by Diane Ehrensaft to describe children who 'live outside gender boxes'. While some adult genderqueer and gender non-conforming individuals find the description affirming, others consider the term condescending. Use with caution.

On this, see: Ehrensaft, *Gender Creative Child*.
*See also: **Gender-Expansive, Gender Non-Conformity; Gender Non-Conforming, Genderfluid; Gender Fluidity, Genderqueer***

Gender-Critical (adjective)
'Gender-critical' is a term adopted by *TERFs* to indicate their distaste for current levels of acceptance of trans, genderqueer, and gender non-conforming identities. TERFs' criticism of gender is essentially that it does not exist as such; their argument is that sex is a real, biological attribute, with genuine real-world consequences, while gender is merely a social effect. Thus, what they consider excessive emphasis on gender undermines efforts to fight for equality for the sexes. Gender-critical thought is therefore biologically *Essentialist*.

According to a gender-critical viewpoint, trans men are 'copping out' on their lived experience of women's inequality, whereas trans women are asserting their male privilege to grotesquely usurp even the very state of oppression into which the patriarchy forces women. In this scenario, trans men are deluded by society's misogyny, which they have internalized, with the result that they turn this hatred of women against themselves and attempt to erase their 'intrinsic' female identity. At the same time, trans women are cast as dangerous and predatory figures, invading women's safe spaces and appropriating support meant for 'real' women. This plays into the insidious narrative of trans-ness as a deceitful disguise or *Trap*, leading to real-world violence against the trans community, especially trans women (*Transmisogyny*), and even more so trans women of colour (*Transmisogynoir*).
See also: **Essentialism; Essentializing; Essentialist, Transphobia; Transphobic, Transmisogyny, Transmisogynoir, Trap**

Gender Dysphoria; Gender Dysphoric (noun; adjective)
There are two broad categories of gender dysphoria: physical and social dysphoria. Not every trans person experiences dysphoria in the same way or to the same degree, or at all.

Physical dysphoria may be described as visceral feelings of discomfort arising from an individual's lack of identification with physical features which are not typically recognized as 'matching' their identified gender. For example: a trans man may feel dysphoric about the appearance and/or feeling of his chest, the way it looks, makes his clothes fit, and the way it influences people's assumptions about him. In addition, the appearance and/or feeling of his chest may influence his own assessment of his own identity, in a form of *Internalized Transphobia*.

Social dysphoria may be described as visceral feelings of discomfort arising not from the physical body, but from the way in which others perceive and react to that body, as well as from body language and behaviours deemed to 'belong' to a particular gender. For example, a non-binary person may not experience dysphoria around their physical body, but find it extremely distressing to be referred to with gendered terms or pronouns.

'Gender euphoria' is a term which originates in trans communities as a play on 'gender dysphoria'. It is used to draw attention to the way in which discussion of trans identities and existences, as well as conversations surrounding transition, tend to focus on trans people's discomfort in their assigned gender, without ever mentioning the sometimes exhilarating feeling of discovering and embodying the gender identity and presentation which is fitting, truthful, and right.

See also: *Bind; Binding; Binder, Internalized Transphobia, Pack; Packing; Packer, Pass; Passing, Pronouns*

Gender-Expansive (adjective)
'Gender-expansive' is a term sometimes used of and by genderqueer and/or gender non-conforming people, particularly children. The term works to counteract rigid views of the gender binary, and to combat *Cisnormativity*. Some consider the term condescending and/or infantilizing. The designation is sometimes used to skirt the issue of trans, genderqueer, and gender non-conforming identity, by offering a euphemistic, non-specific, and therefore more 'palatable' alternative to direct discussion of trans, genderqueer and gender non-conforming experiences. Avoid this usage. Use with caution if referring to individuals.

See also: *Binary, Cisnormativity; Cisnormative, Gender-Creative, Gender Non-Conformity; Gender Non-Conforming, Genderfluid; Gender Fluidity, Genderqueer*

Genderfluid (or Gender-Fluid); Gender Fluidity (adjective; noun)
Some individuals experience their identified gender as a stable form, whereas for others their gender identity varies. Gender fluidity is not the same as becoming aware that one's identified gender is at odds with one's assigned gender, but rather refers to an identified gender which inherently fluctuates. Genderfluid individuals are included under the trans umbrella. Some genderfluid individuals describe themselves as non-binary, whereas others do not feel the need for another identifier other than genderfluid. Some individuals alter their gender expression or presentation, or use different pronouns, depending on their current experience of their gender. Genderfluid individuals may use any pronouns, and may present in feminine, masculine, or androgynous ways. Genderfluid (no hyphen) and gender-fluid (hyphen) are used interchangeably.

APPENDIX

See also: **Agender, Non-Binary, Transition; Transitioning, Transfeminine, Transmasculine**

Gender Non-Conformity; Gender Non-Conforming (noun and adjective)
Gender non-conforming individuals are individuals whose gender expression does not match what is culturally normative for their assigned (and/or identified) gender. Gender non-conforming individuals may not reject their assigned gender, but reject the conventional rules governing gendered behaviour, activities, appearance, and so on. Other gender non-conforming individuals may identify as non-cis and/or trans. Gender non-conformity may reflect an individual's rejection of the system of assigned binary gender. Gender non-conforming individuals are often included alongside trans individuals in discussion and activism, in phrases such as 'trans and gender non-conforming'. This is due to the fact that, although gender non-conforming individuals may not be trans, they are likely to face similar oppressions since both groups are perceived as flouting gender norms. 'Gender non-conforming' may be abbreviated to 'GNC'.
See also: **Gender, Gender-Creative, Gender-Expansive, Genderfluid; Gender Fluidity, Genderqueer, Non-Binary, Non-Normative Gender**

Genderqueer (adjective)
Genderqueer individuals experience their assigned gender as inadequate to encompass their gender identity. Genderqueer individuals may identify as trans, though this is not always the case. Genderqueer individuals may additionally identify as **Non-Binary, Genderfluid, Gender Non-Conforming, Transfeminine** or **Transmasculine**. Genderqueer individuals may present in feminine, masculine, or androgynous ways, and may use feminine, masculine, or gender-neutral pronouns. As always, defer to individuals' preference.

For further reading, see in particular: Nestle, Howell, and Wilchins, *Genderqueer*.
See also: **Assigned Sex; Assigned Gender, Genderfluid; Gender Fluidity, Gender Non-Conformity; Gender Non-Conforming, Non-Binary, Non-Normative Gender, Transfeminine, Transmasculine**

He-She (noun and pronoun)
Avoid, for example, 'Ashley is a he-she'; 'he-she reads novels'. This is an offensive, derogatory term. It dismissively combines binary categories of gender whilst underscoring the rigidity of the binary itself, disallowing potential

subject positions beyond 'he' or 'she'. Do not use, unless an individual has explicitly told you that this is the pronoun they use.
See also: **Pronouns**

He/She (noun and pronoun)
Avoid in noun form, as in *He-She*. This is an offensive, derogatory term. Use with caution, if at all, as pronoun. 'He/she' is commonly used to denote, superficially at least, a generalized or inclusive reference – for example, if an author does not wish to stipulate 'he' or 'she'. However, when 'he/she' is used to refer to an individual, it may function to erase non-binary identities by constructing them as a failure of the binary, nevertheless comprehensible only on the binary's terms. In addition, this usage may denote the author's dismissive unwillingness to consider a more accurate and respectful pronoun set beyond the binary, such as *'They/Them' (singular)*.
See also: **He-She, Pronouns, They/Them** (*singular*)

Hermaphrodite (noun)
This is an antiquated term for individuals who would now be referred to as intersex. It is offensive in modern usage; do not use unless an individual explicitly tells you that this is the correct way to refer to them. For the most part, the intersex community has rejected the term as both pathologizing (because of its relation to medical abuse and authority) and socially stigmatizing. However, some reclaim the term.

The word 'hermaphrodite' references the Greek myth of Hermaphroditus. In a premodern context, the term could signify individuals other than those who would now be considered intersex, including individuals we would now describe as queer, trans, non-binary, or otherwise gender or sexually non-conforming. In addition, 'hermaphrodite' was used to refer to mythical beings who were half men and half women. Given this context, the term 'hermaphrodite' could also convey mythological connotations. As such, trans and intersex bodies become 'unnatural', 'unreal', or merely metaphorical.

When discussing premodern 'hermaphrodites', it is important to distinguish between intersex individuals and mythological beings. Avoid 'hermaphrodite' when it has othering implications. It is important to be clear when using the term that it is not a modern usage: use **Intersex** when referring in general to individuals whose biological characteristics do not fit neatly within binary cultural definitions of 'male' and 'female'. When using the term 'hermaphrodite', indicate that this is the term which would have been current in the premodern era, and clarify its meaning in context.
See also: **Binary, Intersex, Sex**

Hijra (noun and adjective)
A trans-feminine, non-binary, or intersex gender identity in South Asia, historically occupying specific socio-religious function(s) in Hindu and Islamic cultures. The word 'hijra' is used in Hindustani and Bengali, whereas in Urdu 'hijra' is considered derogatory, and the respectful term 'khwaja sara' is used instead. Hijras are an officially recognized third gender in some countries in the Indian subcontinent, such as Bangladesh, and are recognized within a broader grouping of third-gender identities (encompassing intersex, trans, and hijra individuals) elsewhere, such as in Pakistan, and India. Hijras often live in 'structured communities' (Pamment, 'Performing Piety', p. 297), in which older members of the community mentor younger members. The imposition of normatively binaristic Western mores of sex and gender by British colonizers increased the stigmatization faced by the hijra community. Today, hijras routinely face poverty and experience significant social marginalization.

See: Hinchy, *Governing Gender*; Moorti, 'Queer Romance'; Pamment, 'Performing Piety'; Reddy, *With Respect to Sex*.
See also: **White Supremacy**

Identify (As); Identifying (As) (verb; present participle)
See: **Identified Gender**

Identified Gender (noun)
Everyone has both an assigned gender and an identified gender. An individual's identified gender is who they understand themself to be; it is their identity. Thus, both trans women and cis women *identify as* women because they *are* women.

Be precise in your usage of the verb forms '*Identify (As); Identifying (As)*' to avoid delegitimizing trans people's identities. Do not, for example, state: '[Name] identifies as a woman', when you wouldn't use that formulation to refer to a cis woman. Instead, say: '[Name] is a woman'. Or, if it is relevant in the context – which is the case less often than many people assume – state: '[Name] is a trans woman'. 'Identify as' is relevant when distinguishing between assigned and identified gender; otherwise just use 'is'. The construction '[Name] identifies *themself* as' is unnecessary and incorrect; just use '[Name] identifies as'.
See also: **Assigned Sex; Assigned Gender, Pass; Passing, Read (Someone) As; Reading (Someone) As**

Internalized Transphobia (noun)
Internalized transphobia is transphobia absorbed by a trans person through exposure to cultural norms, and subsequently directed against themself, as well as other trans people, either consciously or unconsciously.
See also: **Transphobia; Transphobic**

Intersex (adjective)
The correct modern word for a person whose biological characteristics do not fit neatly within cultural **Binary** definitions of 'male' and 'female'. Intersex individuals are (almost) always assigned a binary gender at birth, and in most of the world are still subjected to non-consensual surgical or hormonal treatment. These medical interventions aim to align intersex bodies more closely with normative binary gender/sex definitions. This type of intervention is viewed by most intersex people as a violent and unnecessary medicalized imposition of cultural norms. Some intersex individuals identify as trans, some as cis, and some as neither.
See: Chase, 'Hermaphrodites with Attitude'
See also: **AFAB, AMAB, Assigned Sex; Assigned Gender, CAFAB, CAMAB, Cis(gender), Hermaphrodite, Sex, Trans(gender)**

It (noun and pronoun)
Some people use 'it' as their pronoun. Avoid unless an individual has specifically told you that it is correctly referred to as 'it'. The derogatory use of 'it' as a pronoun is very offensive. It can function as an exceptionally dismissive way of referring to trans and genderqueer people, focusing on and stigmatizing their non-conformity to cisgender/heterosexual constructs of gender.
See also: **Preferred Pronouns, Pronouns**

Medical Transition
See: **Transition; Transitioning**

Misgender; Misgendering (verb; present participle)
'Misgendering' is the act of using the wrong pronouns and/or gendered nouns to refer to an individual. Both trans and cis people may be misgendered, although the experience is likely to be more distressing to a transgender person. For a trans person, the gender incorrectly ascribed is likely to be the gender they were assigned at birth, and thus echoes the message which society as a whole has attempted to enforce, that the individual is 'really' the gender that they were assigned at birth, and that being trans is

'wrong', 'unnatural', or is not 'real'. As such, misgendering can be a form of micro-aggression.

Misgendering may be deliberate or accidental. Accidental misgendering may happen for a variety of reasons: it may be a mistake which occurs when an individual sees another individual and incorrectly identifies their gender based on socially accepted cues. This can happen to both cis and trans people. It may be a simple slip of the tongue – again, this happens to both cis and trans people. Or it may be an unthinking, habitual use of gendered language which references a trans person's assigned gender. This can be particularly hurtful, since it can feel like a rejection of the trans individual's expressed and identified gender. Misgendering is often a trigger for dysphoria. Deliberate misgendering is an act of violence.

In the context of literature or history, pay particular attention to context, and what is visible of the character's intentions and identification. If the character's identity is unclear, it can be useful to refer to them using singular *They/Them* pronouns, which are typically viewed as a respectful default. Be clear and precise about the choices you are making, and articulate these to the reader.

See also: **Dead Name; Dead-Naming; Dead Name, Gender Dysphoria; Gender Dysphoric, Pronouns, Transphobia; Transphobic, 'They/Them'** (*singular*)

MTF (*adjective and noun*)

The acronym 'MTF' stands for 'Male to Female'. The term is used by many trans women to describe themselves affirmatively. Other trans women find 'MTF' problematic for a number of reasons, chiefly because the term foregrounds transition over identity, which many feel is inaccurate both practically and conceptually.

The practical issue is the following: a trans woman may transition, then live for decades in her identified gender. Fifty years after the process of transitioning is over, the term 'MTF' may seem to define her by a stage in her life which is long past and of little relative importance. For many trans women, *Transition* is a finite process, a ring-fenced, relatively brief period compared to the rest of an individual's life, marking a 'before' and an 'after'. In contrast, many other individuals (both trans and cis) feel that their identity is more accurately represented by a process of constant becoming. As a rule, transition is a personal process which is both irrelevant and inaccessible to external parties. Thus, identifications made on the basis of an individual's transition status are based on invasive assumptions and should be avoided.

The conceptual issue is that the term 'MTF' presents both male and female gender identities as valid and important parts of the trans woman's identity. Yet many trans people experience recognizing and coming to understand their identified gender as a process of realizing that they have always been this gender, although they may not have been able to understand their gender in this way previously due to social conditioning and the effects of *Essentialist* assumptions in the cultural climate. Thus, *Transition* is experienced as a process of understanding and expressing their innate gender. By transitioning, they are moving to live and present in ways which are (socially coded as, or innately felt to be) congruent with that identity, rather than (as the term 'MTF' may be considered to suggest) undertaking a process which *produces* or *enacts* a new gender.

The foregrounding of 'M' in 'MTF', for some, suggests that trans women are 'really' or 'naturally' men, and that their female identity is either an 'unnatural' replacement for their innate maleness or an accretion layered on top of it. This plays into pernicious stereotypes of trans (and particularly *Transfeminine*) identities as 'disguises' intended to *Trap* and deceive others. This is a dangerous and pervasive cultural assumption, which leads to real and often deadly violence against trans women, especially trans women of colour (see *Transmisogyny, Transmisogynoir*).

By contrast, some consider the positioning of 'M' in 'MTF' to signify the way in which an individual has left the 'M' behind, and thus constitutes full recognition of their gender identity, while others consider that they were never 'M' in the first place, but were incorrectly assigned this identity due to essentialist socio-cultural assumptions. These individuals may prefer the acronym 'FTF' ('Female to Female'), which acknowledges their trans identity and their transition, whilst affirming the fact that they were always women.

Whilst plenty of trans women still use the term 'MTF', it is a complicated and contested designation. For this reason, do not use unless you know that this is an individual's preferred term.

See also: *Essentialism; Essentializing; Essentialist, FTM, FTN/FT*, MTN/ MT*, TERF, Transfemininity; Transfeminine, Transition; Transitioning, Transmisogyny, Transmisogynoir, Transphobia; Transphobic, Trap*

MTN/MT (adjectives, nouns)*

The acronyms 'MTN' and 'MT*' signify 'Male to *Neutrois*' and 'Male to [other gender]'. 'MTX' is another variant of these acronyms, for 'Male to X-gender', with 'X-gender' referring, broadly speaking, to agender or non-binary identities. The terms follow the same logic as *MTF,* whilst acknowledging that not every *AMAB* person who transitions is a binary trans woman.

See also: AMAB, Essentialism; Essentializing; Essentialist, FTM, FTN/FT*, MTF, Neutrois, TERF, Transition; Transitioning. Transphobia; Transphobic, Trap

Names

When an individual permanently transitions to presenting as their identified gender, always use their post-transition name to refer to them, adding clarifications if necessary. For example, a text may introduce a character by stating: 'Marie entranced the court with her fine gown.' Later in the text, the character transitions and assumes a different name, David. Correct usage would thus be: 'David [i.e. post-transition name] is introduced to the reader before his [i.e. post-transition pronoun] transition, wearing a beautiful dress'. Avoid using gendered nouns which do not match an individual's identified gender, even when referring to the pre-transition phase (unless this is the preference of the individual in question): 'David was married to Peter', not 'David was Peter's wife'.

When an individual's transition is not presented as definitive or permanent, or if the pre- and post-transition identities are presented as equally valid, use the name and pronouns which reflect the period under discussion. In order to make these determinations in a sensitive manner, pay close attention to context, and to what is visible of the character's intentions and identification. Be clear and precise about the choices you are making, and articulate these to the reader.

A name which a trans person no longer uses – usually the name they were given at birth – is often referred to as their **'Dead Name'**. 'Dead-naming', or calling someone by their dead name, is taboo in the transgender community. Deliberate dead-naming is a violent act of interpellation, similar to the deliberate use of the wrong pronouns (see **Misgender; Misgendering**). When citing an author who has transitioned, always refer to them by their new name, even when discussing works published before they transitioned. Where it is necessary to include the dead name to enable readers to find a previous publication (e.g. if John Smith previously published as Mary Smith), use formulations such as: 'John Smith's book *Medieval Mermen* (published as M. Smith)'. It is respectful to use initials in this way to avoid using forenames whose gender does not match the author's identified gender. There is no standard, or one-size-fits-all rule for bibliographies. Nevertheless, a respectful citation would be something like the following: 'Smith, John [publishing as Smith, M], *Medieval Mermen* (Oxford: Oxford University, 2014).'

On practices for citing trans scholars, see: Coman, 'Trans Citation Practices'; Thieme and Saunders, 'How Do You Wish To Be Cited?'.

See also: **Identified Gender, Misgender; Misgendering, Pronouns**

Neutrois (adjective)
'Neutrois' is a gender identity which may fall within the agender and/or non-binary spectrum. The word 'neutrois' refers to a neutral gender. Neutrois individuals may use any pronoun set, and may present in masculine, feminine, or neutral/*Androgynous* ways.
See also: **Agender, Non-Binary**

Non-Binary (adjective)
Non-binary is an umbrella term for a range of identities which are neither wholly female nor wholly male. Individuals may simply describe their identity as 'non-binary', or may use additional descriptors for their identity. Non-binary people may or may not identify as trans, since they reject their assigned sex/gender in favour of their identified gender.

Some non-binary people use singular *They/Them* pronouns; some use *Ze/Hir* or other pronouns, or no pronouns; some use binary pronouns. This does not make people more or less non-binary. Some non-binary people present in a masculine way, some in a feminine way, and some in an androgynous way. Some non-binary people's presentation varies. This does not make people more or less non-binary.

'Non-binary' is sometimes abbreviated to 'NB' or 'enby'. Some non-binary people refer to themselves as enbies; don't use this term for someone without asking whether they are comfortable with it. Avoid writing, for example, 'David is gender non-binary', since 'gender' is redundant in this phrasing, just as 'gender' is redundant in the phrase 'David is gender male'.

Other non-binary genders include, but are not limited to: *Neutrois*, multigender, polygender, intergender. Note that trans people are not non-binary merely by virtue of being trans. Many non-binary individuals identify as trans, but there are also many *binary* trans people (trans women and trans men). Both binary and non-binary trans people are non-cis. Non-binary refers to a specific set of identities; it is not a synonym for non-cis.
See also: ***Androgynous; Androgyny, Assigned Sex; Assigned Gender, Gender, Genderfluid; Gender Fluidity, Genderqueer, Identified Gender, Pronouns, Trans(gender)***

Non-Normative Gender (noun)
'Non-normative gender' can serve as a useful, neutral umbrella term when describing identities in the past which were not necessarily understood by the individuals in question in the same ways in which *Trans(gender)*, *Genderqueer* and *Gender Non-Conforming* identities are understood today. The term can also be used when linking identities in the past to identities

in the present. This term also reflects the fact that what is considered 'non-normative' will vary according to temporal and cultural location.

'Non-normative gender' can also be used as an adjective in phrases such as 'non-normative gender identity' or 'non-normatively gendered behaviour'.
See also: **Gender, Gender Non-Conformity; Gender Non-Conforming**

Out; Outing (verb and adjective; present participle)
As with non-straight sexualities, a person who is 'out' as trans or genderqueer is someone who has disclosed this identity to (an)other individual(s). It is possible to be out to some people, or in some situations, but not to/in others. '*Coming out*' is often seen as a significant, dramatic, and potentially traumatic singular event; however, coming out is an ongoing process, since once an individual has come out (i.e. decided that particular information about their identity should be made public), they inevitably find themself repeatedly disclosing this information to different people, in different settings and at different times. 'Outing' someone without their permission is a violent act, with potentially lethal ramifications for the outed individual.
See also: **Closet (In The); Closeted, Pass; Passing, Trap**

Pack; Packing; Packer (verb; present participle; noun)
'Packing' refers to the practice of using a 'prosthetic' penis. Packers can be differentiated from dildos or strap-ons (worn dildos), which are 'erect' and carry stronger associations with sex acts, while packers are 'flaccid'. Their primary purpose is to give the look and feeling of a penis, usually under clothing. The term 'packer' encompasses anything (from a commercially manufactured packer, in the shape of a penis and testicles, to a piece of cloth or a balled-up pair of socks) which can be literally packed into underwear or other clothing covering the lower body in order to produce the desired effect. Like a dildo or a strap-on, however, packers may also be considered a part of the wider assemblage that makes up a person's gendered and sexual embodiment. For instance, the term 'packer' may be used to clarify the type or enactment of a trans man's penis; alternatively the term may be omitted, and the 'prosthetic' penis simply affirmed as a penis (i.e. some penises are made of flesh and others of cloth or silicone). People who may pack include *Trans Men* (although not all trans men pack); *Non-Binary* or *Agender* individuals; and cisgender female *Drag* kings. People who pack may do so intermittently, or on certain occasions and not on others.
See also: **Bind; Binding; Binder, Gender Dysphoria; Gender Dysphoric, Pad; Padding, Pass; Passing, Tuck; Tucking**

Pad; Padding (verb; present participle)
'Padding' refers to the practice of using materials and undergarments to create a preferred body silhouette, typically by adding volume and shape to the chest, hips, and buttocks. Padding in this way is used to produces a more stereotypically feminine appearance, which may improve the fit of female clothes, alongside reducing an individual's **Gender Dysphoria**. Padding may also be considered a part of the wider assemblage that makes up a person's gendered and sexual embodiment. People who may pad include trans women (although not all trans women pad); non-binary or agender individuals; and cisgender male **Drag** queens. People who pad may do so intermittently, or on certain occasions and not on others.
See also: **Bind; Binding; Binder, Gender Dysphoria; Gender Dysphoric, Pack; Packing, Pass; Passing, Tuck; Tucking**

Pass; Passing (verb; present participle)
The verb 'passing' refers to being 'read' socially (particularly by strangers) as one's identified gender. The verb may be transitive or intransitive; trans people talk about 'passing' or 'passing as cis'. The phrase 'passing as male/female' should be avoided since it plays into narratives of deception (see **Trap**). The notion of passing is problematic because it reinforces notions of trans people's identified genders a) being secondary to their assigned genders and b) amounting to a kind of disguise. However, the term is still used by transgender individuals because it is a convenient shorthand which also encapsulates the way in which, due to the pervasiveness of oppressive social gender norms, the individual feels pressure to *be readable* as their identified gender, and cannot expect others to make any effort to recognize them as who they are.

The term '**Stealth**' may be used within trans communities to refer to a trans individual who is consistently read as their identified gender, and chooses not to make their trans-ness public. Like 'passing', this term is commonly used among trans individuals as a shorthand to describe the navigation of cisnormative society. However, this is another term which problematically reinscribes narratives of secrecy and disguise, with an individual's trans-ness situated as something to be hidden. Being 'stealth' can be contrasted to being '**Closeted**'. Whereas 'stealth' refers to an individual who is not **Out** as trans but is known as their identified gender, a closeted individual is not out as trans, and is known as their assigned gender. Being stealth and being closeted may both reflect shame, and/or safety concerns if the individual's trans identity were to be disclosed. 'Stealth' refers to a specifically trans form of outness, since a trans woman may be known to

APPENDIX 309

all as ('out' as) her identified gender, while concealing her trans status. This distinction does not have an analogue for queer cis individuals.

Instead of 'passing', use: ***Read (Someone) As***, as in: 'Before he cut his hair, he was often read as a woman'. The use of 'passing' as an adjective is problematic and offensive, since it unwarrantedly locates value in the 'ability' to be read as one's identified gender. 'Passable' (adjective) is an older iteration of 'passing' (adjective). It is now generally perceived as offensive. *See also:* ***Cisnormativity; Cisnormative, Cissexism; Cissexist, Closet (In The); Closeted; Out; Outing, Read (Someone) As; Reading (Someone) As, Transition; Transitioning, Trap***

Preferred Pronouns (noun)
Avoid. The term 'preferred pronouns' is well-meaning, yet problematic. Intended to introduce the idea that people may prefer to be referred to using pronouns other than the ones which socialization may lead others to unthinkingly use for them, the term ultimately entrenches difference between trans and cis people. This implies that cis people simply have 'pronouns', whereas trans people have 'preferred pronouns'. This also suggests that trans individuals have 'normal', 'natural', or 'original' pronouns, which they simply 'prefer' not to use; this implication returns to the trope of trans identity as disguise.

In addition, the phrase 'preferred pronouns' suggests that others have a choice in how they address a trans person. Merely 'preferring' particular pronouns is not a very strong argument for their use, and leaves cis people to make their own judgement as to whether the trans individual's 'preference' trumps the potential discomfort which may be experienced by the cis person. This discomfort stems from the requirement for the cis individual to challenge social gender norms by ignoring 'cues' such as physical morphology or vocal pitch which are socially encoded, and internalized, as gender markers. Discomfort may also be generated by the fact that the cis individual is required to correct reflexive, socialized speech conventions with which they have conformed for their entire life, possibly for the first time.

In short: do not use this phrase. Trans people, like cis people, simply have pronouns.
See: **Pronouns**

Pronouns
Pronouns are vastly overdetermined, freighted with an enormous weight of cultural signification: they are used to label, but also to interpellate, and to reprimand. Thus, for trans people, usage of the correct pronouns is immensely meaningful both in terms of social perception and of self-image.

The most common pronoun sets are: 'she/her', 'he/him', and singular ***They/Them***. Avoid referring to 'male' or 'female', 'masculine' or 'feminine' pronouns, as this implies a link between gender identity and pronoun use which is not necessarily accurate. Other neutral or non-binary pronoun sets include '***Ze/Hir***', '***Ze/Zir***', and '***Ey/Em***', among others. An individual's pronouns are often given in the form 'they [nominative]/them [dative]' as a compromise between brevity and giving the full inflected form which may be necessary for someone to understand how to use less familiar pronoun sets. Some individuals do not use pronouns; in this case, the individual's name is used instead, for instance, 'Ashley picked up Ashley's book'. Note also that some people use more than one pronoun set concurrently and flexibly, for example, 'Ashley's pronouns are "she/her" or "they/them"'.

When making pronoun determinations regarding a literary or historical character, pay particular attention to context, and what is visible of the character's intentions and identification. If the character's identity is unclear, it can be useful to refer to them using singular 'they/them' pronouns. Note, however, that 'they/them' is only a superficially neutral choice, and has some disadvantages. These are discussed in detail in the entry for ***They/Them (singular)*** below.

As a basic rule, avoid the following pronouns: '***It***', '***He-She***', '***She-He***', '***Shim***'. '***She/He***', '***He/She***' and '***S/He***' should be used with caution, if at all, as they can be problematic. These pronouns are offensive when used to refer to an intersex or non-binary person, or to someone of whose gender the speaker/writer is uncertain. This is because these pronouns deny the validity of these individuals' identities by reducing these identities to something meaningless, incomprehensible or not worth comprehending in the terms of the binary system. These identities are thus presented as 'wrong' according to the binary system, yet only imaginable in terms of the narrow confines of that system. However, these constructions may, at times, be used to represent identities which are both male/masculine and female/feminine.

For example, ***She/He*** might be used to refer to a literary character who is miraculously transformed from female to male, but is presented as first female, then male, in temporally distinct phases. Here, the use of ***She/He*** highlights that those identities form part of one overarching identity, and acknowledges the fact that the character never appears to be, or to understand her/himself as, non-binary. Once again, attention to context and the character's identification is key. Articulate the choices you are making to the reader and be explicit about your thinking. If in doubt, use ***They/Them (singular)***, with full awareness of the drawbacks and nuances of this usage.

For declension tables of neutral/non-binary pronouns, see: the 'Gender Pronouns' fact sheet produced by the University of Wisconsin-Milwaukee's Lesbian, Gay, Bisexual, Transgender Resource Center. For more detail on gender-inclusive pronouns, including their history, see: Baron, *What's Your Pronoun*; Zimman, 'Transgender Language Reform'. For an example of nuanced usage of '*She/He*', see: Gutt, 'Transgender Genealogy'. For comparative analyses of gender-neutrality across languages (English, French, German, Swedish), see: Hord, 'Bucking the Linguistic Binary'. On the history of non-binary pronouns, see: Baron, *What's Your Pronoun*, esp. chs. 3-4.
See also: **Misgender; Misgendering**, **Non-Binary**, **They/Them** (*singular*)

Queer (noun and adjective)
Formerly a slur, now reclaimed by many as an umbrella term for anyone who does not conform to social gender norms, including gender expression and identity, and gay/lesbian/bi/pan identity. Increasingly used to denote a disruption of or divergence from structural norms, such as queer temporality, that is, the ways in which normative expectations of biological and reproductive teleology may fail to describe queer lives. Notably used in academia – queer theory, queer studies, etc. – but still offensive to some. May be referred to as 'the q-slur'.

For an overview of queer studies, see: Hall, Jagose, Bebell and Potter, *Queer Studies Reader*. On reclamation of the word 'queer', see: Rocheleau, 'Former Slur'.

Read (Someone) As; Reading (Someone) As (verb; present participle)
To 'read' someone as a particular gender is to gain an impression of their identity based on their presentation. This impression may or may not be accurate. Use 'read (someone) as' instead of '*Pass; Passing*'.
See also: **Pass; Passing**

Sex (noun)
Sex is supposedly a biological determination dependent on bodily morphology and reproductive capacity. **Gender** is supposedly derived from sex: that is, the 'bodily truth' of sex characteristics, primarily genitalia. However, the 'objective' determination of sex is already a culturally contingent, gendered process. 'Physical sex' is less a biological truth than a social construct: where we in our culture have chosen to draw the line between what we see as a male sex and what we see as a female sex is more or less arbitrary. For example, for many years, **Intersex** infants were coercively assigned a binary sex at birth (often through genital surgery and/or hormone treatment)

(see *CAFAB, CAMAB*). Such classifications were dependent on normative calculations derived from genital measurement, and assumptions about whether the infant would grow up to be capable of being the penetrating partner in penis-in-vagina sex. 'Ambiguous' genitalia would be assigned male or female with the aid of a tape measure, with a 'short' phallus classified as female (a clitoris), and a 'long' phallus classified as male (a penis).

Thus it is, in fact, *gender*, and the cultural norms and assumptions which surround it, which necessitates the rigid and insistent categorization of sex. The malleability and fluidity of gender threatens to unsettle the fixity of sex, and to reveal the always already gendered nature of its construction. Thus it becomes necessary, precisely because of the destabilizing effect of the interactions of sex and gender, to deny that these interactions take place, and to attempt to locate sex beyond gender's reach. Gender precedes and establishes sex, only to posit itself as an effect of sex.

For more on this, see in particular: Butler, *Bodies That Matter*; *Gender Trouble*; Kralick, 'Human Bones'; Wade, 'Phall-O-Meter'.
See also: **Assigned Sex; Assigned Gender, Binary, Essentialism, Essentializing, Essentialist, Gender, Intersex, Sex Change**

Sex Change (noun)
Avoid. The term 'sex change' implies a total, and temporally localizable (i.e. it happens at a specific time, has a 'before' and an 'after') switch from one binary sex category to the other. This term (and its cognates, e.g. 'change of sex') is offensive and should never be used. Use instead: '***Transition***' or 'transformation', depending on temporal context(s) and the circumstances of the events.

The notion of the 'sex change' grounds sex/gender in bodily classification and assigns it the status of biological 'truth'. Thus, it rests not only on a straightforward sex binarism, which is easily and unequivocally diagnosable, but also on a simplistic view of anchoring within these categories. Having erased intersex bodies in order to reduce sex to two clear and discrete categories, this logic then locates sex solely in the body (and mostly in the genitals). Sex is thereby posited as an unassailable truth, and located as such within a prediscursive domain, where it cannot be subject to interrogation or questioning. Yet sex itself is produced by and through gender, and processes of gendering.

'Sex changes' do not exist, because the construction of 'sex' on which this concept is predicated is no more than a sociocultural fantasy – and transgender subjects are those for whom this fantasy rings most false. Non-normatively gendered individuals are subjects whose lived experience has viscerally demonstrated to them that the sociocultural fantasy of the natural and automatic congruence of sex/gender/sexuality is in no way natural or inevitable.

NB. Depending on context, constructions such as 'Tiresias changed sex' can be a neutral way to describe the physical transformation of a literary or mythical character. This usage is different to the noun form, 'sex change' (i.e. 'Tiresias's sex change'), which tends to reify (and essentialize) an event rather than describing an effect.

For more analysis on this, see: Butler, *Gender Trouble*
See also: **Gender, Intersex, Sex, Transition; Transitioning, Trans(gender)**

Sexual Reassignment Surgery (noun)
Avoid as antiquated; use 'gender-affirming surgery' instead.
See: **Transition; Transitioning**

S/He (pronoun)
This pronoun foregrounds the feminine in a reference to a generalized subject position. As such, it has been used as a powerful means of feminist action, destabilising the patriarchal hierarchy which positions men as the 'default' subject. Use with caution, if at all, when referring to an individual, for reasons discussed in the entries for *He/She* and *She/He*.
See also: **Pronouns**

She-He (noun and pronoun)
Avoid, for example, 'Ashley is a she-he'; 'she-he reads novels'. This is an offensive, derogatory term. It dismissively combines binary categories of gender whilst underscoring the rigidity of the binary itself, disallowing potential subject positions beyond 'he' or 'she'. Do not use, unless an individual has explicitly told you that this is the pronoun they use.
See also: **Pronouns**

She/He (noun and pronoun)
Avoid in noun form, as in *She-He*. This is an offensive, derogatory term. Use with caution, if at all, as pronoun. 'She/he' or '*S/He*' is commonly used to denote, superficially at least, a generalized or inclusive reference – for example, if an author does not wish to stipulate 'she' or 'he'. However, when 'she/he' or 's/he' is used to refer to an individual, it may function to erase non-binary identities by constructing them as a failure of the binary, nevertheless comprehensible only on the binary's terms. In addition, this

usage may denote the author's dismissive unwillingness to consider a more accurate and respectful pronoun set beyond the binary.
See also: **She-He; Pronouns**

Shemale (noun)
Avoid. This is an offensive, derogatory term.

Shim (noun and pronoun)
Avoid. This is an offensive, derogatory term. Never use as a noun, and do not use as a pronoun, unless an individual has explicitly asked you to.
See also: **Pronouns**

Social Transition (noun)
See: **Transition; Transitioning**

Stealth (adjective)
See: **Pass; Passing**

TERF (noun)
This is an acronym for 'Trans-Exclusionary Radical Feminist'. TERFs are a subset of (typically) second-wave feminists who explicitly reject trans women from their definition of 'woman' due to essentialist claims about genitals and reproductive capacity. They view the supposed 'trans agenda' as entrenching the gender binary, and thus harmful to women. Radical feminists with such views typically reject the label of 'TERF', considering it to be a slur. In recent years, TERF has become widely used, especially on social media, to refer to a transphobic individual, whether or not that individual is a radical feminist to boot. For archetypal frameworks underpinning TERF thinking, see: **Gender-Critical**.
See also: **Essentialism; Essentializing; Essentialist, Gender-Critical, Transmisogyny, Transphobia; Transphobic**

They/Them (singular) (pronoun)
A non-binary or gender-neutral pronoun, also used as a 'generic' pronoun which aims to avoid offensive, irrelevant and/or inaccurate phraseology. It is often used by non-binary individuals, for whom binary 'he/him' or 'she/her' are inaccurate, and the supposedly generic (yet still binaristic) '*S/He*' (or similar) is equally problematic. Other neutral or non-binary pronoun sets include '*Ze/Hir*', '*Ze/Zir*', and '*Ey/Em*', among others. 'They' uses an already well-known pronoun for a purpose which it has already been in use for some

time. In recent years, dictionaries have formally recognized 'they' in the singular as a 'legitimate' pronoun. This shift follows the evolution of 'you' in English from a plural to a singular a few hundred years ago. 'They' singular has been in use in English for hundreds of years, and is routinely used in casual conversations today. In 2019, for instance, the Merriam-Webster Dictionary updated the entry for 'they' to include its usage by non-binary individuals, supporting existing remarks as to the usage of singular 'they' as 'well established in speech and writing, even in literary and formal contexts'.

Note that 'they/them' pronouns tend to be used in two separate ways currently. Firstly, as the correct and specific pronoun set, or one of such sets, for people who have indicated that these are the correct pronouns for them. Secondly, as a 'courtesy' or 'proxy' pronoun set when a person's correct gender pronouns are unknown. Thus, using 'they/them' is not a wholly neutral choice, nor without ramifications. For instance, using 'they/them' as a default pronoun for the categories of 'unknown' and 'other' erases the existence of individuals for whom 'they/them' is the correct pronoun set, the one which accurately reflects their identity. Moreover, referring to an individual with 'they/them' pronouns can function to deny or wilfully reject their gender identity, if deployed to 'overwrite' in bad faith the identified gender of a literary or historical figure, or if an individual has communicated that 'they/them' is not the correct pronoun set. In such cases, the use of 'they/them' to refer to an individual other than oneself may signal a refusal to acknowledge that individual's identified gender. Thus, paradoxically, 'they/them' can underscore that an individual's gender presentation is flawed, or illegible. Nevertheless, using 'they/them' as a default pronoun has significant advantages. It is better than the old-fashioned practice of defaulting to 'he' (for an unknown/unspecified subject), and of default gendering based on external appearance and/or cultural bias. Above all, be clear and precise about the choices you are making and why – including when using 'they/them' – and articulate this to the reader.

For additional guidance on 'they/them' pronouns, see in particular: Bongiovanni and Jimerson, *Guide*. On the historical usage of 'they' (singular), see: Baron, *What's Your Pronoun*, ch. 5. For an example of usage of 'they' (singular) in medieval scholarship, see: Spencer-Hall, *Medieval Saints*, passim, and the explanatory note on p. 59.
See also: **Misgender; Misgendering, Non-Binary, Pronouns**

Tranny (adjective and noun)
Avoid. 'Tranny' is generally considered to be a slur. It is most commonly used in reference to trans women. The term has been reclaimed by some

trans, non-binary, and queer persons as a term of identity or endearment. It may be represented graphically as 'tr*nny', or referred to as 'the t-slur'.

For more information, see: Serano, 'Personal History'.

*See also: **Transmisogyny**, **Transmisogynoir***

Trans(gender) (adjective)

A transgender (or simply trans) individual is someone whose **Identified Gender** does not match their **Assigned Gender**. It is a description of a state, rather than a process. For this reason, avoid the term 'transgender*ed*'. However, it may take some time for a transgender individual to realize and/or understand their identified gender, since the normative cultural imperative to be cisgender is so strong.

The neutral antonym of 'transgender', or 'trans', is 'cisgender' or 'cis'. The Latin prefixes 'trans' and 'cis' mean, respectively: 'across, over' (i.e. crossing from one gender (the gender assigned at birth) to another (the identified gender); and 'on this side of' (i.e. not crossing over, but remaining in the gender assigned at birth).

The sole determinant for being trans is identification. Many trans people **Transition** (medically, socially, and/or otherwise), but others cannot, for a variety of reasons, or choose not to. This does not make the individuals any less trans. Similarly, being transgender is not determined by embodiment.

To refer to the state of being trans, use the noun '**Trans-ness**'. For example: 'An individual in the closet is someone that has not told anyone about their trans-ness.' Avoid **Transgenderism,** for reasons explained in the relevant entry.

'Trans' is sometimes also written as 'trans*'. The **Asterisk (*)** is a wildcard character, a placeholder indicating that these five letters may be followed by any combination of other letters, such as transfeminine, transgender, transmasculine, transsexual, transvestite, and so on. This formulation is intended to broaden the possible meanings of 'trans', rendering the term more inclusive. However, many argue that 'trans' is already inclusive, and that the asterisk is therefore unnecessary. This is a polemical debate in trans studies. For a summary, see: Trans Student Educational Resources, 'Why We Used Trans*'. Note, however, that while trans is now generally preferred to trans* when referring to individuals, trans* is frequently used in trans(*) studies to refer to broader cultural aspects of trans(*) experience, and 'trans(*)' as a discursive construct, for instance, trans(*) thought, trans(*) affect, etc. On the trans asterisk and its uses, see: van Kessel, Minnaard and Steinbock, 'Trans*'; Stryker, Currah, and Moore, 'Trans-, Trans, or

APPENDIX

Transgender?'. For an example of the productive use of the trans asterisk, see: Bey, 'Trans*-ness of Blackness'.

For further reading, see: Stryker, 'Transgender Studies 2.0'; Stryker and Aizura, *Reader 2*; Stryker and Whittle, *Reader*. On the intersection of race with trans-ness and genderqueer identities, see in particular: Aizura, et al., 'Transgender Imaginary'; Marlon M. Bailey, *Butch Queens*; Driskill, *Asegi Stories*; Ellison, et al., 'Issue of Blackness'; Johnson, *No Tea, No Shade*; Snorton, *Black on Both Sides*.

*See also: **Assigned Sex; Assigned Gender, Cis(gender), Identified Gender, Transition; Transitioning, Trans(gender) Man, Trans(gender) Woman, Transgenderism; Transgenderist***

Transgendered (past participle)
Avoid. Transgender is an adjective. 'Transgendered' (like 'gendered') is a past tense verb. Generally, most people are 'transgender' people and not 'transgendered' unless in the uncommon circumstances of being made trans by outside forces. This is the reason most pro-trans writers and speakers have mostly abandoned 'transgendered' for 'transgender'. Likewise, this is why anti-trans writers and speakers use 'transgendered': either because they are using out-of-date information, or because they view trans-ness as a lifestyle that is indoctrinated into otherwise cisgender men and women. For these reasons, be intentional whenever (trans)gender or (trans)gendered is used, for both grammatical and rhetorical reasons.
*See also: **TERF, Trans(gender), Transgenderism; Transgenderist***

Transgenderism; Transgenderist (noun; adjective)
Avoid. 'Transgenderism' is a term used by trans-antagonistic people to imply that being trans is a 'lifestyle choice' and/or an aberration from 'natural' and universal cisgender identity. To describe the state of being trans, use instead the noun ***Trans-ness***.
*See also: **TERF, Trans(gender), Transgendered***

Trans(gender) Man (noun phrase)
A person assigned female at birth (*AFAB*) who identifies as a man, regardless of whether they have medically or socially transitioned. Note: not a 'transman' or a 'trans-man', nouns implying that 'trans(-)men' and 'men' are different categories, but a 'trans man'. In the latter, the adjective 'trans' modifies the noun 'man', which is a category common to both trans men and cis men.

Trans(gender) Woman (noun phrase)
A person assigned male at birth (***AMAB***) who identifies as a woman, regardless of whether they have medically or socially transitioned. Note: not a 'transwoman' or a 'trans-women', a noun implying that 'trans(-)women' and 'women' are different categories, but a 'trans woman'. In the latter, the adjective 'trans' modifies the noun 'woman', which is a descriptor common to both trans women and cis women.

Transition; Transitioning (verb and noun; present participle and adjective)
Transition refers to the process of assuming or openly declaring a different gendered identity or social role. This may be a temporary or permanent shift. The use of 'transition' moves away from calling such events 'changes' (e.g. ***'Sex Change'***) because most trans individuals see transition as a process of expressing what has always been their identified gender (even if they were unable to recognize this identification previously, due to ***Cisnormative*** culture) rather than taking on a new or 'changed' gender. Yet transition is likely also to include changing, correcting, and/or affirming gender on legal and medical documents, in familial and professional arenas, in clothing and pronoun usage, as well as by using various medical technologies.

Transitions will look different depending on the formulation of genders in the individual's cultural and temporal location, and on the technologies and procedures for transition which are available, as well as the personal inclinations of the individual transitioning. Transition can occur relatively quickly, seemingly all at once, or may occur in fits and starts over a lifetime. Transitions may involve explorations which are later set aside as the person's gender identity evolves.

Social transition refers to non-medical steps taken to alleviate ***Dysphoria*** and establish one's identified gender, including, but not limited to, changing one's name and/or pronouns; wearing different clothes; wearing or not wearing make-up; wearing different hairstyles; taking on a different social role. Social transition likely to be determined by an individual's cultural and temporal location, as what is socially normative for a particular gender changes in different times and places.

Medical transition refers to hormonal or surgical steps taken to change characteristics or appearance typically in order to reduce physical and/or social ***Gender Dysphoria***. Medical transition does not *make* a person trans; people who medically transition do so *because* they are trans. Therefore, it is incorrect to assume that trans people did not exist before medical transition was possible. The term ***'Sexual Reassignment Surgery'*** (or 'SRS') denotes surgical steps undertaken as part of medical transition. It is used by some trans people to describe their own experiences, though it is somewhat dated. Avoid, unless you are referring to yourself or you know that this term is used by the person in question. Use *'Gender-Affirming Surgery'* or *'Gender Confirmation Surgery'* instead. Note, 'surgery' is used here as non-countable, i.e. potentially plural, and does not denote a singular, definitive surgery that enacts trans-ness. There are, instead, many kinds of surgery which a trans individual may or may not undertake, as part of their transition. Transition is not a single pathway, but looks different for every individual.

Not transitioning does not make someone not trans. An individual might not be able to express their identity outwardly at a given moment for various reasons. They may wait until a better time to do so, or they may never be able to express their identity, depending on their social/cultural/historical position.

See also: Assigned Sex; Assigned Gender, Pass; Passing

Transfemininity; Transfeminine (noun; adjective)
'Transfeminine' is an umbrella term which encompasses the identities of individuals whose identified gender is more feminine than their assigned gender. Trans women are transfeminine, but so, too, are some feminine non-binary, genderqueer or genderfluid individuals. The term 'trans woman' generally suggests that femininity is a defining feature of an individual's identified gender. However, a transfeminine person may feel that, while femininity constitutes part of their gender identity, there are other aspects of their gender which are equally or more important. This may, for example, may be the case for feminine non-binary, genderqueer or genderfluid individuals.

See also: Femme; Genderfluid; Gender Fluidity, Genderqueer, Non-Binary, Trans(gender), Transmasculine

Transman (noun)
Avoid. This noun implies that 'transmen' and 'men' are different categories. Use instead 'trans man': here, the adjective 'trans' modifies the noun 'man', which is a descriptor common to both trans men and cis men.

See also: Trans(gender) Man

Transmasculinity; Transmasculine (noun; adjective)
'Transmasculine' is an umbrella term which encompasses the identities of individuals whose identified gender is more masculine than their assigned gender. Trans men are transmasculine, but so, too, are some masculine non-binary, genderqueer, or genderfluid individuals. The term 'trans man'

generally suggests that masculinity is a defining feature of an individual's identified gender. However, a transmasculine person may feel that, while masculinity constitutes part of their gender identity, there are other aspects of their gender which are equally or more important. This may, for example, be the case for masculine non-binary, genderqueer, or genderfluid individuals.

For further reading, see: Parker, *Black Transmasculine Compilation*.
See also: **Butch, Genderfluid; Gender Fluidity, Genderqueer, Non-Binary, Transfeminine, Trans(gender)**

Transmisogynoir (noun)
Moya Bailey invented the term 'misogynoir' in the late 2000s to name the nuanced, intersectional experience Black women face when dealing with gender-based hatred. Though Bailey explicitly limits the term's remit to Black women, it has become used more broadly to refer to the misogyny experienced by all women of colour. 'Misogynoir' came to be popularized online, especially by the work of the blogger Trudy. She developed Bailey's concept further, coining the term 'transmisogynoir'. Transmisogynoir is the intersection of transmisogyny and (anti-Black) racism. Trans women, and in particular trans women of colour, face high levels of abuse, violence and murder. As with misogynoir, transmisogynoir is often used to refer to an experience faced by all trans women of colour, not specifically Black trans women.

On this, see: Moya Bailey, 'They Aren't Talking About Me…'; Bailey and Trudy, 'On Misogynoir'; Trudy (@thetrudz), tweet (14 August 2013); Trudy, 'Explanation'.

On violence against trans women, see: Smith, *Transgender Day of Remembrance*.
See also: **Internalized Transphobia, Transmisogyny, Transphobia; Transphobic, White Supremacy**

Transmisogyny (noun)
Transmisogyny is the intersection of transphobia and misogyny. Trans women, and in particular trans women of colour, face high levels of abuse, violence, and murder.

On this, see: Smith, *Transgender Day of Remembrance*.
See also: **Internalized Transphobia, Transmisogynoir, Transphobia; Transphobic**

Trans-ness; Transness (noun)
See: **Trans(gender)**

APPENDIX   321

Transphobia; Transphobic (noun; adjective)
Transphobia is discrimination against trans people, or people perceived to be trans, on the basis of their gender identity. At the core of transphobia is the assumption that transgender bodies, identities, and experiences are unreal, deceptive, invalid or illegitimate in comparison to cisgender bodies, identities and experiences. Transphobia is a form of structural and systemic marginalization. It occurs in interpersonal interactions as well as in discourse, including in academic work which relies on trans-exclusionary and/or transphobic assumptions.

For more on this, see in particular: Montgomerie, 'Addressing'; Serano, 'Detransition'; Smith, *Transgender Day of Remembrance.*
See also: **Internalized Transphobia, Transmisogyny, Transmisogynoir**

Transsexual (noun and adjective)
The term 'transsexual' is an older term for identities which are now more commonly described as transgender. A line is sometimes drawn between the two terms, stating that a transsexual person is someone who has taken surgical and/or hormonal steps to change their physical embodiment/sexed body (the implicit, binaristic assumption being that the change is to the 'other' of the two sexes), while a transgender person is someone who (merely) identifies as a gender other than the gender they were assigned at birth. Thus, all transsexuals may be considered transgender, but not all transgender individuals may be considered transsexual.

The term 'transgender' moves beyond the term 'transsexual' in two key ways. First, it surpasses the binaristic framework which 'transsexual' always implies in its attachment, and adherence, to the contours of, 'sex'. 'Transgender' facilitates the conceptualizing of non-binary, agender, and genderqueer identities by opening up possibilities of existence and identification. Secondly, 'transgender' ceases to rely on bodily morphology (and bodily modification) as indicators of identity. In the 'transgender' model, identification is enough; no more evidence of identity is required. Thus, 'transgender' allows the separation of identity and embodied existence, revealing different ways in which bodies can be understood and refusing the limitations of binaristic thinking.

For these reasons, 'transsexual' is now often perceived as a reductive term. It may signal a lack of familiarity regarding current thought on trans identities, and also, in its cleaving to sex, an unwelcome medicalization and pathologization of bodies and experiences. 'Transsexual' remains close to the '*Sex Change*' narrative, in which a wholesale shift from one binary sex to the other is enacted by medical means, localizable to a specific moment in time. 'Transgender', meanwhile, can encompass complex processes of *Transition* (or lack thereof), and relocates the emphasis of 'trans' from 'objectively' visible medical processes originating outside the self, to affirm the significance and the validity of internal, subjective experiences.

Many trans people, particularly trans elders who grew up with the term 'transsexual', use it to refer to themselves, and others are reclaiming it as an affirming designation. Avoid using this term unless you are referring to yourself, or you know that the individual to whom you are referring prefers this term. Instead, use ***Trans(gender)***.

See also: ***Sex Change, Trans(gender), Transition; Transitioning***

Transvestite; Transvestism (adjective and noun; noun)
In popular usage, 'transvestite' is often used synonymously with 'cross-dresser' to describe an individual who wears clothes typically worn by individuals of the 'opposite' gender. Historically, however, 'transvestite' was used in psychiatric texts to describe cross-dressing behaviour as 'deviance' with particular links to the 'deviance' of homosexuality. Thus, it carried – and to a certain degree still carries – a connotation of fetish, deployed in a stigmatizing and derogatory way. As such, this terminology should be used with extreme caution. If the context is appropriate, replace with 'cross-dresser', etc., which is stigmatizing to a lesser degree.

Using the term 'transvestite' (or 'transvestism') in relation to trans individuals demonstrates a fundamental misunderstanding of trans identity. This misunderstanding is founded upon the perception that trans individuals wear clothing associated with the 'opposite' assigned sex/gender, when they are in fact wearing clothing associated with their identified gender. Describing a transgender individual as a 'transvestite' reduces their identity to an 'incorrect' application of cultural norms regarding clothing, and implies that they are 'really' their assigned sex/gender, but masquerading as the 'opposite' sex/gender. For example, a trans woman may be incorrectly perceived as a transvestite: a man wearing women's clothing. However, since she is in fact a woman wearing women's clothing, she is not a transvestite; to describe her as such erases and dismisses her female identity.

See also: ***Cross-Dress; Cross-Dressing; Cross-Dresser, Drag, Tranny***

Transwoman (noun)
Avoid. This noun implies that 'transwomen' and 'women' are different categories. Use instead 'trans woman': here, the adjective 'trans' modifies the noun 'woman', which is a descriptor common to both trans women and cis women.

See also: ***Trans(gender) Woman***

Trap (*verb; noun; adjectival noun*)

The notion of 'trap' and 'trapping' is a persistent, pervasive, derogatory trope which serves to normalize transphobia and justify transphobic violence. This trope casts trans-ness as insidiously deceptive – in other words, a trap that the trans individual is laying for an 'unsuspecting' cis-het victim. A particularly prevalent 'trap' narrative presents a trans woman 'deceiving' a male love interest, simply by presenting as her identified gender and thereby being an object of the suitor's lust. The eventual 'revelation' that his date is 'really' a man is portrayed as a betrayal of trust and an offense to his heterosexual masculinity which throws him into existential chaos. This 'legitimizes' the suitor's violent retribution against the trans woman, even up to the point of murder. If the revelation occurs before (much) physical contact, the suitor is typically portrayed as deeply relieved, having only barely 'escaped' an 'atrocity'. Even if the suitor does not respond with physical violence, he may still do harm to the trans woman, by *Outing* her to others. This narrative places emphasis on the cis-het man's experience and worldview, denying both the validity of the trans woman's identified gender, and the horrifying reality that in a sexual encounter between a trans woman and a cis man, the woman is, statistically speaking, exposed to the risk of transmisogynistic murder, even more so if she is a woman of colour. Similar narratives circulate regarding trans men, but these tend to be less virulent, and are less likely to result in violence.

'Trap' as a noun can be a derogatory term for a trans person, in particular a trans woman. Do not use.

On this trope, see: Gossett, Stanley, and Burton, *Trap Door*.
See also: **Out; Outing, Pass; Passing, Transmisogyny, Transmisogynoir**

Tuck; Tucking (*verb and noun; present participle*)

The practice of manipulating, that is, 'tucking', the genitals to provide a flatter appearance between the legs. Tucking is most often associated with trans women and cisgender male drag queens, although it may be practiced by a wide variety of genders, including intersex and non-binary persons. The flatter appearance is generally supposed to make the body appear more 'feminine' and allow the body to 'pass' more readily as cis female, especially when skintight or revealing clothing, such as swimwear, evening wear, or lingerie, is worn. Yet a person may tuck for a wider variety of reasons, including to alleviate feelings of gender dysphoria, or due to an affinity for/enjoyment of the flat forms produced. The noun 'tuck' may be used to refer to the result of tucking. People who tuck may do so intermittently, or on certain occasions and not on others.

See also: **Bind; Binding; Binder, Gender Dysphoria; Gender Dysphoric, Pack; Packing; Packer, Pad; Padding, Pass; Passing**

Two-Spirit (*adjective*)

An indigenous North American gender identity. This is an 'umbrella' term, agreed upon at an international conference in 1990 by members of the of Native American and First Nations gay and lesbian community. It refers to people who are indigenous to Turtle Island (North America) and whose gender, gender roles, or gender expressions differ from the normative roles of men and women in their respective cultures.

   On this, see: Driskill, *Asegi Stories*; Jacob, Thomas and Lang, *Two-Spirit People*; Rifkin, *When Did Indians Become Straight?*; de Vries, '(Berdache) Two-Spirit'; Wilson, 'Our Coming In Stories'.
See also: **White Supremacy**

White Supremacy

Gender is inextricably bound up with racialization. White supremacy imposes and centres (white) binary gender, relentlessly othering what it views as non-normative genders, especially when these are expressed by indigenous people and/or people of colour. For this reason, the assumption that indigenous and/or non-white identities such as bakla, *Hijra*, kathoey, *Two-Spirit*, and many others, are equivalent to or part of the spectrum of trans identities is an overtly colonizing gesture which presumes the primacy and completeness of the white (trans)gender system. This does not mean, of course, that individuals with these identities cannot or do not include themselves under or see themselves as represented by the LGBTQIA+ umbrella; indeed, some versions of the acronym, such as LGBTQ2S (commonly used in Canada) explicitly reference indigenous two-spirit identities. The distinction to be drawn is between assumptions which flatten the gender of non-white subjects into reductive and marginalizing white paradigms, and the consensual participation of subjects in cultural expressions (such as Pride) which they feel represent, respect, and celebrate their identities. Racialized gender descriptors or identities should not be appropriated by those of other heritages.

   On this, see: Aizura et al., 'Transgender Imaginary'; binaohan, *decolonizing*; Camminga, 'Umbrella?'; Dutta and Roy, 'Decolonizing'; Paramo, 'Transphobia'; Snorton, *Black on Both Sides*. On gender in North American indigenous cultures, see: Driskill, *Asegi Stories*; Jacob, Thomas and Lang, *Two-Spirit People*; Lang, *Men as Women, Women as Men*; Rifkin, *When Did Indians Become Straight?*. On hijra identities, see: Hinchy, *Governing Gender*;

Moorti, 'Queer Romance'; Reddy, *With Respect to Sex*. On Black trans identities, see: Bey, 'Trans*-ness of Blackness'; Ellison et al., 'Issue of Blackness'; Johnson, *No Tea, No Shade*; Snorton, *Black on Both Sides*.
See also: Transmisogynoir

Ze/Hir (pronouns)
An example of gender neutral or non-binary pronouns, to replace 'he/him' and 'she/her'. 'Ze' may also be spelled 'zie'.
See also: Pronouns

Ze/Zir (pronouns)
An example of gender neutral or non-binary pronouns, to replace 'he/him' and 'she/her'. 'Ze' may also be spelled 'zie'.
See also: Pronouns

Bibliography

Aizura, Aren Z., Trystan Cotten, Carsten Balzer/Carla LaGata, Marcia Ochoa, and Salvador Vidal-Ortiz, eds., 'Decolonizing the Transgender Imaginary', *TSQ: Transgender Studies Quarterly*, 1.3 (2014).

Bailey, Marlon M., *Butch Queens Up in Pumps: Gender, Performance, and Ballroom Culture in Detroit* (Ann Arbor: University of Michigan, 2013).

Bailey, Moya, 'They Aren't Talking About Me...', *The Crunk Feminist Collection*, 14 March 2010. <http://www.crunkfeministcollective.com/2010/03/14/they-arent-talking-about-me/> [accessed 29 November 2018].

Bailey, Moya and Trudy, 'On Misogynoir: Citation, Erasure, and Plagiarism', *Feminist Media Studies*, 18.4 (2018), 762-68. <https://doi.org/10.1080/14680777.2018.1447395> [accessed 12 August 2020].

Barker, Meg-John, and Alex Iantaffi, *Life Isn't Binary: On Being Both, Beyond, and In-Between* (London: Jessica Kingsley, 2019).

Baron, Dennis, *What's Your Pronoun?: Beyond He and She* (New York: Liveright, 2020).

* binaohan, b., *decolonizing trans/gender 101* (Toronto: biyuti, 2014).

Bergman, S. Bear, *Butch is a Noun* (Vancouver: Arsenal Pulp, 2006).

—, *The Nearest Exit May Be Behind You* (Vancouver: Arsenal Pulp, 2009).

Bey, Marquis, 'The Trans*-ness of Blackness, the Blackness of Trans*-ness', *TSQ: Transgender Studies Quarterly*, 4.2 (2017), 275-95.

Bongiovanni, Archie, and Tristan Jimerson, *A Quick & Easy Guide to They/Them Pronouns* (Portland: Limerence, 2018).

* Bornstein, Kate, *My New Gender Workbook: A Step-by-Step Guide to Achieving World Peace Through Gender Anarchy and Sex Positivity* (New York: Routledge, 2013).

Boswell, John, *Christianity, Social Tolerance, and Homosexuality* (Chicago: University of Chicago, 1980).

* Butler, Judith, *Bodies That Matter: On the Discursive Limits of "Sex"* (New York: Routledge, 1993).

* —, *Gender Trouble: Feminism and the Subversion of Identity* (London: Routledge, 1990).

* —, 'Imitation and Gender Insubordination', in *Inside/Out: Lesbian Theories, Gay Theories*, ed. by Dianna Fuss (London: Routledge, 1991), pp. 13-31.

Burgwinkle, William, *Sodomy, Masculinity, and Law in Medieval Literature: France and England, 1050-1230* (Cambridge: Cambridge University, 2004).

Burgwinkle, Bill, and Cary Howie, *Sanctity and Pornography in Medieval Culture: On the Verge.* (Manchester: Manchester University, 2010).

Burke, Jennifer Clare, ed., *Visible: A Femmethology, Volume 1* (Ypsilanti: Homofactus, 2009).

Bychowski, M.W., 'Gender Terminology', *Transliterature: Things Transform* <http://www.thingstransform.com/p/terminology-on-gender.html> [accessed 11 June 2020].

Cadden, Joan, *Meanings of Sex Difference in the Middle Ages: Medicine, Science, and Culture.* (Cambridge: Cambridge University, 1993).

Camminga, B. 'Where's Your Umbrella?: Decolonisation and Transgender Studies in South Africa', *Postamble*, 10.1 (2017). <https://www.academia.edu/31979917/Wheres_Your_Umbrella_Decolonisation_and_Transgender_Studies_in_South_Africa> [accessed 16 June 2019].

* Chase, Cheryl, 'Hermaphrodites with Attitude: Mapping the Emergence of Intersex Political Activism', *GLQ*, 4:2 (1998), 189-211.

Coman, Jonah, 'Trans Citation Practices – A Quick-and-Dirty Guideline', *Medium*, 27 November 2018 <https://medium.com/@MxComan/trans-citation-practices-a-quick-and-dirty-guideline-9f4168117115> [accessed 11 April 2019].

Dinshaw, Carolyn, *Getting Medieval: Sexualities and Communities, Pre- and Postmodern* (Durham: Duke University, 1999).

—, *How Soon Is Now? Medieval Texts, Amateur Readers, and the Queerness of Time* (Durham: Duke University, 2012).

Driskill, Qwo-Li, *Asegi Stories: Cherokee Queer and Two-Spirit Memory* (Tucson: University of Arizona, 2016).

Dutta, Aniruddha, and Raina Roy. 'Decolonizing Transgender in India: Some Reflections', *TSQ: Transgender Studies Quarterly*, 1.3 (2014), 320-36.

Ehrensaft, Diane, *The Gender Creative Child: Pathways for Nurturing and Supporting Children Who Live Outside Gender Boxes* (New York: Experiment, 2016).

Ellison, Treva, Kai. M. Green, Matt Richardson, and C. Riley Snorton, eds., 'The Issue of Blackness,' *TSQ: Transgender Studies Quarterly*, 4.2 (2017).

* Feinberg, Leslie, *Transgender Warriors* (Boston: Beacon, 1996).

Gossett, Reina, Eric A. Stanley and Johanna Burton, eds., *Trap Door: Trans Cultural Production and the Politics of Visibility* (Cambridge: MIT, 2017).

Gutt, Blake, 'Transgender Genealogy in Tristan de Nanteuil', *Exemplaria*, 30.2 (2018), 129-46. <https://www.tandfonline.com/doi/abs/10.1080/10412573.2018.1453652> [accessed 12 August 2020].

* Halberstam, J., *Female Masculinity* (Durham: Duke University, 1998).

Hall, Donald E., Annamarie Jagose, Andrea Bebell, and Susan Potter, eds., *The Routledge Queer Studies Reader* (New York: Routledge, 2013)

Harris, Laura, and Elizabeth Crocker, eds. *Femme: Feminists, Lesbians and Bad Girls* (New York: Routledge, 1997).

Hinchy, Jessica, *Governing Gender and Sexuality in Colonial India: The Hijra, c.1850-1900* (Cambridge: Cambridge University, 2019).

Hord, Levi C.R., 'Bucking the Linguistic Binary: Gender Neutral Language in English, Swedish, French, and German', *Western Papers in Linguistics / Cahiers linguistiques de Western*, 3: article 4 (2016), 1-27 <https://ir.lib.uwo.ca/cgi/viewcontent.cgi?article=1027&context=wpl_clw> [accessed 29 November 2018].

Jacob, Sue-Ellen, Wesley Thomas and Sabine Lang, eds., *Two-Spirit People: Native American Gender Identity, Sexuality, and Spirituality* (Urbana: University of Illinois, 1997).

Johnson, E. Patrick, ed., *No Tea, No Shade: New Writings in Black Queer Studies* (Durham: Duke University, 2016).

Kapitan, Alex, 'The Radical Copyeditor's Guide to Writing About Transgender People', *Radical Copyeditor*, 31 August 2017 <https://radicalcopyeditor.com/2017/08/31/transgender-style-guide/> [accessed 29 November 2018].

van Kessel, Looi, Liesbeth Minnaard and Eliza Steinbock, 'Trans*: Approaches, Methods, and Concepts', *Tijdschrift voor Genderstudies* 20.4 (2017), 335-59.

Kralick, Alexandra, 'How Human Bones Reveal the Fallacy of a Biological Sex Binary', *Pacific Standard*, 25 December 2018 <https://psmag.com/social-justice/our-bones-reveal-sex-is-not-binary> [accessed 11 April 2019].

Lang, Sabine, *Men as Women, Women as Men: Changing Gender in Native American Cultures*, trans. John L. Vantine (Austin: University of Texas, 1998).

Lochrie, Karma, *Heterosyncrasies: Female Sexuality When Normal Wasn't* (Minneapolis: University of Minnesota, 2005).

Lochrie, Karma, Peggy McCracken, and James A. Schultz, eds., *Constructing Medieval Sexuality* (Minneapolis: University of Minnesota, 1997).

Mills, Robert, *Seeing Sodomy in the Middle Ages* (Chicago: University of Chicago, 2015).

Montgomerie, Katy, 'Addressing The Claims In JK Rowling's Justification For Transphobia' *Medium*, 16 June 2020 <https://medium.com/@completelykaty/addressing-the-claims-in-jk-rowlings-justification-for-transphobia-7b6f761e8f8f> [accessed 1 July 2020].

Moorti, Sujata, 'A Queer Romance with the Hijra', *QED: A Journal in GLBTQ Worldmaking*, 3.2 (2016), 18-34.

* Nestle, Joan, Howell, Claire, and Wilchins, Riki Anne, eds., *Genderqueer: Voices from Beyond the Sexual Binary* (Los Angeles: Alyson, 2002).

Pamment, Claire, 'Performing Piety in Pakistan's Transgender Rights Movement', *TSQ* 6.3 (2019), 297-314. <https://doi.org/10.1215/23289252-7549414> [accessed 12 August 2020].

Paramo, Michael, 'Transphobia is a White Supremacist Legacy of Colonialism', *Medium*, 17 July 2018 <https://medium.com/@Michael_Paramo/transphobia-is-a-white-supremacist-legacy-of-colonialism-e50f57240650> [accessed 16 June 2019].

Parker, Ilya, ed., *Black Transmasculine Compilation* [digital collection] (North Carolina: Decolonizing Fitness) <https://decolonizingfitness.com/products/black-transmasculine-compilation> [accessed 12 August 2020].

Reddy, Gayatri, *With Respect to Sex: Negotiating Hijra Identity in South India* (Chicago: University of Chicago, 2005).

Rifkin, Mark, *When Did Indians Become Straight?: Kinship, the History of Sexuality, and Native Sovereignty* (Oxford: Oxford University, 2011).

Rocheleau, Juliette, 'A Former Slur Is Reclaimed, And Listeners Have Mixed Feelings', *NPR*, 21 August 2019 <https://www.npr.org/sections/publiceditor/2019/08/21/752330316/a-former-slur-is-reclaimed-and-listeners-have-mixed-feelings?t=1590509113219> [accessed 26 May 2020].

Rupp, Leila. J., Verta Taylor, and Eve Ilana Shapiro, 'Drag Queens and Drag Kings: The Difference Gender Makes', *Sexualities* 13 (2010), 275-94.

Serano, Julia, 'A Personal History of the "T-word" (and Some More General Reflections on Language and Activism)', *Whipping Girl*, 28 April 2014 <http://juliaserano.blogspot.com/2014/04/a-personal-history-of-t-word-and-some.html> [accessed 11 April 2019].

—, 'Detransition, Desistance, and Disinformation: A Guide for Understanding Transgender Children Debates', *Medium*, 2 August 2016 <https://medium.com/@juliaserano/detransition-desistance-and-disinformation-a-guide-for-understanding-transgender-children-993b7342946e> [accessed 29 November 2018].

—, 'On the "Activist Language Merry-go-round," Stephen Pinker's "Euphemism Treadmill," and "Political Correctness" More Generally', *Whipping Girl*, 2 June 2014 <http://juliaserano.blogspot.com/2014/06/on-activist-language-merry-go-round.html> [accessed 11 April 2019].

* —, *Whipping Girl: A Transsexual Woman on Sexism and the Scapegoating of Femininity* (2nd edn.) (Berkeley: Seal, 2013).
Smith, Gwendolyn Ann, *Transgender Day of Remembrance* <http://tdor.info> [accessed 29 November 2018].
* Snorton, C. Riley, *Black on Both Sides: A Racial History of Trans Identity* (Minneapolis: University of Minnesota, 2017).
Spencer-Hall, Alicia, *Medieval Saints and Modern Screens: Divine Visions as Cinematic Experience* (Amsterdam: Amsterdam University, 2018).
Stryker, Susan, 'Transgender Studies 2.0: New Directions in the Field', paper presented at the Scandinavian Trans* Studies Seminar, University of Copenhagen, Denmark, 9 December 2011. <https://koensforskning.ku.dk/kalender/trans/stryker.pdf> [accessed 29 November 2018].
* Stryker, Susan, and Aren Z. Aizura, eds., *The Transgender Studies Reader 2* (New York: Routledge, 2013).
Stryker, Susan, Paisley Currah, and Lisa Jean Moore, 'Trans-, Trans, or Transgender?', *Women's Studies Quarterly*, 36.3-4 (Fall-Winter, 2008), 11-22.
* Stryker, Susan, and Paisley Currah, eds., 'Postposttranssexual: Key Concepts for a Twenty-First-Century Transgender Studies', *TSQ: Transgender Studies Quarterly*, 1.1-2 (2014).
* Stryker, Susan, and Stephen Whittle, eds., *The Transgender Studies Reader* (New York: Routledge, 2006).
Szabo, Felix, 'Non-Standard Masculinity and Sainthood in Niketas David's *Life* of Patriarch Ignatios', in Alicia Spencer-Hall and Blake Gutt, eds., *Trans and Genderqueer Subjects in Medieval Hagiography* (Amsterdam: Amsterdam University, 2021), pp. 109-29.
Taylor, Verta, and Leila. J. Rupp, 'Chicks with Dicks, Men in Dresses: What It Means to Be a Drag Queen', *Journal of Homosexuality*, 46.4 (2004), 113-33.
Thieme, Katja, and Mary Ann S. Saunders, 'How Do You Wish To Be Cited? Citation Practices and a Scholarly Community of Care in Trans Studies Research Articles', *Journal of English for Academic Purposes*, 32 (2018), 80-90. <https://hcommons.org/deposits/item/hc:20559/> [accessed 11 April 2019].
Tougher, Shaun, 'Holy Eunuchs! Masculinity and Eunuch Saints in Byzantium', in P. H. Cullum and Katherine J. Lewis, eds., *Holiness and Masculinity in the Middle Ages* (Cardiff: University of Wales, 2004), pp. 93-108.
Trans Student Educational Resources, 'Why We Used Trans* and Why We Don't Anymore', <http://www.transstudent.org/asterisk/> [accessed 29 November 2018].
Trudy (@thetrudz), 'The street harassment and violence trans women face is notorious and sickening. Transmisogyny and transmisogynoir are truly awful', 8:35 PM, 14 August 2013. Tweet. <https://twitter.com/thetrudz/status/367731149386174464> [accessed 29 November 2018].

Trudy, 'Explanation of Misogynoir', *Gradient Lair*, 28 April 2014 <http://www.gradientlair.com/post/84107309247/define-misogynoir-anti-black-misogyny-moya-bailey-coined> [accessed 29 November 2018].

University of Wisconsin-Milwaukee's Lesbian, Gay, Bisexual, Transgender Resource Center, 'Gender Pronouns', *University of Wisconsin-Milwaukee's Lesbian, Gay, Bisexual, Transgender Resource Center* <https://uwm.edu/lgbtrc/support/gender-pronouns/> [accessed 29 November 2018].

de Vries, Kylan Mattias, '(Berdache) Two-Spirit', in Jodie O'Brien, ed., *Encyclopedia of Gender and Society, Volume 1* (Thousand Oaks: SAGE, 2009), pp. 62-65.

Wade, Lisa, 'The Phall-O-Meter', *Sociological Images*, 4 September 2008 <https://thesocietypages.org/socimages/2008/09/04/the-phall-o-meter/> [accessed 11 April 2019].

Wilson, Alex, 'Our Coming In Stories: Cree Identity, Body Sovereignty and Gender Self-Determination', *Journal of Global Indigeneity*, 1.1 (2015) <https://ro.uow.edu.au/jgi/vol1/iss1/4> [accessed 23 August 2019].

Zimman, Lal, 'Transgender Language Reform: Some Challenges and Strategies for Promoting Trans-Affirming, Gender-Inclusive Language', *Journal of Language and Discrimination*, 1.1 (2017), 84-105.

Index

abbeys   43-44, 46, 50, 54, 88, 96-97, 103, 211
ability   54, 57, 75, 182, 208, 215, 225, 234, 237-41, 257
   hyper-ability   240
abject, abjection   227, 235
able-bodyminded-ness   226-27, 232-33
   compulsory   227
ableism   227-28
Abraham   67
Acts (Book of)   113
Adam   99-101
Aelred of Rievaulx   50
affective piety   *see* piety, affective
affectivity   13, 31, 65, 133-34, 136, 142, 146-49, 225, 228, 230-31, 252
agape-ic encounter   144-45
Aizura, Aren Z.   21
alchemy   27, 137
Alexandria   65, 69-71, 77, 112, 210, 272
St Alexis   205-07, 211, 213
Alice the Leper   226
allies, allyship   282, 285
America   16, 28-29, 88, 183, 269
American Civil War   269
Amsler, Mark   146-47
St Anastasia/Anastasios   91
androgyneity   73, 286
Androshchuk, Fedir   186
Angela of Foligno   103
angels   48-49, 52-54, 56, 69, 82, 100-01, 119, 125, 229-32, 235, 237, 239
   archangels   98, 100, 123
   castration by in dreams, visions   54, 112
   Gabriel   98, 100
   Michael   123
Annunciation   97, 100
anonymity   9, 67, 71, 73, 203, 215, 224, 229
Anson, John   254
antisociality   70-71
St Apolinaria/Dorotheos   91
apostles   113, 117, 124-25, 215
   Paul   124
   Peter   124
de los Apóstoles, Francisca   88
Arbman, Holger   191
archaeology   28, 30, 177-93
   problematic assumptions of gender   28, 177-93, 270
   trans archaeology   179-80
archives (queer)   70-71, 83
Aristotle   273
arma Christi   138, 140, 145
Arrek (fifth century scholar)   66, 71
Ása, queen of Agder   184
asceticism   24, 102, 119-22, 124, 211, 235-36, 273-74

Assassin's Creed   276
St Athanasia   91
Athos   121, 251
audience   14, 23, 47, 50, 55, 57, 59, 74, 87, 90, 98-99, 102-04, 112-13, 121, 126, 137, 141, 149-50, 202, 204-05, 207, 209, 212, 215-17, 248, 258, 273; *see also* readers
Augsburg   48
St Augustine   47, 73, 254-55, 271
Augustinians   66, 73, 271, 275
authenticity   14, 30, 87-88, 102, 138, 140, 225, 245-65, 271
authority
   authority figures   46, 69, 103, 217, 233
   bodily   228
   poetic   213-15
   religious   46, 69, 103, 171
authorship   69, 71, 73
autohagiography   14
Ávila   91
Azades   113

Baanes Angoures (Byzantine ceremonial eunuch chamberlain)   119
Bacon, Roger   142
Bamberg   46
baptism   68, 88-89, 95, 103, 113, 138, 260
St Barbara of Nicomedia   271-72, 276
Bardas (Byzantine noble)   118-19, 126
Barker, Meg-John   134-35
Basil of Caesarea   113-16
beard, facial hair   91, 111, 118-19, 121, 126, 137, 157-58, 167-68, 186, 257, 274
   bearded (non-eunuch) men   111, 121, 158, 274
de Beauvoir, Simone   267
Bell, Father Francis   95-96
Berlant, Lauren   31
Bernard of Clairvaux   47, 50, 52, 54, 57
de Berneville, Guillaume   211
Bestul, Thomas   134
Bible, the   26, 54, 100, 123, 136
biological essentialism   13, 24, 29, 179, 192, 253, 256, 285
biopolitics   80
Birka chamber grave Bj. 581   *see* graves
birth   18, 51-52, 67, 72, 82, 92, 94-96, 98-99, 115, 124, 135, 138-40, 143, 147, 149, 232, 248, 256, 275; *see also* labour
birthing girdles   138-40, 143, 147, 275
Blanchandin·e   29, 223-44
   Clarinde (cousin)   231, 240
Black Lives Matter movement   269
blood   23, 69, 136, 236, 275
bodyminds   225-27, 229, 232-33, 235, 239
St Bonaventure   92-93, 103

Bonne of Luxembourg   143-46, 149
Book of the Holy Trinity, The (Frater Ulmannus)   137
Book of Margery Kempe, The   78
Books of Hours   139, 143-49
Boon, Jessica A.   22, 97, 102, 104
Bosporus strait   123
Boswell, John   284
Bouman, Walter Pierre   134-35
Bride of Christ   24, 47, 54-55, 59, 75, 78-79, 93, 103, 213
Bridegroom (Christ)   47, 54, 78, 103
Brock, Sebastian P.   258
Burgwinkle, William (Bill)   25, 284
burials   *see also* graves
   Kaupang boat burial (Ka. 294-296)   178, 187-89
   Oseberg ship burial   178, 184-87
Butler, Judith   227, 230, 268, 285
Bychowski, M.W.   12, 19, 22-23, 29-30, 270, 272-74, 285
Bynum, Caroline Walker   24, 136, 140-41, 224, 275
Byzantium   13, 28, 30, 109-27, 157-58

Cadden, Joan   284
Caesarius of Heisterbach   56
Campbell, Emma   74, 76, 157, 207, 211
canonization   14, 102, 275
Capgrave, John   29, 65-85, 272
Cardinal Cisneros   88, 93, 103
Carthusians   161, 173
castration   109, 111-12, 114, 117-19, 121, 126, 157, 274
   in dreams   54, 112
   self-castration   293
St Catherine   201, 218; *see also* St Katherine of Alexandria
Caxton, William   67
Cazelles, Brigitte   223
celibacy   66, 201-02, 212, 257
charity   211, 276
Charles IV of France   162, 173
Charles V of Spain   88
chastity   78, 80-81, 110-11, 113-16, 119-23, 126, 202, 259
Chaudhry, V. Varun   20
Chess, Simone   23
Chevalier d'Éon   277
childbirth   *see* birth
Christ   25, 53, 56-57, 69, 78, 82, 88-90, 92-95, 98, 103, 115, 117, 127, 136-37, 145, 208, 230, 237, 252-53, 255, 259, 270, 275, 277; *see also imitatio Christi*
   artistic representations of   125, 133-36, 138-41, 143-49, Fig 5.1 (144), Fig E.1 (273)
   beyond gender   27
   body in/as Eucharist   43, 136
   as bridegroom/husband   24, 47, 54, 67-68, 75, 77-79, 81-82, 95, 103
   as brother   94
   contact and/or identification with   25, 88, 93-94, 133-34, 141-43, 146-48, 275
   crip/disabled   238
   as father   92, 240
   feminine and/or feminized body   24, 135-137, 139, 149, 240, 274-75
   as foetus   99, 101
   gender fluidity, gender non-conformity, genderqueerness   24, 27, 29-30, 87, 91, 133-50, 240, 275
   genitalia   137-41, 143, 146-49
   as hermaphrodite   27, 137
   humanity   89, 133-37, 149, 208
   Incarnation   89, 208
   as Man of Sorrows   148
   as model for transgender saints   253-54, 258
   as monster   146
   as mother   24, 93-94, 136, 149, 228, 275
   as non-binary   133-50
   pregnant   102
   queer erotics of   136, 141
   as son   80-81, 92, 100, 272
   as suffering   133-34, 138-40, 238, 275
   wounds   29-30, 133-50, Fig 5.2 (145), 275
chromosomes   *see* sex, assigned
chronic illness   *see* illness
chronic pain   *see* pain
Chu, Andrea Long   20
Church Fathers   121, 237; *see also* Holy Fathers
cis-essentialism   249
cisgender identity assignment, compulsory   250
cisheteronormativity   13, 177, 237
cisheterosexuality   17, 227, 233
   compulsory   227
Cistercians   43-50, 54-55, 57-59, 226, 228
Cîteaux   58
civil rights   18, 262
class, social   28, 74, 268-69
Clairvaux   59
St Clare   92, 103
Clare, Eli   233
clothing   12, 50, 91, 159, 163, 168-69, 171, 202, 204, 215, 246-47, 251-52, 257-58, 276
Cologne   48-49
Colwill, Lee   13, 28-30, 270, 275
Coman, Jonah   front matter (cover image credit), 17
communion, cross-temporal   14, 20, 83, 142, 150, 203, 216, 218
Complainte Nostre Dame   160
completeness, completion   81, 91, 93, 102, 117, 122, 144, 210-11, 223-25, 233, 237, 239
confession   24, 48, 57, 124-25, 260-61
Congregation for Catholic Education   17
Constantine VII   112
Constantinople   110, 118, 123, 125-26
Constas, Nicholas   251

conversion   47, 50-52, 55, 67-69, 77-78, 82, 113,
    182-83, 209, 229, 232, 272
coresthesia   142
Corinthians   89
Council of Toledo   99
Cox, Laverne   16
creation   15, 59, 89-90, 251, 253-55, 272, 276-77
Crenshaw, Kimberlé   268
crip theory   28-29, 227, 237-38
cripistemologies   228, 232-34, 237, 239
cross-dressing   12, 27, 44, 202, 245, 247, 249,
    276, 291-92; *see also* saints, 'transvestite'
    and/or 'cross-dressing'
Crusades   112
cure   29, 69, 124, 223-44
Currah, Paisley   20

David (Scottish king)   50
Davis, Stephen J.   249, 253-54, 258
Daza, Friar Antonio   95
death   12-13, 18, 28, 43-63, 60, 66, 68-69, 76,
    82, 91, 122-26, 138, 140, 156-57, 168-69, 180,
    184-90, 202, 206, 208, 210, 217, 223-25, 230-31,
    235-38, 246-47, 249, 259-62, 283
debate   17, 21, 68-69, 74, 148, 161-62, 183, 185,
    192, 251, 275
deceit, deception   26, 214-15, 248, 260; *see also*
    disguise
Defence of Eunuchs (Theophylact of Ochrid)   115
Denmark   178, 188
depoliticization   66
De Trinitate (Augustine)   254
devil, the   57, 137, 257
DeVun, Leah   27, 137
*Diagnostic and Statistical Manual of Mental
    Disorders* (*DSM*)   247, 256
Diest   161
Dinshaw, Carolyn   45, 83, 284
Diocletianic persecutions   113
disability   19, 28-30, 223-44, 275
    and intersectionality   268
    medical model   233
    political/relational model   224, 232-33
    social model   224, 233
disembodiment   140, 224
disguise   26-27, 29, 44, 49-52, 159, 229, 248,
    252, 258, 262
Dit de l'unicorne   160
divine will   77, 79, 98, 137, 207, 209, 212, 231,
    235, 237, 240-41, 253
domesticity   66, 80, 98, 178
dreams, dream visions   47, 54, 72, 112, 119;
    see also visions
Duggan, Lisa   65, 80
Duke of Tyre   75
dysphoria   *see* gender dysphoria

East Anglia   79
Easton, Martha   139-41

ecstasy (mystical)   15, 142, 144
Edelman, Lee   70
Eiríks saga rauða   *see* sagas
El Conhorte (Juana de la Cruz)   88
elites   28, 74, 125
Elphick, Kevin C.A.   29-30, 270, 274
embodiment   12-13, 15, 20, 28, 30, 71, 91, 213,
    223-44, 253-54, 261
emotion   14, 31, 74, 139, 147, 186, 206-08
'The Empire Strikes Back: A Posttranssexual
    Manifesto' (Stone)   20, 262
Les enfances nostre sire Jhesu Crist   160
Engelhard of Langheim   43-60
England   66-67, 78-79, 191, 201
enslavement   21, 109, 181, 269
epistemologies, trans   234, 239
Erbo, abbot of Prüfening   46, 57
Eucharist   43-44
St Eufrosine/Euphrosine/Euphrosyn/Esma-
    rade/Smaragdus   29-30, 91, 112, 155-76,
    201-21, 273, 276
    illuminations of Life   29, 155-76, 274
    Panuze/Pasnutius (saint's father)   156,
        204-14, 217
St Eugenia/Eugenios/Eugenius   91, 113, 159
    Hyacinth (companion)   113
    Protas (companion)   113
eunuchs   13, 27, 29-30, 109-29, 155-58, 167-69,
    171-73, 257-58, 274, 293
    Ethiopian eunuch baptized by St Philip   113
    eunuch saints   *see* saints
Europe   13, 28, 48, 51, 78, 133, 139, 202, 276-77
Eusebius of Caesarea   113
Eve   99-102
evil   114-15, 121, 125
    evil thoughts   204
    evil twin   20
exceptionality   13-14, 28, 73, 75, 77, 79, 110, 204,
    210, 212, 247, 258
exempla, exemplary tales   45-46, 50, 58
exemplarity   46, 76, 79, 121, 201, 205, 209, 212,
    248, 274

facial hair   *see* beard, facial hair
Fall, the   99-101, 205, 271
Fauvel Master   160-62, 165-73
Feinberg, Leslie   11-12, 14
Fisher, Will   23
Fradenburg, Louise   203
France   12, 155, 162, 173, 201, 224, 229, 269
Pope Francis   102
St Francis   92-93, 96-97, 103
    Bernard (follower)   92
    Leo (companion)   92
Franciscans   29, 88, 92-95, 97, 103, 137
Freccero, Carla   203
Frederick Barbarossa   48
Freyja   182
Frijhoff, Willem   269

futures 11, 19, 23, 26, 28, 45, 49, 65-85, 116, 206, 234, 237, 284

Galatians 56, 88
Game of Thrones 276
Gansum, Terje 185
Garber, Marjorie 249
Gardeła, Leszek 188
Gaunt, Simon 213, 216
gender 295-96
   in Byzantium 111, 157-58
   of Christ 24-25, 27, 30, 134-50, 274-75
   of divinity 272, 274-75, 277
   essentialism 20, 45, 47, 56-57, 178, 292-93
   'gender-critical' 21, 297
   of God 90, 94, 104, 272, 275, 277
   and grooming, clothing 29, 164-71, 230; see also facial hair, beard; clothing; hair; tonsure
   hierarchies 205, 212, 237, 258
   identified gender 15, 17, 30, 134-35, 156, 159, 165, 169-70, 172, 181, 230, 247, 249, 252, 256-57, 282, 285, 301
   indigenous American gender systems 183, 324
   and language 30-31, 53, 55, 59, 156, 169, 203-04, 215, 268, 282; see also names; pronouns
   medieval theorizations of 12, 14, 24-25, 27, 30, 79, 149, 181, 201-03, 217, 273, 276-77
   modern theorizations of 14, 17, 134-35, 230, 268, 277, 284
   norms, roles 13-14, 19, 60, 70, 74-75, 88, 97, 177, 179, 181, 184, 191, 204-06, 209, 212, 217, 256, 275-76, 283
   predominance of colonialist, white-centric frameworks 20-21, 28-29, 283; see also white supremacy
   and racialization 283
   of saints 24-25, 27, 29, 72, 75, 83, 87, 90-94, 102-03, 109-110, 112, 126, 137, 155-59, 163-65, 167-72, 202-04, 210, 213-15, 228, 246-50, 252-261, 271-77
   social gender 157, 180, 186, 192, 270, 275
   'third' gender 16, 25, 27, 56, 158, 183
gender binary 11-12, 25-28, 30, 45, 59-60, 94, 102-03, 134-37, 149, 157-58, 165, 178-80, 183, 193, 204-05, 253, 256, 274, 277, 282, 288
gender dysphoria 15, 255-57, 259, 297-98
gender essentialism 20, 24, 45, 47, 56-57, 178, 253, 256, 292-93
gender euphoria 15, 298
gender fluidity 11, 23, 49, 95, 135, 204, 214, 273, 275-77, 298-99
   Christ 24, 91, 135-37, 139, 141-42, 149, 275
   Cistercian 47
   Joseph of Schönau 53, 55, 59, 60
   Juana de la Cruz 29, 87, 97, 102-04
   saints 23, 204, 275-77

genderqueer 11-12, 14, 16-17, 23, 27, 29-30, 66, 69, 72-74, 76, 79-80, 82-83, 104, 134-35, 155-56, 158, 167, 169-70, 174, 179, 191, 218, 267, 270, 277, 281-83, 285, 299
Gender Recognition Act (2004) 17-18
genealogy 23, 29-30, 66-67, 73, 83, 231, 239
Genesis (Book of) 67, 100-01, 253
genetics *see* sex, assigned
genitalia 18, 54, 137-41, 146, 237, 239, 247, 257, 259, 275
   genitalia, Christ's 148-49
      phallus 143, 149
      vagina 137-39, 146
      vulva 139-41, 146-47, 149
St George 201, 218
Gérard of Diest 161
Gerdrup 188
gestation 82, 97, 102, 273-74
St Gilles 211, 224, 229, 231-32, 235, 237, 239-41
   Clarinde (mother) 231, 240
glory 57, 75, 103, 125, 144, 234
God 24-25, 48-50, 52-55, 57-58, 69, 73, 79, 87, 89-90, 93, 95-98, 102, 124-25, 156, 164, 171, 205, 208-09, 212-13, 215-16, 231, 234, 236-38, 240, 251-55, 257, 261-62, 270-72, 274-77; *see also* Christ; Holy Spirit; Trinity
   beyond gender 103, 272, 275, 277
   as cause/source of non-normative gender 91, 94, 103, 155, 274
   as feminine 97
   as gender non-conforming, gender-fluid 87, 102-04
   as husband 157
   as lover 204, 211, 213
   as maternal, as mother 228, 277
   pregnant with Christ 99-100, 102
   pregnant with the Virgin Mary 101
   union with 134, 142, 204, 239
God's will *see* divine will
Golden Legend (Caxton) 67
Gordon, Colby 23
Gospels, the 97-98, 148
Gousset, Marie-Thérèse 161
government 17-18, 74, 76, 112, 118
grace 52, 59, 73, 88-89, 93, 124, 224, 270
grammar and sex/gender 59, 89-90, 112, 163, 169
grave goods 180-82, 184-93, 270, 275
   animal sacrifices 184-85, 188, 191
   apparel and fabrics 185-86, 188-89
   cannabis seeds 183-85
   harness mounts 186
   jewellery 181, 187-90
   rattles 183, 185
   staffs (iron, wooden) 184-85, 188
   weapons 181, 187-92
graves 178-85, 187-92, 270, 275; *see also* burials
   Birka chamber grave Bj. 581 178-79, 181-82, 191-92

as hagiographic narratives 178, 180-81
Klinta double cremation (59:2, 59:3) 178, 189-90
Grayson, Saisha 159
Greek 66-67, 71, 112, 125, 251, 300
Greenland 182
Gregory of Nazianzus 114
The Guardian 21
Gutt, Blake 23, 27-30, 49, 269, 275

Hagia Sophia 119
hagiographers 24, 78, 82, 110, 157, 204-07, 211-18, 249, 251, 258, 271; *see also* Capgrave, John; Engelhard of Langheim; Niketas David
hagiography 27, 91, 103, 155, 201-02, 228, 245, 248, 251, 254, 258, 267-68, 271; *see also* graves
   audiences of 14, 47, 50, 55, 57, 59, 74, 112, 121, 126, 137, 141, 149, 201-02, 204-05, 207, 209, 212, 215-17, 248, 258, 274-75
   Byzantine 111-12, 114, 118, 120, 124, 126-27
   definition, usage 13-14, 27
   feminist and queer scholarship on 22-25, 30, 136, 268, 270
   trans 247-48, 251
   trans memoirs as 14
hair 124, 156-57, 159, 164-65, 167-69, 171, 186, 258, 274; *see also* beard, facial hair; tonsure
Halberstam, Jack 141, 144, 148
haptics *see* touch; trans haptics
Harvey, Susan Ashbrook 258
healing, miraculous 157, 225, 228, 235, 240, 261, 275
heaven 49, 52, 54-55, 66, 71, 74, 77, 100-01, 104, 110, 113, 115, 120, 125, 224, 234, 239
Herman of Tournay 58
hermaphrodites *see* intersex bodies and identities
hermits 68, 77, 91, 271
Hernández, Francisca 88
heteronormativity 66, 70, 78, 80, 82-83, 103, 136, 177; *see also* cisheteronormativity
heterosexuality 25, 45, 70, 82, 136, 227, 277; *see also* cisheterosexuality
   reproductive heterosexuality 80
hijras 29, 301
St Hilaria/Hilarion 91
Hildegard of Bingen 104
Hildegund of Schönau *see* Joseph of Schönau
Hirschfeld, Magnus 12, 29-30, 245-53, 255-56, 258, 262
historicism 26, 65, 136, 245
history 11-15, 17, 19-21, 25-28, 30-31, 47, 67, 70-71, 73-74, 80, 89, 97, 111, 114, 116, 123, 127, 136, 150, 182-83, 191-93, 201-03, 205, 245, 247-49, 251, 261, 267-69; *see also* time
   appropriation by white supremacists 177-78, 276; *see also* white supremacy
   feminist approaches to 22-25, 30, 268, 270

genderqueer history 218
impossibility of 'neutrality', 'objectivity' 20, 26, 30-31, 191, 205, 217-18
non-binary history 149
queer history 82-83
racialization of 28
(re)constructed in the present 19, 25, 150, 177-78, 193, 201-03, 205, 268-70, 276
relevance of medieval history to modern subjects 25, 26, 30-31, 149-50, 217-18, 270, 277
reliance on historians as subjects 19, 26-27, 30, 177-78, 181-82, 193, 203, 205, 270
salvation history 89, 101, 103
trans history 13, 15, 19, 21-23, 28, 218, 249-50, 261, 263, 276-77
Holck, Per 186
holiness 28, 44, 53, 56, 92, 95, 121, 165, 209
   and trans-ness 13-14, 17, 92, 137, 165, 258
Holy Fathers 116; *see also* Church Fathers
Holy Land 140
Holy Spirit 89, 98, 122
homonormativity 29, 65-66, 80, 82
homosexuality 231, 246
Hotchkiss, Valerie R. 254, 258
Howie, Cary 25
humility 57, 93, 98, 119, 213-14, 216
humoural theory 273-74

Iconoclasm 117-20, 124-25, 127
identifications 15-17, 45, 54, 58-59, 65, 73, 83, 103, 119, 134-35, 147, 156, 159, 165, 169, 172, 203, 214, 217, 230, 247, 249, 256, 273, 276, 283
Patriarch Ignatios of Constantinople 29-30, 109-29, 274
   Georgo (sister) 124
   Prokopia (mother) 123-24
   Theophano (sister) 124
illness 140, 226, 228
   chronic 227, 231
imago Dei 209, 251-61
imago mundi, imagines mundi 252-57, 260
imago transvesti 250-59
imitatio Christi 102-03, 137, 147, 149, 238, 245-65, 270
imitatio transvesti 250-53, 258-61
imitation 59, 78, 103, 113, 201, 208-09, 211-13, 215-16, 225, 227, 249, 252-53, 255, 258-60, 270-71
immortality 68, 75
impairment 29-30, 224-29, 231-35, 238-41
imperfection 27, 30, 225, 231, 283
imprisonment 48, 69
impurity 122
incarnation 68, 89, 94-102
incompleteness, incompletion 225, 237
inheritance 65-66, 74-75, 77, 94, 123, 206, 210-11, 256
Inquisition, the 88, 91, 97, 103-04

intercession 69, 92, 208, 212-13, 216, 224-25, 236
internet 18, 21, 262, 285
intersectionality 12-13, 19-21, 28, 74, 83, 157, 249, 251, 253, 268, 282
intersex bodies and identities 104, 137, 253, 281-82, 302
   in archaeology 179, 181
   Christ as intersex 27, 137
   'hermaphrodites' 25, 27, 137, 273, 300
   in history 25-27, 179
   legal recognition 18
   and medieval humoural theory 273-74
Irigaray, Luce 268
Iron Age, Late 13, 28-29, 177-93
Isaiah (Book of) 123
Islamophobia 276

Jacobus de Voragine 67
Jean le Noir 142
Jeanne of Flanders 161
Jenner, Caitlin 16
St Jerome 237
Jerusalem 48, 52
Jesus *see* Christ
Jesus as Mother (Bynum) 24, 136
Joan of Arc 12-13, 23, 91, 269, 276
Johannes of Wackerzele 271
John Chrysostom 114
John, Duke of Normandy 143
John of Laverna 93-94
Johnson, Marsha P. 14
Joseph of Schönau 27-30, 43-60, 274
   named as Hildegund 44-45, 55
Joseph, Stephan 248
Journal for Early Modern Cultural Studies 23
Juana de la Cruz 22, 29-30, 87-107, 274
   Vida 91, 93-95
Judaism 14, 89
Julian of Norwich 23

Kafer, Alison 224, 232-33
Kapitan, Alex 285
St Katherine of Alexandria 29, 65-85, 272; *see also* St Catherine
   Adrian (hermit, advisor) 68, 77, 80-82
   Athanasius (disciple) 66, 71
   Meliades (mother) 67-68, 75
Kaupang boat burial (Ka. 294-296) *see* burials
Keegan, Cáel M. 15
Kim, Dorothy 19, 22, 23
kinship 14, 74, 157, 241
Klinta double cremation (59:2, 59:3) *see* graves
Kłosowska, Anna 23
Kristeva, Julia 268

labour
   birth 72-73, 138-40, 275
   intellectual 71-73, 120-22, 273

   physical 186
   poetic 72-73, 216
   religious 46, 120-22, 217
Lactantius 113
LaFleur, Greta 23
Lagarde, Christine 277
language 30-31, 47-49, 57, 67, 73, 93, 95, 98, 102, 122, 141, 202-03, 212-15, 250, 256, 281-325; *see also* grammar and sex/gender; pronouns
   and expansion of gender possibilities 47, 59-60, 102, 104, 134, 151, 215, 256, 268
   gendered 47, 156, 213
   granularity of terminology 282-83
   and lived experience(s) 283, 285
   and normalization of gender binary 282
   of sanctity 47
   shifts in terminology 282-84
   and/as violence 281-82
Laon 58
Last Judgement 213, 216
Latin 45, 66-67, 71, 90, 112, 203-04, 250, 271
Lausus 113
Lee, Robert E. 269
Legenda Aurea (Jacobus de Voragine) 67, 169
Legenda Maior (St Bonaventure) 92
Le Goff, Jacques 268
Leo V (Byzantine emperor) 117-18
Lewis, Flora 139
libraires 160-61, 173
Light, Ellis 15, 23
liminality 29, 81, 90-97, 183, 212
lineages 30, 70-71, 73, 77, 80-82, 237, 239; *see also* genealogy
Little Flowers of St Francis, The 93-94
Lochrie, Karma 136, 139, 141, 205, 284
Loki 183
Lombardi-Nash, Michael A. 252, 256
London 66
Longinus (biblical character) 139-40
love 54, 68, 73, 77, 81-82, 92, 94, 101, 134, 204-09, 211-17, 226, 234, 276
Love, Heather 70
St Luke 97-98, 102
Lynne, Norfolk 73

Madrid 88
Mahaut, Countess of Artois 160-61
Maid of Orléans *see* Joan of Arc
Maillet, Clovis 23, 285
manuscript illuminations 29, 135, 137-50, 155-74, 274
manuscripts 29, 58, 67, 134-50, 155, 158-74, 203, 229, 251, 274-75
   Brussels, Bibliothèque royale de Belgique, MS 9229-30 159-62, 165-69, Fig 6.2 (166), 172-73
   The Hague, Koninklijke Bibliotheek, MS 71 A 24 159-62, 165, 169-73, Fig 6.3 (170)

INDEX

haptic interaction with   138-43, 146-48, 166-67, 172, 275
The Loftie Hours   147
London, Wellcome Collection, Wellcome MS 632   138-39
Munich, Bayerische Staatsbibliothek München, MS CLM 10177   169-70, Fig 6.4 (170)
Oxford, Bodleian Library, Canonici Miscellaneous   74, 159
Paris, Bibliothèque de l'Arsenal, MS 5204   159-63, Fig. 6.1 (163), 165, 173
Psalter and Prayer Book of Bonne of Luxembourg, New York, Metropolitan Museum of Art, The Cloisters Collection, MS 69.86   143-46, Fig. 5.1 (144), Fig. 5.2 (145), 149
Rothschild Canticles   148-49
St Margaret of Antioch   201
marginality, marginalization   16, 19, 21, 23, 26, 74, 83, 110, 127, 234, 248, 252, 269-70, 281, 284
margins   143, 145-46, 149, 173
St Marina/Mary/Marin/Marinos/Marinus   29-30, 91, 112, 137, 159, 245-65, 274
Eugenius (father)   246, 256
vita antiqua   251, 255
marriage   66, 68, 74-79, 81-83, 91, 95-97, 103, 120, 156, 170-71, 272, 276
mystical/spiritual   67-68, 74, 76-79, 81-82, 96, 103, 157
same-sex   66, 79
martyrdom   67, 69-70, 76, 78-79, 110, 113, 117, 120
martyrs   75, 82, 110, 114, 117, 125
St Mary Magdalene   93-94
Master of BnF fr. 160   160
Masters of the Delft Grisailles   147
maternity   24, 69, 136, 209, 228
St Matrona/Babylas   91, 112
Matthew (Book of)   113-15, 120
Maubeuge Master   160-65, 173
de Maubeuge, Thomas   160-62
Maxentius (Persian emperor)   68-69
Mayburd, Miriam   183
McCulloch, Florence   214, 216-17
McLoughlin, Caitlyn   29-30, 65-85, 272
McRuer, Robert   227, 233
medicine   27, 79, 109, 118, 140, 180, 230, 233, 236, 248, 250, 262
Medieval Feminist Forum   22-23
medieval trans studies   *see* trans studies, medieval trans studies
memorialization   14, 70, 117, 184, 187, 189
memory   187, 189, 193, 224, 269
menstruation   140, 275
Merkel, Angela   277
Messiah, the   92
metaphor   47, 59, 71, 76, 92, 98, 102-04, 113, 115, 211

Methodios (ninth-century patriarch)   112
Michael I (Byzantine emperor)   123
Michael III (Byzantine emperor)   118
milk   23, 69, 93, 124, 136
Mills, Robert   22, 25, 146, 149-50, 164, 284
miracles   45, 52-54, 60, 69, 87-88, 91, 94-95, 97, 102-03, 118, 124-26, 157, 160, 162, 224-25, 228, 232, 235, 240; *see also* healing, miraculous
misogyny   17, 26, 202, 217-18, 237; *see also* transmisogyny; transmisogynoir
Mitchell, David T.   235
Mock, Janet   16
monasteries   44, 50-55, 59, 95-96, 112-13, 121, 123, 155-58, 163, 165-66, 168-71, 173, 204, 209-12, 246-47, 255, 257, 259-60, 273
monks   24-25, 27, 43-59, 91, 112, 120-21, 126, 156-57, 159, 162-72, 201-02, 204, 212, 217, 228, 246-47, 251, 254-64, 273-74
trans monks   *see* St Eufrosine/Euphrosine/Euphrosyne/Esmarade/Smaragdus; Joseph of Schönau; St Marina/Mary/Marin/Marinos/Marinus
More, Alison   209
Morgagni-Stewart-Morel syndrome   186
mortification, bodily   *see* asceticism
Mother Juana   *see* Juana de la Cruz
Mount Athos   *see* Athos
Mount Sinai   *see* Sinai
Mughal, Aisha   16
Muñoz, José Esteban   81-82
Murray, Jacqueline   202-03
'My Words to Victor Frankenstein' (Stryker)   20
mysticism   15, 23, 25, 92-93, 95-96, 103-04, 136, 228, 268, 272; *see also* marriage, mystical/spiritual
mythology, Norse   178, 183

names   29-30, 45, 156-57, 203-04, 250
dead names, dead-naming   45n4, 249-50, 292
neo-pagans   177
Newman, Barbara   24, 104
Newman, Martha G.   27-30, 274
New Testament   115
New World   88
Nikephoros of Miletos   110
Niketas David   109-29
Niketas the Patrician   110
nobility   74-75, 79, 81, 117, 171, 216, 238
non-binary   11, 134-35, 156, 253, 270, 276, 282, 306
Christ as   29, 134-50
discrimination against non-binary individuals   17
eunuchs as   158
legal recognition of non-binary identities   16
non-binary historical subjects   134-35, 149-50
Nora, Pierre   267, 269
Nordeide, Sæbjørg Walaker   185

Norfolk 73
Norway 178, 184-89
Numancia 88
nuns 43, 45-47, 58-59, 95-96, 112, 156-57, 164, 171, 201, 211, 226

Odin 182-83
Ogden, Amy V. 29-30, 158n15, 168, 171, 248, 270, 272-73, 276
oil 69, 124
Öland *see* Klinta double cremation (59:2, 59:3)
optical theory, medieval 141-42, 146
orality, oral tradition, oral narratives 45-47, 55, 180
Orange is the New Black 16
Orléans 13, 91
Oseberg ship burial *see* burials
Ousthazades 113

pagans 68, 78, 120, 117, 207, 232
pain 15, 72, 135, 139-40, 208, 226-28, 231, 233-34, 236, 238, 260
  chronic 227, 231
Palladius 113
parables 50, 52, 57, 92, 102
paradise 101, 239; *see also* heaven
Paris 29, 50, 159-60, 268
part, partiality 19, 103, 113, 137, 139, 141-42, 145-46, 149, 157, 165, 172-73, 178, 184-85, 187, 192, 208, 210-11, 224, 233, 259, 261, 271
passion 67, 134, 138-40, 148
Patlagean, Evelyne 254
Patsavas, Alyson 233
St Paul 56, 92, 124
St Paula Barbada 91
St Pelagia/Pelagien/Pelagius 91, 137, 159, 169
perfection 27, 30, 54, 120, 137, 148, 204, 209, 223-25, 232, 235, 238, 270, 274
persecution 69, 75, 113, 117, 124, 207, 271, 277
perversion, perversity 16, 70, 117, 182-83
Peterson, Christopher 247
St Philip 113
Photios I 110, 117-20, 125-26
piety 25, 77, 117, 123, 202, 210, 226, 240
  affective 133-34, 146-48
pilgrimage 48, 50
pleasure 72, 203, 218, 276
  carnal 276
Poor Clare nuns 95
prayer 46, 69, 91, 93, 95-96, 137-38, 140, 147, 170, 204, 212-14, 235, 240
  prayer books, prayer rolls 29, 134, 139, 143, Fig. 5.1 (144), 145, Fig. 5.2 (145), 147
precarity, academic 22-23
pregnancy 72, 97, 99-100, 102, 116, 247, 259-61; *see also* gestation
Price, Neil 188, 190
Princes' Islands 123

prison *see* imprisonment
privilege 19, 23, 29, 65-85, 125, 228, 238, 269, 297
procreation 51, 69, 81-83
pronouns 49, 55, 156, 169, 203-04, 217, 229, 246n60, 249-50, 309-11; *see also* grammar and sex/gender; language
prostheses 230, 232, 240, 307
  narrative 235-37, 239-40
Proverbs (Book of) 98
psalms 99
psalters Fig. 5.1 (144), Fig. 5.2 (145)
Pseudo-Dionysius the Areopagite 272
purity 50, 54-55, 77, 121, 138

queerness 12-13, 19, 28-29, 31, 51, 54, 87, 136, 141-42, 150, 157, 159, 165, 171, 173, 178, 182-92, 209, 217, 311
  in the Academy 23-25, 284
  and disability 233, 237
  and genealogy, reproduction 29-30, 51, 65-85, 237
  intersection with trans-ness 12
  and order 54
  queer privilege 65-85
  and religion 17, 25, 136, 141, 155, 157, 182-84, 201; *see also* seiðr
  and time 20, 29, 83, 150
  and whiteness 24
queerphobia 13, 17, 26, 150, 282
queer studies, readings 20, 23-25, 217
queer theory 12, 20, 227

racialization 20-21, 28-29, 178, 276, 283
Raskolnikov, Masha 23
Raymond, Janice 18
readers 14, 29, 58, 65-66, 69-70, 73-75, 78-79, 81, 83, 100, 122, 125-26, 142-43, 146-50, 157, 162-63, 166, 168, 172, 178-79, 212, 215-17, 234, 248-49, 252, 254, 257-58, 274-75, 283, 285; *see also* audience; manuscripts
reading, trans modes of 15, 141-43, 149-50; *see also* trans haptics
reason 74
rebirth 52
recluses 49, 51, 55
recognition 12-14, 51-52, 65, 81, 83, 139, 147, 179, 186, 248, 250, 260
relics 88, 124, 224-25, 239
religiosity 13, 44, 46
Rennes 78
reproduction
  biological 66, 69-70, 74-76, 79-80, 82-83, 237, 257
  disabled 237
  genderqueer 66
  heterosexual 70, 80, 237
  queer 70, 237
  textual 65-85
reproductive futurism 70, 75, 237

Revelation (Julian of Norwich)   23
Richard, M.   251
Richards, Christina   134-35
Ringrose, Kathryn M.   27, 158
Rivera, Sylvia   14
Roem, Danica   16
Rome   48, 69, 113, 139, 157-58, 206
Rose of Viterbo   103
Rouse, Mary A.   160-62, 172
Rouse, Richard H.   160-62, 172
Rowling, J.K.   18
Rudy, Kathryn   172
rulership   68, 70, 74-76, 101-02, 182, 184, 277

Saami people   183
sagas   178, 182-84, 188
   Eiríks saga rauða   182, 188
   Ynglinga saga   182-84
Saint Pancras, London   66
saints   *passim*
   assigned female at birth   30, 272-73;
     see also St Eufrosine/Euphrosine/
     Euphrosyne/Esmarade/Smaragdus;
     Joseph of Schönau; St Marina/Mary/
     Marin/Marinos/Marinus
   basic characteristics   24, 270-71, 276-77
   eunuch saints   13, 29; *see also* Patriarch
     Ignatios of Constantinople
   and flexibility of gender identity   27,
     201-02, 204-05, 271-77
   as models for imitation   201, 204, 209-10,
     212-16, 271, 273
   patron saints   229, 232
   sexualization of   25
   'transvestite' and/or 'cross-dressing'   26-
     27, 91, 112, 159, 202, 228, 247, 250, 252,
     254-55, 258
   and virginity   69, 92, 98, 116, 156, 272
   visual portrayals of   25, 29, 271, 274; *see
     also* manuscript illuminations
salvation   52-53, 79, 89, 91, 101-03, 116-17, 125,
   205, 212, 217, 225, 236, 255-57, 262
sanctity   14, 53, 74-75, 79, 99-100, 122, 223-28,
   232, 256
   and cure   234
   and disability   30, 224-28
   and embodiment   30, 99-100, 224-28, 241
   and eunuchs   110-11, 116, 126
   and gender   14-15, 24, 29, 47, 50, 53, 79, 91,
     110-11, 126, 149, 227-28, 256
   and haptics   140, 147
   and healing   240
   and identity   241
   and knowledge   239
   odour of   49, 53, 225
   and queerness   14, 25, 110-11
   as relational   233, 238-39
   and trans-ness   12, 14-15, 28, 53, 91, 149,
     224-28

Sandler, Lucy Freeman   139
Sarah (wife of Abraham)   67
Scandinavia   13, 28-29, 177-97
Schalk, Sami   238
Schleif, Corine   148
scholasticism   66, 272
Schönau (Cistercian abbey)   44-46, 49-53, 55-56
Scotland   50, 67
Scottish Legendary   67
scribes   55, 160-62, 249
Seelen-Einschlag   252
Seelenregungen   256
seiðr   13, 29, 178, 182-92, 275
Seligman, Martin   247
de Senlis, Jean   160-62
Serano, Julia   256, 261-62, 285
Sermon on the Incarnation (Juana de la
   Cruz)   94, 97-102
Sermon on the Trinity (Juana de la Cruz)   99,
   102
sermons
   Basil of Caesarea   113
   Bernard of Clairvaux   47, 54
   Cistercian   50, 57
   and eunuchs   113
   and gender   29, 102, 104
   Juana de la Cruz   29, 87-90, 94, 97-104, 274
   Tristan de Nanteuil   234
sex, assigned   51, 54-59, 88, 102, 134-37, 157,
   167-68, 179-80, 214, 246-47, 257, 268, 272, 274,
   276-77, 284-85, 287-88, 292-93
   and genetics, genomic/chromosomal
     sexing   179-82, 191-92, 270
   historical conceptualizations   273, 277
   legal redefinitions   18
   osteological sexing   179-81, 186-87, 190-92
   secondary sex characteristics   137, 157, 186
Sexon, Sophie   29-30, 275
sexuality   12, 19, 28, 54-55, 80, 111, 115-16, 122,
   136, 148, 158, 257, 268, 274
sexualization of saints   25
shamanism   183
Shapur II   113
Siberia, native peoples of   183
sin   48, 88, 99, 121, 207-09, 213-17, 226, 248,
   259-60, 273
   original   101
Sinai   69
skin   30, 141, 148, 188, 190
Skoglund, Pontus   180
St Smaragdus   *see* St Eufrosine/Euphrosine/
   Euphrosyne/Esmarade/Smaragdus
Snorton, C. Riley   21, 285
Snyder, Sharon L.   235
social class   *see* class, social
Society for French Studies   22
Society for Medievalist Feminist
   Scholarship   22
Song of Songs   24-25, 47, 54, 59, 93-94

St Sophia 204
soul-impact, soul-affect *see* Seelen-Einschlag
soul-movement, soul-stirring, soul-
　striving *see* Seelenregungen
souls 49, 52, 54, 93, 101, 205, 250, 253, 255-56
　as Bride 47
　fed by Christ's blood 136
　gendered 43, 90, 252
　genderless 208
　judged by Christ 101
　trans 30, 43, 247-48, 250-62
South England Legendary 67
Spencer-Hall, Alicia 142, 144, 226, 235, 269
spirit 90, 117; *see also* Holy Spirit
spirituality, the spiritual
　and the body 225, 227
　gendered forms of spirituality 46-47,
　　103-04, 125, 136, 211, 253, 270
　spiritual alterity 83
　spiritual confidants 114
　spiritual devotion 79
　spiritual dryness 93
　spiritual fatherhood 124
　spiritual fertility 127
　spiritual formation 52, 59
　spiritual friendship 208
　spiritual guides, leaders 208, 270
　spiritual haptics 141
　spiritual exceptionality, spiritual
　　ideal 66, 77
　spiritual imitation 211
　spiritual imperceptiveness 208
　spiritual kinship 14
　spiritual life 82
　spiritual love 204, 207-09
　spiritual marriage 74, 78, 96, 157
　spiritual meditation 133-34, 136, 141, 146, 149
　spiritual perfection 120, 274
　spiritual progress 207
　spiritual power 78
　spiritual significance 14
　spiritual status 226
　spiritual struggle 116
　spiritual texts 24
　spiritual transcendence of gender 88, 95,
　　103-04, 136, 211, 253
　spiritual understanding 208
　spiritual virility 125
　spiritual wounds 226
sterility 70-71, 123-24
Stock, Kathleen 21
St Omers 95
Stone, Sandy 20, 262
Stones, Alison 161
Storey, Christopher 214
Stryker, Susan 20, 285
Sub-*Fauvel* Master 161
suffering 17, 117, 133-35, 138-39, 147-48, 236,
　238, 252, 259, 269, 275

suicide 14, 17
Supreme Court of the United States 18
Surtz, Ronald 99, 102
St Susannah/John 91
Sweden 178, 189-92
Symeon the New Theologian 110
Syria 251
Szabo, Felix 13, 28-30, 274

temporality 13, 51, 65, 78, 80-83, 142, 150, 186,
　224, 232, 235, 284; *see also* time
temptation 50, 54, 56-57, 99-100, 110, 115-16, 121
TERFs *see* transphobia
St Thais 165
St Thekla 92
St Theodora/Theodoros 92
Theodosius II 113
Theophylact of Ochrid 115
'third' gender *see* gender
Thorbjorg 182, 188
time 14, 20, 26, 53, 80, 143, 150, 172-73, 180,
　184-87, 189, 229, 236, 247, 268, 282; *see also*
　communion, cross-temporal; history;
　temporality
　touching across/through time; times
　　touching 14, 20, 45, 59, 83, 142, 150,
　　202, 218
Time magazine 16
Title VII of the US Civil Rights Act (1964) 18
Toledo 88, 99
Tolley, Clive 183
tonsure 92, 157, 163-64, 166-68, 170-71; *see
　also* hair
torture 25, 68-69, 201
touch 45, 49, 59, 83, 138-39, 140-43, 146-50,
　166-67, 172, 261, 275; *see also* trans haptics
Tougher, Shaun 158
tradition 17, 24, 26, 30, 52, 74, 79, 88, 90-94,
　97-98, 102-04, 111, 115-16, 120-22, 126, 178, 183,
　201, 249-51, 253, 269, 271, 274
transcendence 14-15, 24-25, 29, 44, 53, 79,
　87-90, 93-94, 102, 104, 137, 139, 144, 202, 204,
　207-08, 212, 215, 217, 226, 231, 273
transfemininity 17, 319
transformation 29, 54, 90-91, 95-97, 103, 215,
　224, 229-32, 234-37, 239-40, 259, 283
transgender *see also* trans-ness
　definition(s), usage(s) 11-14
　intersection with genderqueer, genderfluid,
　　and non-binary identities 11
Transgender Studies Quarterly 20-21
transgression 14, 25, 27, 29, 65, 70, 73, 79, 83,
　103-04, 147, 178, 183, 201-21, 226, 275
trans haptics 141-43
transition 96-97, 102, 136, 159, 171-72, 225, 247,
　249, 252, 254-58, 260-61, 318-19
　legal 248
　medical 248
　into religious orders 96, 251, 255, 258

as salvation 256
social 229
translation 66-67, 71-72, 76, 91, 93, 95-96, 99, 102, 112, 150, 204, 209, 212-15, 225, 249, 251-52, 256, 260, 271
Transliterature: Things Transform 22
transmasculinity 12, 17, 319-20
transmisogynoir 16, 28, 283, 320
transmisogyny 16, 18, 320
trans-ness *passim*
   and/as authenticity 14-15, 245-65
   and embodiment 13, 223-44
   and genealogy 23, 30, 65-85
   in history 11, 13-15, 27, 30-31, 134-35, 190-92, 214-18, 276-77; *see also* archaeology
   and/as holiness 12-15, 17, 87-107, 276; *see also* sanctity; *seiðr*; spirituality, the spiritual
   legibility thereof 15, 26-27, 155-97
   and whiteness 20-21, 28-29, 283, 324-25
transphobia 26, 228, 321
   in the Academy 15, 21-22, 28
   historical justifications for 19, 218
   internalized 302
   medieval 12, 218-19
   modern 13, 16-18, 150, 262, 281-82
   notion of 'disguise' 26-27; *see also* disguise
   TERFs 17-18, 314
   and white supremacy 20-21, 28-29
trans rights 15-18, 277
   and Trump administration 18
trans studies 12, 14-15, 30
   backlash to 21
   Black trans studies 21
   and dismantling white supremacy 13, 19-20, 178
   ethics thereof, for cis academics 15, 22-23, 27-28, 30
   and feminist scholarship 23-25, 30
   gatekeeping in 21
   overview of field 20-22
   medieval trans studies
      as additive 25-26
      anglocentrism of 23
      ascendency of 22-23
      core methodologies of 26-28, 30
      further work to do 25-26
      overview 22-23, 26
      prominence of precarious and junior scholars in 23
   and queer studies 13, 20, 23-25
   relevance for cis-heterosexual culture 13, 27, 277
   representation in 22-23
   spurious claims of 'anachronism' 19
   whiteness of, in academic context 20-21, 28
trans theory 12-14, 20, 23, 53, 246, 249
transvestites 245-252, 255, 322; *see also* saints, 'transvestite' and/or 'cross-dressing'

Transvestites (*Die Transvestiten*) (Hirschfeld) 29, 245, 247-49, 251-53, 256, 262
'transvestite monks' 228; *see also* 'transvestite nuns'
'transvestite nuns' 112; *see also* 'transvestite monks'
'transvestite' saints *see* saints, 'transvestite' and/or 'cross-dressing'
trap 261-63, 323; *see also* disguise
Trier 48
Trinity, the 89, 92, 98-99, 102, 104, 137, 142, 254, 272
Tripoli 251
Tristan de Nanteuil (text) 23, 29, 223-44, 275
Tristan de Nanteuil (character) 229-31, 235-37, 240
   Doon (half brother) 237
Twitter 17-18
Two-Spirit identities 29, 324
Tyre 48, 52, 75

Frater Ulmannus 137
UN Convention on the Elimination of all Forms of Discrimination against Women 16

vanity 51, 56
Vatican, the 17, 102
vernacular texts and translations
   Middle Dutch 147, 271
   Middle English 67, 271
   Middle French 29, 224, 229
   Middle German 137, 271
   Middle Spanish 89, 91, 93, 95, 99
   Old English 203
   Old French 29, 155-56, 158, 202-03, 214-15
   Old Norse 177-78, 182-84
Verona 48-49
St Veronica 95-97, 103
Vestfold *see* Oseberg ship burial
via negativa 102, 104
Vie des saints 160
Vie de saint Alexis 205-07, 211, 213
Vie de saint Gilles (Guillaume de Berneville) 211
Villiers (Cistercian abbey) 54
violence 16, 21, 69, 117, 191-92, 201, 225, 281
   against trans people 14, 16, 262, 281, 283
   of cure 233
   of language 281-2
   systemic 283
   white-supremacist 19, 21; *see also* transmisogynoir
Virgin Mary 24, 68, 77, 80-82, 87, 92, 94, 96-103, 125, 133, 135, 137-38, 164-65, 169, 240, 274
virginity 50, 69, 75-81, 92, 97-99, 114-16, 156, 202, 257, 272, 277
virtue 50, 57, 77, 101, 110-11, 114-17, 119-24, 126, 204-05, 208-13, 217, 247-48, 258

visions   12, 25, 47, 52-53, 72, 95, 112, 140, 142, 144, 204; *see also* dreams, dream visions; optical theory, medieval
vocation   91-92, 95-97, 103

warriors   182; *see also* Birka chamber grave Bj. 581
Wechterswinkel (abbey)   43, 46, 58-59
Whipping Girl (Serano)   261
whiteness of academic fields   20-21, 24
white supremacy   13, 16, 19-21, 24, 28-29, 269, 283, 324-25
    appropriation of medieval history   12-13, 19-20, 177-78, 269, 276
Whittington, Karl   26

wholeness   149, 215-16, 223-24, 232, 235, 239
Wikipedia   18
St Wilgefortis   137
William (abbot of Villiers)   54
Williams, Howard   180
will of God   *see* divine will
Winstead, Karen   74, 78
womanism   24
womb   20, 72, 81, 97-102, 113, 206, 273
World Health Organization   16
wounds   29-30, 133-50, 226, 239, 275
Wright, Vanessa   29-30, 203, 274

Ynglinga saga   *see* sagas

Printed and bound by CPI Group (UK) Ltd, Croydon, CR0 4YY
18/10/2023

08152642-0002